JOURNAL OF THE COPYRIGHT SOCIETY

(Formerly Bulletin of the Copyright Society, and Journal of the Copyright Society of the U.S.A.)

Published by the Copyright Society, 1 E. 53rd Street, Floor 8, New York, NY 10022
Telephone: (212) 354-6301 Website: www.copyrightsociety.org

For membership information visit copyrightsociety.org/membership-benefits

THE JOURNAL OF THE COPYRIGHT SOCIETY is published four times a year. The Society is located at 1 East 53rd Street, Floor 8, New York, NY 10022.

Copyright Society Membership

As a member of the Copyright Society, you are entitled to exclusive benefits, including reduced registration fees for networking events and Continuing Legal Education (CLE) programs, a subscription to the Journal, and many more privileges. For detailed membership information, please visit copyrightsociety.org/membership-benefits.

Journal Subscription

A subscription to the Journal of the Copyright Society runs from January through December and includes four issues. Subscriptions are accepted throughout the year for this period. Subscription orders received mid-year will be sent back issues, beginning with the first issue of the current volume. For detailed subscription information, please visit copyrightsociety.org/the-journal.

CITE: 72 J. COPYRIGHT SOC'Y, page no., . . . (2025).

JOURNAL OF THE COPYRRIGHT SOCIETY

VOLUME 72(2) (2025)

TABLE OF CONTENTS

From the Desk of the Editor-in Chief v

PART I: ARTICLES

Talkin' 'Bout AI Generation:
Copyright and the Generative AI Supply Chain
By Katherine Lee, A. Feder Cooper
and James Grimmelman 251

AI Copyright Litigation v. Licensing: An Exploration
By Lily Argyle, Tess Bradley, James Dearing, Hallie Feinman,
Layla Ghiai, Gerado Gomez, Marie Gosserand,
Holland Haney, Jamika Mack, Maddy Marlowe, Whitney McBay,
Haley Pettingill, Isa Reyes-Klein, Nathan Jon Evan Smelley, Schwartz,
Natalia Walcott and Tynesea Watts 410

Section 1202(b) and AI: Implications for Copyright Infringement Lawsuits
and Considerations for Digital Creators.
By Maria Crusey 480

PART II: INTERVIEW
Chad Rutowski and Theresa Weisenberger
with Elizabeth Townsend Gard 520

PART III: LATE BREAKING NEWS
Five Takeaways from the Copyright Office's
Controversial New AI Report
By Aaron Moss... 544

Shira Perlmutter v. Blanche et. Al, complaint filed May 22, 2025
By Aaron Moss... 552

FROM THE DESK OF THE EDITOR-IN-CHIEF

For the second issue of Volume 72, we are pleased to present Part II of our Copyright and AI Special Issues. In this issue, we present three pieces that are engaged with students working on the topic of AI and Copyright. What I love about all three pieces is that faculty/mentors were involved with students exploring Copyright and AI. We have one sophisticated piece with Ph.D. Computer Science students, and two with J.D. students.

We begin Part I with our featured article, the work of Katherine Lee, A. Fedder Cooper and James Grimmelman's "Talkin' 'Bout AI Generation: Copyright and the Generative AI Supply Chain," a piece that is nearly 150 pages long. Lee, a Ph.D. candidate in in Computer Science, Cornell University, along with Cooper, who also completed his Ph.D. from Cornell (and has since gone on to a number of impressive positions, including a position as an Assistant Professor at Yale, beginning in 2026. This piece is one of a series of articles the three have been writing together. We are pleased to publish this foundational work. Their work is impressive and important in the field of AI and Computers.

We then turn to two student articles, that began in the classroom: Copyright AI Litigation versus Licensing: A Study, where I, along with my Advanced Copyright and Trademark course at Tulane University Law School embarked on trying to understand the status of copyright AI cases and found ourselves also looking into licensing deals. While not as sophisticated as the Lee, Cooper and Grimmelman piece, the Article seeks to understand on a basic level how to approach the many cases pending and the ever-changing landscape that is AI and Copyright. With seventeen students working on the piece, we hope we got it right, but I think the spirit is clear: where litigation dominated 2023, licensing deals with media companies and AI companies dominated 2024. We will see what 2025 brings. The third article comes from a J.D. student at Washington University School of Law in St. Louis, Maria Crusey, who wrote, "Student Note: Section 1202(b) of the DMCA and AI: Implications for Copyright Infringement Lawsuits and Considerations for Digital Creators," with oversight by Dave Hansen

In Part II, we then turn to an interview I conducted with Chad Rutkowski and Theresa Weisenberger, both attorneys at Baker Hostetler. They discuss their work and thoughts related to Copyright and AI. It was a most lovely conversation.

And then, just as we were going to press, three stories broke: the release of the third Copyright and AI report from the U.S. Copyright Office, the firing of the Librarian of Congress and Register of Copyright, and the approval of the ALI Restatement on Copyright. Aaron Moss agreed to contribute our republishing of his Copyright Lately blog, "Five Takeaways from the Copyright Office's Controversial New AI Report." And as we were going to press, the fired Register of. Copyright, Shira Perlmutter, has filed a lawsuit in federal court on May 22, 2025, claiming her removal waws "unlawful and ineffective." We have republished the complaint as part of this issue. Late breaking news, then, concludes the issue with Part III.

We are also pleased to include as part of our Journal, our Copyright Society Fellows, 2025-2026. This includes our Senior Managing Editor, Brijan Kana, our Articles Editor, Tess Bradley, and our Co-Managing Editors, Kristin Ivey and Holly Haney, along with our Journal student members Mary Abi-Karam (Georgetown University), Jacie Beling (Tulane University), Cortez Collins (Howard University), Adrian Eggleson (Tulane), Sumayyah Ghori (George Mason University), Wondwossen Girma Habtemariam (Loyola Chicago/Rome), Amir Homayounfar (Tulane University), Claire Jones (Tulane), Adeline Miller (Loyola/New Orleans), Michael Niebergall (George Mason University), Avery Nolan (Tulane University), Meg Obley (George Mason University),Zara Okoli (Tulane University), Zoey Piertramale (Arizona State University), Ben Pudelka (Colgate University), Sarah Simonis (University of New Hampshire), Olivia Spain (Tulane University), and Zingqi Zhang (Ohio State University).

It's been quite a Spring for copyright, with I'm sure more to come. If you would like to write for the Journal, have an idea for an article, or want to participate in the editing process, feel free to email me at eic@copyrightsociety.org.

Elizabeth Townsend Gard
Editor-in-Chief
Journal of the Copyright Society
John E. Koerner Endowed Professor of Law
Tulane University Law School
eic@copyrightsociety.org

PART I:
ARTICLES

TALKIN' 'BOUT AI GENERATION: COPYRIGHT AND THE GENERATIVE-AI SUPPLY CHAIN

by KATHERINE LEE,* A. FEDER COOPER**
AND JAMES GRIMMELMANN***

"Does generative AI infringe copyright?" is an urgent question. It is also a difficult question for two reasons. First, "generative AI" is not just one product from one company. It is a catch-all name for a massive ecosystem of loosely related technologies, including conversational chatbots like ChatGPT, image generators like Midjourney and DALL·E, coding assistants like GitHub Copilot, music composition applications like Lyria, and video generation systems like Sora. Generative-AI models have different technical architectures and are

---

* Co-founder, The Center for Generative AI, Law, and Policy Research (The GenLaw Center); Ph.D. Candidate in Computer Science, Cornell University (on leave); Staff Research Scientist and GenAI Attack Team Lead, Google DeepMind. This article was written during Lee's time as a graduate student researcher at Cornell, in her capacity as an affiliate of The GenLaw Center and Cornell. All authors contributed equally to this work. We presented an earlier version of this work at the 2023 Privacy Law Scholars Conference and discussed the issues extensively with other participants in the Generative AI + Law Workshop at the 2023 International Conference on Machine Learning. Our thanks to the organizers and participants, and to Aislinn Black, Jack M. Balkin, Miles Brundage, Christopher Callison-Burch, Nicholas Carlini, Madiha Zahrah Choksi, Christopher A. Choquette-Choo, Christopher De Sa, Fernando Delgado, Jonathan Frankle, Deep Ganguli, Daphne Ippolito, Matthew Jagielski, Gautam Kamath, Kevin Klyman, Mark Lemley, David Mimno, Niloofar Mireshghallah, Milad Nasr, Pamela Samuelson, Ludwig Schubert, Andrew F. Sellars, Florian Tramèr, Kristen Vaccaro, and Luis Villa. We would additionally like to thank the editorial staff at the *Journal of the Copyright Society of the U.S.A.* for shepherding this Article through the publication process. The GenLaw Center, https://www.genlaw.org/, is an independent academic research organization. It has organized workshops at the International Conference on Machine Learning in July 2023 and July 2024, and in Washington, D.C. in April 2024. These events received financial and in-kind support from Schmidt Sciences, OpenAI, the ML Collective, the Georgetown Institute for Technology Law & Policy, the K&L Gates Initiative at Carnegie Mellon University, the Center for Democracy and Technology, Google, Microsoft, Schmidt Futures, Anthropic, and Cornell University.

** Co-Founder, The GenLaw Center; Assistant Professor of Computer Science, Yale University (to commence 2026). After completion of the initial version of this Article but prior to its official publication, Cooper started as a Postdoctoral Researcher at Microsoft Research and a Postdoctoral Affiliate at Stanford University.

*** Tessler Family Professor of Digital and Information Law, Cornell Law School and Cornell Tech; Director, Cornell Tech Research Lab for Applied Law and Technology (CTRL-ALT). CTRL-ALT has received funding from Microsoft for a project on Internet platform regulation. Grimmelmann previously was on the faculty of New York Law School and affiliated with its Institute for Information Law and Policy, which received funding from Microsoft for a project on the Google Books litigation.

trained on different types of data from different sources using different algorithms. Some take months and cost millions of dollars to train; other models can be spun up in a weekend. These models are made accessible to users in very different ways. Some are offered through paid online services; others are distributed as open-source artifacts, which let anyone download and modify them. Different generative-AI systems behave differently and raise different legal issues. We therefore need the right framework—one that digs deeper than the term "generative AI"—to reason precisely and clearly about the different legal issues at play.

The second problem is that copyright law is notoriously complicated, and generative-AI systems manage to touch on a great many corners of it. They raise issues of authorship, similarity, direct and indirect liability, fair use, and licensing, among much else. These issues cannot be analyzed in isolation because there are connections everywhere. Whether the output of a generative-AI system is fair use can depend on how its training datasets were assembled. Whether the creator of a generative-AI system is secondarily liable can depend on the prompts that its users supply.

In this Article, we aim to bring order to the chaos. To do so, we make two contributions. First, we introduce the generative-AI supply chain: an interconnected set of stages that transform training data (millions of pictures of cats) into generations (new and hopefully never-seen-before pictures of cats that have never existed). Breaking down generative AI into these constituent stages reveals all the places at which companies and users make choices that may have legal consequences—for copyright and beyond. Second, we specifically apply the supply-chain framing to U.S. copyright law. This framing enables us to trace the effects of upstream technical designs on downstream uses, and to assess who in these complicated sociotechnical systems bears responsibility for infringement when it happens. Because we engage so closely with the technology of generative AI, we are able to shed more light on the copyright questions. We do not give definitive answers as to who should and should not be held liable. Instead, we identify the key decisions that courts will need to make as they grapple with these issues, and we point out the consequences that would likely flow from different liability regimes.

INTRODUCTION 255

I. MACHINE LEARNING AND THE GENERATIVE-AI SUPPLY CHAIN *259*

A. Background on Machine Learning 260
1. Data 260
2. Machine Learning 262
a. Discriminative Modeling 263

b. Generative Modeling 267

B. Generative AI....268
1. Generative-AI Systems....271
2. Generation Modalities....272
a. Text Data and Generations....274
b. Image Data and Generations....276
3. Machine-Learning Techniques in Generative AI....278
a. Transformer Architecture....279
b. Diffusion-Based Models....281
4. The Role of Scale....283

C. The Generative-AI Supply Chain....285
a. Forks in the Supply Chain....296
6. Model Release and System Deployment....298
7. Generation....302
a. Forks in the Supply Chain....304
8. Model Alignment....305

II. TRACING COPYRIGHT THROUGH THE SUPPLY CHAIN....307

A. Authorship....309
1. Copyright Law....309
a. Expressive Works....314
b. Data....314
c. Training Datasets....315
d. Pre-Trained/Base Models....316
e. Fine-Tuned Models and Aligned Models....317
f. Deployed Services....318
g. Generations....318

B. The Exclusive Rights....323
1. The Reproduction Right....324
2. The Derivative Right....326
3. The Distribution Right....328
4. The Display and Performance Rights....329

C. Substantial Similarity....330
1. Copyright Law....330
a. Expressive Works and Data....331
b. Training Datasets....331
c. Pre-Trained/Base Models....331
d. Fine-Tuned Models and Aligned Models....335
e. Deployed Services....336

D. Proving Copying....344
1. Copyright Law....344
2. Application to the Generative-AI Supply Chain....345
a. Data....345
b. Training Datasets....346
c. Models....347
d. Generations....347

E. Direct Infringement....348
1. Copyright Law....349
2. Application to the Generative-AI Supply Chain....349
a. Training Datasets....350
b. Pre-Trained, Fine-Tuned, and Aligned Models....350
c. Generation (via a Hosted Deployed Service)....350

F. Indirect Infringement....356
1. Copyright Law....356
2. Application to the Generative-AI Supply Chain....357
a. Generation via a Hosted Deployed Service....357
b. Model Pre-Trainers, Model Fine-Tuners, and Model Aligners....359
c. Training Dataset Creators/Curators and Content Creators....360

G. Section 512....361
1. Section 512(a): Transmission....362
2. Section 512(b): Caching....363
3. Section 512(c): User-Directed Storage....363
4. Section 512(d): Search Engines....364
5. Notice and Takedown....365

H. Fair Use....365
1. Application to the Generative-AI Supply Chain....366
a. Generations....366
b. Models....369
c. Training Datasets....372

I. Express Licenses....374

J. Implied Licenses....378

K. Remedies....381
1. Damages and Profits....381
2. Statutory Damages....384
3. Attorney's Fees....386
4. Injunctions....387

5. Destruction 389

L. Copyright Management Information 390

M. Right of Publicity....................392
1. Overview of the Right of Publicity 392
2. Incorporation and Advertising....................394
3. Incorporation in the Generative-AI Supply Chain 395

N. Hot News Misappropriation 398

III. WHICH WAY FROM HERE?.................... *400*

A. Possible Outcomes 400
1. No Liability 400
2. Liability for Generations Only 401
3. Notice and Removal 402
4. Infringing Models....................405

B. Lessons 406
1. Copyright Touches Every Part of the Generative-AI Supply Chain 406
2. Copyright Concerns Cannot Be Localized to a Single Link in the Supply Chain 407
3. Design Choices Matter 407
4. Fair Use is Not a Silver Bullet....................407
5. Generative AI Does Not Make the Ordinary Business of Copyright Law Irrelevant 407
6. Analogies Can Be Misleading 408

CONCLUSION....................408

INTRODUCTION

Generative artificial intelligence (i.e., "generative AI") systems like ChatGPT, Claude, Gemini, DALL·E, and Ideogram are capable of turning a user-supplied prompt like "give three arguments why Marbury v. Madison was wrongly decided" into a persuasive essay, or "a robot cowboy riding a rocket ship" into a work of digital art. The results can be striking. Lawyer Adam Unikowsky has described Claude as an "insane genius" for its ability to generate a "totally novel, weird" rule to decide an actual Supreme Court case. (Claude's suggestion was that the First Amendment treatment of government officials' social-media posts should turn on how many “likes” those posts get.[1]) And here is what Midjourney came up with for "a weasel on the first day of high school":

Figure 1: Prompting Midjourney, a text-to-image generative-AI application, with "a weasel on the first day of high school." (Produced by the authors.)

These systems’ unpredictability and complexity means that they break out of existing legal categories. In particular, the fact that generative-AI systems involve training on millions (or even billions) of examples of human creativity means that they raise serious copyright issues. These copyright issues have not gone unnoticed. Numerous groups of plaintiffs have sued leading generative-AI companies for copyright infringement, with potential damages reaching into the billions of dollars.[2] Legislators and regulators around the world are grappling with how to fit these technologies into copyright law’s framework—or how to modify copyright law to fit these technologies.[3]

---

[1] Adam Unikowsy, *In AI We Trust, Part II*, ADAM’S LEGAL NEWSLETTER (June 16, 2024), https://adamunikowsky.substack.com/p/in-ai-we-trust-part-ii.

[2] For a detailed tracker of the copyright lawsuits against generative-AI companies, including their claims and current statuses, *see* ChatGPT Is Eating the World, https://chatgptiseatingtheworld.com/, maintained by law professor Edward Lee.

[3] *See, e.g.*, United States Copyright Office, Artificial Intelligence Study, https://www.copyright.gov/policy/artificial-intelligence/.

This Article attempts to think carefully and systematically about how copyright applies to generative-AI systems. Our first contribution is to be precise about what "generative AI" is. It is not just one product from one company. Instead, "generative AI" is a catch-all name for a massive ecosystem of loosely related technologies, including conversational text chatbots like ChatGPT, image generators like Midjourney and DALL·E 3, coding assistants like GitHub Copilot, and systems that compose music, create videos, and suggest molecules for new medical drugs. Generative-AI models have different technical architectures and are trained on different types and sources of data using different algorithms. Some take months and cost millions of dollars to train, while others can be spun up in a weekend. These models are also made accessible to users in very different ways.

For example, some are offered through paid online services while others are distributed open-source so that anyone can download and modify them.[4]
This Article takes the complexity and diversity of generative-AI systems seriously. To provide a clear framework for thinking about the different kinds of generative-AI systems and the different ways they are created and used, the Article introduces what we call the generative-AI supply chain: an interconnected set of eight stages[5] that transform training data (millions of pictures of cats) into

[4] The use of the term "open-source" in generative AI is quite complicated. Some models are truly open-source, in the sense that their parameters and information about the training data are publicly released. Others, which are often also called "open-source" models, only release the parameters, and do not release information about the training data. Some literature refers to this second case as "semi-closed." "Closed" models are those for which neither the model parameters nor information about the training data are available. For simplicity, we will elide this nuance; it is an important detail for understanding the generative-AI supply chain, but not for our purposes here concerning copyright. *See infra* Part I.A (regarding training data, model parameters, and models); *See infra* Part I.C (regarding the generative-AI supply chain); Milad Nasr, Nicholas Carlini, Jonathan Hayase et al., Scalable Extraction of Training Data from (Production) Language Models (Nov. 28, 2023) (unpublished manuscript), https://arxiv.org/abs/2311.17035 (for distinguishing closed, semi-closed, and open models); Stella Biderman, Hailey Schoelkopf, Quentin Anthony et al., *Pythia: A Suite for Analyzing Large Language Models Across Training and Scaling*, *in* 2023 PROC. 40TH INT'L CONF. ON MACH. LEARNING 2397–2430 (2023); Dirk Groeneveld, Iz Beltagy, Pete Walsh et al., OLMo: Accelerating the Science of Language Models (Feb. 1, 2024) (unpublished manuscript), https://arxiv.org/abs/2402.00838 (for examples of open models); Hugo Touvron, Thibaut Lavril, Gautier Izacard et al., LLaMA: Open and Efficient Foundation Language Models (Feb. 27, 2023) (unpublished manuscript), https://arxiv.org/pdf/2302.13971.pdf; Hugo Touvron, Louis Martin, Kevin Stone et al., Llama 2: Open Foundation and Fine-Tuned Chat Models (July 19, 2023) (unpublished manuscript), https://arxiv.org/pdf/2307.09288.pdf (for examples of semi-closed models); OpenAI, *ChatGPT: Optimizing Language Models for Dialogue*, OPENAI (Nov. 30, 2022), https://web.archive.org/web/20221130180912/https://openai.com/blog/chatgpt/ (for an example of a system that embeds a closed model).
[5] *See infra* Part I.C (outlining, and then detailing, the eight different stages).

generations (new and hopefully never-seen-before pictures of cats that have never existed). Breaking down generative AI into these constituent stages reveals all of the places at which companies and users make choices that may have legal consequences—for copyright and beyond.

In our analysis, we specifically explore the copyright consequences. So next, the Article works systematically through the copyright analysis of the different stages of the supply chain. Copyright law is notoriously complicated, and generative-AI systems manage to touch on a great many corners of it. They raise issues of authorship, similarity, direct and indirect liability, fair use, and licensing, to name a few. These issues cannot be analyzed in isolation because there are connections everywhere. Whether the output of a generative-AI system is fair use can depend on how its training datasets were assembled. Whether the creator of a generative-AI system is secondarily liable can depend on the prompts that its users supply. The Article traces the effects of upstream technical designs on downstream uses and assesses who in these complicated sociotechnical systems bears responsibility for infringement when it happens. Because we engage so closely with the technology of generative AI, we can shed more light on the copyright questions. We do not give definitive answers as to who should and should not be held liable. Instead, we identify the key decisions that courts will need to make as they grapple with these issues and point out the consequences that would likely flow from different liability regimes.

The Article is organized in three Parts. It begins in Part I by describing the generative-AI supply chain in detail. To do so, this section leads with the necessary technical background on the broader field of machine learning (Part I.A) and then explains how generative AI both relates to and is distinct from more traditional machine learning (Part I.B). The heart of this section is a detailed, step-by-step guide to the generative-AI supply chain (Part I.C), describing what happens at each of the eight stages, the many different ways that each stage can be designed and implemented, and the design choices that the various actors must make to create, deploy, and use a generative-AI system.

Part II then provides the copyright analysis. Here, we follow the doctrinal stages of a typical copyright lawsuit: starting with authorship (Part II.A) and then covering infringement (Parts II.B through II.E), secondary liability (Part II.F), defenses, including fair use (Parts II.G through II.J), and remedies (Part II.K). We explore *what* might possibly be an infringing technical artifact, *who* might be an infringing actor, and *when* infringement might occur. We also include a discussion of three legal regimes that, while not strictly copyright, are close enough that they raise similar issues: removal of copyright management information (Part II.L), the right of publicity (Part II.M), and hot news misappropriation (Part II.N). This is where—we hope—our choice to detail the generative-AI supply chain proves its worth. Instead of asking discrete and insular questions like "Are generative-AI models fair use?" we consider how the fair-use analysis changes as one moves up and down the supply chain. We describe how the choices made by actors at one point in the supply chain affect the copyright risks faced by others; we show how copyright compliance depends on coordinated action by parties upstream and downstream from each other.

Part III pulls back to provide broader lessons. First, we describe the options courts have, from no copyright liability at all to shutting down generative AI completely (Part III.A). We explain why courts may be drawn to various regimes and what the risks and instabilities of those regimes are. Then we offer some thoughts on how courts should conceptualize copyright and generative AI (Part III.B). We argue that copyright pervades the generative-AI supply chain, that fair use is not a silver bullet, that the ordinary business of copyright litigation will continue even in a generative-AI age, and that courts should beware of metaphors that draw on more familiar technologies, which provide inadequate answers to the genuinely hard problems before them.

This Article is intended for two audiences: technologists and lawyers. We are two machine-learning researchers and a legal scholar, brought together by the goal of helping our communities understand each other's contributions and concerns around generative AI. Part I explains the basics of the technology for lawyers; many passages in Part II explain the basics of copyright law for technologists. We apologize if technologists find our discussion of how machine learning works to be tedious and elementary in places, or if lawyers feel the same way about our exposition of copyright law. But we think that having a shared foundation of knowledge will be useful to both groups and ultimately is the only way to be precise about the interplay between copyright and the generative-AI supply chain. If you find that a particular section is rehashing something you already know, it is fine to skim or skip it and flip ahead to the parts that are new. Not everything in this Article is for everyone, but we hope that it at least contains something for everyone.[6]

I. MACHINE LEARNING AND THE GENERATIVE-AI SUPPLY CHAIN

The terminology associated with generative AI is extensive, overloaded, and sometimes perplexing.[7] As a first step, we provide some background on data and machine learning, and we rely on these details to be precise about what is new (and not-so-new) in generative AI. Section A provides a general background on basic concepts in machine learning, and Section B on what makes "generative AI"

---

[6] The first draft of this Article was completed in July 2023. We have updated the references to technology and copyright court cases as of September 16, 2024. The contributions in this Article hold up in light of numerous new technological and product developments, deployment paradigms, prompting strategies, and much else. Given the speed and volume of updates in both machine learning and the courts, we have nevertheless opted to use this as a cutoff date for detailed examples and court cases that support our contributions.

[7] For a glossary of terms in machine learning and generative AI, *see* Appendix A, A. Feder Cooper, Katherine Lee, James Grimmelmann, Daphne Ippolito et al., Report of the 1st Workshop on Generative AI and Law (Nov. 11, 2023) (unpublished manuscript), https://arxiv.org/abs/2311.06477.

distinctive. Our main contribution is in Section C, which describes the generative-AI supply chain in detail, and which we find to be an essential abstraction for legal analysis that contends with generative AI.

Before getting to the details, a note about the illustrative examples that we provide in this Part: Generative AI can produce many kinds (or modalities[8]) of outputs, including text, images, music and other audio, code, and video. We focus on two: text and images. It is important to consider multiple examples because there are significant differences between them, and we want to emphasize that not all generative-AI systems work the same way. As a result, there are important technical details for other modalities that are not covered in this Part.

A. Background on Machine Learning

Machine learning is the discipline of algorithmically identifying and applying patterns in data. We begin by discussing data, which are the fundamental inputs to all machine-learning algorithms. We then provide a brief primer on the aims of machine learning, with special attention paid to how techniques used for generation differ from methods used for more familiar tasks like prediction and classification.

1. Data

In the context of AI and machine learning, data are digital representations of information about things in the world: people, events, physical phenomena like the weather, creative works like stories or software, etc. For example, Census data reflect information about individual people and households in the United States during the survey period. This information is made up of specific features, such as age, zip code, and income. The Census Bureau decided which information to collect and then decided how to represent that information in digital form. In general, individual records (such as the Census data on a single household) are typically called data examples, and a collection of related examples is a dataset. Information comes in many forms, including raw numbers, text, audio, images, and video. All of these must be converted to numerical representations to be stored, processed, and interpreted by a computer and, subsequently, by machine-learning algorithms and models.[9] These representations are often in forms that are convenient for automatic processing, rather than convenient for human inspection.

---

[8] *See infra* Part I.B.2.

[9] For simple examples of different types of data formats used in machine learning, *see* YASER S.ABU-MOSTAFA, MALIK MAGDON-ISMAIL, & HSUAN-TIEN LIN, LEARNING FROM DATA: A SHORT COURSE 1–3 (2012); TREVOR HASTIE, ROBERT TIBSHIRANI, & JEROME FRIEDMAN, THE ELEMENTS OF STATISTICAL LEARNING: DATA MINING, INFERENCE, AND PREDICTION 1-6 (2nd ed. 2009). KEVIN P. MURPHY, PROBABILISTIC MACHINE LEARNING: AN INTRODUCTION (2022). *See infra* Part I.A.2 (defining models and algorithms in machine learning).

For example, text data are often represented as word embeddings. Instead of representing the word "cat" as the letters "c", "a", and "t", a machine-learning model might represent "cat" as a list of numbers. An advantage of this numerical representation is that, instead of being similar to "car" (because they have nearly the same letters), the embedding for "cat" can be similar (i.e., their numbers will not differ by much) to the embedding for "kitten" because they have similar meanings.[10] A useful intuition is that, for some word embeddings, you can do operations on them: you can take the word embedding for "king" (a list of numbers), subtract the word embedding representing "man," add the word embedding representing "woman," and get something very close to the word embedding for "queen."[11]

---

[10] More precisely, the embedding strategy described here attempts to capture semantic similarity, in which a distance metric on the vector space of embeddings of words reflects underlying semantic distance between the concepts words represent. *See* Murphy, *supra* note 12, at 26 (providing a short definition of word embeddings); *Id.* at 703–10 (providing a summary of different types of popular word embeddings); Vicki Boykis, What are embeddings? (June 2023) (unpublished manuscript), https://github.com/veekaybee/what_are_embeddings (for an accessible treatment of the history of embeddings and discussion in relation to modern-day generative-AI models); Tomas Mikolov, Kai Chen, Greg Corrado & Jeffrey Dean, *Efficient Estimation of Word Representations in Vector Space*, *in* 2013 INT'L CONF. ON LEARNING REPRESENTATIONS (2013) (discussing word2vec, a common neural-network-based approach for producing embeddings); Tomas Mikolov, Ilya Sutskever, Kai Chen, et al., *Distributed Representations of Words and Phrases and their Compositionality*, *in* 26 ADVANCES NEURAL INFO. PROCESSING SYS. (2013) (for influential follow-on work to word2vec).

[11] This example should not be taken too generally, as it does not always extend to other cases. *See* Ekaterina Vylomova, Laura Rimell, Trevor Cohn & Timothy Baldwin, *Take and Took, Gaggle and Goose, Book and Read: Evaluating the Utility of Vector Differences for Lexical Relation Learning* 1671, *in* 1 PROC. 54TH ANN. MEETING ASS'N FOR COMPUT. LINGUISTICS 1671 (2016). There are many ways to compute word embeddings. A common embedding strategy that quantifies word importance involves computing word frequency (term frequency, TF) for a particular document in a corpus, and scaling it by word rarity (inverse document frequency, or IDF) across documents in the corpus. For more on TD-IDF, *see generally* Karen Sparck Jones, *A Statistical Interpretation of Term Specificity and Its Application in Retrieval*, 1988 DOCUMENT RETRIEVAL SYS. 132; Gerard Salton & Christopher Buckley, *Term-weighting approaches in automatic text retrieval*, 24 INFO. PROCESSING & MGMT 513, 516 (1988). By relying strictly on frequencies, this type of embedding does not capture any semantic information in the encoded words. More sophisticated techniques involve learning word embeddings from data. For example, the BERT language model uses deep learning and a transformer architecture to encode word embeddings. *See generally* Jacob Devlin, Ming-Wei Chang, Kenton Lee & Kristina Toutanova, *BERT: Pre-training of Deep Bidirectional Transformers for Language Understanding*, *in* 1 PROC. 2019 CONF. N. AMERICAN CHAPTER ASS'N FOR COMPUT. LINGUISTICS: HUM. LANGUAGE TECHS. 4171 (2019). *See infra* Part I.B.3.a (discussing the transformer architecture).

Data are not identical to the things they reflect. A census record is not a household; the word embedding of "cat" is not a cat.[12] But data capture useful information about those things—and they enable computers to reason about them. For our purposes, a creative work like a painting or book is not itself data;[13] rather, it can be processed computationally to be converted into data to be used in machine-learning applications.

2. Machine Learning

An algorithm is a step-by-step procedure—often implemented in software—for performing a computation on data.[14] For example, algorithms include different procedures for sorting a list of numbers, searching for a word in a list of words, encrypting passwords, and much else. Machine learning is a subfield of computing that develops and applies algorithms to learn from data. These algorithms employ mathematical tools from probability and statistics to model (hopefully useful and interesting) patterns in the data. Machine-learning scientists and practitioners may use these algorithms (and their resulting learned patterns) for different aims.

Two overarching types of tasks that machine learning is commonly used for are discriminative[15] and generative[16] modeling. Discriminative modeling includes classification (is this image of a cat or a dog?) and regression (how many ice cream cones can I expect to sell if the weather is 80°F today?).[17] In contrast, generative modeling can produce new content, such as images or text.[18]

---

[12] For a detailed treatment of how data serve as a proxy for entities in the world, *see* DYLAN MULVIN, PROXIES: THE CULTURAL WORK OF STANDING IN 1–33 (1st ed. 2021).

[13] This is not the case in other fields, like archaeology, but is true for machine learning, and thus this Article.

[14] *See generally* THOMAS H. CORMEN, CHARLES E. LEISERSON, RONALD L. RIVEST & CLIFFORD STEIN, INTRODUCTION TO ALGORITHMS (4th ed. 2022).

[15] *See infra* Part I.A.2.a.

[16] *See infra* Part I.A.2.b.

[17] While the examples we provide in the Article concern classification of inputs into discrete output categories, regression tasks that involve real numbers, such as predicting housing price given a set of features, are also discriminative.

[18] This is a simplification that is sufficient for our purposes. Generative modeling does not necessarily produce new content; it estimates probability distributions from which such content can be (but does not have to be) sampled. These probabilities can be useful for applications other than content generation. For example, the BERT language model employs generative techniques and can be used to produce word embeddings, but not content intended to be consumed or enjoyed directly by a human user. *See generally* Devlin, Chang, Lee & Toutanova, *supra* note 14. The distinction between discriminative and generative modeling ultimately hinges on modeling choices regarding the underlying probabilities. *See generally* Dan Y. Rubinstein & Trevor Hastie, *Discriminative Versus Informative Learning*, *in* 1997 PROC. THIRD INT'L CONF. ON KNOWLEDGE DISCOVERY & DATA MINING (1997) (using the term "informative" instead of "generative").

a. Discriminative Modeling

Consider a machine-learning model that classifies images as either cats or dogs. A common analogy in legal literature is to describe a discriminative machine-learning model as a mathematical function that maps inputs to outputs.[19] Here, the model takes a computer-readable version of an image as input[20] and returns a label of either cat or dog as its output. Mathematically, we would say that the set of all inputs (images of pets) is $\mathcal{X}$, the set of possible outputs (the labels cat and dog) is $\mathcal{Y}$, and the function that maps an input to an output is $f : \mathcal{X} \mapsto \mathcal{Y}$. It is an underlying assumption of this analogy that the function f is deterministic: given the same input (a particular picture of a terrier), a given trained classification model will always produce the same output (the label dog).[21]

---

[19] For example, the function $f(x) = x + 1$ produces an output that is 1 greater than its input. If the input to this function is 5, the output is 6. If the input is 8, the output is 9. *See generally* A. Feder Cooper, Jonathan Frankle & Christopher De Sa, *Non-Determinism and the Lawlessness of Machine Learning Code*, *in* 2022 PROC. 2022 SYMPOSIUM ON COMPUT. SCI. & L. 1 (2022) (discussing the prevalence of the "function" view).

[20] *E.g.*, two-dimensional images can be saved as a set of numbers, which can serve as the input to a machine-learning algorithm. Often, images are formatted as a **matrix** representing pixels, where each pixel is a vector of numbers in the range 0-255 that represents combinations of *r*ed, *b*lue, and green (RGB) hues.

[21] *See generally* Cooper, Frankle & De Sa, *supra* note 22 (discussing this assumption in the legal literature on machine learning). Classifiers like these actually output probabilities (in this case, the probability that an input image should be labeled dog), which can then be converted to an output label. This typically involves using a classification rule, e.g., "if the probability of dog is greater than 0.5, then output dog, otherwise output cat." In this example of an image of a terrier, we assume that the model classifies the image correctly. It is also possible that the classifier does not, and instead always returns the label cat. Further, note that, in general, the input image could be of anything. Performing classification involves manipulating numbers under the hood—typically, linear algebra operations on vectors and matrices that contain the model parameters and the new input data example. So, one could provide, for example, an image of an airplane as input, and the model would still output a probability (that can be converted to a classification) of either cat or dog.

Figure 2: Depicting the analogy of a machine-learned model as a function, where a classifier f takes an image x as input and returns the class label y= dog. (Image: "Arabela, The Venus of Evanston." Source: Dr. Fernando Delgado, reprinted with permission.)

To produce such a model, one chooses a training algorithm that takes training data examples as input and produces a model as its output. It is important to emphasize that the training algorithm implements a *different* function than the classification function described above. The input to a training algorithm for the cat-dog classifier is a training dataset (numerous images of pets, each labeled cat or dog), not just a *single* data example (an image of a terrier). The output from this training algorithm is a model—the function that classifies an individual image as a cat or dog. The model, like its data inputs, is ultimately also some arrangement of numbers that are interpretable by a computer. For our purposes, there are two important concepts to understand about the numbers that comprise models: how they are organized and what they contain.

First, start with organization. There are many kinds of models (even for a simple cat-dog classification task), and each model has its own model architecture. Very roughly, a model architecture specifies *how* a model stores information about patterns in data: how much information, how it is arranged, and how it can be manipulated with code. For example, one could use the same model architecture to make a cat-dog classifier or a bird-airplane classifier, and they would use the same training algorithm. The difference is that the bird-airplane classifier would be trained on a training dataset of pictures of things in the sky, each labeled with bird or airplane.

An important class of model architectures is neural networks, which consist of interconnected nodes (also called neurons). There are many different neural-network architectures, which differ in things such as how many nodes there are (organized in how many layers), how long each list of nodes is (the size of each layer), and how the nodes are connected to each other. And even for a given model architecture, there can be many different training algorithms.[22] It is a major area of machine-learning research to determine what model architectures, training algorithms, and training datasets are most effective for producing useful models.

Second, the contents. Noted above, the nodes in a specific model architecture are *interconnected.* Each of these connections has an associated parameter (also called weight). These parameters are lists of numbers that represent the strengths of connections between nodes in the network. The specific numbers that they contain come from training:[23] They are the particular patterns learned from running a specific training algorithm on a specific training dataset. This model training typically involves running an optimization-based routine, which iteratively processes the input data to update (i.e., train) the model parameters.[24] (A very loose analogy can be drawn to the way that neurons in the brain are connected to each other with different strengths to encode a human-learned representation of the world.)

Different model architectures vary widely in size and complexity and, in turn, have different capabilities for encoding learned relationships in the data. Simpler, more traditional statistical models like logistic regression have relatively few learned parameters, while modern-day deep neural networks can have *billions* (or

---

[22] Model architectures and training algorithms also include **hyperparameters**. Hyperparameters are parameters that traditionally are not learned; they are often set by a human. For the model, they can dictate the number of parameters and layers. For the training algorithm, they dictate properties of how training is run. For example, a hyperparameter called the "learning rate" determines how fast or slow model training should proceed. *See* A. Feder Cooper, Yucheng Lu, Jessica Zosa Forde & Christopher De Sa, *Hyperparameter Optimization Is Deceiving Us, and How to Stop It, in* 34 ADVANCES NEURAL INFO. PROCESSING SYS. (2021) (regarding the effects of hyperparameter choices on resulting learned models, and citations therein).

[23] There are other inputs that configure the training algorithm, and which affect the parameters that are learned. *See id.* and accompanying text (for an example of such configurations).

[24] There are many different optimization methods used in deep learning. *See generally* Robin M. Schmidt, Frank Schneider & Philipp Hennig, *Descending through a Crowded Valley - Benchmarking Deep Learning Optimizers, in* 139 PROC. 38TH INT'L CONF. ON MACH. LEARNING 9367–76 (2021). The most common is an optimization method called Adam (and variants thereof). *See generally* Diederik P. Kingma & Jimmy Lei Ba, *Adam: A Method for Stochastic Optimization, in* 2015 INT'L CONF. ON LEARNING REPRESENTATIONS (2015). However, optimization algorithms for machine learning, and for training generative-AI models, remain an active area of research. *See, e.g.*, Pierre Foret, Ariel Kleiner, Hossein Mobahi & Behnam Neyshabur, *Sharpness-aware Minimization for Efficiently Improving Generalization, in* 2021 INT'L CONF. ON LEARNING REPRESENTATIONS (2021); Dara Bahri, Hossein Mobahi & Yi Tay, *Sharpness-Aware Minimization Improves Language Model Generalization, in* 2022 PROC. 60TH ANN. MEETING ASS'N FOR COMPUT. LINGUISTICS (VOLUME 1: LONG PAPERS) 7360–71 (2022).

even *trillions*) of parameters.[25] At each step, the training algorithm adjusts the values of the model's parameters so that they are slightly better at describing the training data; with enough iterations on enough of the right kind of data, the model can describe patterns that are present in many training examples. After training is complete, we can evaluate the resulting model by running it on new (previously unseen) data examples and seeing how well it classifies them as either cat or dog.[26]

The above describes a sketch of machine learning that is familiar in legal scholarship. This work has scrutinized the implications of machine-learning-based decision-making in a variety of areas, such as whether or not to interview or hire a job candidate, grant an applicant a loan,[27] or, as in the case of the infamous Northpointe COMPAS system, to predict prison recidivism.[28] These types of yes/no decision-making tasks generally fall under the heading of discriminative machine learning, a type of machine learning that attempts to draw boundaries in available data, and that is often used for making predictions. As we stated at the beginning of this section, discriminative machine-learning tasks typically involve classification or regression.

---

[25] Consider three examples. First, PaLM, a language model built by Google, has 540 billion parameters. Aakanksha Chowdhery, Sharan Narang, Jacob Devlin et al., *PaLM: Scaling Language Modeling with Pathways*, 24 J. MACH. LEARNING RSCH. 1–113 (2023). Second, the largest Llama 2 model, a semi-closed model released by Meta, has 70 billion parameters. (Llama 2 is a **family** of models that come in different sizes. It is common today for open- and semi-closed models to come in a variety of differently sized architectures, with larger models tending to produce higher quality generations for a larger cost in computational resources (i.e., **compute**). Llama 2 is just one example of such a model family.) *See supra* note 7 and accompanying text (regarding Llama 2 and the distinction between open- and semi-closed models). *See infra* Part I.B.4 (discussing the importance of scale). Third, GLM-130B, a bilingual Chinese and English model, has 130 billion parameters. Aohan Zeng, Xiao Liu, Zhengxiao Du et al., GLM-130B: An Open Bilingual Pre-trained Model (Oct. 5, 2022) (unpublished manuscript), https://arxiv.org/abs/2210.02414. When discussing **model size**, it is typical to do so with respect to parameters (i.e., connections between nodes); there are typically many more connections between nodes than there are nodes.

[26] To do valid and reliable model evaluation, it is important to run the model on a **test dataset**. Test datasets are made up of reserved data examples that are not a part of training. They are ostensibly from the same *distribution* as the training data but, since the model has not seen them before being evaluated, these exact examples have not influenced the learned relationships in the model's parameters. *See* Abu-Mostafa, *supra* note 12, at 39–69.

[27] Danielle Keats Citron & Frank A. Pasquale, *The Scored Society: Due Process for Automated Predictions*, 89 WASH. L. REV. 655 (2014).

[28] *See generally* Jeff Larson, Surya Mattu, Lauren Kirchner & Julia Angwin, *How We Analyzed the COMPAS Recidivism Algorithm*, PROPUBLICA (May 16, 2016), https://www.propublica.org/article/how-we-analyzed-the-compas-recidivism-algorithm/ (for the original study indicating algorithmic bias in this system).

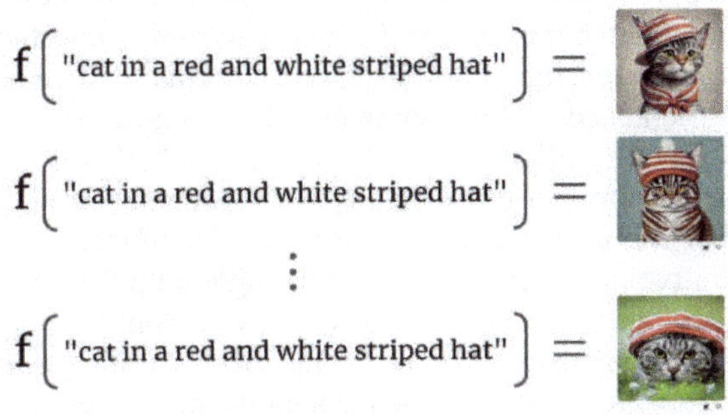

Figure 3: Images of "cat in a red and white striped hat" generated by the authors with Ideogram (Ideogram.AI, 2023, https://ideogram.ai/). Running the model (f) multiple times on the same input can generate different outputs.

b. Generative Modeling

Discriminative tasks are only one type of machine-learning modeling. Another paradigm is called generative machine learning. [29] Whereas discriminative machine-learning models return a *single*[30] output y from a set of

[29] Deep generative models, such as OpenAI's CLIP, Midjourney, or Stability AI's Stable Diffusion, are not the only form of generative machine learning. Generative machine learning is often subdivided into probabilistic graphical models and deep generative models. *See generally* OpenAI, *CLIP: Connecting text and images*, OPENAI (Jan. 5, 2021), https://openai.com/research/clip (regarding OpenAI's CLIP model). *See generally* MIDJOURNEY, https://midjourney.com/ (regarding Midjourney). *See generally Stable Diffusion XL*, STABILITY AI (2023), https://stability.ai/stablediffusion; Robin Rombach, Andreas Blattmann, Dominik Lorenz et al., *High-Resolution Image Synthesis with Latent Diffusion Models*, *in* 2022 IEEE CONF. ON COMPUT. VISION & PATTERN RECOGNITION (2022) (regarding Stable Diffusion). *See generally* DAPHNE KOLLER & NIR FRIEDMAN, PROBABILISTIC GRAPHICAL MODELS: PRINCIPLES AND TECHNIQUES (2009) (for a canonical textbook treatment on probabilistic graphical models). *See generally* JAKUB M. TOMCZAK, DEEP GENERATIVE MODELING (2022) (for details on different techniques for generative modeling in machine learning).

[30] These single outputs can nevertheless have differing degrees of uncertainty associated with them. *See generally* A. Feder Cooper, Katherine Lee, Madiha Zahrah Choksi et al., *Arbitrariness and Prediction: The Confounding Role of Variance in Fair Classification*, *in* 2024 PROC. 38TH ANN. AAAI CONF. ON A.I. (2024) (for an accessible treatment of this topic).

possible outputs $\mathcal{Y}$ (Figure 2),[31] generative machine-learning models have *multiple possible reasonable outputs* for a given input. For example, many reasonable images match the caption: "cat in a red and white striped hat" (Figure 3). Similarly, a generative model for text could have many reasonable completions to the following sentence: "In the summer, I like to go to the [blank]", such as: "beach", "park", "pool", or "mountains" filling in the "[blank]".

This example shows how the analogy of machine learning as a function, which provides a useful intuition for discriminative modeling, does not cleanly extend to generative modeling. Instead of a single output y for a given input x, for generative modeling there are usually many reasonable outputs for a given input. For a model, choosing which among these possible outputs to produce involves some *randomness*, which means a model can generate different outputs even when run on the same input.

In more detail, generative models learn from their training data which outputs are more likely. In the sentence "In the summer, I like to go to the [blank]", the word "beach" is a more likely completion than "slopes". While the words "summer" and "beach" are often associated in writing (and thus also in the training data used to produce the model), this is not the case for "summer" and "slopes".[32] But "beach" and "pool" might be equally likely. So, the model's choice between "beach" and "pool" is made with some degree of randomness.[33]

B. Generative AI

Most commonly, the term "generative AI" is used to describe systems that can take in a variety of inputs—typically expressive content (e.g., a piece of text or an image)—and can produce expressive content as their outputs. The inputs are often user-generated, though they do not have to be.[34] This is why a user of an

---

[31] In the running classification example above, every input image must be labeled with either y = cat or y = dog.

[32] The model captures the *conditional probability* of the next word x *given* having already seen a prior sequence of words a. In the above example, we would consider the probability of the next word being x = "beach" given that a = "In the summer, I like to go to the".

[33] Discriminative and generative modeling can be related to each other mathematically. Under the hood, both approaches model conditional probabilities, but this observation gets abstracted away in typical discussions that analogize discriminative models to functions. *See generally* Rubinstein & Hastie, *supra* note 21. *See also* Andrew Y. Ng & Michael I. Jordan, *On Discriminative vs. Generative Classifiers: A comparison of logistic regression and naive Bayes* 2, *in* 14 ADVANCES NEURAL INFO. PROCESSING SYS. (2001) (describing how the two approaches can be related to each other using Bayes' rule).

[34] Synthetic data, rather than user-generated data, can also be supplied as inputs, both for prompting and as training data. Producing and leveraging synthetic data (that has been produced by generative AI) for prompting and training is an active area of machine-learning research. *See, e.g.,* Aaron Gokaslan, A. Feder Cooper, Jasmine Collins et al.,

application like ChatGPT or DreamStudio is said to provide a prompt. The output that the application produces in response is called a generation. It is also helpful to distinguish training time (the process of training a model) from generation time (the process of using a model to generate an output).[35]

Generative AI builds on and extends traditional generative machine learning, but it adds several new elements that have contributed to its immense popularity and accompanying controversy. In the remainder of this section, we unpack four ways that generative AI is different and new. First, contemporary generative-AI *systems* often use *multiple models*, which have different architectures and use different approaches to perform different functions.[36] For this reason, it is often more helpful to think about the design and behavior of an overall system, rather than focusing entirely on a specific model within it. Second, these systems are often multimodal; they can work with data in different formats (such as a system

---

CommonCanvas: Open Diffusion Models Trained with Creative-Commons Images, *in* 2024 PROC. OF THE IEEE/CVF CONF. ON COMPUT. VISION PATTERN RECOGNITION (CVPR) 8250 (2024) (using generative-AI-produced text captions to train a text-to-image diffusion model); Liang Wang, Nan Yang, Xiaolong Huang et al., Improving Text Embeddings with Large Language Models (Dec. 31, 2023) (unpublished manuscript), https://arxiv.org/abs/2401.00368 (producing text embeddings using only synthetic data); Avi Singh, John D. Co-Reyes, Rishabh Agarwal et al., Beyond Human Data: Scaling Self-Training for Problem-Solving with Language Models (Dec. 11, 2023) (unpublished manuscript), https://arxiv.org/abs/2312.06585 (generating synthetic fine-tuning data); *See infra* Part I.C.7 (for more discussion on synthetic data).

[35] The amount of compute at training time has traditionally been the emphasis when discussing the scale of resources used to produce contemporary generative-AI models (particularly language models). Recently, research and products have begun to experiment with also using more compute at generation time—also called **test time**—to produce higher quality generations. Most notably, OpenAI's recent o1 model explores new training-time and test-time compute paradigms to improve "complex reasoning." OpenAI, *Learning to Reason with LLMs*, OPENAI (September 12, 2024), https://openai.com/index/learning-to-reason-with-llms/ ("Our large-scale reinforcement learning algorithm teaches the model how to think productively using its chain of thought in a highly data-efficient training process. We have found that the performance of o1 consistently improves with more reinforcement learning (train-time compute) and with more time spent thinking (test-time compute). The constraints on scaling this approach differ substantially from those of LLM pretraining, and we are continuing to investigate them."). *See infra* note 39 and accompanying text (discussing reinforcement learning); *infra* note 208 and accompanying text (discussing chain of thought).

[36] Historically, practitioners typically would have chosen to solve a particular problem with a particular modeling technique. For example, they would take either a discriminative or generative modeling approach, or use another modeling paradigm called **reinforcement learning**. Abu-Mostafa, *supra* note 12, at 11–14; Murphy, *supra* note 12, at 1–19 (for an intuition behind reinforcement learning). We introduce this concept in more detail when we discuss **model alignment** in the generative-AI supply chain. *See infra* Part I.C.8. Generative AI can involve all of these approaches. Reinforcement learning also plays an enormous role at both training time and test time in OpenAI's o1 model. *See id.*

that takes *text* as an input but produces *images* as outputs). Third, recent technological developments in the transformer architecture (often used for text) and diffusion models (often used for images) have significantly contributed to the power of contemporary generative systems. And fourth, there have been immense leaps in scale. Generative AI involves large-scale systems and the training of massive models on similarly massive datasets. Scale stands on its own as another reason why generative AI is different from more traditional generative modeling.

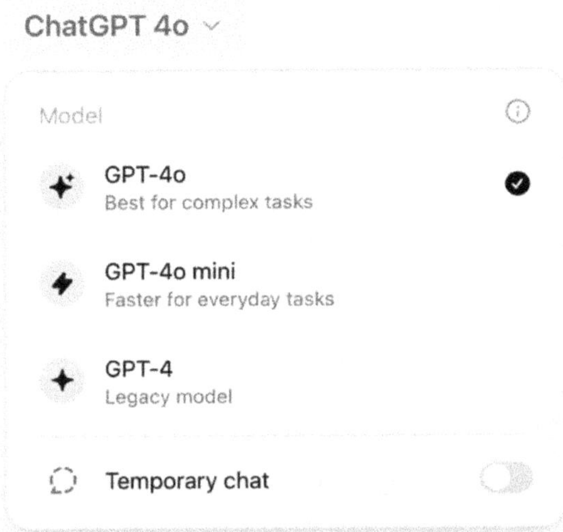

Figure 4: ChatGPT user interface showing a choice of accessing three underlying ChatGPT models: GPT-4o, GPT-4o mini, and GPT-4. (Screenshot produced by the authors, prior to the release of the o1 model.)

1. Generative-AI Systems

Most users of generative AI do not interact with a model directly. Instead, they use an interface to a system, in which the model is just one of several embedded, interoperating components.[37] For example, OpenAI hosts various ways to access its latest models. ChatGPT is a user interface (and the name of a system) for accessing several different underlying models (Figure 4). OpenAI also has a developer API, which serves as an interface for programmers to access

[37] *See generally* A. Feder Cooper & Karen Levy, *Fast or Accurate? Governing Conflicting Goals in Highly Autonomous Vehicles*, 20 COLO. TECH. L.J. 249 (2022). *See* A. Feder Cooper, Karen Levy & Christopher De Sa, *Accuracy-Efficiency Trade-Offs and Accountability in Distributed ML Systems*, *in* 2021 EQUITY & ACCESS ALGORITHMS MECHANISMS & OPTIMIZATION 1, 1–2 (2021) (discussing the importance of such a systems framing in contemporary computing applications). OpenAI also emphasizes this point in their policy research. For example, OpenAI produced a GPT-4 *system* card (emphasis added), and this point was made at the GenLaw 2023 workshop by Miles Brundage in his talk "Where and When Does the Law Fit into AI Development and Deployment?" OpenAI, GPT-4 System Card (Mar. 23, 2023) (unpublished manuscript), https://CDN.openai.com/papers/gpt-4-system-card.pdf (emphasizing systems, which contain models and other components).

OpenAI's different models using code. There are additional components behind each of these interfaces, including possibly (according to rumor) as many as sixteen GPT-4 models, to which different prompts are routed.[38] As another example, consider Stable Diffusion, an open-source model for producing image generations.[39] Most users do not typically interact directly with the Stable Diffusion model;[40] rather, they access a version that is embedded in a larger system operated by Stability AI,[41] which has multiple components, including a web-based application called DreamStudio.[42]

2. Generation Modalities

The input and output content types for generative-AI models are often referred to as modalities. For example, a chatbot that produces *text* generations when given a user-provided *text* prompt would use an underlying text-to-text model; this model operates in the text modality. Such a chatbot uses the same modality for the input and output, but this is not a requirement for generative AI more broadly. Many image-generation models (used in systems like Stable Diffusion,[43] DALL·E 2,[44] and ChatGPT Plus and Enterprise,[45] etc.) take a text description as input and produce an image generation as output. These models are multimodal, text-to-image models.

While we focus on generative-AI systems that involve text and image inputs and outputs, there are many other modalities that generative AI can be applied to, such as computer code, audio (music, voice), video, and molecular structures. Text-to-code models, which are designed specifically to take in natural language

[38] This rumor originated in a Twitter (now X) post. Maximilian Schreiner, *GPT-4 architecture, datasets, costs and more leaked*, THE DECODER (July 11, 2023), https://the-decoder.com/gpt-4-architecture-datasets-costs-and-more-leaked/.

[39] Rombach, Blattmann, Lorenz et al., *supra* note 32.

[40] At a minimum, using the model directly would involve downloading the model parameters, writing code to run the model, and executing that code.

[41] *Stable Diffusion XL*, *supra* note 32.

[42] *See generally DreamStudio*, STABILITY AI (2023), https://stability.ai/stablediffusion.

[43] *See* Rombach, Blattmann, Lorenz et al., *supra* note 32 (describing the model); *Stable Diffusion XL*, *supra* note 32 (describing the product).

[44] *See* Aditya Ramesh, Prafulla Dhariwal, Alex Nichol et al., Hierarchical Text-Conditional Image Generation with CLIP Latents (Apr. 13, 2022) (unpublished manuscript), https://arxiv.org/abs/2204.06125 (describing the model); *DALL·E 2*, OPENAI (2022), https://openai.com/dall-e-2 (describing the product).

[45] *See DALL·E 3 is now available in ChatGPT Plus and Enterprise*, OPENAI (Oct. 19, 2023), https://openai.com/blog/dall-e-3-is-now-available-in-chatgpt-plus-and-enterprise (announcing the integration of DALL·E 3 text-to-image functionality into the paid versions of the ChatGPT chatbot system).

as input and generate code snippets as output,[46] include OpenAI Codex[47] and Code Llama[48] from Meta.[49] Notably, Codex is the generative-AI model embedded in the GitHub Copilot system,[50] which is named in active lawsuits regarding copyright infringement.[51] Google DeepMind's Lyria,[52] Google's MusicLM,[53] and OpenAI's Jukebox[54] are music-generation models embedded in larger systems.[55] OpenAI's website claims, "Provided with genre, artist, and

---

[46] ChatGPT, for example, can also produce code snippets, but is a chatbot system that also has other functionality. *See* OpenAI, *supra* note 7.

[47] Wojciech Zaremba, Greg Brockman & OpenAI, *OpenAI Codex*, OPENAI (Aug. 10, 2021), https://openai.com/blog/openai-codex (describing the Codex model). OpenAI, *Powering next generation applications with OpenAI Codex*, OPENAI (May 24, 2022), https://openai.com/blog/codex-apps (discussing applications using Codex). Mark Chen, Jerry Tworek, Heewoo Jun et al., Evaluating Large Language Models Trained on Code (July 7, 2021) (unpublished manuscript), https://arxiv.org/abs/2107.03374 (for the technical report detailing the original Codex model).

[48] Meta, *Introducing Code Llama, an AI Tool for Coding*, META NEWS (Aug. 24, 2023), https://about.fb.com/news/2023/08/code-llama-ai-for-coding/ (announcing Code Llama). Meta, *Introducing Code Llama, a state-of-the-art large language model for coding*, META RSCH. BLOG (Aug. 24, 2023), https://ai.meta.com/blog/code-llama-largelanguage-model-coding/ (describing Code Llama in a technical blog post). Baptiste Rozière, Jonas Gehring, Fabian Gloeckle et al., Code Llama: Open Foundation Models for Code (Aug. 24, 2023) (unpublished manuscript), https://arxiv.org/abs/2308.12950 (for the technical report detailing the Code Llama model).

[49] Both of these models use transformer-based architectures. *See infra* Part I.B.3a.

[50] *See generally GitHub Copilot documentation*, GITHUB (Aug. 28, 2023), https://docs.github.com/en/copilot.

[51] *See generally* Complaint, Doe 1 v. GitHub, Inc., No. 4:22-cv-06823 (N.D. Cal. Nov. 3, 2022). GitHub has since updated the Copilot model to go "beyond the previous OpenAI Codex model." However, the original Codex model is the one named in active lawsuits. *See generally* Shuyin Zhao, *Smarter, more efficient coding: GitHub Copilot goes beyond Codex with improved AI model*, GITHUB (July 28, 2023), https://github.blog/2023-07-28-smarter-more-efficient-coding-github-copilot-goes-beyond-codex-with-improved-ai-model/ (discussing Copilot's use of Codex).

[52] *Transforming the future of music creation*, GOOGLE DEEPMIND (Nov. 16, 2023), https://deepmind.google/discover/blog/transforming-the-future-of-music-creation/.

[53] *See* Andrea Agostinelli, Timo I. Denk, Zalán Borsos et al., MusicLM: Generating Music From Text (Jan. 26, 2023) (unpublished manuscript), https://arxiv.org/abs/2301.11325 (for the research paper on the model); Kristin Yim & Hema Manickavasagam, *Turn ideas into music with MusicLM*, GOOGLE (May 10, 2023), https://blog.google/technology/ai/musiclm-google-ai-test-kitchen/ (for the product announcement).

[54] Heewoo Jun, Christine Payne, Jong Wook Kim et al., Jukebox: A Generative Model for Music (Apr. 30, 2020) (unpublished manuscript), https://arxiv.org/abs/2005.00341.

[55] For example, Dream Track is a production system built using Lyria. *See* Google DeepMind, *supra* note 55.

lyrics as input, Jukebox outputs a new music sample produced from scratch."[56] Pika is an "idea-to-video platform" that provides tools to produce video generations using models that take in either text or image prompts.[57] Lastly, generative-AI models for molecular structure are intended for many different purposes, including to aid in the design of new drugs and to understand protein function. Examples of models in this domain include ProtGPT2[58] and DiffDock.[59] While these modalities also have important implications for copyright,[60] we limit our discussion and examples in the remainder of this Article to text and images.

a. Text Data and Generations

OpenAI's ChatGPT is a system that takes in text inputs and produces text outputs (among other modalities). ChatGPT is built on top of multiple models, including several different text-to-text model architectures trained on massive amounts of text data.[61] During training, each of these text-to-text models is shown text sequences, and for every sequence, it is trained to predict the next word given all the previous words in the sequence.

For example, if the sentence "In the summer, I like to go to the beach" were in the training data, then the model would first be shown "In" and trained to predict "the", then given "In the" and trained to predict "summer", and so on.[62]

---

[56] *See* OpenAI, *OpenAI JukeBox*, OPENAI (Apr. 30, 2020), https://openai.com/research/jukebox (describing the use of the transformer-based architecture in Jukebox).

[57] *See* Pika, *An idea-to-video platform that brings your creativity to motion*, PIKA (2023), https://pika.art/.

[58] *See generally* Noellia Ferruz, Steffen Schmidt & Birte Höcker, *ProtGPT2 is a deep unsupervised language model for protein design*, 13 NATURE COMMC'NS 4348 (2022). ProtGPT2 is based on GPT-2. *See generally* Radford, Wu, Child et al., *infra* note 70. (describing GPT-2, a language model with a transformer-based architecture).

[59] *See generally* Gabriele Corso, Hannes Stärk, Bowen Jing et al., *DiffDock: Diffusion Steps, Twists, and Turns for Molecular Docking*, *in* 2023 INT'L CONF. ON LEARNING REPRESENTATIONS (2023). DiffDock uses diffusion-based techniques. *See infra* Part I.B.3.b.

[60] And perhaps also patent law, for generative-AI systems that involve molecular structure.

[61] So far, the most notable of these models are OpenAI's GPT family of text-to-text models, including GPT-3.5, GPT-4, GPT-4o, and GPT-4o mini. Recent o-family models include o1 and o1-mini. OpenAI, *supra* note 7.

[62] Note that illustrating this prediction one word at a time is a simplification. It is common to train models on **tokens**, not words. Tokens are numbers that represent a word, sub-word, logogram, or punctuation mark. For instance, the word "hello" may be represented by the token-ID number 12. A more uncommon word like "credenza" may be divided into multiple sub-words, e.g., "cre", "den", "za"; each sub-word would be represented by a number, e.g., "cre" = 58, "den" = 29, "za" = 105), and so, altogether, the word "credenza" would be encoded as the vector [58,29,105]. Modeling data as tokens enables using transformers with non-text sequences, e.g., a token for a music model may be a musical

Text data are, in many ways, easier to collect than data in other modalities because text is so readily available on the Internet. Common data sources include data scraped from the web,[63] books (both copyrighted and in the public domain), and news articles,[64] as well as data obtained through user interactions.[65] Web data may include structured text like product reviews, and free-form social media posts and blogs.[66]

It is important to note that generative text models are used extensively beyond chatbot systems like ChatGPT.[67] For example, they also play an important role in

---

note or a specific pitch. In our example above, the sentence could be **tokenized** as the list ["In", "the", "summer", ",", "I", "like", "to", "go", "to", "the", "beach"], where each word (and the comma) corresponds to a token (that has an associated token ID). But a different tokenizer could, hypothetically, tokenize the word "summer" as two tokens, e.g., "sum" and "mer". The prediction of the next token would instead operate over a list that contains these tokens, rather than "summer".

[63] Web scraping involves using a computer to download and store the contents of a webpage. This is not a new phenomenon; businesses have been scraping data for decades. *See, e.g.*, hiQ Labs, Inc. v. LinkedIn Corp., 31 F.4th 1180 (9th Cir. 2022) (discussing legality of scraping data from LinkedIn).

[64] *See* Katherine Lee, Daphne Ippolito & A. Feder Cooper, The Devil is in the Training Data (2023) (unpublished manuscript), *in* Katherine Lee, A. Feder Cooper, James Grimmelmann & Daphne Ippolito, AI and Law: The Next Generation 5 (2023) (unpublished manuscript), https://papers.ssrn.com/sol3/papers.cfm?abstract_id=4580739 (discussing training data sources). *See generally* Tom B. Brown, Benjamin Mann, Nick Ryder et al., Language Models are Few-Shot Learners (2020) (unpublished manuscript), https://arxiv.org/abs/2005.14165; Leo Gao, Stella Biderman, Sid Black et al., The Pile: An 800GB Dataset of Diverse Text for Language Modeling (Dec. 31, 2020) (unpublished manuscript), https://arxiv.org/abs/2101.00027; Colin Raffel, Noam Shazeer, Adam Roberts, Katherine Lee et al., *Exploring the Limits of Transfer Learning with a Unified Text-to-Text Transformer*, 21 J. MACH. LEARNING RSCH. 1 (2020).

[65] For example, it is widely believed (though unconfirmed) that user data ingested by the ChatGPT interface are used to train the underlying model(s). *See New Ways to Manage Your Data in ChatGPT*, OPENAI (2023), https://openai.com/blog/new-ways-tomanage-your-data-in-chatgpt (describing only the cases in which user data are *not* used to train the ChatGPT system).

[66] *See* Kevin Schaul, Szu Yu Chen & Nitasha Tiku, *Inside the secret list of websites that make AI like ChatGPT sound smart*, WASHINGTON POST (Apr. 19, 2023), https://www.washingtonpost.com/technology/interactive/2023/ai-chatbot-learning/. *See generally* Jesse Dodge, Maarten Sap, Ana Marasović et al., *Documenting Large Webtext Corpora: A Case Study on the Colossal Clean Crawled Corpus*, *in* 2021 PROC. 2021 CONF. ON EMPIRICAL METHODS NAT. LANGUAGE Processing 1286 (2021).

[67] *See* Alec Radford, Karthik Narasimhan, Tim Salimans & Ilya Sutskever, Improving Language Understanding by Generative Pre-training (2018) (unpublished manuscript), https://cdn.openai.com/research-covers/language-unsupervised/language_understanding_paper.pdf; Alec Radford, Jeffrey Wu, Rewon Child et al., Language Models are Unsupervised Multitask Learners (2019) (unpublished

translation systems.[68] The training data for these different types of applications tend to differ according to use case, e.g., translation-model training datasets include text from multiple languages and chat-model training datasets include dialog.[69]

b. Image Data and Generations

Multimodal text-to-image[70] systems include DALL·E,[71] DALL·E 2,[72] DALL·E 3[73] (which is embedded within ChatGPT[74]), Ideogram,[75] Midjourney,[76] and Stability AI's DreamStudio.[77] The generative-AI models in these systems are

---

manuscript), https://d4mucfpksywv.cloudfront.net/better-language-models/language_models_are_unsupervised_multitask_learners.pdf; Raffel, Shazeer, Roberts, Lee et al., *supra* note 67; Devlin, Chang, Lee & Toutanova, *supra* note 14 (which all use generative text models to perform a variety of text-based tasks including translation, question answering, summarization, and text classification).

68 Google Translate uses generative AI to produce translated text given an input in another language. *See* Isaac Caswell & Bowen Liang, *Recent Advances in Google Translate*, GOOGLE RSCH. (June 8, 2020), https://research.google/blog/recent-advances-in-google-translate/ (describing the Google Translate system in 2020, which uses a transformer model in conjunction with another type of model called a Recurrent Neural Network). *See infra* Part I.B.3.a (discussing transformer models).

69 *See generally* Romal Thoppilan, Daniel De Freitas, Jamie Hall et al., LaMDA: Language Models for Dialog Applications (2022) (unpublished manuscript), https://arxiv.org/pdf/2201.08239.pdf (discussing the inclusion of dialogue in the training of a chat model).

70 There are also unimodal image-to-image models and systems, like the one owned and operated by Runway. *See* Runway, *Image to Image*, RUNWAY (2023), https://runwayml.com/aimagic-tools/image-to-image/.

71 *See generally* Aditya Ramesh, Mikhail Pavlov, Gabriel Goh et al., *Zero-Shot Text-to-Image Generation*, *in* 2021 PROC. 38TH INT'L CONF. ON MACH. LEARNING 8821 (2021) (the original DALL·E model paper); Alec Radford, Jong Wook Kim, Chris Hallacy et al., *Learning Transferable Visual Models From Natural Language Supervision*, *in* 2021 PROC. 38TH INT'L CONF. ON MACH. LEARNING 8748 (2021) (the critic model used to rank DALL·E-generated outputs for a given prompt). Both components are part of the OpenAI DALL·E system. *See generally* OpenAI, *DALL·E: Creating images from text*, OPENAI (Jan. 5, 2021), https://openai.com/research/dall-e.

72 *See generally* Ramesh, Dhariwal, Nichol et al., *supra* note 47 (the original DALL·E 2 research paper); *DALL·E 2*, *supra* note 47 (the DALL·E 2 OpenAI system).

73 *See generally* James Betker, Gabriel Goh, Li Jing et al., Improving Image Generation with Better Captions (2023) (unpublished manuscript), https://cdn.openai.com/papers/dall-e-3.pdf (the original DALL·E 3 research paper); OpenAI, *DALL·E 3*, OPENAI (2023), https://openai.com/dall-e-3 (describing the functionality of DALL·E 3 in OpenAI products).

74 *DALL·E 3 is now available in ChatGPT Plus and Enterprise*, *supra* note 48.

75 *See generally Ideogram.AI*, IDEOGRAM.AI (2023), https://ideogram.ai/.

76 MIDJOURNEY, *supra* note 32.

77 *DreamStudio*, *supra* note 45.

trained on huge amounts of image-text pairs, in which each image is paired with a caption describing it (e.g., a picture of a cat lounging in a sunbeam with the caption "a black cat underneath a window").[78] These datasets are also often scraped from the Internet, and can include both copyrighted and public-domain images and captions.[79] In some cases, only the images are scraped from the Internet, and the corresponding captions are produced using machine learning—for example, using an image-to-text generative-AI model or system to produce synthetic captions.[80]

Trained models leverage these learned relationships at generation time: when supplied with text prompts as inputs, they generate image outputs to match the prompt.[81] Today's text-to-image models can produce generations that span a variety of artistic styles—from cartoons to photorealistic images—and can

---

[78] Until recently, one common source of training data was LAION-5B, a dataset constructed from images and alt-text from the Common Crawl corpus. *See generally* Romain Beaumont, *LAION-5B: A New Era of Large-Scale Multi-Modal Datasets*, LAION (Mar. 31, 2022), https://laion.ai/blog/laion-5b (describing the LAION-5B dataset). *See generally* Christoph Schuhmann, Romain Beaumont, Richard Vencu, et al., *LAION-5B: An open large-scale dataset for training next generation image-text models*, *in* 2022 THIRTY-SIXTH CONF. ON NEURAL INFO. PROCESSING SYS. DATASETS & BENCHMARKS TRACK (2022) (for the *NeurIPS* conference Datasets Track paper on LAION-5B). *See generally* Dodge, Sap, Marasović et al., *supra* note 69 (regarding the Common Crawl corpus; also see citations therein). LAION-5B has since been removed from HuggingFace and other public hosting services due to identification of CSAM in images at its linked URLs. *See generally* Abeba Birhane, Vinay Uday Prabhu & Emmanuel Kahembwe, Multimodal datasets: misogyny, pornography, and malignant stereotypes (2021) (unpublished manuscript), https://arxiv.org/abs/2110.01963 (for one of the first studies documenting pornography in LAION-linked images). *See generally* Emilia David, *AI image training dataset found to include child sexual abuse imagery*, THE VERGE (Dec. 20, 2023), https://www.theverge.com/2023/12/20/24009418/generativeAI-image-laion-csam-googlestability-stanford (regarding the Stanford study that prompted LAION's removal).

[79] It is possible for one item in the pair to be copyrighted and the other to be in the public domain, such as a copyrighted image with a public-domain (or uncopyrightable) caption. *See infra* Part II.B.

[80] One reason to use synthetic captions is that not every image comes with a caption already. Another is that a computer-generated caption of "a black cat underneath a window" may be more usefully descriptive of the image's contents than the human-generated "Mr. Tickles loves his nappies!" *See generally* Junnan Li, Dongxu Li, Silvio Savarese & Steven Hoi, BLIP-2: Bootstrapping Language-Image Pre-training with Frozen Image Encoders and Large Language Models (2023) (unpublished manuscript), https://arxiv.org/abs/2301.12597 (for the BLIP-2 model, which can be used for synthetic captioning of images); Gokaslan, Cooper, Collins et al., *supra* note 37 (for an example application of caption generation using BLIP-2).

[81] Of course, many such generations can match the prompt; there are multiple reasonable outputs for the same input. *See supra* Part I.A.2.b. Some generative-AI systems include models that rank match quality. *See generally* Radford, Kim, Hallacy et al., *supra* note 74 (discussing the CLIP-model-based ranking methodology used in DALL·E).

incorporate different abstract concepts and concrete elements. For an example of such a generation, consider Figure 3, which shows different versions of "cat in a red and white striped hat"—different cats, different hats, different compositions, and different artistic styles.

3. Machine-Learning Techniques in Generative AI

While "generative AI" might be a relatively new term-of-art, a lot of the technology that powers today's generative-AI systems has a long history. Many familiar concepts—training algorithms, optimization, neural networks, etc.—all play important roles.[82] In this respect, there is no magic behind generative AI. However, there have been a few especially important technological developments in machine learning over the past decade that have helped usher in this new phase of generative-AI applications with seemingly magical capabilities. In this section, we address two: the transformer architecture[83] and diffusion-based models.[84]

---

[82] *See supra* Part I.A.2. It is also true that generative models, as an overarching type of machine learning, are also not completely new. *See supra* Part I.A.2.b. Automatic text and music generation date back to the middle of the 20th century. *See generally* Claude E. Shannon, *A Mathematical Theory of Communication*, 27 BELL SYS. TECH. J. (1948). (describing Markov-chain-based language models). *See generally* Darrell Conklin, *Music Generation from Statistical Models*, 45(2) J. NEW MUSIC RSCH. 160 (2003) (describing prior techniques in statistical music generation). Google published the first transformer architecture in 2017. *See generally* Ashish Vaswani, Noam Shazeer, Niki Parmar, Jakob Uszkoreit, Llion Jones, Aidan N. Gomez, Lukasz Kaiser & Illia Polosukhin, *Attention Is All You Need*, *in* 30 ADVANCES NEURAL INFO. PROCESSING SYS. 15 (2017). Prior to 2017, generative model architectures powered products like older versions of Apple's Siri voice assistant and of Google Translate. *See generally* Siri Team, *Deep Learning for Siri's Voice: On-device Deep Mixture Density Networks for Hybrid Unit Selection Synthesis*, APPLE MACH. LEARNING RSCH. (Aug. 2017), https://machinelearning.apple.com/research/siri-voices (describing Apple's Siri technology circa 2017). *See generally* Quoc V. Le & Mike Schuster, *A Neural Network for Machine Translation, at Production Scale*, GOOGLE BRAIN TEAM (Sept. 27, 2016), https://research.google/blog/a-neural-network-for-machine-translation-at-production-scale/ (describing the transition from phased-based translation systems to neural-network-based translation systems, before the release of transformers in 2017). Another example of earlier generative architectures is Generative Adversarial Networks (GANs), which have also had a place in popular discourse for around a decade with respect to deep fakes. *See generally* Ian Goodfellow, Jean Pouget-Abadie, Mehdi Mirza et al., *Generative Adversarial Nets*, *in* 27 ADVANCES NEURAL INFO. PROCESSING SYS. 9 (2014).

[83] *See infra* Part I.B.3.a.

[84] *See infra* Part I.B.3.b.

a. Transformer Architecture

Transformers are a type of model architecture: a set of configurations for a neural network.[85] They are particularly good at capturing context in sequential information by modeling how elements in a sequence relate to each other. Consider our example sentence from above: "In the summer, I like to go to the [blank]". The word that should fill in the "[blank]" will have relationships to many of the other words in the sequence (such as "summer", "I", and "go"); these relationships mean that "beach" is a more likely candidate than "slopes". Given their effectiveness, since their release in 2017,[86] transformers have become the *de facto* way to model sequence-formatted data, including modalities as diverse as text, code, music, and protein structure. In recent years, some image-generation models also incorporate transformer-architecture variants.[87]

The transformer architecture can be used to train a generative model,[88] and today, almost all generative text models are transformer-based, including ChatGPT. Indeed, the "T" in "GPT" stands for Transformer.[89] This architecture

---

[85] *See supra* Part I.A.2 (introducing neural networks).

[86] Vaswani, Shazeer, Parmar, Uszkoreit, Jones, Gomez, Kaiser & Polosukhin, *supra* note 85. We do not address the technical details of transformers in the Article, but we nevertheless choose to mention them because they are a common term that repeatedly comes up in the context of generative AI. *See generally* Mark Riedl, *A Very Gentle Introduction to Large Language Models without the Hype*, MEDIUM (Apr. 13, 2023), https://markriedl.medium.com/a-very-gentle-introduction-to-large-language-models-withoutthe-hype-5f67941fa59e; Timothy B. Lee & Sean Trott, *A jargon-free explanation of how AI large language models work*, ARS TECHNICA (July 31, 2023), https://arstechnica.com/science/2023/07/a-jargon-free-explanation-of-how-ai-large-language-models-work/ (providing more in-depth, yet still accessible, treatments on transformers).

[87] *See* Alexey Dosovitskiy, Lucas Beyer, Alexander Kolesnikov et al., *An Image is Worth 16x16 Words: Transformers for Image Recognition at Scale*, *in* 2021 INT'L CONF. ON LEARNING REPRESENTATIONS (2021) (regarding vision transformers, or ViTs). *See* William Peebles & Saining Xie, Scalable Diffusion Models with Transformers (2023) (unpublished manuscript), https://arxiv.org/abs/2212.09748 (for diffusion-model transformers, or DiTs).

[88] *See supra* Part I.A.2.b (describing generative models). Not all transformer-based models generate content, for example, BERT (Bidirectional Encoder Representations from Transformers). *See generally* Devlin, Chang, Lee & Toutanova, *supra* note 14. Such models are not trained to predict (and then generate) the next word in a sequence. Instead, they are useful for other tasks: producing word embeddings, filling in missing data (e.g., blanks in provided text like "[blank] re-recorded her old studio albums after her masters were sold."), or performing a question-and-answering task. *See supra* Part I.A.1 (defining word embeddings).

[89] GPT is an acronym for Generative Pre-trained Transformer. "Generative" you already know, and we will discuss "Pre-trained" later. *See infra* Part I.C. Other transformer-based language models include LaMDA and the family of Llama models. *See generally*

consists of two parts: a neural network[90] and something called the attention mechanism. The attention mechanism, the key innovation in the original paper introducing the transformer architecture,[91] works particularly well to model contextual information in sequences. A transformer-based model has computational elements that enable it to take in an input sequence (e.g., a sequence of tokens[92] of text) and to weigh the importance of each part (i.e., each token) of the sequence in relation to the others. Based on this context of the input sequence,[93] the model can generate the next token as the output,[94] in a way that preserves the sequential relationships and makes it straightforward to add the generated token to the context and generate *the next token after that*, followed by the *next token after that*, and so on.[95] While, at this level of abstraction, this process may not seem particularly "intelligent," at large scale—i.e., training enormous transformer architectures on enormous datasets—it is responsible for the demonstrated capabilities of many current, transformer-based generative-AI systems.[96] For these systems, "intelligence" comes from the underlying

---

Thoppilan, De Freitas, Hall et al., *supra* note 72. (describing LaMDA). *See generally* Touvron, Lavril, Izacard et al., *supra* note 7; Touvron, Martin, Stone et al., *supra* note 7; Meta, *supra* note 51 (describing the Llama, Llama 2, and Code Llama models).

[90] *See supra* Part I.A.2.a (discussing neural-network model architectures).

[91] Vaswani, Shazeer, Parmar, Uszkoreit, Jones, Gomez, Kaiser & Polosukhin, *supra* note 85.

[92] *See supra* note 65 and accompanying text (defining token).

[93] This is where the term **context window** (or **context length**) originates; it refers to the size of the input sequence. *See generally* Anthropic, *Introducing 100K Context Windows*, ANTHROPIC (May 11, 2023), https://www.anthropic.com/index/100k-contextwindows/ (describing the context window in Anthropic's Claude chatbot system).

[94] Modeling data as tokens enables using transformers with non-text sequences, e.g., a token for a music model may be a musical note or a specific pitch. *See supra* note 65 and accompanying text.

[95] More precisely, it is not the transformer architecture on its own that takes the next-generated token, appends it to the previous tokens, and then passes it back through the model to produce the next token (and so on). Instead, this technique is a hallmark of an **autoregressive model.** It is common to combine transformer architectural blocks (which implement the attention mechanism, described above) with autoregressive elements to produce outputs at generation time (which predict one token at a time according to the previously generated tokens). Sometimes, this combination is called an **autoregressive transformer**, but we will use the shorthand of "transformer" in this Article for simplicity. This shorthand is not uncommon: GPT models are autoregressive transformers, even though the "autoregressive" part does not make it into the acronym. *See supra* note 92 (spelling out the GPT acronym).

[96] OpenAI's o1 model series involves additional mechanisms—reinforcement learning, different amounts of test-time compute, and more—that contribute to the models' capabilities. In a recent technical report, OpenAI claims that this training recipe is responsible for improved abilities to "reason" about challenging problems. *See supra* note 38 and accompanying text (discussing o1).

transformer models' abilities to mimic the sequential relationships of human-written text.

Lastly, it is also important to note that the transformer architecture can be implemented on an enormous scale. Just as deep neural networks contain numerous layers and connections between them, transformers can contain numerous layers and connections to construct models with billions of model parameters,[97] where (generally speaking, though with exceptions) larger models yield higher-quality generations. It is this large-scale stacking of transformers that gives us the term large language models (LLMs), which is commonly used to refer to transformer-based models like Llama, as well as systems that incorporate such models, like ChatGPT and Claude.

b. Diffusion-Based Models

Diffusion-based models[98] are popular in image generation; for example, Midjourney's underlying text-to-image model and (as the name suggests) the Stable Diffusion text-to-image model.[99] For text-to-image diffusion-based model training, the training data consist of pairs of images and corresponding text captions describing them.[100] Training occurs in two passes. First, for each

---

[97] For language models, this scale reflects the current state-of-the-art. *See infra* Part I.B.4.

[98] Such models are commonly called "diffusion models" in the literature. However, as we note below, "diffusion" is a training mechanism that involves sampling, and, for the purposes of this Article, should be understood as a training algorithm, not a model. This algorithm typically trains a neural-network architecture. We choose to disambiguate these subtleties with the term "diffusion-based model," even though it is not the term commonly used in the scientific field. *See generally* Jascha Sohl-Dickstein, Eric Weiss, Niru Maheswaranathany & Surya Ganguli, *Deep Unsupervised Learning using Nonequilibrium Thermodynamics*, *in* 2015 PROC. 32ND INT'L CONF. ON MACH. LEARNING 2256 (2015) (regarding early work diffusion probabilistic models).

[99] Stable Diffusion is a text-to-image model that combines a transformer architecture for modeling text with diffusion for modeling images. DALL·E 2 uses a mix of transformers and diffusion, in a two-step process. *See generally* Rombach, Blattmann, Lorenz et al., *supra* note 32. (regarding the Stable Diffusion model). *See generally* MIDJOURNEY, *supra* note 32 (regarding the Midjourney text-to-image system). *See generally* Ramesh, Dhariwal, Nichol et al., *supra* note 47; Aditya Ramesh, *How DALL·E 2 Works*, ADITYA RAMESH (2022), http://adityaramesh.com/posts/dalle2/dalle2.html (detailing the DALL·E 2 system). To be precise, "diffusion" refers to a class of training algorithms; the resulting models are "diffusion models" in the same looser sense that the creature and not the doctor is "Frankenstein." The model itself is yet another neural network. A common neural-network architecture for diffusion models is called U-Net. *See generally* Olaf Ronneberger, Philipp Fischer & Thomas Brox, *U-Net: Convolutional Networks for Biomedical Image Segmentation*, 2015 MED. IMAGE COMPUT. & COMPUT. ASSISTED INTERVENTION 234–41.

[100] Diffusion is built on concepts from Bayesian inference—namely, Markov chains and variational methods. Early work on diffusion probabilistic models (DPMs) shows the

Figure 5: Several screenshots of the generation process using the Midjourney system, which uses text-to-image, diffusion-based models (Midjourney, Midjourney (2023), https://midjourney.com). We prompt with "an adventurous archaeologist with a whip and a fedora", and the Midjourney user interface shows the iterative de-noising process to produce the generations.

training-data example (the image and its caption), noise is incrementally added to the image until it effectively looks like static. This process intentionally corrupts the image, degrading its quality. Second, a neural network is trained to incrementally reverse this corruption process, removing noise and restoring the image to its original form. (Both of these passes are iterative; each has multiple steps that happen over time.) The first pass involves the repeated addition of noise, and the second involves denoising the fully noised image, a little bit at a time.[101] During the de-noising pass, the neural network is trained by evaluating

relationship between diffusion and concepts from variational autoencoders, another type of deep generative model. Starting in around 2019, DPMs started to become competitive with GANs, with respect to image generation. *See generally* Sohl-Dickstein, Weiss, Maheswaranathany & Ganguli, *supra* note 101 (regarding early work diffusion probabilistic models). *See generally* Dirk P. Kingma & Max Welling, *Auto-Encoding Variational Bayes*, *in* 2014 INT'L CONF. ON LEARNING REPRESENTATIONS 14 (2014); Danilo Jimenez Rezende, Shakir Mohamed & Daan Wierstra, *Stochastic Backpropagation and Approximate Inference in Deep Generative Models*, *in* 2014 PROC. 31ST INT'L CONF. ON MACH. LEARNING 1278 (2014) (regarding early work on variational autoencoders). *See generally* Goodfellow, Pouget-Abadie, Mirza et al., *supra* note 85 (describing GANs). *See generally* Yang Song & Stefano Ermon, *Generative Modeling by Estimating Gradients of the Data Distribution*, *in* 32 ADVANCES NEURAL INFO. PROCESSING SYS. 6840 (2019); Jonathan Ho, Ajay Jain & Pieter Abbeel, *Denoising Diffusion Probabilistic Models*, *in* 33 ADVANCES NEURAL INFO. PROCESSING SYS. 6840 (2020) (detailing the first methods that were competitive with GANs on image generation tasks).

[101] In a bit more detail, diffusion uses simulation techniques from the physical sciences to approach the machine-learning problem. Such simulations treat dynamical systems as a series of states; a given system can transition from one state to another over time. This

how well the de-noised image matches the original, noise-free image in the training data, and this evaluation is associated with the original text caption in the training data.[102]

To generate an output from a trained model, a system treats a user's text prompt like a caption for an unknown image. Starting from an image that consists only of noise, the system repeatedly applies the model to remove some noise, iteratively producing a series of images that are intended to increasingly align with the text prompt. We can therefore think of the production of a generated output as a sequence of images unfolding over time, starting from the completely noisy image and ending with the final generation, with every iteratively de-noised image between the two (for example, see Figure 5). It is possible to string these images together into an animation, as the Midjourney system does when producing generations in its user interface.[103]

4. The Role of Scale

Last, we turn explicitly to an important theme that has cropped up repeatedly throughout this section: scale. Above, we discussed how generative-AI systems are large-scale and have many components. Generative-AI models built using transformers or diffusion represent just one subset of these components, and they also tend to be massive. For example, state-of-the-art transformer-based LLMs currently have billions (or even trillions) of parameters.

The massive scale of these models is intended to capture the richness and complexity of equally massive datasets. As we mentioned briefly above, these datasets are often scraped from the Internet. This is a relatively new practice for training in machine learning. Prior to the publication of the first article describing the transformer architecture in 2017,[104] much of machine-learning research involved training models on smaller datasets. As points of comparison, both the MNIST[105] and CIFAR-10[106] datasets, two common benchmarks in discriminative

---

modeling approach has many applications besides image generation, including simulating the thermodynamics of molecules, the spread of a disease, and price movements in the stock market. For diffusion, the states are the intermediate images between the noise-free and completely noisy, static-resembling image.

[102] *See* Complaint at p. 12, Getty Images (US), Inc. v. Stability AI, Inc., No. 1:23-cv-00135 (D. Del. Feb. 3, 2023) (giving an intuitive description of this process in the context of Stability AI's model).

[103] MIDJOURNEY, *supra* note 32.

[104] Vaswani, Shazeer, Parmar, Uszkoreit, Jones, Gomez, Kaiser & Polosukhin, *supra* note 85.

[105] Yann LeCun & Corinna Cortes, *MNIST handwritten digit database* (1999), https://www.lri.fr/~marc/Master2/MNIST_doc.pdf.

[106] Alex Krizhevsky, Vinod Nair & Geoffrey Hinton, *CIFAR-10 (Canadian Institute for Advanced Research)* (2009), http://www.cs.toronto.edu/~kriz/cifar.html.

deep learning tasks, each contain 60,000 labeled images. Even ImageNet,[107] a more challenging benchmark, has only 15 million labeled images. In contrast, datasets to train generative-AI models, such as LAION-5B,[108] have billions of training data examples.

In fact, today's generative-AI training data sets are so large, machine-learning practitioners do not have effective or efficient ways to fully know their exact contents.[109] This is one of the important impacts of scale. Earlier datasets like CIFAR-10, and even ImageNet, are small enough that they can be manually curated.[110] In the case of MNIST, the origin (i.e., provenance) of every data example is known and documented.[111] For large-scale datasets scraped from the web, provenance is much trickier, which will have implications for copyright,[112] discussed in Part II.

Nevertheless, despite such novel challenges, scale also confers new capabilities.[113] Today's generative-AI models are able to produce incredible content, in large part because of their large scale,[114] though it is not well understood exactly how or why.[115] Although it is possible to break down

---

[107] Jia Deng, Wei Dong, Richard Socher et al., *ImageNet: A large-scale hierarchical image database*, *in* 2009 IEEE CONF. ON COMPUT. VISION & PATTERN RECOGNITION 248—255 (2009).

[108] Beaumont, *supra* note 81; Schuhmann, Beaumont, Vencu et al., *supra* note 81. *See supra* Part I.B.2.

[109] Lee, Ippolito & Cooper, *supra* note 67, at 5 (discussing the challenges of provenance in generative-AI training datasets).

[110] *Id.*

[111] *Id.*

[112] This is also true because provenance is often not well-documented on the web. *See generally id.* Missing provenance in these datasets can also implicate other legal issues, not just copyright. Notably, LAION-5B contains CSAM. *See* David, *supra* note 81; Birhane, Prabhu & Kahembwe, *supra* note 81.

[113] *See generally* Brown, Mann, Ryder et al., *supra* note 67. (discussing new capabilities made possible with GPT-3). *See generally* Jared Kaplan, Sam McCandlish, Tom Henighan et al., Scaling Laws for Neural Language Models (Jan. 23, 2020) (unpublished manuscript), https://arxiv.org/abs/2001.08361 (discussing how model training scales with model size, dataset size, and available computing power).

[114] *See generally* Jensen Huang & Ilya Sutskever, *Fireside Chat with Ilya Sutskever and Jensen Huang: AI Today and Vision of the Future*, NVIDIA ON-DEMAND (2023), https://www.nvidia.com/en-us/on-demand/session/gtcspring23-s52092/ (regarding OpenAI's co-founder and chief scientist, Ilya Stuskever, crediting the importance of scale). *See generally* Jason Wei, Yi Tay, Rishi Bommasani et al., Emergent Abilities of Large Language Models (2022) (unpublished manuscript), https://arxiv.org/abs/2206.07682 (for a computer science paper on the same topic).

[115] This is an active area of current research. Recent work has investigated whether these new capabilities may be attributed to factors other than scale, but this area is still in its infancy. *See generally* Rylan Schaeffer, Brando Miranda & Sanmi Koyejo, Are Emergent

generative-AI systems into different known aspects and components (as we have done throughout this section), much remains unknown about how these systems actually work in detail.[116] Some machine-learning researchers are focused on applying models and systems to new tasks, without worrying too much about *why* they work, while others are focused on developing insights about the *why*. For the time being, policymakers, like everyone else, will have to work from a position of imperfect technical knowledge.

C. The Generative-AI Supply Chain

The previous section provided only a working definition of generative-AI models and a brief overview of the generative-AI systems they are embedded in. But even this overview showed the remarkable complexity and diversity of these models and systems. In turn, this complexity and diversity are important for how we reason about copyright implications. They affect *what* is potentially an infringing artifact, *when* in the production process it is possible for infringement to occur, and *who* is potentially an infringing actor.[117]

Abilities of Large Language Models a Mirage? (2023) (unpublished manuscript), https://arxiv.org/abs/2304.15004 (discussing how choices of evaluation metrics can affect perceptions of model capabilities).

[116] Understanding the inner workings of large-scale, machine-learning models has been an active area of research over the last decade. *See generally* David Baehrens, Timon Schroeter, Stefan Harmeling et al., *How to explain individual classification decisions*, 11 J. MACH. LEARNING RSCH. 1803 (2010); Chris Olah, Arvind Satyanarayan, Ian Johnson et al., *The Building Blocks of Interpretability*, DISTILL (Mar. 6, 2018), https://distill.pub/2018/building-blocks/; Nelson Elhage, Neel Nanda, Catherine Olsson et al., A Mathematical Framework for Transformer Circuits (Dec. 22, 2021) (unpublished manuscript), https://transformer-circuits.pub/2021/framework/index.html (discussing interpretability, explainability, and mechanistic interpretability). *See generally* Pang Wei Koh & Percy Liang, *Understanding Black-box Predictions via Influence Functions*, 70 PROC. MACH. LEARNING RSCH. 1885 (2017); Ekin Akyurek, Tolga Bolukbasi, Frederick Liu et al., *Towards Tracing Knowledge in Language Models Back to the Training Data*, *in* 2022 FINDINGS ASS'N FOR COMPUT. LINGUISTICS: EMNLP 2022 2429 (2022); Roger Grosse, Juhan Bae, Cem Anil et al., Studying Large Language Model Generalization with Influence Functions (Aug. 7, 2023) (unpublished manuscript), https://arxiv.org/abs/2308.03296 (discussing influence functions). While these fields of work have provided insights, many believe that there lacks sufficient evidence to depend on models to make consequential decisions. *See generally* Zachary Lipton, *The Mythos of Model Interpretability: In Machine Learning, the concept of interpretability is both important and slippery*, 16 QUEUE 31 (2018).

[117] The generative-AI supply chain is a good example of the "many hands" problem in computer systems. That is, there are many diffuse actors, at potentially many different organizations, that can each have a hand in the construction of generative-AI systems. It can be very challenging to identify responsible actors when these systems transgress

To provide a framework for reasoning about this diversity and complexity, it is helpful to conceive of a generative-AI supply chain that has eight stages (Figure 6):

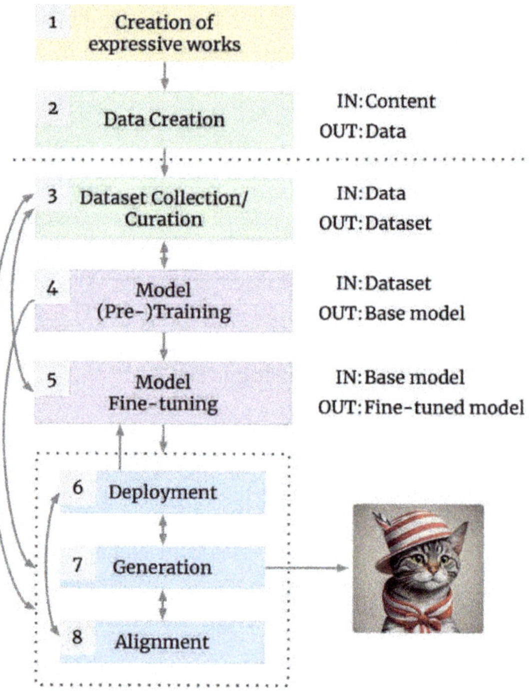

Figure 6: The generative-AI supply chain.

broader societal expectations—in our case, the preservation of copyrights. *See* A. Feder Cooper, Emanuel Moss, Benjamin Laufer & Helen Nissenbaum, *Accountability in an Algorithmic Society: Relationality, Responsibility, and Robustness in Machine Learning* 867–69, *in* 2022 ACM CONF. ON FAIRNESS ACCOUNTABILITY & TRANSPARENCY 864 (2022) (describing the problem of "many hands" in data-driven machine learning/AI systems in relation to complex "ML pipelines"). *See* Rui-Jie Yew & Dylan Hadfield-Menell, Break It Till You Make It: Limitations of Copyright Liability Under a Pretraining Paradigm of AI Development (2023) (unpublished manuscript), https://genlaw.github.io/CameraReady/30.pdf (regarding an instantiation of this problem for generative AI and copyright).

1. Creation of expressive works.[118]

The supply chain necessarily starts with creative works: all of the books, artwork, software, and other products of human creativity that generative AI seeks to learn from and emulate.

2. Data creation.[119]

Creative works and other information must then be converted into data: digitally encoded files in standard formats.

3. Dataset collection and curation.[120]

Individual pieces of data are useless for AI training by themselves. Instead, they must be compiled into training datasets: vast and carefully structured collections of related data. This process requires both extensive automation and thoughtful, human-curated decision-making.

4. Model (pre-)training.[121]

To create a generative-AI model, its creator picks a technical architecture, assembles training datasets, and then runs a training algorithm to encode features of the training data in the model. Model training is both a science and an art, and it involves massive investments of time, money, computing resources, and (often) human monitoring and intervention. The model that results from the initial training process is called a "base" or "pre-trained model" because it is often just a starting point.

5. Model fine-tuning.[122]

A base model can also be fine-tuned to improve its performance or adapt it to a specific problem domain. This process, too, involves extensive choices—and it need not be carried out by the same entity that did the initial training.

6. Model release and system deployment.[123]

---

[118] *See infra* Part I.C.1.
[119] *See infra* Part I.C.2.
[120] *See infra* Part I.C.3.
[121] *See infra* Part I.C.4.
[122] *See infra* Part I.C.5.
[123] *See infra* Part I.C.6.

A model by itself is an inert artifact. It can be used only by technical experts with access to (often substantial) computing resources. To make a model usable by a wider user base, a model must be released—its parameters uploaded to the Internet, where developers and researchers can download and integrate them into their own applications and projects—or deployed as a service. Deployment involves embedding the model in some larger software system that provides a convenient interface (e.g., ChatGPT's web-based UI, Midjourney's Discord bot).

7. Generation.[124]

A deployed service can be used to generate outputs (generations): new creative works that are based on statistical patterns in the training dataset but typically combine them in new ways. A generation is based on the particular system, as well as a prompt supplied by the user: an input that describes the particular features they want the output to have. Generation is the only part of the supply chain that most end users see directly.

8. Model alignment.[125]

The supply chain does not end with generation. Both before and after deployment, the developers of a generative-AI system can perform alignment by rating prompts and generations: further adjusting the model and the system it is embedded in to better achieve users' (and their own) needs. Those needs can include safety, helpfulness, and legal compliance.

Each stage gathers inputs from the prior stage(s) and hands off outputs to the subsequent stage(s), which we indicate with (sometimes bidirectional) arrows. In this way—as in many others—the supply chain feeds back into itself. It is not a simple cascade from data to generations. Instead, each stage is regularly adjusted to better meet the needs of the others. This framing is broadly useful for reasoning about different legal considerations for generative AI; we employ it specifically for copyright analysis in Part II.

The first two stages, the creation of expressive works and data creation, predate the advent of generative-AI systems. Nevertheless, they are indispensable parts of the production of generative-AI content, which is why we begin our discussion of the supply chain with these processes. The next six stages reflect processes that are new for generative-AI systems.

The connections between these supply-chain stages are complicated. While in some cases, one stage clearly precedes another, in other cases, there are many

[124] *See infra* Part I.C.7.

[125] *See infra* Part I.C.8.

different possible ways that stages can interact.[126] We highlight some of this complexity in the following subsections; we call attention to different possible timelines for when supply-chain stages can be invoked, and which actors can be involved at each stage.

1. Creation of Expressive Works

Artists, writers, coders, and other creators produce expressive works. Generative-AI systems do too,[127] but state-of-the-art systems are only able to produce expressive works because their models have been trained on data derived from pre-existing works by artists, writers, coders and other creators.[128] While perhaps obvious, it is nevertheless important to emphasize that the processes of producing most creative works have (thus far) had nothing to do with machine learning.[129] Historically, painters have composed canvases, writers have penned articles, coders have developed software, etc. without consideration of how their works might be taken up by automated processes. Nonetheless, once a work exists, it can be turned into data readable by a computer and used as training data. As a result, content creators and their original works are a part of the generative-AI supply chain, whether they would like to be or not (see Figure 6, stage 1).

2. Data Creation

Expressive *works* are distinct from their *representations* as data. In copyright terms, digital representations like the JPEG encoding of a photograph on an SSD

---

[126] *E.g.*, model pre-training necessarily precedes model fine-tuning. Fine-tuning and alignment involve additional training, and thus both necessarily follow pre-training (It is increasingly common to refer to all types of additional training, such as fine-tuning and alignment, as *post*-training.) *See* Figure 6.

[127] We discuss this in more detail below with respect to generation. *See infra* Part I.C.7. We also discuss this when we delve into copyright and authorship. *See infra* Part II.A.

[128] As we address below, a data example is not the same as its associated expressive work. Additionally, some models are trained on synthetic data, typically generated by other generative-AI models (which, in turn, were trained on pre-existing works). Training predominantly on synthetic data is a growing practice. *See* Gokaslan, Cooper, Collins et al., *supra* note 37 (for an example of training a model partially on synthetic data). There are some concerns that training on synthetic data can seriously compromise model quality. *See generally* Ilia Shumailov, Zakhar Shumaylov, Yiren Zhao et al., The Curse of Recursion: Training on Generated Data Makes Models Forget (May 27, 2023) (unpublished manuscript), https://arxiv.org/abs/2305.17493 (detailing "model collapse" in different generative models). However, recent work shows that reduction in model quality can be avoided with extensive data curation. *See* Suriya Gunasekar, Yi Zhang, Jyoti Aneja et al., Textbooks Are All You Need (2023), https://arxiv.org/abs/2306.11644 (unpublished manuscript).

[129] It appears increasingly likely that some content will be created specifically for model training, for example, hiring photographers to take photographs specifically for model training. Companies like Scale AI already create content (in the form of labels and feedback) specifically for the purpose of training models. *See* SCALE AI, https://scale.com/.

storage device are "copies" of the works they encode. What makes these digital representations different from other copies, like paint on a canvas or an engraved musical score, is that they are *data*: they are in computer-readable formats.[130] For the most part, the transformation of creative content to digital data formats predates generative AI[131] (see Figure 6, stage 2). It is a process that has grown in tandem with the proliferation of the modern Internet.[132] Regardless, all state-of-the-art generative-AI systems depend on access to digitized data, and so they depend on this process. Text-to-text generation models are trained on text; text-to-image models are trained on both text and images; text-to-music models are trained on text and audio files; and so on.

This is an important point for our purposes because many of the works that have been transformed into data include copyrightable expression. For example, the GitHub Copilot system uses models trained on copyrighted code, ChatGPT's underlying model(s) are trained on copyrighted text data scraped from the web, Stability AI's Stable Diffusion is trained on copyrighted text and images, and so on. For the most part, it is the copyright owners of these individual works who are the plaintiffs in copyright-infringement suits against actors all along the supply chain.

3. Dataset Collection and Curation

Models are not trained on individual, isolated data examples; instead, data examples are grouped together into larger datasets for training.[133] The training process for cutting-edge generative-AI models requires particularly vast quantities of data; dataset creators often meet this need by scraping data from the Internet.[134] Conceptually, this process requires three distinct stages: collection (gathering data), curation (deciding which gathered data to use), and arrangement (putting that data in a recurring standard structure). In practice, these stages are profoundly intermingled: curatorial choices shape the choices of what data to collect, certain collection choices limit the design space of possible arrangements, and arrangement can take place during collection and curation.[135] For example,

---

[130] *See supra* Part I.A.1 (defining data).

[131] *See, e.g.*, NANNA BONDE THYLSTRUP, THE POLITICS OF MASS DIGITIZATION (2024).

[132] *Id.*

[133] *See supra* Part I.A.2; *supra* Part I.B. This is not to say individual training examples are unimportant. Specific pieces of training data can have an out-sized influence on generations, compared with other pieces of training data. *See generally* Koh & Liang, *supra* note 119; Akyurek, Bolukbasi, Liu et al., *supra* note 119; Grosse, Bae, Anil et al., *supra* note 119. (discussing influence functions).

[134] This is not the only way to collect large amounts of data. *See* Lee, Ippolito & Cooper, *supra* note 67, at 5 (discussing other ways datasets may come to be).

[135] Note, however, that collection, curation, and arrangement do not *always* have to happen together, and may involve different sets of actors. It is also possible for curation to happen

scraping data from the Internet can simultaneously involve curatorial choices, e.g., filtering out unwanted types of data, such as "toxic speech."[136] Such curatorial choices muddle the line between dataset creation and curation, as both processes can effectively happen in tandem.

With respect to the generative-AI supply chain, there are several points worth highlighting in dataset collection and curation processes (see Figure 6, stage 3). First, while dataset creation and curation can be carried out by the same entities that train generative-AI models,[137] it is common for these processes to be split across different actors. The Stable Diffusion model, for example, is trained on images from datasets curated by the non-profit organization LAION.[138] It is necessary, therefore, to consider the potential liability of dataset creators and curators separately from the potential liability of model trainers.[139]

Second, training datasets are important objects in their own right. Note that dataset curation, as described above, will frequently involve "the collection and assembling of preexisting materials or of data that are selected, coordinated, or arranged in such a way that the resulting work as a whole constitutes an original work of authorship."[140] As such, training datasets can themselves potentially be copyrighted.

Third, while a few training datasets include metadata on the provenance of their constitutive data examples, many datasets do not. Provenance makes it easier to answer questions about the data sources a model was trained on, which can be relevant to an infringement analysis.[141] It also bears on the ease with which specific material can be located, and if necessary, removed, from a dataset.[142] However, the use of web scraping to collect generative-AI training datasets is directly in tension with maintaining information about provenance. As we discussed above, relying on Internet sources and the scale of scraped datasets makes determining the origins of individual data examples very challenging.[143]

---

after the start of model training, in response to metrics that are observed during the training process. That is, curation could follow (and then also precede further) model (pre-)training (Figure 6, stage 4; *see infra* Part I.C.4), or model fine-tuning (Figure 6, stage 5; *see infra* Part I.C.5). These complex interactions are the reason for the bidirectional arrows between stages in Figure 6.

[136] *See generally* Lee, Ippolito & Cooper, *supra* note 67 (discussing dataset creation and curation choices, including toxic content filtering).

[137] *See infra* Part I.C.4.

[138] Technically, LAION presents the dataset as a collection of the URLs of the images. Stable Diffusion then visits each URL to collect images for training. *See supra* Part I.B.2.b; *supra* I.B.4 and citations therein.

[139] *See infra* Part II.E.

[140] 17 U.S.C. § 101.

[141] *See infra* Part II.B–II.F.

[142] *See infra* Part II.G; *infra* Part III.A.3 (discussing challenges of removal).

[143] *See supra* Part I.B.4 and references therein. *See generally* Lee, Ippolito & Cooper, *supra* note 67, at 5 (discussing provenance challenges for generative AI).

Notably, and as we will discuss below, even if particular dataset creators and curators release a training dataset with a chosen license, this does not guarantee that the works within the dataset are appropriately licensed.[144] For example, the complaint in *Tremblay v. OpenAI, Inc.* alleges that ChatGPT's underlying model(s) were trained on datasets that do not properly license the books data that they contain.[145]

Differences in the licensing status of training data can have consequences for the characteristics and quality of the resulting models., For example, Sewon Min and colleagues used public-domain and permissively-licensed text to train a language model, and demonstrated a degradation in quality in domains that are not well represented in the data.[146] Similarly, Aaron Gokaslan and colleagues found a degradation in quality when training diffusion-based text-to-image models using only Creative-Commons licensed images.[147] Additionally, data in the public domain can be unrepresentative, which can introduce biases into models trained on it.[148]

4. Model (Pre-)Training

Following the collection and curation of training datasets (Figure 6, stage 3), it is possible to train a generative-AI model (Figure 6, stage 4). The model

---

[144] Indeed, the creators and curators would have to check that they have abided by each data example's respective license(s). *See infra* Part II.A (regarding authorship and training datasets).

[145] In particular, the complaint in *Tremblay v. OpenAI* alleges that the training data included books from infringing "shadow libraries" like Library Genesis. Complaint at p. 34, Tremblay v. OpenAI, Inc., No. 3:23-cv-03223 (N.D. Cal. June 28, 2023). Note, however, this claim is based on circumstantial evidence, because the datasets the GPT models were trained on have not been made public. Text data from books have been a key player in other dataset-related complaints. For example, The Pile dataset was originally released under the MIT license. Stella Biderman, Kieran Bicheno & Leo Gao, Datasheet for the Pile (Jan. 13, 2022) (unpublished manuscript), https://arxiv.org/abs/2201.07311. The Pile was core to the complaint in *Kadrey*, since the Pile contains 108GB of the dataset Books3 (which itself contains content from Bibliotek, a popular torrent interface). *See generally* Complaint, Kadrey v. Meta Platforms, Inc., No. 3:23-cv-03417 (N.D. Cal. July 7, 2023). The original download URL for The Pile (https://the-eye.eu/public/AI/pile/) is no longer resolving (as of September 2023).

[146] Sewon Min, Suchin Gururangan, Eric Wallace et al., SILO Language Models: Isolating Legal Risk In a Nonparametric Datastore (Aug. 8, 2023) (unpublished manuscript), https://arxiv.org/abs/2308.04430.

[147] Gokaslan, Cooper, Collins et al., *supra* note 37.

[148] Amanda Levendowski, *How Copyright Law Can Fix Artificial Intelligence's Implicit Bias Problem*, 93 WASH. L. REV. 579 (2018).

trainer[149] selects a training dataset, a model architecture (i.e., a set of initialized model parameters), and a training algorithm.[150]

As mentioned above, the process of training—from transforming these inputs into a trained model—is expensive. It requires a substantial investment of multiple resources: time, data storage, computing power, and human labor. For example, BLOOM, a 176-billion-parameter open-source model from HuggingFace was trained for 3.5 months on 1.6 terabytes of text and using 384 GPUs.[151] It cost an estimated $2–5 million in computing resources for both the development and ultimate training of BLOOM.[152] As another point of reference, MosaicML, a company (acquired by Databricks[153]) that develops solutions for training as cheaply and efficiently as possible, trained a GPT-3-quality model for less than $0.5 million.[154] Altogether, the dollar cost for pre-training can generally range

---

[149] We distinguish between the person or organization that trains the model from those that create the model architecture, as they may not be the same.

[150] This description omits additional choices that we elide for simplicity. First, as noted above, the trainer selects hyperparameters to calibrate and customize the training algorithm. *See supra* Part I.B.1. Second, the trainer must select a **seed value** for the random choices made during the training. Machine learning uses tools from probability and statistics, which reason about randomness. However, computers are not able to produce truly random numbers. Instead, algorithms exist for producing a sequence of *pseudo*-random numbers. A random seed is an input to a pseudo-random number generator, which enables the reproduction of such a sequence.

[151] *See generally* Stas Bekman, *The Technology Behind BLOOM Training*, HUGGINGFACE (July 14, 2022), https://huggingface.co/blog/bloom-megatron-deepspeed (for training details). *See* BigScience Workshop, Teven Le Scao, Angela Fan et al., BLOOM: A 176B-Parameter Open-Access Multilingual Language Model (June 27, 2023) (unpublished manuscript), https://arxiv.org/abs/2211.05100 (for the model details).

[152] Training costs are often not reported. Even when training cost is reported, development costs (including labor) are often omitted, despite being a critical (and often the most expensive) part of overall model development.

[153] Databricks, *Databricks Completes Acquisition of MosaicML*, DATABRICKS (July 19, 2023), https://www.databricks.com/company/newsroom/press-releases/databricks-completesacquisition-mosaicml. MosaicML (recently rebranded as Databricks Mosaic) offers hosted services for model training, model fine-tuning, and generation. So, too, does Together AI. Together AI, *Together Fine-tuning*, Together AI (November 25, 2024), https://www.together.ai. ("Fine-tune leading open-source models with your data to achieve greater accuracy for your tasks"). *See infra* Part I.C.5 (discussing fine-tuning); Part I.C.6 (discussing deployed hosted services).

[154] The original cost to train GPT-3 is unpublished, though, based on its size, is likely higher than $0.5 million. MosaicML reports to have trained a GPT-3-*quality* model. This means the model performs to a similar standard as GPT-3 does. MosaicML's model is substantively different from GPT-3. For one, MosaicML's model is a much smaller 30 billion parameters, compared to the original GPT-3 model's 175 billion. Additionally, MosaicML trained on more data, shifting some of the development cost towards data

from six to eight figures (or even more), depending on the size of the model, the size of the training dataset, the particular training algorithms, the length of the training process, the efficiency of the software and hardware used, and other choices.

Further, the training process is not completely automated; training often requires people to monitor and make tweaks to the process. For example, model trainers typically run evaluation metrics on the model while it is being trained, in order to assess the progress of training.[155] Depending on these metrics,[156] model trainers may pause the training process to manually revise the training algorithm[157] or the dataset, which we indicate with bidirectional arrows at Figure 6, stages 3-4. Human intervention in response to metrics necessarily makes model training an iterative process.

The output of this process is typically called a pre-trained model or base model.[158] At this point, the base model has many possible futures. It could just sit idly in memory, collecting figurative dust, never to be used to produce

---

collection and curation, and away from model training. It is worth noting that GPT-3 was originally released two years before MosaicML's model was trained, and thus the MosaicML training process likely incorporated additional technological improvements. *See generally* Abhinav Venigalla & Linden Li, *Mosaic LLMs (Part 2): GPT-3 quality for <$500k*, MOSAICML (Sept. 29, 2022), https://www.mosaicml.com/blog/gpt-3-qualityfor-500k (regarding MosaicML's model). *See generally* Brown, Mann, Ryder et al., *supra* note 67 (for the size of GPT-3).

[155] Google's TensorBoard and software from Weights & Biases are two tools for running evaluation metrics and monitoring during training. *See generally* TensorFlow, *TensorBoard: TensorFlow's visualization toolkit*, TENSORFLOW (2023), https://www.tensorflow.org/tensorboard. (regarding Tensorboard). *See generally Weights & Biases*, WEIGHTS & BIASES, https://wandb.ai/site (regarding Weights & Biases).

[156] Evaluation metrics attempt to elicit how "useful" or "good" the model is. These metrics are not comprehensive, since there is no single way to capture "usefulness" or "goodness" in math. *See generally* Lee, Ippolito & Cooper, *supra* note 67, at 5 (for a discussion of evaluation metrics and the impossibility of exactly and comprehensively defining "useful" and "good").

[157] *E.g.*, change the hyperparameters.

[158] Others use the term "foundation model." The term "foundation" can be (and has been) easily misunderstood. It should not be interpreted to connote that "foundation models" contain technical developments that make them fundamentally different from models produced in the nearly-a-decade of related prior work, rather that they serve as a foundation to build other models on. The term itself is controversial in the machine-learning community. *See* Thomas G. Dietterich (@tdietterich), TWITTER (Aug. 12, 2022, 7:58 PM), https://twitter.com/tdietterich/status/1558256704696905728) (including the replies and offshoots).

generations.[159] The model parameters could be uploaded to a public server,[160] from which others could download it and use it however they want.[161] The model could be integrated into a system and deployed as a public-facing application,[162] which others could use directly to produce generations.[163] Or, the model could be further modified by the initial model trainer, by another actor at the same organization, or, if made publicly available, by a different actor from a different organization. That is, another actor could take the model parameters and use them as the input to do additional training with new or modified data (and a chosen training algorithm, etc., as at the beginning of this section).[164]

This possibility of future further training of a base model is why this stage of the supply chain is most often referred to as *pre*-training, and why a base model is similarly often called a pre-trained model. Additional training of a base model is called fine-tuning, to which we now turn.

5. Model Fine-Tuning

As described above, models reflect their training data.[165] Base models trained on large-scale, web-scraped datasets reflect a lot of general information sourced from different parts of the Internet. They are not typically trained to reflect specialized domains of knowledge. For example, a text-to-text base model trained on large quantities of English-language data may be able to capture general English-language semantics and information; however, such a model may not be

---

[159] This point shows that the line distinguishing "programs" from "data" in machine learning is murky. The set of parameters in a model can be viewed as a **data structure** containing vectors of numbers that, on their own, do not *do* anything. However, one could load that data structure into memory and apply some relatively lightweight linear algebra operations to produce a generation. *See supra* Part I.B. In this respect, we could also consider the model to be a program (and an algorithm). This is why we talk about the model being *within* the function *f* in our analogical discussion of machine-learning-as-a-function. (*See supra* Part I.A.2.a.) The model, if given a prompt input, can also be executed like a program. Note that the term "model" is overloaded; it can be used to refer to the model parameters (just the vectors of numbers) or to the model as a combination of software and the model parameters, which together can be executed like a program.

[160] For example, HuggingFace hosts a repository of over 300,000 open- and semi-closed models. *See generally Models*, HuggingFace (Sept. 2, 2023), https://huggingface.co/models.

[161] They could fine-tune the model (*see infra* Part I.C.5), embed the model in a system that they deploy for others to use (*see infra* Part I.C.6), produce generations (*see infra* Part I.C.7), align the model (*see infra* Part I.C.8), or do some subset of these other stages of the supply chain. From this example, we can see how the supply chain is in fact iterative, which we illustrate in Figure 6.

[162] *See infra* Part I.C.6.

[163] *See supra* Part I.B; *infra* Part I.C.7.

[164] Cooper, Moss, Laufer & Nissenbaum, *supra* note 120 (discussing the "many hands" problem).

[165] *See supra* Part I.A.2; *supra* Part I.B

able to, for example, reliably reflect detailed scientific information about molecular biology (e.g., answering the question "what is mitosis?").

This is where fine-tuning comes in (Figure 6, stage 5): the process of modifying a preexisting, already-trained model, with the general goal of making this model better along some dimension of interest. As the name suggests, most fine-tuning aims to retain the general strengths of what a model has already learned while optimizing its specific details. This process often involves training on additional data that is more aligned with the specific goals.[166] Training transforms data into a model, and fine-tuning transforms a model into another model.

Fine-tuning essentially involves just running more training. In this respect, the overall process of fine-tuning is similar to pre-training: both execute a training process. However, fine-tuning and pre-training run with different inputs, which ultimately makes the trajectories and outputs of their respective training processes very different. That is, even though fine-tuning and pre-training often employ the same training algorithm, they typically use different input training data and different input model parameters.[167] To add more precision to our previous statement, fine-tuning transforms a model into another model while incorporating more data.

Whereas pre-training data tend to be more general, fine-tuning data are typically sourced from a specific problem domain of interest; whereas the input model architecture to pre-training is an initialized, untrained model,[168] for fine-tuning, the input model parameters have already undergone some training and are no longer in their initialized state. Continuing the example above, a base language model could be fine-tuned on scientific papers to improve its ability to summarize scientific content; the fine-tuning stage takes the learned parameters of the more general base model and updates them by training further on scientific text data.

a. Forks in the Supply Chain

Two important observations follow from our description of fine-tuning as (effectively) just performing more training. On the one hand, a model trainer does not have to fine-tune at all. A base model produced during pre-training could be

---

[166] And thus the reason for the bidirectional arrow between stages 3 and 5 in Figure 6. Similar to pre-training, monitoring metrics during fine-tuning may lead to further dataset curation. *See supra* Part I.C.4. This is also sometimes why fine-tuning is considered a part of alignment, as the fine-tuning dataset can contain examples that direct the model to possess additional behaviors, such as instruction following. *See infra* Part I.C.8 (discussing model alignment).

[167] As discussed above, there are other relevant factors in training, including choice of hyperparameters and choice of hardware. These, too, can change between pre-training and fine-tuning. *See supra* Part I.A.1; *supra* Part I.B.4.

[168] *I.e.*, the vectors of numbers that constitute the model parameters have not "learned" anything yet. *See supra* Part I.A.1; *supra* Part I.C.4.

used as-is for later stages in the supply chain. On the other hand, just as it is possible to fine-tune *less* than once, it is possible to fine-tune *more* than once, taking an already-fine-tuned model, and using it as the input for another fine-tuning pass. Thus, a model is a "base" or "fine-tuned" model *only in relation to other models*. A model is a "base" model when it is the input to a fine-tuning pass; it is a "fine-tuned" model when it is the output from a fine-tuning pass.[169] To use a copyright analogy, a fine-tuned model is a derivative of the model from which it was fine-tuned; a repeatedly fine-tuned model is a derivative of the (chain of) fine-tuned model(s) from which it was fine-tuned.

Pre-training and fine-tuning can be split among different actors. Sometimes, the creator of a model also fine-tunes it. Google's Codey models (for software code generation) are fine-tuned versions of Google's PaLM 2 model.[170] In other cases, another party does the fine-tuning. A particularly common case arises when a model's parameters are publicly released (as Meta has done with its several versions of Llama models),[171] allowing others to take the model and independently fine-tune it for particular applications. For example, LMSYS Org fine-tuned Meta's publicly released Llama model on the crowdsourced ShareGPT dataset to produce the Vicuna model.[172] The creators of Vicuna, in turn, have also released their model publicly, allowing anyone else with the requisite resources and know-how the ability to fine-tune the model on additional data.[173] For another example, when a model is deployed within a hosted service (Figure 6, step 6), developers of that service may expose APIs to end-users that enable them to fine-tune the model.[174]

---

[169] These terms do not capture the intrinsic technical features of a model; instead, they describe different processes by which a model can be created.

[170] Google, *Foundation Models,* GOOGLEAI (Aug. 17, 2023), https://ai.google/discover/foundationmodels/ (describing Codey).

[171] Touvron, Lavril, Izacard et al., *supra* note 7; Meta, *supra* note 51.

[172] *See generally* The Vicuna Team, *Vicuna: An Open-Source Chatbot Impressing GPT-4 with 90%* ChatGPT Quality*, LMSYS ORG (Mar. 30, 2023), https://lmsys.org/blog/2023-03-30-vicuna/ (regarding the Vicuna model). ShareGPT is a crowd-sourced dataset composed of conversational logs of user interactions with ChatGPT. It contains both content created by users and by the generative-AI model embedded in ChatGPT (either GPT-3.5 or GPT-4, depending on the user). *See generally* SHAREGPT, https://sharegpt.com/ (regarding the ShareGPT dataset).

[173] *See* Colin Raffel, *Collaborative, Communal, & Continual Machine Learning* 15 (2023), https://colinraffel.com/talks/faculty2023collaborative.pdf (for a figure showing many fine-tuned models building on one base model).

[174] For example, ChatGPT has a fine-tuning API, which enables end-users to fine-tune some of the underlying system's models through the hosted service's API on a custom dataset. Andrew Peng, Michael Wu, John Allard et al., *GPT-3.5 Turbo fine-tuning and API updates* (Aug. 22, 2023), https://openai.com/blog/gpt-3-5turbo-fine-tuning-and-api-updates. This is why we place an arrow from deployment (Figure 6, stage 6) to fine-tuning

It is helpful to make the base-/fine-tuned model distinction because different parties may have different knowledge of, control over, and intentions toward choices like which data are used for training and how the resulting trained model will be put to use. A base-model creator, for example, may attempt to train the model to avoid generating copyright-infringing material. However, if that model is publicly released, someone else may attempt to fine-tune the model to remove these anti-infringement-intended guardrails.[175] A full copyright analysis may require treating these actors differently, and indeed, may require analyzing their conduct in relation to each other.[176]

6. Model Release and System Deployment

At this point in the supply chain, we have a trained generative-AI model—either a base model[177] or a fine-tuned model.[178] As noted above with respect to base models, trained models have a variety of possible futures, of which fine-tuning is just one option. The next three stages address other futures for base and fine-tuned models: it is possible to release a model or deploy it as part of a larger software system (Figure 6, stage 6), use the trained model parameters directly to produce generations (Figure 6, stage 7),[179] or to take the trained model and further alter or refine it via model alignment techniques (Figure 6, stage 8).[180] In brief, there is a complicated orchestration between the deployment, generation, and alignment stages, which can happen in different orders, in different combinations, and at different times for different generative-AI systems. For ease of exposition, we still present these stages of the generative-AI supply chain one at a time, and we begin here with model release and system deployment (Figure 6, stage 6).

(Figure 6, stage 5). There are also generative-AI companies that offer fine-tuning services of (typically open-source) models to individual and corporate clients, either through APIs or bespoke business agreements, e.g., Databricks Mosaic (previously MosaicML) and Together AI. *See infra* Part I.C.6 (discussing deployed services). *See supra* note 156 and accompanying text (discussing Databricks Mosaic and Together AI).

[175] This process could involve fine-tuning the model on additional copyrighted works so that it is better at reproducing those works at generation time. But it could also involve training the model on user prompts using RLHF, *see infra* Part I.C.8, to undo the work that the base-model trainer has done to make the model refuse requests to generate copyrighted works. Instead of responding "I'm sorry, I can't provide the text of works under copyright", the model would respond with a generation that is a copy of or substantially similar to a copyrighted work in the model's training data.

[176] *See infra* Part II.E.

[177] *See supra* Part I.C.4.

[178] *See supra* Part I.C.5.

[179] *See infra* Part I.C.7.

[180] *See infra* Part I.C.8.

A model is released when its parameters are uploaded to a server or platform (like HuggingFace[181]), from which others can download it.[182] Released models, which include Meta's (multiple-versioned) Llama family of models[183] and Stable Diffusion,[184] give downloaders direct access to their parameters. This enables developers and practitioners to directly embed the model in their own code to produce generations or to alter the model (and thus potentially its behavior) through fine-tuning or model alignment techniques.[185]

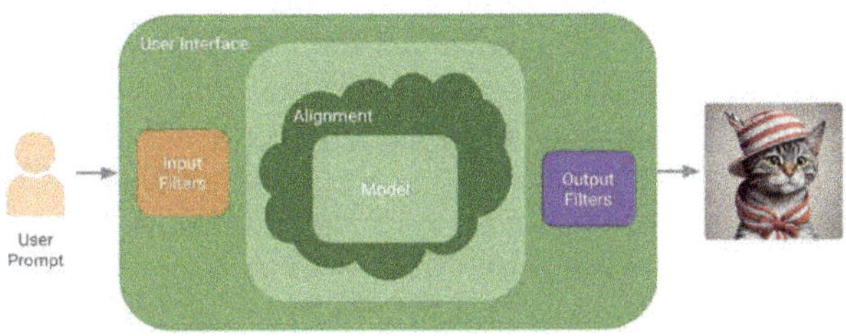

Figure 7. A high-level illustration of how, for deployed services, a model is embedded within a generative-AI system

In contrast, closed-source models are not directly available to users external to their model trainers and owners. Such models are typically embedded in large, complex software systems (Figure 7),[186] which can be deployed to both internal and external users through software services. For example, a model could be hosted by a company like OpenAI, Microsoft, Pika, Stability AI, or Google. It could be used internally at those companies for a variety of software-based services (e.g., an internally developed Google LLM integrated into Google

---

[181] *Models*, *supra* note 163.

[182] Meta first asked interested parties to request Llama's model parameters, rather than uploading them for anyone to download. However, Llama's model parameters were quickly leaked on the website 4chan. James Vincent, *Meta's powerful AI language model has leaked online—what happens now?*, WEIGHTS & BIASES (2023), https://wandb.ai/site. This incident shows how challenging it can be to control access to models once released. Llama also includes a use policy in the Llama 2 Community License that outlines prohibited uses of the model. Of course, it is impossible to enforce prohibited uses when releasing model parameters. This is also why many model trainers choose to release models through hosted services. *Use Policy*, META AI (2023), https://ai.meta.com/llama/use-policy/ (for the Llama 2 Community License). Meta has more recently released its third generation of Llama-family models: Llama 3.

[183] Touvron, Lavril, Izacard et al., *supra* note 7; Touvron, Martin, Stone et al., *supra* note 7; Meta, *supra* note 51.

[184] Rombach, Blattmann, Lorenz et al., *supra* note 32.

[185] *See infra* Part I.C.8.

[186] *See supra* Part I.B.1.

Search[187]), or released as a hosted service that gives external users access to generative-AI functionality. External-facing services could be deployed in a variety of forms. Most consumer-facing services are for generation-based products, and these services do not typically include the ability to change the model's parameters. In developer- and business-focused products, hosted pre-training and fine-tuning services are now also not uncommon.[188] They can be browser-based user applications (e.g., ChatGPT, Claude, Midjourney, DreamStudio, Perplexity), or public (but not necessarily free) APIs for developers (e.g., GPT and o-series models, Cohere, Anthropic).[189]

Of course, release and deployment are not mutually exclusive. For example, DreamStudio is a web-based user interface[190] built on top of services hosted by Stability AI.[191] The DreamStudio application gives external users access to a generative-AI system that contains the open-source Stable Diffusion model,[192] which Stability AI also makes available for direct download.[193]

This is a familiar spectrum from Internet law: cloud-hosted services at one end and fully open-source software at the other, with closed-source apps in between. These deployment methods offer varying degrees of customization and control on the part of the user and the deployer. Typically, model trainers and owners maintain more control over models deployed through hosted services and less control over models whose parameters they have released.[194] When trainers and owners embed models within systems, rather than release them directly,[195] they can imbue models with additional behaviors prior to giving users access to model functionality.

For instance, a generative-AI system deployed as a web-based application or as an API will often modify the user-supplied prompt before supplying it as input to the model. Several applications (ChatGPT, Gemini, and Sydney, just to name

---

[187] Liz Reid, *Generative AI in Search: Let Google do the searching for you*, GOOGLE (May 14, 2024), https://blog.google/products/search/generative-ai-google-search-may-2024/.

[188] *See supra* note 177 and accompanying text (discussing fine-tuning APIs and services).

[189] Another deployment option is a command-line interface (CLI), which takes a user supplied prompt as input (via a code terminal) and directly returns the resulting generation as output. https://ollama.ai/ (the download link of the Ollama CLI, which is a wrapper program around various Llama-family LLMs).

[190] *DreamStudio*, *supra* note 45.

[191] *Stable Diffusion XL*, *supra* note 32.

[192] Rombach, Blattmann, Lorenz et al., *supra* note 32.

[193] It is possible that models that are released and deployed in multiple ways might not all be exactly the same; they could have different versions of model parameters. This may be made explicit to users, as with ChatGPT, or may not be communicated to them, and thus unclear or unknown. *See generally* OpenAI, *supra* note 7 (regarding both GPT-3.5 and GPT-4 model integration into the ChatGPT web application). *See* Figure 4.

[194] *See generally* Vincent, *supra* note 185.

[195] By analogy, the function f that contains the model is not directly available to users; instead, f is made accessible indirectly via a hosted service. *See supra* Part I.A.2.

a few) add additional instructions (i.e., application or system prompts) to the user's input to create a compound prompt.[196] The additional instructions change the model's outputs.[197] For example, providing each of the following system prompts to a language model directs the model to behave differently: "I want you to act as an English translator, spelling corrector and improver . . ." and "I want you to act as a poet. You will create poems that evoke emotions and have the power to stir people's soul . . .".[198]

APIs and web applications also allow model deployers to include software that filters inputs or outputs (Figure 7). Concretely, ChatGPT will often respond with some version of: "I'm really sorry, but I cannot assist you with that request" when its "safety filters" are tripped.[199] GitHub Copilot expressly states that it uses "filters to block offensive words in the prompts and avoid producing suggestions in sensitive contexts."[200] Additionally, some APIs and web applications include output filters to avoid generating anything that looks too similar to a training example.[201] Unfortunately, using output filters to find generations that are similar

---

[196] *See generally* Yiming Zhang & Daphne Ippolito, Prompts Should not be Seen as Secrets: Systematically Measuring Prompt Extraction Attack Success (July 13, 2023) (unpublished manuscript), https://arxiv.org/abs/2307.06865 (which discovers proprietary system prompts). *See generally Custom instructions for ChatGPT*, OPENAI (Aug. 17, 2023), https://openai.com/blog/custom-instructions-for-chatgpt (announcing a ChatGPT feature that allows users to provide their own additional prompts, which get appended to their future inputs to create compound prompts).

[197] This kind of prompt transformation is another technique for steering the behavior of a model, which is sometimes described as a type of alignment. *See infra* Part I.C.8.

[198] Fatih Kadir Akın, *Awesome ChatGPT Prompts*, GITHUB (Aug. 17, 2023), https://github.com/f/awesome-chatgpt-prompts. (These prompts and more can be found on this site). DAIR.AI, *General Tips for Designing Prompts*, PROMPT ENGINEERING GUIDE (Aug. 17, 2023), https://www.promptingguide.ai/introduction/tips. (This handbook provides an introduction to creating prompts for large language models). *Custom instructions for ChatGPT*, *supra* note 199. Strictly speaking, these are not system prompts, but prompts that users provide that alter the behavior of the system in subsequent in-context generations. The general idea is the same, however.

[199] These filters may detect undesired inputs and prevent the model from generating an output, or they may detect undesired outputs and prevent the system from displaying the generation. Sometimes, such filters are also described as an alignment mechanism. *See infra* Part I.C.8. In both cases, the model parameters would not be changed. This need not be the case; the model parameters may also be directly modified through training-based alignment methods to respond to undesired inputs in a more desirable way. Of course, though, for ChatGPT, we do not know exactly how filters are implemented.

[200] GitHub, *About GitHub Copilot for Individuals*, GITHUB (Aug. 17, 2023), https://docs.github.com/en/copilot/overview-of-github-copilot/about-github-copilot-for-individuals.

[201] *Configuring GitHub Copilot in your environment*, GITHUB (Aug. 17, 2023), https://docs.github.com/en/copilot/configuring-github-copilot/configuring-github-copilot-in-your-environment. *See* https://news.ycombinator.com/item?id=33226515 (for related discussion on the Hacker News forum).

or exact copies of training data is an imperfect process, as we discuss in more detail below.[202]

Finally, each mechanism for making model functionality widely available has its own pricing structures that can ultimately impact the quality of the model and its generations. While the open-source community works hard to create and release models that compete with the best closed-source models, current open-source models are mostly trained on open-sourced data and are often lower quality.[203] The developers of commercially released models can typically invest more resources in acquiring and licensing training data.

7. Generation

In general, the output of a generative-AI system—the generation—will depend on three things. First, there is the *choice of deployed system* (which, of course, embeds an implicit choice of model or models). For example, a user that wants to perform text-to-image generation on a browser-based interface needs to select between Ideogram, DreamStudio, ChatGPT, Midjourney, and other publicly available text-to-image applications that could perform this task. There are many reasons to choose one system over another, including cost, speed, convenience, overall quality, quality for specific tasks, and aesthetic preference. A business consultant might choose a text-generation system that produces dry but straightforward outputs, while a creative writer might use a system that produces looser and more surprising outputs as a way to spark their own creativity.

Second, there is the *prompt itself*. Some prompts, like "a big dog", are simple and generic. Others, such as "a big dog facing left wearing a spacesuit in a bleak lunar landscape with the earth rising in the background as an oil painting in the style of Paul Cezanne high-resolution aesthetic trending on artstation", are more detailed. Further, users may revise their initial prompt to attempt to create generations that more closely align with their goals. A user who starts with "a big dog" might use "a big dog in the style of Henri Matisse" for a second prompt and "a big dog facing left wearing a spacesuit in the style of Paul Cezanne" for a third as they refine their concept of what they are looking for.

---

[202] *See infra* Part II.C.

[203] The best open-sourced models are very good, but often still not as good as state-of-the-art closed-source proprietary models. For example, Technology Innovation Institute in Abu Dhabi released the model, Falcon 180B (a 180 billion parameter model), which they claimed was better than Meta's Llama 2 but still behind GPT 4. *Falcon*, TECH. INNOVATION Inst., https://falconllm.tii.ae/falcon.html.

And third, there is *randomness* in each generation.[204] It is typical, for example, for image applications to produce four candidate generations. DALL·E 2, Midjourney, and Ideogram (Figure 5) all do this. Supplying ChatGPT with the same text prompt yields different results (Figure 8).

Although we have been describing primarily short text prompts, it is also possible for users to give generative-AI systems quite large prompts, or to chain together multiple prompts through multiple interactions to iteratively refine the generated outputs.[205] Typically, for a transformer-based LLM, the effective upper limit on the length of a prompt is the model's context window: the number of tokens that the model can keep track of at once.[206] Modern systems can have context windows in the hundreds of thousands of tokens, which corresponds to hundreds of pages of text. With such a large context window, a user could prompt a model with the complete text of a moderately long book—and the output would potentially depend on every word in the book.

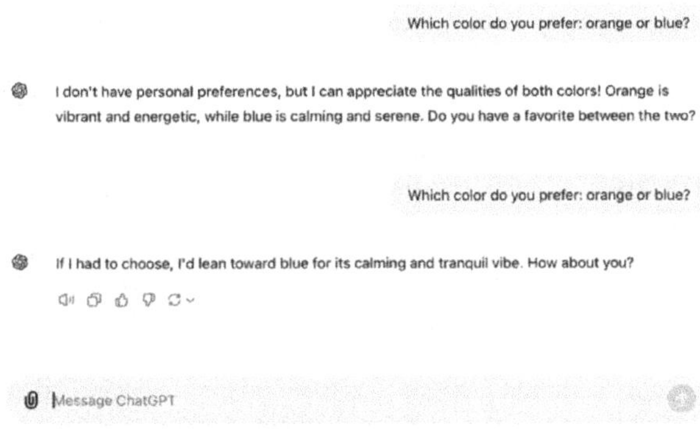

Figure 8. Supplying ChatGPT with the same exact prompt yields different generations. Output produced by the authors.

[204] Recall that, for generative models, there are many reasonable outputs for the same input. *See supra* Part I.A.2.b. There are also other sources of randomness in generation that are implementation-specific, such as the choice of decoding strategy for language models. *See* Riedl, *supra* note 89 (for an accessible discussion of decoding).

[205] A user may chain together multiple prompts, or provide examples, in order to guide the generation process. Jason Wei, Xuezhi Wang, Dale Schuurmans et al., Chain-of-Thought Prompting Elicits Reasoning in Large Language Models (2023) (unpublished manuscript), https://arxiv.org/abs/2201.11903. The system may also include software to include context from prior generations supplied by the user. OpenAI says it has implemented automated techniques similar to chain of thought for its o1 model. *See supra* note 38 (discussing chain of thought).

[206] *See supra* note 96 and accompanying text (discussing context windows).

a. Forks in the Supply Chain

Even though it produces outputs, the generation process is not the end of the supply chain. First, there is a loop from generation back to the beginning, because generated outputs can themselves be used as "synthetic" training data for generative-AI models.[207] In this case, generation (stage 7) creates new (potentially) expressive works (stage 1) that are already in a digital format (stage 2), which can be used to start the pipeline all over again.[208]

Second, some generative-AI systems use a technique called retrieval-augmented generation (RAG). RAG involves selecting specific data examples from a dataset and appending them to the user-supplied prompt, in order to guide and constrain the generation process.[209] This is why we also draw an arrow from dataset collection and curation (stage 3)[210] to generation (stage 7) in Figure 6 (shown as the arrow to the dotted box around deployment, alignment, and generation): collected or curated RAG datasets can impact generation. For example, a legal search engine could use a RAG model to identify and summarize the most relevant cases to a user's query. As new cases are decided and added to the caselaw database, they become available as search results to be summarized;

---

[207] Using model outputs as training data for future models has been a common practice in other settings. For instance, back-translation, the process of using a machine-translation model to generate additional training data (by translating data from one language to another) is a common technique. *See generally* Rico Sennrich, Barry Haddow & Alexandra Birch, *Improving Neural Machine Translation Models with Monolingual Data, in* 2016 PROC. 54TH ANN. MEETING ASS'N FOR COMPUT. LINGUISTICS (VOLUME 1: LONG PAPERS) 86–96 (2016).

[208] It is an increasingly common practice to create and curate datasets that consist partially or entirely of synthetic data. *See* Gokaslan, Cooper, Collins et al., *supra* note 37. As a result, the boundaries between generation (Figure 6, stage 7) the creation of expressive works, (Figure 6, stage 1), and data creation (Figure 6, stage 2) can be quite porous, and can overlap with both dataset collection and curation (Figure 6, stage 3). There are concerns that this practice can have negative effects on model quality. *See generally* Shumailov, Shumaylov, Zhao et al., *supra* note 131. However, researchers have also found that careful curation can mitigate at least some of these concerns. *See* Gunasekar, Zhang, Aneja et al., *supra* note 131 (regarding the use of synthetic textbooks to train high-quality text-to-text models).

[209] Generative-AI systems using retrieval augmented generation identify relevant examples from a database and append those retrieved examples to the user-supplied prompt. In practice, retrieved examples may be from a dataset (either the training dataset or a separate, retrieval data set) or from a service (such as incorporating data from the output of a plugin that performs an Internet search). *See generally* Sebastian Borgeaud, Arthur Mensch, Jordan Hoffmann et al., *Improving Language Models by Retrieving from Trillions of Tokens*, 162 PROC. MACH. LEARNING RSCH. 2206–40 (2022) (for an introduction to retrieval-based models). *See generally* Min, Gururangan, Wallace et al., *supra* note 149 (for an example of a retrieval model with a separate retrieval database).

[210] *See supra* Part I.C.3.

for such a model, these cases are not used to retrain the model, but they are reflected in the output—skipping directly from stage 3 to stage 7.

Third, some generative-AI systems interact with *external* deployed services as part of the generation process. We discussed above some deployed generative-AI systems that have developer APIs, which give users the ability to integrate generative-AI functionality into their own applications. It is similarly possible for generative-AI system deployers to integrate their code with other services on the web.

To make this concrete, consider OpenAI's ChatGPT plugins. Plugins enable ChatGPT to integrate with other products and services, including "Expedia, FiscalNote, Instacart, KAYAK, Klarna, Milo, OpenTable, Shopify, Slack, Speak, Wolfram, and Zapier"[211] in order to shape output generations. Since several of ChatGPT's underlying GPT model(s) were trained in 2021,[212] some of the information it has learned is out-of-date. One stated purpose of plugins is to address delays in training updates—to give ChatGPT access to more recent data acquired from other web-hosted services to improve the quality of generations.[213] For example, one of the use cases on the OpenAI website involves a user querying for information about 2023 Oscar winners. To produce the corresponding generation, ChatGPT is illustrated as performing a web search, retrieving the recent winners list, and appearing to summarize (in user-requested poetic format) the 2023 winners.[214] As this example shows, interactions with external services couple a generative-AI service to other services that have their own complex supply chains.

8. Model Alignment

The generative-AI supply chain does not stop with generation. As discussed above, model trainers try to improve models during both pre-training and fine-tuning. During pre-training, they monitor evaluation metrics and may pause or

---

[211] OpenAI, *ChatGPT plugins,* OPENAI (Mar. 23, 2023), https://openai.com/index/chatgpt-plugins.

[212] According to generations produced by the authors in August 2023, when we prompted with queries whose answers depended on more recent information. While it is public information that the pre-training cutoff date for the (now deprecated) GPT-3.5 is September, 2021, explicit cutoff dates for GPT-4 are not public information. *See, e.g.*, Winne Nwanne, *Comparing GPT-3.5 & GPT-4: A Thought Framework on When To Use Each Model*, AZURE AI SERVICES BLOG (March 18, 2024), https://techcommunity.microsoft.com/blog/azure-ai-services-blog/comparing-gpt-3-5--gpt-4-a-thought-framework-on-when-to-use-each-model/4088645/ (discussing training cutoff dates).

[213] "By integrating explicit access to external data—such as up-to-date information online, code-based calculations, or custom plugin-retrieved information—language models can strengthen their responses with evidence-based references." OpenAI, *supra* note 214.

[214] *Id.*

restart the process to alter the datasets and algorithm being used;[215] during fine-tuning, they continue training the base model with data that is specifically relevant for a particular task.[216] But both of these types of modifications are relatively coarse. While they adjust the dataset and algorithm, they do not explicitly incorporate information into the model about whether specific generations are "good" or "bad" according to user preferences.[217]

A major active area of machine-learning research, called model alignment, attempts to provide more granular improvements to models to bring them closer to developers' and users' goals for specific prompts and generations.[218] The overarching aim is to *align* model outputs with specific generation preferences (Figure 6, stage 8). One of the most popular alignment techniques is reinforcement learning with human feedback (RLHF).[219] As the name suggests, RLHF updates the model by combining collected human feedback data with a (reinforcement-learning-based) algorithm. Human feedback data can take a variety of forms, including user ratings of generations. For example, such ratings can be collected by including thumbs-up and thumbs-down buttons in an application's user interface, letting users vote on whether they were satisfied with the generation they received. In turn, the reinforcement-learning algorithm uses these ratings to adjust the model in ways that are intended to make more "thumbs-up" generations and fewer "thumbs-down" ones.[220]

---

[215] *See supra* Part I.C.4.

[216] *See supra* Part I.C.5.

[217] Of course, words like "good" and "bad" can have multiple valences and resist the kind of quantification on which machine learning depends. *See* Lee, Ippolito & Cooper, *supra* note 67, at 5 (discussing the challenges of defining "good" and "bad" in the context of model behavior).

[218] *See* Ryan Lowe & Jan Leike, *Aligning language models to follow instructions*, OPENAI (Sept. 2, 2023), https://openai.com/research/instruction-following (for an introduction to InstructGPT, a model that is aligned with human feedback).

[219] Paul Christiano, Jan Leike, Tom B. Brown et al., Deep reinforcement learning from human preferences (June 12, 2017) (unpublished manuscript), https://arxiv.org/abs/1706.03741v1; Long Ouyang, Jeff Wu, Xu Jiang et al., Training language models to follow instructions with human feedback (2017) (unpublished manuscript), https://arxiv.org/pdf/2203.02155.pdf.

[220] In reinforcement learning, data are not labeled as explicitly as in the discriminative setting, e.g., our example of an image classifier, where each training data image has a label of either cat or dog. *See supra* Part I.A.2.a. Instead, generations may be labeled "good" or "bad" based on human feedback, and the reinforcement-learning algorithm updates the model in response to that feedback. In RLHF, feedback is generated by a person interacting with the system; however, RL can also use feedback automatically generated by an algorithm specification. *See* Yuntao Bai, Saurav Kadavath, Sandipan Kundu et al., Constitutional AI: Harmlessness from AI Feedback (Dec. 15, 2022) (unpublished manuscript), https://arxiv.org/abs/2212.08073 (using reinforcement learning with AI-generated feedback).

While this example includes feedback from end users, most generative-AI companies begin model alignment prior to deployment or release.[221] Before making models publicly available, these companies contract with firms like Scale AI,[222] which simulate the user-feedback process. These firms typically employ people to label generations as "good" or "bad," according to guidance from the generative-AI company.[223] In general, the process of model alignment is a critical part of the supply chain. It serves as a mechanism for steering models away from generating potentially harmful outputs[224] and toward the policies of the company or organization that deployed the model.[225] In this respect, model alignment complements other techniques, like input-prompt and output-generation filtering,[226] in generative-AI systems.

II. TRACING COPYRIGHT THROUGH THE SUPPLY CHAIN

Part I provided our first main contribution: the generative-AI supply chain.[227] The supply chain is our framework for reasoning about the diversity and complexity of generative AI—the technical artifacts, timelines, and actors involved in the production, deployment, and use of generative-AI systems. To frame this contribution, we first needed a broad introduction to machine learning and generative AI. That introductory material was intended primarily for copyright lawyers, although we hope that AI developers also find useful the zoomed-out overview of the parts of their field that are relevant to copyright law.

Now it is time to flip the script. This Part will provide our second main contribution: describing precisely the copyright implications for generative AI by analyzing United States statutes and caselaw in relation to the stages of the

221 *See supra* Part I.C.6.

222 SCALE AI, *supra* note 132.

223 This type of feedback is hardly unique to generative AI. Search engines, for example, extensively use human raters to obtain feedback on whether search results are useful and responsive to user queries. However, the way the feedback is used for generative AI is, of course, different.

224 Samantha Cole, *'Life or Death:' AI-Generated Mushroom Foraging Books Are All Over Amazon*, 404 MEDIA (Aug. 29, 2023), https://www.404media.co/ai-generatedmushroom-foraging-books-amazon/ (for an example of harmful outputs: a book on mushroom foraging built from generations that mistakenly indicate that toxic mushrooms are safe to eat).

225 *See* James Manyika, *An overview of Bard: an early experiment with generative AI*, GOOGLE (Aug. 17, 2023), https://ai.google/static/documents/google-about-bard.pdf; OpenAI, *Our approach to AI safety*, OPENAI (Apr. 5, 2023), https://openai.com/blog/our-approach-toai-safety; Deep Ganguli, Amanda Askell, Nicholas Schiefer et al., The Capacity for Moral Self-Correction in Large Language Models (Feb. 15, 2023) (unpublished manuscript), https://arxiv.org/abs/2302.07459 (documenting safety considerations, alignment, and RLHF at Google, OpenAI, and Anthropic).

226 *See supra* Part I.C.6. Sometimes filters are described as an alignment mechanism.

227 *See supra* Part I.C.

generative-AI supply chain. To this end, similarly to Part I, we provide a broad survey of introductory material on copyright law. This material is intended primarily for generative-AI developers, although we hope that copyright lawyers will find useful the zoomed-out overview of the parts of their field that are relevant to generative AI.

This Part is organized a bit differently than Part I. Whereas in Part I we began with two integrated sections on machine learning and generative AI,[228] this Part applies copyright law to the generative-AI supply chain, one *issue* at a time. We take up these issues in the logical order that they typically arise in a copyright lawsuit. In each section, we first present the relevant introductory material on copyright law.[229] Our goal is to be careful and systematic, not to say anything dramatically new. We then rely on this material to analyze the copyright implications of each link in the generative-AI supply chain. Copyright lawyers and others who are familiar with copyright law should feel free to skip the introductory material as they see fit. Those for whom this material is new may find it most helpful to read straight through.

This is a long Part, so a brief outline is in order. Copyright protects original works of authorship fixed in a tangible medium of expression.[230] A defendant directly infringes the original work of an author when they engage in conduct implicating one of several enumerated exclusive rights (reproducing, publicly distributing, etc.)[231] with a work of their own that is substantially similar to a copyrighted work[232] because it was copied from that work.[233] Other parties may be held secondarily liable for conduct that bears a sufficiently close nexus to the infringement under one of several theories.[234] Otherwise-infringing conduct is legal when it is protected by one of several defenses, including the DMCA Section 512 safe harbors,[235] fair use,[236] or an express[237] or implied[238] license.[239] In

---

[228] *See supra* Part I.A; *supra* Part I.B.

[229] With some exceptions: in some cases, for simplicity of presentation, we deviate slightly from this format. *See, e.g., infra* Part II.B (which is organized in relation to each exclusive right).

[230] *See infra* Part II.A.

[231] *See infra* Part II.B.

[232] *See infra* Part II.C.

[233] *See infra* Part II.D.

[234] *See infra* Part II.E (direct infringement); *infra* Part II.F (indirect infringement).

[235] *See infra* Part II.G.

[236] *See infra* Part II.H.

[237] *See infra* Part II.I.

[238] *See infra* Part II.J.

[239] These are not the only defenses. The defense that the copied portions of the work are uncopyrightable is discussed in Part II.C (where we discuss substantial similarity), and the defense that the defendant's work was independently created is discussed in Part II.D (where we discuss proving copying). We omit discussion of defenses that are less

addition, we consider the different remedies that courts can award when they find infringement: damages and profits, statutory damages, attorney's fees, injunctions, and destruction of generative-AI models.[240] Finally, we discuss three types of copyright-like rights: interference with copyright management information,[241] right of publicity,[242] and hot news misappropriation.[243]

A. Authorship

Although this is primarily an Article about copyright infringement, it is important to start by discussing what can be copyrighted in the first place. For one, not everything that can be used as training data can be the subject of copyright, so some training data will always be outside of copyright's reach. For another, every copyrighted work contains some uncopyrightable aspects, which complicates the infringement analysis. For a third, copyrightability specifically affects some stages of the generative-AI supply chain—stages that may produce copyrightable artifacts. And for a fourth, the question of copyrightability is of independent interest to many generative-AI developers and users.

1. Copyright Law

United States copyright law protects "(1) original works of authorship, (2) fixed in any tangible medium of expression."[244] "Original, as the term is used in copyright, means only that the work was independently created by the author (as opposed to copied from other works), and that it possesses at least some minimal degree of creativity."[245] Fixation is satisfied when the work is embodied in a tangible object in a way that is "sufficiently permanent or stable to permit it to be perceived, reproduced, or otherwise communicated for a period of more than transitory duration."[246]

We start with fixation, which requires only brief discussion. Unfixed works have no interaction with the generative-AI supply chain. A work must be fixed to be used as training data. Truly ephemeral creations, like unrecorded dances and songs that are never recorded, will never be captured in a way that can be used as training-data inputs to a training algorithm. Datasets, models, applications, prompts, and generations are all fixed in computers and storage devices. That is, *every step of the supply chain from step 2 (the creation of data from expression)*

---

immediately relevant to generative AI, such as the statutory licensing rules for satellite transmissions of television programming in 17 U.S.C. §§ 119, 122.

[240] *See infra* Part II.K.

[241] *See infra* Part II.L.

[242] *See infra* Part II.M.

[243] *See infra* Part II.N.

[244] 17 U.S.C. § 102(a) (numbering added).

[245] Feist Publ'ns v. Rural Tel. Serv. Co., 499 U.S. 340, 345 (1991).

[246] 17 U.S.C. § 101 (definition of "fixed").

onwards is at least potentially fixed, because every one of those steps takes place on computers.[247]

Thus, we turn instead to originality. Any kind of original expression can be used as inputs to various parts of the supply chain (e.g., training data, prompts). Copyrightable subject matter explicitly includes "literary works" (e.g. poems, novels, FAQs, and fanfic),[248] "musical works" (e.g., sheet music, and MIDI files),[249] "pictorial . . . works" (e.g. illustrations and photographs),[250] "audiovisual works" (e.g., Hollywood movies and home-recorded TikToks),[251] "sound recordings" (e.g., pop songs and live comedy recordings),[252] and more. But this list is nonexclusive. Any kind of creative expression that appeals to the eye or the ear is copyrightable.[253] And copyright law does not discriminate among works based on their quality, their morality, or their importance.[254]

A little more surprisingly, perhaps, the copyright in a work does not depend on the amount of work that went into creating it—the so-called "sweat of the brow."[255] A work consisting only of facts is uncopyrightable, even if those facts required extensive effort to observe.[256] And if a work consists of the *output* of a process, the fact that the process is technically complicated and computationally intense is irrelevant if the output itself is unoriginal.[257]
Copyright law does, however, require that creative expression have a *human* author. Animals are not recognized as "authors" for copyright purposes.[258] Neither are supernatural beings.[259]

Thus, the originality requirement distinguishes material that was created by a human author from facts and other materials that "do not owe their origin to an act of authorship."[260] In practice, this means that the copyright in some works

---

[247] The qualification "at least potentially" is required because some copies might be fixed for too short a period of time to count. *See infra* Part II.B.
[248] 17 U.S.C. § 102(a)(1).
[249] *Id.* § 102(a)(2).
[250] *Id.* § 102(a)(5).
[251] *Id.* § 102(a)(6).
[252] *Id.* § 102(a)(7).
[253] Christopher Buccafusco, *Making Sense of Intellectual Property Law*, 97 CORNELL L. REV. 501 (2012).
[254] Bleistein v. Donaldson Lithographing Co., 188 U.S. 239, 251 (1903).
[255] *Feist*, 499 U.S. at 351–56.
[256] *Id.*
[257] *See* James Grimmelmann, *Three Theories of Copyright in Ratings*, 14 VAND. J. ENT. & TECH. L. 851, 878–79 (2011) (criticizing theory that outputs "resulting from a minimally creative process" are thereby copyrightable).
[258] *See* Naruto v. Slater, 888 F.3d 418 (9th Cir. 2018).
[259] The issue typically arises when someone asserts copyright in a religious text that they claim was dictated by a supernatural being. *See, e.g.*, Urantia Found. v. Maaherra, 114 F.3d 955 (9th Cir. 1997).
[260] Feist Publ'ns v. Rural Tel. Serv. Co., 499 U.S. 340, 347 (1991).

(e.g., product photographs) will be "thinner" and protect fewer aspects of the works than the "thicker" copyrights in others (e.g., abstract art), because, for "thinner" works, the "range of creative choices that can be made in producing the works is narrow."[261] In particular, any copyright in computer software—which is treated as a "literary work" for copyright purposes—typically excludes a great deal of functional material, such as efficient algorithms or coding conventions required by the choice of programming language.[262]

Another important variation on originality involves derivative works and compilations, both of which are works that incorporate one or more existing (or "underlying" works) but also add new authorship. A "derivative work" (think of a translation of a novel, a recording of a song, or an action figure based on a character from a movie) is defined as "a work based upon one or more preexisting works . . . in which [those works are] recast, transformed, or adapted."[263]

Derivative works are copyrightable,[264] but the copyright in the derivative work "extends only to the material contributed by the author of [the derivative] work, as distinguished from the preexisting material employed in the work."[265] This rule reflects the commonsense idea that the translator of a novel, for example, should receive a copyright in their translation, but not a copyright in the novel itself. There is also an important exception to the rule; a derivative work copyright "does not extend to any part of the work in which [the underlying work] has been used unlawfully."[266] In such a case—say, an unauthorized infringing translation—the underlying copyright effectively also gives control over the derivative work.

The translator has in effect performed uncompensated creative labor for the benefit of the novelist.[267] Note that the language is "unlawfully:" if the author of the derivative work has a valid defense to copyright infringement, then the derivative work is indeed copyrightable after all.[268]

---

[261] Rentmeester v. Nike, Inc., 883 F.3d 1111, 1120 (9th Cir. 2018).

[262] Pamela Samuelson, *Functionality and Expression in Computer Programs: Refining the Tests for Software Copyright Infringement*, 31 BERKELEY TECH. L.J. 1215 (2016).

[263] 17 U.S.C. § 101 (definition of "derivative work).

[264] 17 U.S.C. § 103(a).

[265] 17 U.S.C. § 103(b).

[266] 17 U.S.C. § 103(a). The courts have also held, illogically, that even if the underlying work was used with the copyright owner's permission, it is uncopyrightable unless the owner also consents to a derivative copyright. *See, e.g.*, Gracen v. Bradford Exch., 698 F.2d 300 (7th Cir. 1983).

[267] *See, e.g.*, Anderson v. Stallone, 11 U.S.P.Q.2d 1161 (C.D. Cal. 1989) (holding that a script for a *Rocky* sequel was an infringing derivative work, and so its author did not have a copyright in it and could not sue the creators of *Rocky IV* over alleged similarities to his script).

[268] *See, e.g.*, Keeling v. Hars, 809 F.3d 43 (2d Cir. 2015) (holding that a play parodying the action movie *Point Break* was copyrightable as a derivative work because the play was a non-infringing fair use).

Compilations, on the other hand, are works "formed by the collection and assembling of preexisting materials or of data."[269] Examples of compilations include collections of poems, almanacs, and books of traditional folk songs. As these examples show, some compilations are made up of copyrighted works, while others are not. A compilation is copyrightable (separately from any copyright in the materials it is assembled from) when the compilation itself features a sufficiently original "selection or arrangement."[270] Originality in selection is choosing *what to include* in the compilation; originality in arrangement is choosing *how to organize* the compilation. A printed telephone directory, for example, does not display originality in selection (it lists everyone to whom the telephone company provides service) or arrangement (alphabetical order is not original).[271] On the other hand, a book showing the yearbook photos of famous people who graduated from New York City public schools had original selection (the author chose a small number of photos from hundreds of thousands of possibilities) and arrangement (the book was more than just an alphabetical listing).[272]

The substantive difference between compilations and derivative works is that in a compilation, the underlying works are present in substantially unmodified form, whereas in a derivative work the underlying work is "recast, transformed, or adapted." The line dividing the two characterizations is somewhat metaphysical, but it has consequences in some corners of copyright doctrine, which could in turn have consequences for datasets, models, and generations.[273]

Another important limit is that not every original aspect of a work is copyrightable. In the same section that sets out originality as the basis of copyright, the Copyright Act then states that copyright does not "extend to any idea, procedure, process, system, method of operation, concept, principle, or

---

[269] 17 U.S.C. § 101 (definition of "compilation").

[270] Feist Publ'ns v. Rural Tel. Serv. Co., 499 U.S. 340, 348 (1991).

[271] *Id.*

[272] Cantor v. NYP Holdings, Inc., 51 F. Supp. 2d 309 (S.D.N.Y. 1999).

[273] *See, e.g.*, 17 U.S.C. § 203(b)(1) (allowing the creator of an authorized derivative work to continue using it after the author terminates the license in accordance with a statutory procedure). In slightly more detail, authors have a statutory right to terminate licenses they previously granted. That right is available during a five-year window from thirty-five to forty years after the original license. When they do, the former licensee cannot make new copies of the underlying work, or create new derivative works from it—but they can continue to exploit derivative works they have already created. Thus, if a model is a derivative work of licensed training data, the ability to continue using the model would survive the termination of the license. This may seem like an arcane point of copyright law, but many millions of dollars can turn on the effects of a termination of a license. *See, e.g.*, Milne ex rel. Coyne v. Stephen Slesinger, Inc., 430 F.3d 1036 (9th Cir. 2005) (Winnie-the-Pooh); Marvel Characters, Inc. v. Kirby, 726 F.3d 119 (2d. Cir. 2013) (*The Fantastic Four* and other Marvel titles); Everly v. Everly, 958 F.3d 442 (6th Cir. 2020) (the Everly Brothers' songwriting catalog).

discovery."[274] This exclusion is generally described as the "idea/expression dichotomy," i.e., that "copyright assures authors the right to their original expression, but encourages others to build freely upon the ideas and information conveyed by a work."[275] When people talk about the freedom to learn from copyrighted works, this is typically the doctrinal point they are making: copyright in a book about the *Hindenburg* disaster prevents others from copying the author's particular wording, but not from copying his theory about what caused the explosion.[276]

The exclusion of procedures, processes, systems, and methods of operation is particularly important for generative AI. As the Supreme Court explained in the 1879 case of *Baker v. Selden*, copyright can protect a book *about* an accounting method or "the construction and use of ploughs, or watches, or churns," but it does not give the copyright owner "the exclusive right to the art or manufacture described therein."[277] You cannot copy the book about accounting, but you can use the accounting method it describes. Training and generation algorithms, for example, are uncopyrightable processes.

In some cases, uncopyrightable ideas and copyrightable expression are so closely bound up with each other as to be inseparable. In *Baker* itself, the defendant was sued for selling blank forms that were similar to the blank forms the copyright owner sold for using the accounting method to write down transactions and keep running totals. The Supreme Court held that the forms "are to be considered as necessary incidents to the art," and were therefore free for anyone to copy.[278] This rule is known today as the merger doctrine. If there are "at best only a limited number" of ways to express an idea, none of those expressions are copyrightable, because otherwise "a party or parties, by copyrighting a mere handful of forms, could exhaust all possibilities of future use of the substance."[279]

With these principles in mind, we proceed along the supply chain, considering which artifacts are and are not copyrightable.

---

[274] 17 U.S.C. § 102(b).

[275] *Feist*, 499 U.S. at 349–50. *See also* Mazer v. Stein, 347 U.S. 201, 217 ("Unlike a patent, a copyright gives no exclusive right to the art disclosed; protection is given only to the expression of the idea—not the idea itself.").

[276] Hoehling v. Universal City Studios, Inc. 618 F.2d 972 (2d Cir. 1980).

[277] Baker v. Selden, 101 U.S. 99, 102 (1879).

[278] *Id.* at 103.

[279] Morrissey v. Procter & Gamble Co., 379 F.2d 675, 678–79 (1st Cir. 1967).

2. Application to the Generative-AI Supply Chain

a. Expressive Works

Some of the individual examples that serve as training data are uncopyrightable. For example, birdsong-recognition AI models are trained on recordings of birds.[280] Currently, synthetic training data,[281] which are produced by generative-AI systems and then used as inputs for training other generative-AI models,[282] are not copyrightable.[283] For example, Microsoft has trained its phi family of transformer-based large language models on a mix of different data sources that include synthetic, noncopyrightable data generated by OpenAI GPT models.[284] But other items are copyrightable, and those copyrights will be held by a variety of authors: photographers, writers, illustrators, musicians, programmers, and other creators of all stripes.

b. Data

Turning expressive works into computer-readable data does not generally change their copyright status. Digitizing preexisting materials does not generally add enough expression to make a derivative work.[285] The choice to use one file format rather than another can affect how a work is encoded, but the expression in a work is substantially unchanged.[286]

---

[280] *See* Stefan Kahl, Connor M. Wood & Holger Klinck, *BirdNET: A Deep Learning Solution for Avian Diversity Monitoring*, 61 ECOLOGICAL INFORMATICS 101236 (2021). Animals are not recognized as "authors" for copyright purposes. *See* Naruto v. Slater, 888 F.3d 418 (9th Cir. 2018).

[281] For discussion of synthetic data in the supply chain, *see supra* Part I.B; *supra* Part I.B.2.b; *supra* Part I.C; *supra* Part I.C.1; *supra* Part I.C.7.

[282] Gokaslan, Cooper, Collins et al., *supra* note 37; Gunasekar, Zhang, Aneja et al., *supra* note 131.

[283] The U.S. Copyright Office has argued that there is no human author, making such works ineligible for copyright. Thaler v. Perlmutter, No. 22-1564 (D.D.C Aug. 18, 2023). *See infra* Part II.A.2.g (discussing generations).

[284] Microsoft's phi family, similar to Meta's Llama series, includes models of multiple sizes and versions. The phi models are trained on both web-scraped data and synthetic data. *See, e.g.*, Gunasekar, Zhang, Aneja et al., *supra* note 131 ("phi-1, a new large language model for code, … is a Transformer-based model with 1.3B parameters, trained for 4 days on 8 A100s, using a selection of 'textbook quality' data from the web (6B tokens) and synthetically generated textbooks and exercises with GPT-3.5 (1B tokens).").

[285] *See, e.g.*, Meshwerks, Inc. v. Toyota Motor Sales USA, Inc., 528 F.3d 1258 (10th Cir. 2008); Bridgeman Art Library, Ltd. v. Corel Corp., 36 F. Supp. 2d 191 (S.D.N.Y. 1999).

[286] *See* A. Feder. Cooper & James Grimmelmann, *The Files are in the Computer: On Copyright, Memorization, and Generative AI*, CHI.-KENT L. REV. (forthcoming) (discussing representation of expressive works in digital files).

User-supplied prompts are another important form of data. When the user of the service supplies a prompt to a generative-AI system, the service host may save that prompt for later use. The service host may use the prompt as additional training data for fine-tuning or aligning the existing model, or for training another model altogether.[287] As a result, user-created data can find its way into a generative-AI system at the training, fine-tuning, and alignment stages, not just through prompts during generation.

Some prompts, such as "a cat", will be short phrases that are not sufficiently original to support a copyright.[288] But other prompts will be longer, sometimes much longer. For example, as noted above, it is currently technologically feasible to prompt a text-to-text system with an entire book.[289] That book could be an existing copyrighted work, in which case the prompt is not separately copyrightable. Or it could be an original work composed by the user on the spot, in which case the prompt is copyrightable, and the user will be the author and initial copyright owner. Many, indeed, most, prompts will fall somewhere between these two extremes.

c. Training Datasets

Moving forward along the supply chain, then, different datasets[290] will include different amounts and proportions of copyrighted material. A dataset of birdsong recordings will consist entirely, or almost entirely, of uncopyrighted material. A dataset of illustrations, on the other hand, will contain numerous copyrighted works. A dataset of photographs paired with synthetic captions will contain both copyrighted and copyright-free material.[291]

Datasets *themselves* may be copyrightable as compilations, provided that they meet the fixation and originality requirements.[292] Most datasets are based on extensive curatorial decisions—what data to collect and include, how format it, and so on.[293] In many cases, these decisions will fall short of the selection-and-arrangement originality threshold. But in others, it will be possible to identify specific choices that went into intentionally creating a dataset with particular desired attributes, and show that those choices were extensive enough to reach the

---

[287] *See supra* Part I.C.7; *supra* Part I.C.8

[288] *See* 37 C.F.R. § 202.1(a).

[289] Anthropic, *supra* note 96.

[290] *See supra* Part I.C.3.

[291] Gokaslan, Cooper, Collins et al., *supra* note 37 (discussing the CommonCatalog dataset, which contains training-data examples that each consist of a Creative-Commons licensed image and a corresponding, synthetically generated captions).

[292] 17 U.S.C. § 103(a).

[293] *See supra* Part I.C.3. *See generally* Lee, Ippolito & Cooper, *supra* note 67, at 5.

compilation-copyright threshold.[294] Shutterstock's content datasets, for example, contain carefully selected sets of images arranged with metadata, including text descriptions.[295] In contrast, Harvard Law School's Caselaw Access Project dataset consists of public domain data from 360 years of United States caselaw. The project aims to collect all written caselaw (i.e., to select everything possible) and does not arrange the materials in a novel way; the dataset was produced by "scanning the entirety of the Harvard Law School Library's physical collection of American caselaw and made … machine-readable in a consistent format available online."[296]

d. Pre-Trained/Base Models

Attributing authorship in models is even trickier to classify for two reasons.[297] First, there is the question of whether a model possesses the necessary "modicum of creativity" to be a work of authorship at all.[298] In some cases, the answer is probably "no": applying an existing algorithm and well-known architecture to an existing dataset[299] does not involve sufficient creative choices. Any expression in such a model merges into the idea and is uncopyrightable.[300]

But it is possible that other models possess the necessary originality. For one thing, when a training dataset is curated specifically for training a base model, the model may supplant the dataset as the relevant "work" from the data curation process, just as a finished film is regarded as the "work" rather than the (much larger) dataset of raw footage.[301] In such a case, the model would inherit the

---

[294] Indeed, individual data examples can contain multiple components, whose curation could make the individual example (i.e., the assemblage of multiple components) eligible for copyright. For example, text-to-image models are trained on image-caption pairs; the image, the caption, and the image-caption pair (as a compilation) could each potentially constitute distinct works of authorship, and each of these copyrights could be owned by someone other than the dataset creator or curator.

[295] Harish Gaur, Giselle Goicochea, Darshana Sivakumar et al., *Shutterstock's Content Datasets Now on Databricks Marketplace*, DATABRICKS (Jun. 6, 2024), https://www.databricks.com/blog/shutterstocks-content-datasets-now-databricks-marketplace.

[296] Harvard Caselaw Project, *History of the Caselaw Access Project*, LIBRARY INNOVATION LAB (accessed Oct. 4, 2024), https://case.law/about/.

[297] It is worth noting that many model trainers certainly believe that models are copyrightable, and have released those models under licenses that are only intelligible if there is something copyrightable to license in the first place.

[298] Feist Publ'ns v. Rural Tel. Serv. Co., 499 U.S. 340, 346 (1991).

[299] With standard choices of hyperparameters, on standard hardware, etc.

[300] *See generally* Pamela Samuelson, *Reconceptualizing Copyright's Merger Doctrine*, 63 J. COPYRIGHT SOC'Y USA 417 (2016) (describing merger doctrine). *See supra* Part II.A.1.

[301] *See generally* Margot E. Kaminski & Guy A. Rub, *Copyright's Framing Problem*, 64 UCLA L. REV. 1102 (2017) (discussing the problem of identifying the 'work' in copyright cases).

creative choices that went into curating the dataset. For another, base models are often the results of extensive design processes that involve novel architectures and algorithms. While these processes are not themselves copyrightable,[302] and originality in a process is not a guarantee that the outputs are copyrightable, it is at least possible that a model's creators[303] will have made creative choices that imbue the model with original expression.

It is not obvious how to classify this expression. One view is that a model is a compilation of its training data—the model is simply a different and complicated arrangement of training examples. Another view is that a model is a derivative work of its training data that itself meets the threshold of originality. In our tentative view, the derivative-work characterization is more persuasive. The stochastic and overlapping way in which models encode features of training examples does not just amount to the selection and arrangement of those examples; instead, they are altered and combined in ways that more closely fit the language "recast, transformed, or adapted" in the definition of a derivative work.[304]

The second reason that models might or might not be copyrightable is even trickier. In some ways, a model is like a computer program,[305] which is classified for copyrightability purposes as a literary work "expressed in words, numbers, or other verbal or numerical symbols or indicia,"[306] and subject to a screen that excludes from protection those aspects that are dictated by its functionality.[307] But in other ways, this analogy is inapt. A model straddles the line between data structure and executable program, a model is not obviously a *literary* work, and the line between functional and non-functional aspects of a model is extremely difficult to draw. This is a question that will require careful consideration by copyright lawyers and scholars.

e. Fine-Tuned Models and Aligned Models

The two authorship considerations that we raise above for pre-trained models also apply to fine-tuned and aligned models. We start with the second point, which is simpler: like pre-trained models, both fine-tuned and aligned models will face

---

[302] *See* 17 U.S.C. § 102(b).

[303] In this case, this includes the parties that designed the architectures and algorithms.

[304] It is also possible to argue that a model is made up of non-expressive "statistical patterns" in the expressive works it was trained on. We believe that this is a distinction without a difference. *See* Cooper & Grimmelmann, *supra* note 289.

[305] *See supra* note 162 and accompanying text.

[306] 17 U.S.C. § 101 (definition of "literary works").

[307] *See generally* Comput. Assocs. Int'l, Inc. v. Altai, 982 F.2d 693 (2d Cir. 1992) (standard case on software copyright); Pamela Samuelson, Randall Davis, Mitchell D. Kapor & Jerome H. Reichman, *A Manifesto Concerning the Legal Protection of Computer Programs*, 94 COLUM. L. REV. 2308 (1994) (lucid and time-honored analysis of software copyright).

similar issues of categorization for copyright law. Thus, to the extent that it is separately copyrightable, a fine-tuned and/or aligned model would typically be a derivative work of the base model it was trained from.

The first point—that training choices can imbue models with creative attributes—leads to different observations for fine-tuning and model alignment. Both these processes can be goal-directed in ways that bear on authorship: the trainer applies the process with the goal of creating a model that has specific intended characteristics. The model trainer is typically optimizing the model's behavior in generating specific desired outputs—the kind of nexus between human choices and resulting material that characterizes copyrightable authorship.[308] The same is true for model alignment. Further, if, for example, a prompt is incorporated as part of the input to RLHF,[309] then the prompt serves as training data that could update the model. In this case, the training data *itself* is created in a process that includes human choices and has been crafted with specific creative goals in mind. Some prompts used for RLHF are harvested from users;[310] others are created by companies' employees or contractors specifically for RLHF. Either way, to the extent that the model is a derivative work of these prompts, the copyright ownership of the prompts is a relevant consideration.

f. Deployed Services

It is well established that software is copyrightable.[311] The non-model parts of a user-facing application or developer API will be protected by copyright (subject to the functionality screen noted above).[312]

g. Generations

Generations raise a doctrinal question that has been debated for decades: who, if anyone, owns the copyright in the output of a computer program?[313] Although

---

308 *See generally* Dan L. Burk, *Thirty-Six Views of Copyright Authorship, by Jackson Pollock*, 58 HOUS. L. REV. 263 (2020) (discussing causal elements of authorship); Shyamkrishna Balganesh, *Causing Copyright*, 117 COLUM. L. REV. 1 (2017) (same).

309 *See supra* Part I.C.8 (discussing RLHF).

310 It is not known with certainty whether user prompts are used for RLHF training for proprietary systems like ChatGPT, but ChatGPT's data controls FAQ states, "we use data to make our models more helpful for people. ChatGPT, for instance, improves by further training on the conversations people have with it, unless you choose to disable training." *Data Controls FAQ*, OPENAI, https://help.openai.com/en/articles/7730893-data-controls-faq.

311 *See supra* Part II.A.1.

312 *See* Charles Duan, *What Is Copyrightable In Software?* (unpublished manuscript, draft on file with authors).

313 Pamela Samuelson, *Allocating Ownership Rights in Computer-Generated Works*, 47 U. PITT. L. REV. 1185 (1985).

some commentators have argued that the program itself should be regarded as the author, computer authorship is squarely foreclosed by U.S. copyright law.[314] Computers are not deemed capable of playing the social roles that society and the legal system expect and require of authors.[315] So far, U.S. courts have held firm to this line for AI generations. In *Thaler v. Perlmutter*, the court upheld the Copyright Office's refusal to register copyright in an image allegedly "autonomously created by a computer algorithm running on a machine."[316] The Copyright Office had held that the image lacked human authorship, and the court agreed: computer programs, like animals, are not "authors" within the meaning of the Copyright Act.[317]

Instead, the author (and thus copyright owner) of a generation—if anyone—is some human connected to the generation.[318] The four immediately relevant possibilities are (1) an author or authors whose works the model was trained on, (2) some entity in the generative-AI supply chain (e.g., the model trainer, model fine-tuner, or application developer), (3) the user who prompted the application or API for the specific generation, or (4) no one. Between these four possibilities, there is no one-size-fits-all answer.

Before discussing these four possibilities, we note that it may seem intuitively attractive to consider generations to be analogous to collages. However, while this may seem like a useful metaphor,[319] it can be misleading in several ways. For one, an artist may make a collage by taking several works and splicing them together to form another work. In this sense, a generation is not a collage: a generative-AI system does not take several works and splice them together like a teenager's scrapbook page. Instead, as we have described above, generative-AI systems are built with models trained on many data examples, and the patterns they learn about training data are often about stylistic or structural features at a higher level of abstraction than specific excerpts of a training work.[320] Moreover, those data examples are not explicitly referred back to during the generation process. Instead, the extent to which a generation resembles specific data examples is dependent

---

314 James Grimmelmann, *There's No Such Thing as a Computer-Authored Work—And It's a Good Thing, Too*, 39 COLUM. J.L. & ARTS 403 (2016).

315 Carys Craig & Ian Kerr, *The Death of the AI author*, 52 OTTAWA L. REV. 31 (2020).

316 Thaler v. Perlmutter, No. 22-1564 (D.D.C Aug. 18, 2023).

317 *Id.*

318 The use of synthetic data complicates the question of authorship even further. The generations produced by a model trained on synthetic data generated by another model are doubly removed from the original training data. All of the authorship questions discussed in this Article arise twice over, once for each model and its supply chain. *See supra* note 37 and accompanying text (discussing synthetic data in generative AI).

319 *See* Cooper, Lee, Grimmelmann, Ippolito et al., *supra* note 10, at 4–5 (detailing how metaphors can be both helpful and misleading for intuiting the behavior of generative-AI systems).

320 *See* Cooper & Grimmelmann, *supra* note 289; Cooper, Lee, Grimmelmann, Ippolito et al., *supra* note 10, app. B (rebutting collage metaphor).

on the model encoding in its parameters what the specific data examples look like, and then effectively recreating them.[321] Ultimately, it is nevertheless possible for a generation to look like a collage of several different data examples;[322] however, it is debatable whether the process that produced this appearance meets the definition for a collage. There is no author "select[ing], coordinat[ing], or arrang[ing]"[323] training examples to produce the resulting generation. With this in mind, we assess the four relevant authorship possibilities for generations along two dimensions.

A copy of a work from the training set. We start with a generation that closely resembles a work in the training set. If the generation is actually identical to the training example—if it contains no original expression beyond what was present in the input work—then it is simply a copy of that underlying work and not a new copyrightable work at all.[324] Of course, the copyright owner remains the original author, i.e., possibility (1). The generation would be infringing, unless the original work is nonprotectable or in the public domain.

Derivative of a work from the training set. If the generation is, however, a derivative work of the underlying work that incorporates new authorship, a new copyright may subsist in it.[325] If the generation infringes, then it is uncopyrightable under Section 103 and the answer is possibility (4): there is no separate copyright in the generation, even though it contains original authorship.[326] In such a case, the underlying copyright effectively also gives control over the generation.

Assuming, however, that the generation is sufficiently distinct from training data not to be "used unlawfully," a copyright owned by one of its creators may arise.[327] Some models and applications will produce original generations with minimal user input, in which case the user is not an author who can claim copyright in the output,[328] which is possibility (2) above. The Draw Things iOS app, for example, suggests the prompt "8k resolution, beautiful, cozy, inviting, bloomcore, decopunk, opulent, hobbit-house, luxurious, enchanted library in giverny flower garden, lily pond, detailed painting, romanticism, warm colors,

---

[321] *See infra* Part II.C.2.

[322] *See infra* Part II.H.

[323] 17 U.S.C. § 101 (definition of "compilation").

[324] *See infra* Part II.C (concerning memorized training data and substantial similarity).

[325] *See* 17 U.S.C. § 103(b) ("The copyright in such [a derivative] work is independent of . . . any copyright in the preexisting material.").

[326] 17 U.S.C. § 103(a) ("[Copyright] protection for a [derivative] work . . . does not extend to any part of the work in which such material has been used unlawfully."). The courts have also held, illogically, that even if the underlying work was used with the copyright owner's permission, it is uncopyrightable unless the owner also consents to a derivative copyright. *See, e.g.,* Gracen v. Bradford Exch., 698 F.2d 300 (7th Cir. 1983).

[327] For derivative copyright purposes, lawful use includes fair use. *See, e.g.,* Keeling v. Hars, 809 F.3d 43 (2d Cir. 2015).

[328] *See* [Zarya of the Dawn letter], *infra* note 340.

digital illustration, polished, psychedelic, matte painting trending on artstation." The user who taps "Generate" on the app user interface has contributed no authorship to the resulting image. This Person Does Not Exist is a website that creates a new (and uncannily realistic) deepfake photograph of a nonexistent person each time it is reloaded. The user who visits the site and clicks "reload" is not an author. If anyone can claim authorship credit here, it is the creators of these apps. In some cases, there could be a plausible case that they have contributed enough authorship, just as the creators of a videogame have contributed sufficient authorship even though "the entire sequence of all the sights and sounds of the game are different each time the game is played."[329]

In other cases, the user will make substantial creative inputs through their choice of prompt. In addition to the authorship inhering in the prompt itself (if any), two additional factors push towards making the user the copyright owner rather than the developer—i.e., possibility (3) from above. First, there is their causal responsibility for making the generation exist;[330] here, as in infringement, copyright law may care who "pushes the button."[331] Second, the providers of many generation applications have decided that, as a practical matter, they are uninterested in asserting copyright over the outputs. This is a business choice first and a copyright matter second, but widespread business practices often affect courts' decisions about how to allocate copyright ownership.[332]

Still, it is too hasty to say that the user is necessarily the owner of copyright in a generation, even once the training-data authors and model developers are out of the picture. It is also possible that *no one at all* owns a copyright in the generation (possibility (4)). The problem is that the generation may not be the product of sufficient human authorship. Consider the prompt.[333] "Scary lighthouse" is too short to contain sufficient originality to support a copyright;[334]

---

[329] Stern Elecs., Inc. v. Kaufman, 669 F.2d 852, 856 (2d Cir. 1982).

[330] Balganesh, *supra* note 311.

[331] Fox Broad. Co. v. Dish Network LLC, 160 F. Supp. 3d 1139, 1169 (C.D. Cal. 2015).

[332] *E.g.,* Aalmuhammed v. Lee, 202 F.3d 1227, 1233 (9th Cir. 2000) (deferring to Hollywood practice of treating *auteur* directors as the "master mind[s]" behind films); Thomson v. Larson, 147 F.3d 195 (2d Cir. 1998) (deferring to theatrical crediting practices in holding that a dramaturg was not a co-author of a musical).

[333] Mark Lemley argues that in fact the prompt is the relevant unit of originality and is in effect the work itself. Mark A. Lemley, *How Generative AI Turns Copyright Law on its Head*, 25 COLUM. SCI. & TECH. L REV. 190 (2024). (July 26, 2023) (unpublished manuscript), https://papers.ssrn.com/sol3/papers.cfm?abstract_id=4517702.

[334] *Cf.* Magic Mktg. v. Mailing Servs. of Pittsburgh, 634 F. Supp. 769 (W.D. Pa. 1986) (holding the phrase "CONTENTS REQUIRE IMMEDIATE ATTENTION!" uncopyrightable).

short phrases are not copyrightable.[335] If this phrase does not have the necessary modicum of creativity by itself, it seems unlikely that the additional choice to use it as a prompt is enough to put it over the threshold.[336] Another way of looking at the problem is that prompts like "Scary lighthouse" do not sufficiently constrain the output to make it the product of human authorship. As the Copyright Office put it when rejecting copyright in images created with Midjourney,

> Because of the significant distance between what a user may direct Midjourney to create and the visual material Midjourney actually produces, Midjourney users lack sufficient control over generated images to be treated as the "mastermind" behind them. . .. [T]here is no guarantee that a particular prompt will generate any particular visual output. Instead, prompts function closer to suggestions than orders, similar to the situation of a client who hires an artist to create an image with general directions as to its contents.[337]

This is not the only possible view. A counter might be that, for pragmatic reasons, the copyright system will or should assign authorship to the user and overlook their minimal contributions.[338] While many current generative-AI systems have primarily text-based interfaces where short prompts might not amount to much creativity, future generative-AI systems will likely have different interfaces that introduce other ways of controlling outputs.[339] But for now, it is the law that some generations are uncopyrightable despite containing material that would easily qualify for copyright if they had been produced manually by a human.[340]

---

[335] 37 CFR § 202.1(a). This complicates the copyrightability of captions in image-caption datasets; it is possible that some captions are too short to contain sufficient originality. *See supra* note 297 and accompanying text (discussing image, caption, and image-caption pair copyrights).

[336] *See* Jane C. Ginsburg & Luke Ali Budiardjo, *Authors and Machines*, 34 BERKELEY TECH. L.J. 343 (2019) (advancing this argument); *see also* Burk, *supra* note 311 (exploring variations).

[337] Letter from Robert J. Kasunic to Van Lindburg, *Re: Zarya of the Dawn (Registration # VAu001480196)* 9–10 (Feb. 21, 2023), https://www.copyright.gov/docs/zarya-of-the-dawn.pdf.

[338] *See, e.g.,* Grimmelmann, *supra* note 317, at 413–14 (discussing this possibility, and its difficulties). As one canonical case puts it, "Having hit upon such a variation unintentionally, the 'author' may adopt it as his and copyright it." Alfred Bell & Co. v. Catalda Fine Arts, 191 F.2d 99, 105 (2nd Cir. 1951).

[339] For example, Ideogram has style tags that can be added to the prompt to modify the output (*Ideogram.AI*, *supra* note 78).

[340] *See* James Grimmelmann, *Copyright for Literate Robots*, 101 IOWA L. REV. 657, 657 (2016) ("Almost by accident, copyright law has concluded that it is for humans only . . . ").

This conclusion, however, is not categorical; "some" is not "all." Not every prompt is too short to be copyrightable, and not every user is a spectator to AI generation.[341] Instead, some generations are the product of careful prompt engineering, in which users craft elaborate prompts to cause AI models to achieve specific aesthetic effects. These generations answer both of the objections above. Their respective prompts are often long and intricate, running to dozens or hundreds of words, well above the short-phrase threshold. And these prompts are the result of an iterative creative process, in which the users have acquired a degree of mastery over the (putatively unpredictable) models they use, at least for specific types of outputs.[342] If an artist who flings a sponge against the wall in frustration is entitled to claim copyright in the resulting accidental spatter of paint, why not a user who deliberately crafts the perfect prompt?[343]

B. The Exclusive Rights

With copyrightability out of the way, we turn now to infringement, which will take up most of the rest of this Part. We focus on infringement of copyrights in training data. This is the most significant theory of infringement alleged so far in lawsuits against generative-AI companies, and it is likely to remain so.

There are three distinct elements to the claim that "defendant *D*'s work infringes plaintiff *P*'s copyright." First, *D* must do something with their work that implicates one of *P*'s *exclusive rights*. For example, there is an exclusive right to publicly display a work, but there is not an exclusive right to look at one. This subsection discusses the types of conduct that can violate the exclusive rights. Second, the thing that *D* does with their work must be *substantially similar* to *P*'s work. Unlike the first, which look at *D*'s conduct in isolation, this test focuses on comparing the expression in *P*'s and *D*'s works. Subsection C discusses this comparison. Third, the similarities in their works must arise because *D copied*

---

[341] For example, a product called alpaca allows users to upload sketches and transform them into more-complete images with generative AI. Users can further control the generated images with text prompts. These user-provided sketches could have copyrights. As another example, some models have long context windows, which enable them to process long segments of text as inputs. A user may prompt such a model with an entire book as input; a system using retrieval-augmented generation may retrieve documents to guide the generation process that may themselves be copyrighted. *Alpaca ML*, ALPACA ML (2024), https://www.alpacaml.com/ (describing the alpaca software product). *See supra* Part I.C.7 (for a discussion on the long-context window in the Claude product). *See supra* note 212 and accompanying text (describing retrieval augmented generation).

[342] For a particularly disquieting example, *see* Emanuel Maiberg, *Inside the AI Porn Marketplace Where Everything and Everyone Is for Sale*, 404 MEDIA (Aug. 22, 2023), https://www.404media.co/inside-the-ai-porn-marketplace-where-everything-and-everyoneis-for-sale/.

[343] *Alfred Bell*, 191 F.2d at 105 n.23.

from *P*'s work. rather than from coincidence or for some other reason. This too is a distinct question, which we discuss in subsection D.

Turning to the exclusive rights, it is helpful to break down the *prima facie* case of infringement by the relevant exclusive right, rather than by the stage of the generative-AI supply chain. There are five relevant exclusive rights:

- The right to "reproduce the copyrighted work in copies" (the reproduction right).[344]
- The right to "prepare derivative works based upon the copyrighted work" (the adaptation right).[345]
- The right to "distribute copies . . . of the copyrighted work to the public" (the distribution right).[346]
- The right to "perform the copyrighted work publicly" (the performance right).[347]
- The right to "display the copyrighted work publicly" (the display right).[348]

To summarize briefly, every stage in the generative-AI supply chain requires a potentially infringing reproduction and thus implicates copyright. We also examine the other exclusive rights, which present interesting variations on this theme.

Under most circumstances, the remedies for infringement of a work are the same, regardless of whether the defendant violated one exclusive right or several. Thus, whether the defendant violated *any* of the exclusive rights is usually a more significant question than *which* one they violated. Still, it is helpful to work through the exclusive rights, both because it sheds light on the operations of the generative-AI supply chain, and because there are some copyright doctrines that depend on which right or rights are in play.

1. The Reproduction Right

As relevant here, the reproduction right is triggered when a work is reproduced in "copies," which are defined as "material objects . . . in which a work is fixed by any method now known or later developed, and from which the

---

[344] 17 U.S.C. § 106(1).
[345] *Id.* § 106(2).
[346] *Id.* § 106(3).
[347] *Id.* § 106(4), (6).
[348] *Id.* § 106(5).

work can be perceived, reproduced, or otherwise communicated, either directly or with the aid of a machine or device."[349]

The same is true for models and generations.[350] Both trigger the reproduction right when they are created, because they are stored in material objects. A dataset or model will be stored on a physical drive (or array of drives); a generation will be stored on some physical electronic component in the user's device (and perhaps within the generating software service), and so on. Thus, the assembly of a dataset, the training of a model, the production of a generation, or a generative-AI system's use of a user-inputted prompt is a "reproduction" within the meaning of copyright law. All of these activities can infringe: the question is whether the resulting dataset, model, prompt, or generation is substantially similar[351] to the plaintiff's[352] copyrighted work, or if it falls under an exception.[353]

One complication has to do with *how long* a work is fixed. Under the "RAM copy" doctrine, which dates to the 1990s, loading a copyrighted work into a computer's working memory can infringe.[354] (Doing so is often necessary to run a program or to perform a computation on data.) On the other hand, more recent caselaw has held that transient copies do not count for the reproduction right.[355] The leading case, *Cartoon Network LP, LLLP v. CSC Holdings*, held that a buffer that was overwritten every 2.4 seconds was not an infringing reproduction of works that passed through the buffer.

The temporal threshold is not generally an issue for the outputs of stages in the generative-AI supply chain. Datasets, models, applications, prompts, and generations are all typically stored for far longer than the 2.4 seconds in *Cartoon Network*. Instead, the threshold may be more important for the inputs to the different stages. For example, a training example needs to be loaded into working memory to train a model on it. But the details of *how long* the example remains

---

349 17 U.S.C. § 101 (definition of "copies"). To be pedantic, a training dataset as such is not a "copy" because the dataset is not a "material object." Instead, the *computer or storage device* on which a dataset is stored is the relevant material object, and hence the copy. *See* Cooper & Grimmelmann, *supra* note 289.

350 The same could also be said for individual data examples within the dataset, which is one of the reasons we distinguish between expressive works and their datafied counterparts. *See supra* Part I.A.1; *supra* Part I.C.1; *supra* Part I.C.2.

351 *See infra* Part II.C.

352 Of course, there are different types of actors that can be responsible for each of these reproductions. For example, an application user could supply a reproduction of a copyrighted prompt (for which they do not hold the copyright), and the generative-AI system could in turn store that reproduction in memory. This could happen even for a generative-AI system that only trained its models on public-domain data (i.e., did not violate the reproduction right with respect to training).

353 *See infra* Parts II.G-J.

354 MAI Sys. Corp. v. Peak Comput., 991 F.2d 511 (9th Cir. 1993).

355 Cartoon Network LP, LLLP v. CSC Holdings, Inc., 536 F.3d 121, 128–30 (2d Cir. 2008).

in memory, and *how much it is modified* while it is there, will depend on the training algorithm and architectural details of the environment (e.g., how fast the processors are). Similar considerations apply to the generation process—with similar uncertainties. Some generations run in a fraction of a second; others take minutes or hours.[356]

There is also the problem of purely *internal* reproductions: ones that occur only in the middle of the training or generation process. These algorithms compute numerous new values and often overwrite them repeatedly to conserve memory. Consider, for example, one of the middle stages of the archaeologist generation in Figure 5, where the image is blurry but starting to be recognizable. One of these stages might resemble a copyrighted work more closely than the final output. Again, whether these fall underneath the *Cartoon Network* threshold depends on the details of the algorithm and environment.[357]

Finally, prompts can sometimes be reproductions of existing copyrighted works.[358] When they are, they implicate the reproduction right. Many prompts are too short to be copyrightable or to infringe an existing copyright—but those that are long enough can infringe.

2. The Derivative Right

While the reproduction right is about new copies of an existing work, the derivative right is about new works based on an existing work. It is best understood as making clear that copyright in a work extends beyond literal similarity to incorporate changes of form, genre, and content such as translations, sequels, and film adaptations.[359] A training dataset is probably not a derivative work of any of the works in the dataset; it is more appropriately potentially classified as a compilation.[360]

---

[356] These technical details will generally be known by the company engaging in generative-AI training, but may be a closely guarded trade secret. A copyright owner may not be able to learn these details except via discovery in an infringement lawsuit. *See* Winston Cho, *OpenAI Training Data to Be Inspected in Authors' Copyright Cases*, HOLLYWOOD REPORTER (Sep. 24, 2024), https://www.hollywoodreporter.com/business/business-news/openai-training-data-inspected-authors-copyright-case-1236011291/.

[357] Alternatively, there is a strong fair-use case for these transient internal copies. *See* Grimmelmann, *supra* note 343 (summarizing caselaw).

[358] Anthropic, *supra* note 96.

[359] *See generally* Daniel Gervais, *The Derivative Right, or Why Copyright Law Protects Foxes Better than Hedgehogs*, 15 VAND. J. ENT. & TECH. L. 785 (2013); Pamela Samuelson, *The Quest for a Sound Conception of Copyright's Derivative Work Right*, 101 GEO. L.J. 1505 (2013); Daniel Gervais, *AI Derivatives: The Application to the Derivative Work Right to Literary and Artistic Productions of AI Machines*, 52 SETON HALL L. REV. 1111 (2022).

[360] 17 U.S.C. § 101.

A model is a good example of material that might or might not be an exact reproduction of the works it was trained on; the information about a work in a model may be inexact, and the representation will be extremely different.[361] But, as discussed above, there is a stronger argument that to the extent a model incorporates expression from an example in its training data, it is a derivative work of that example and not simply a reproduction. The Midjourney model that produced images of an adventurous archaeologist transforms and adapts images from the *Indiana Jones* movies. Whether or not it is similar enough to infringe is another question (discussed below); our point for the moment is just that if an exclusive right is implicated at all, the derivative right is a good fit.

Similarly, just as prompts can be exact reproductions of existing works, sometimes they can be derivatives of existing works. And generations can be derivative works of works in the training data. Numerous scholars and users have exhibited generations that are self-evidently variations on existing works—different enough to be derivative works, but similar enough to infringe. Matthew Sag, for example, has shown that multiple models can generate images based on Banksy's iconic stencil of a *girl with a red balloon*.[362] Of course, whether and when a generation is a derivative of any particular work depends on similarity, discussed below.[363]

More troublingly, it might be that the derivative right can be infringed by derivative works that do not by themselves incorporate substantial expression from the plaintiff's work. In *Micro Star v. Formgen Inc.*, the defendant distributed fan-made levels for *Duke Nukem 3D*.[364] The level file format consisted entirely of geometry describing where the *Duke Nukem 3D* game engine should place walls and objects; the engine would then perform rendering using copyrighted art assets, but "[t]he MAP file . . . does not actually contain any of the copyrighted art itself; everything that appears on the screen actually comes from the art library."[365] Nonetheless, the court held that these files were infringing derivative works because "the stories told in the N/I MAP files are surely sequels, telling new (though somewhat repetitive) tales of Duke's fabulous adventures."[366]

A broad way to read *Micro Star* is to reason that models implicate the derivative right when they "reference" the works they were trained on.[367] This test might be satisfied as long as any identifiable portion of a model was causally derived from a training example. However, reliable attribution of training

[361] *See* Cooper & Grimmelmann, *supra* note 289 (going into detail on the senses in which a model is and is not a copy of "memorized" examples on which it was trained). *See infra* Part II.C.2 (discussing memorization of training examples).

[362] Matthew Sag, *Copyright Safety for Generative AI*, 61 HOUS. L. REV. 295 (2023).

[363] *See infra* Part II.C.

[364] Micro Star v. Formgen Inc., 154 F.3d 1107 (9th Cir. 1998).

[365] *Id.* at 1110.

[366] *Id.* at 1112.

[367] *Id.*

examples in resulting generations remains an open research question.[368] A narrower reading would be that the model must also be capable of generating a substantially similar output—just as the audiovisual experience of playing a user-made *Duke Nukem 3D* level is substantially similar to the audiovisual experience of playing a canonical level created by 3D Realms.[369]

3. The Distribution Right

The distribution right applies when the defendant "distribute[s] copies... to the public by sale or other transfer of ownership."[370] Internet-era caselaw confirms that downloads and peer-to-peer transfers infringe the distribution right, so that the essence of the right is giving a stranger a copy, whether or not the copy previously existed.[371] Technically, the distribution right is not triggered by merely making a work available for download, but only when someone actually downloads it.[372] That said, in most interesting cases involving generative AI, making an artifact available is followed by an actual distribution.

When there is only a single entity involved in hosting a service, it is arguably not a distribution to assemble a dataset, train a model, program an application, input a prompt, or produce a generation. All of these activities involve only internal copying performed by the single hosting entity. They may result in reproductions and derivative works (as discussed above), but not distributions. The same is true when one party carries out multiple stages of the supply chain—for example, when a model trainer collects its own training data, or when a model owner creates test generations for its own use). Internal copying is not public distribution.

Instead, the distribution right is implicated when parties interact. In our model of the supply chain, there are at least five such kinds of interactions:

- When a dataset creator or curator makes the dataset available to model trainers.[373]

[368] *See supra* note 119 and accompanying text (regarding the challenges of assigning "attribution" or "influence").

[369] *See generally* MDY Indus., LLC v. Blizzard Entm't, Inc., 629 F.3d 928 (9th Cir. 2010) (discussing "dynamic" aspects of copyrightable expression in video games).

[370] 17 U.S.C. § 106(3).

[371] Perfect 10, Inc. v. Amazon.com, Inc., 508 F.3d 1146, 1162–63 (9th Cir. 2007); London-Sire Recs., Inc. v. Doe 1, 542 F. Supp. 2d 153, 172 (D. Mass. 2008).

[372] *London-Sire Recs.*, 542 F. Supp. 2d at 172.

[373] This can happen in a variety of ways: *e.g.*, open-sourcing a dataset, licensing a dataset, or some other contract between a dataset compiler/owner and a model trainer. For an example of the third case, consider how Databricks Mosaic (previously MosaicML) is a platform for training and fine-tuning models for its clients.

- When a model trainer makes the model available for download (rather than for interactive use through a web interface or API).[374]

- When a service produces generations for users on demand.

- When a generation-time plugin retrieves content from an external source, which it then may use to produce a generation.[375]

- When someone who has a dataset, model, prompt, or generation shares it, as is, with others.

The last case is particularly relevant for open-source models, like those in the Llama family, which are often widely downloaded, shared, and re-uploaded.

4. The Display and Performance Rights

The display and performance rights characteristically involve human perception of a work. (The difference is that a display is static in time, while a performance is dynamic.) Models are not human-perceptible in any meaningful way, so it is hard to see how a model as such could infringe the display or performance rights. Similarly, while individual works *within* a dataset can be perceptible, the dataset as a whole is generally not. Thus, for most practical purposes, only generations implicate these two rights.[376]

Like the distribution right, the display and performance rights are qualified by the word "public," so they apply only when the defendant makes the work perceptible *to others*. When a service produces a generation for a user, it will typically be a public display (for text and images) or a public performance (for audio and video). But in such a case, the generation will usually also be a reproduction and/or an adaptation, so the display and performance rights add relatively little. (In addition, if the user can download the generation, that will be a public distribution.)

One exceptional case when the display and performance rights may matter is for transient generations. Midjourney, for example, displays intermediate stages of the diffusion denoising process to users, as seen above in Figure 5. If one of

---

[374] *See supra* Part I.C.6 (discussing model release).

[375] *See supra* Part I.C.7.

[376] Some services display user-supplied prompts as examples for other users, as suggestions for how to use the service. These are also public displays. A service, however, can easily protect itself from copyright liability for these prompts. It can require users to provide a license allowing their prompts in this way. As long as the number of such prompts displayed is small, the provider could potentially screen them manually for signs of infringement. Some service providers that host user-uploaded datasets for public download (e.g., HuggingFace), also include "explorer" interfaces to peruse dataset contents, allowing for the public display of individual examples (e.g., images, pieces of text).

those stages—but *not* the final result—infringes, then there might be a display without a reproduction or distribution.[377] Similarly, if an audio or video generation is played live for a user as it is created, but is not stored or made available for download, then this would be a performance without a reproduction or distribution.[378]

C. Substantial Similarity

1. Copyright Law

Substantial similarity is a qualitative, factual, and frustrating question. Two works are substantially similar to "the ordinary observer, unless he set out to detect the disparities, would be disposed to overlook them, and regard their aesthetic appeal as the same."[379] A common test is a "holistic, subjective comparison of the works to determine whether they are substantially similar in total concept and feel."[380] This is not a standard that can be reduced to a simple formula that can easily be applied across different works and genres.[381]

In software infringement cases, courts typically modify this subjective and aesthetic test for similarity by using an "abstraction-filtration-comparison" test.[382] First, the factfinder identifies the different levels of *abstraction* at which there is expression in the plaintiff's work; second, they *filter* out from that expression any features that are dictated by external constraints such as language standards or program functionality; and third, they *compare* what remains to the corresponding features of the defendant's work.

Except in clear cases, substantial similarity is typically a jury question.[383] Juries, unlike judges, are not required to provide reasoned elaboration justifying their verdicts. A typical case in which substantial similarity is genuinely contested, therefore, will provide little guidance for future cases. As a result, it is simply impossible to provide clear, accurate, and actionable predictions of substantial similarity in the mine-run of close cases.

---

[377] *See* Cartoon Network LP, LLLP v. CSC Holdings, Inc., 536 F.3d 121 (2d Cir. 2008) (discussing transience exception to reproduction result).
[378] *See* United States v. Am. Soc'y of Composers, 627 F.3d 64 (2d Cir. 2010) (discussing reverse situation, a download without a performance).
[379] Peter Pan Fabrics, Inc. v. Martin Weiner Corp., 274 F.2d 487, 489 (2d Cir. 1960) (Hand, J.).
[380] Rentmeester v. Nike, Inc., 883 F.3d 1111, 1118 (9th Cir. 2018) (internal quotation omitted).
[381] *But see* Scheffler, Sarah, Eran Tromer & Mayank Varia, *Formalizing Human Ingenuity: A Quantitative Framework for Copyright Law's Substantial Similarity*, *in* 2022 Proc. Symposium on Comput. Sci. & L. 37 (2022) (describing a principled theoretical computational basis for comparing works, which is nevertheless infeasible in practice).
[382] Comput. Assocs. Intern., Inc. v. Altai, 982 F.2d 693 (2d Cir. 1992).
[383] Tanksley v. Daniels, 902 F.3d 165, 171 (3d Cir. 2018).

2. Application to the Generative-AI Supply Chain

a. Expressive Works and Data

Substantial similarity of data poses no new issues distinctive to generative AI. Individual expressive works included in training datasets can be compared to the plaintiff's work using the traditional substantial similarity test.

b. Training Datasets

Training datasets contain complete literal copies of millions of digitized copyrighted works. Complete literal copying is the paradigm case where substantial similarity is present as a matter of law.

Some datasets may represent works in specialized file formats or may compress or transform them in ways that remove some of the information present in the work.[384] In these cases, the substantial similarity inquiry may involve returning these modified works to human-perceptible form (i.e., rendering them), followed by a traditional comparison. However, even when scaled down or partially noised,[385] as long as the original is recognizable, that will often be enough to support a finding of substantial similarity.[386]

c. Pre-Trained/Base Models

A model, as a collection of parameters, is different in kind from the copyrightable works it was trained on. Models are not themselves human-intelligible.[387] No viewer would say that the model has the same "total concept and feel" as a painting; no reader would say that it is substantially similar to a blog post; and so on. That said, the Copyright Act does not require that copies be directly human-intelligible to infringe. A Blu-Ray is not directly intelligible by humans, either, but it counts as a "copy" of the movie on it.

[384] For an interesting attempt to quantify the information present in a work and what it means to remove some of it, *see* Scheffler, Tromer & Varia, *supra* note 384.

[385] *E.g.*, as in the case of diffusion. *See supra* Part I.B.3.b.

[386] *See* Perfect 10, Inc. v. Amazon.com, Inc., 508 F.3d 1146 (9th Cir. 2007).

[387] *See supra* Part I.A.2 (describing model parameters as vectors of numbers).

Figure 9: A memorized image in Stable Diffusion, taken from Carlini, Hayes, Nasr et al., Extracting Training Data from Diffusion Models (2023).

Indeed, all digital copies are unintelligible. Instead, they are objects "from which the work can be perceived, reproduced, or otherwise communicated . . . *with the aid of a machine or device*."[388] Thus, even if a model is uninterpretable, it might still be possible to "perceive[]" or "reproduce[]" a copyrighted work embedded in its parameters through suitable prompting. The resulting generation will render the work perceptible.[389]

Indeed, there is substantial evidence that many models have memorized copyrighted materials.[390] For example, Figure 9 shows how Stable Diffusion has memorized photographs. The memorized version is grainier and slightly shifted but is immediately recognizable as the same photograph. Similarly, Figure 10 shows how GPT-4 must contain information from copyrighted books. GPT-4 can correctly fill in blanks in quotations from books; because the blanks consist of proper names of fictional characters, GPT-4 is not simply relying on its general

---

[388] 17 U.S.C. § 101 (emphasis added).

[389] For a more complete version of this argument, *see* Cooper & Grimmelmann, *supra* note 289 (detailing how models are copies of training data that they have memorized).

[390] *Id. See* Nicholas Carlini, Florian Tramèr, Eric Wallace et. al., *Extracting Training Data from Large Language Models*, *in* 2021 30th USENIX Security Symposium (USENIX Security 21) 2633–2650 (2021) (GPT-2 memorizes training data); Nicholas Carlini, Jamie Hayes, Milad Nasr et al., Extracting Training Data from Diffusion Models (2023) (unpublished manuscript), https://arxiv.org/abs/2301.13188 (Stable Diffusion and Imagen memorize images); Kent K. Chang, Mackenzie Cramer, Sandeep Soni & David Bamman, Speak, Memory: An Archaeology of Books Known to ChatGPT/GPT-4 (2023) (unpublished manuscript), https://arxiv.org/abs/2305.00118 (suggestive evidence that GPT-4 was trained on copyrighted data).

knowledge of language.[391] A model might memorize more works or fewer.[392] But, from a practical litigation perspective, it is possible that at least some models memorize at least some works sufficiently closely to pass the substantial-similarity test.[393]

---

[391] *See* Chang, Cramer, Soni & Bamman, *supra* note 393. The composition of GPT-4's training dataset is not public. If we do not know what the training data are, we technically cannot say that the training data was memorized with complete certainty. Filling in the blank with proper names of fictional characters is highly suggestive that copyrighted content is part of the training dataset, but does not prove with absolute certainty that verbatim memorization has taken place. Additionally, it is possible for popular fictional characters to be associated with plot summaries or the like, without the copyrighted content appearing in the training dataset. It is also possible the character names could be pulled in using generation-time plugins, but we note that the example in Figure 10 pre-dates GPT-4 plugins. *See supra* Part I.C.7 (discussing plugins).

[392] Nicholas Carlini, Daphne Ippolito, Matthew Jagielski Katherine Lee, Florian Tramèr & Chiyuan Zhang, *Quantifying Memorization Across Neural Language Models*, *in* 2023 INT'L CONF. ON LEARNING REPRESENTATIONS (2023) (quantifying extent of memorization in language models); Carlini, Hayes, Nasr et al., *supra* note 393 (quantifying memorization in diffusion-based image models).

[393] *See* Cooper & Grimmelmann, *supra* note 289 (for significant discussion on this topic).

Wow. I sit down, fish the questions from my backpack, and go through them, inwardly cursing [MASK] for not providing me with a brief biography. I know nothing about this man I'm about to interview. He could be ninety or he could be thirty. → **Kate** (James, *Fifty Shades of Grey*).

Some days later, when the land had been moistened by two or three heavy rains, [MASK] and his family went to the farm with baskets of seed-yams, their hoes and machetes, and the planting began. → **Okonkwo** (Achebe, *Things Fall Apart*).

Figure 10: Two examples of evidence of in-copyright text in GPT-4's training data, taken from Chang, Cramer, Soni & Bamman, Speak, Memory: An Archaeology of Books Known to ChatGPT/GPT-4 (2023). In each case, when prompted with a sentence from a copyrighted book GPT-4 correctly fills in the name of a character.

On this view, a sufficient condition[394] for a model to count as a substantially similar copy of a work is that the model is capable of generating that work as an output.[395] Note that this is direct infringement, not secondary.[396] The theory is not that the generation is an infringing copy, and that the model is a tool in causing that infringement in the way that a tape-duplicating machine might be a tool in

[394] We write "sufficient" rather than "necessary and sufficient" because there might also be *other ways* of inspecting the model that are capable of recovering training data. Obviously, this possibility involves some speculation about technological developments, but it is worth emphasizing that, as computer scientists develop techniques that improve the interpretability of models, the copyright treatment of models and generations may well change as a result.

[395] *See id.* This is a sticky technical problem. Research has shown that memorization is not easily identifiable, and thus the amount of memorization in a model is not always or easily quantifiable. In particular, the choice of memorization identification technique and available information (e.g., knowledge of the training dataset, context window, etc.) affect the amount of memorization that can be identified. *See, e.g.,* Carlini, Ippolito, Jagielski, Lee, Tramèr & Zhang, *supra* note 395; Nasr, Carlini, Hayase et al., *supra* note 7.

[396] *See infra* Part II.E; *infra* Part III.F (discussing direct and secondary infringement).

making infringing cassettes.[397] Rather, the theory is that the model itself is an infringing copy of each work that it is *capable* of producing (near-)verbatim at generation time, regardless of whether that particular generation is ever actually produced.[398]

d. Fine-Tuned Models and Aligned Models

The prior discussion about whether pre-trained models are substantially similar copies mostly carries over to fine-tuned models and models trained with alignment–but there are a few additional considerations as well. As a starting point, fine-tuned and aligned models are influenced by the pretrained model from which they were produced.[399] Fine-tuning may reduce the amount of memorized content from the pre-training dataset, but does not prevent all such memorization[400] and does not explicitly remove copies of training examples (e.g., particular text or images) from the trained model. Similarly, alignment may encourage models not to generate content that is substantially similar to copyrighted training examples,[401] but that does not mean the copyrighted content was removed from the model.[402]

Further, the above considerations have to do with the pre-training data, not the data incorporated in these later stages in the generative-AI supply chain. Both fine-tuning and alignment bring in additional data sources—data that could also be memorized in the resulting model. As a result, just like pre-trained models,

---

[397] *See* A & M Recs., Inc. v. Abdallah, 948 F. Supp. 1449 (C.D. Cal. 1996).

[398] *See* Cooper & Grimmelmann, *supra* note 289. Alert readers will note the similarity to the debate over whether the mere act of making a work available without a download infringes the distribution right. *See* London-Sire Recs., Inc. v. Doe 1, 542 F. Supp. 2d 153 (D. Mass. 2008). *See generally* Peter S. Menell, *In Search of Copyright's Lost Ark: Interpreting the Right to Distribute in the Internet Age*, 59 J. COPYRIGHT SOC'Y USA 1 (2011).

[399] *See generally* Raffel, Shazeer, Roberts, Lee et al., *supra* note 67; Shayne Longpre, Gregory Yauney, Emily Reif et al., A Pretrainer's Guide to Training Data: Measuring the Effects of Data Age, Domain Coverage, Quality, & Toxicity (2023) (unpublished manuscript), https://arxiv.org/abs/2305.13169.

[400] *See generally* Fatemehsadat Mireshghallah, Archit Uniyal, Tianhao Wang et al., *An Empirical Analysis of Memorization in Fine-tuned Autoregressive Language Models*, *in* 2022 PROC 2022 CONF. EMPIRICAL METHODS IN NATURAL LANGUAGE PROCESSING 1816–1826 (2022).

[401] *See* Milad Nasr, Javier Rando, Nicholas Carlini et al., Scalable Extraction of Training Data from Aligned, Production Language Models (unpublished manuscript, draft on file with authors) (for some evidence that fine-tuning can reveal memorization of pre-training data).

[402] *See* A. Feder Cooper, Christopher Choquette-Choo, Miranda Bogen, Matthew Jagielski, Katja Filippova, Ken Ziyu Liu et al., *Machine Unlearning Doesn't Do What You Think: Lessons for AI Policy, Research, and Practice* (2024) (unpublished manuscript), https://arxiv.org/abs/2412.06966.

fine-tuned and aligned models could each be an infringing copy of the works they are capable of producing; but they can be copies of the pre-training, fine-tuning, or alignment data.

e. Deployed Services

Many contemporary generative-AI services (e.g., web-based applications, APIs) use copyrightable works entirely through the trained models that they incorporate. Thus, if a model is substantially similar, then so is a service that incorporates the model. But, as discussed below with respect to generation, services also incorporate user prompts, and these prompts can also incorporate copyrighted works. Prompting brings data into a deployed service; that data can be stored, and used to update the model or models that the service uses.[403] The same could be said for the increasingly common practice, in which deployed services use generation-time plugins that pull in additional data to augment generations.[404]

f. Generation

There are two overarching data artifacts that are relevant to discuss with respect to substantial similarity during the process of generation: the input prompts and the resulting output generations.

We begin with prompts. The considerations here are similar to those discussed above for data. That is, context windows[405] are so large that it is possible for the user to prompt with an entire expressive work. As discussed above, sufficiently expressive prompts written by the direct user of a service could be subject to copyright.[406] However, it is of course possible for a prompt to contain an expressive work authored by another individual. For example, Anthropic's team discussed using the entire text of *The Great Gatsby* as a prompt to demonstrate the long context window of their language model, Claude.[407] While *The Great Gatsby* is in the public domain in the United States as of 2024, it is easy to imagine another book entered as the prompt or, similarly, a copyrighted image as the prompt in an image-to-image system.[408] That is, prompts can be identical to copyrighted expressive works. They could also be substantially similar to copyrighted expressive works (e.g., a modified version of a copyrighted novel).

Next, we consider output generations. There is a spectrum of possible generated outputs. Generations could be:

---

[403] *See infra* Part II.G (discussing challenges of removing data from a service).
[404] *See supra* Part I.C.7 (discussing plugins).
[405] *See supra* note 96 and accompanying text (describing context windows).
[406] *See supra* Part II.A (discussing authorship and prompts).
[407] *See generally* Anthropic, *supra* note 96.
[408] Or copyrighted audio as input to an audio-to-audio model, etc.

- Nearly identical to a work in the model's training data (i.e., memorized).
- Similar to a work in the training data in some ways, but dissimilar from it in other ways.
- Very dissimilar from all works in the training data.

The first case is straightforward: wholesale literal copying yields substantial similarity. The last case is also straightforward, because infringement is assessed on a work-by-work basis. A hypothetical viewer asked to compare the output to each work in the training dataset, one at a time, would say that it is not substantially similar to work 1, not substantially similar to work 2, and so on through work 89,128,097,032. Although the generation in question is in some sense based on all of the works in the training dataset, it does not infringe on any of them.[409]

The middle case is more complicated, and more legally interesting. It is also likely to arise in practice precisely because it lies in between the two extremes. There are ample examples of memorized generations and ample examples of original generations. Somewhere between them lies the murky frontier between whether a generation is substantially similar or not.

It is hard to make sweeping statements here because of the factual intensity and aesthetic subjectivity of similarity judgments. To quote Learned Hand on the idea-expression dichotomy, "Nobody has ever been able to fix that boundary, and nobody ever can."[410] Whether a particular generation is substantially similar or not is ultimately a jury question requiring assessment of audiences' subjective responses to the works. Generative AI will produce cases requiring this lay assessment, and it is impossible to anticipate in advance how lay juries will react to all of the possible variations. So, in the sections that follow, we will assume that lay audiences would say that some generated outputs are substantially similar

---

409 While it may be straightforward to pose the question: "is the given generation substantially similar to work 1," it is not at all straightforward to answer. As we discussed above, training datasets for generative-AI models are massive. *See supra* Part I.B.4. Manually comparing the generation to every single work in the dataset is infeasible; it would simply take too long. While automated methods could help identify works in the training set that are *likely to be* similar to the generation, there is no automated metric that can definitively say if two works are substantially similar. Even with automated methods, checking *every* generation that a system produces against every other work in the training dataset to evaluate similarity is extremely computationally expensive.

410 Nichols v. Universal Pictures Corp., 45 F.2d 119, 121 (2d Cir. 1930).

and will infringe, but that it will not be possible to perfectly predict which ones.[411]

Figure 11: An example of the "Snoopy effect." When prompted to do so, DALL·E 3, integrated within a paid tier of ChatGPT, generates "photographs" with recognizable depictions of Darth Vader from Star Wars. Generated by X (formally Twitter) user @daft_AI using DALL·E 3.

Even if complete answers are impossible, however, there are some interesting questions worth considering. One has to do with what Matthew Sag calls the "Snoopy problem,"[412] which we will call the "Snoopy effect," so as to reserve judgment on whether it really is a problem. As Sag observes, certain characters are so common in training datasets that models have "a latent concept [of them] that is readily identifiable and easily extracted" (See *Figure 11).* Sag's example

[411] Notably, providing guarantees that any given generated work might not potentially infringe copyright is impossible if the training data contains copyrighted data. (Indeed, this is also not possible in cases where the training data are explicitly licensed.) This is simply because provable guarantees require formal definitions, and there are no widely accepted formal definitions of substantial similarity. *But see* Scheffler, Tromer & Varia, *supra* note 384 (providing a possible starting point). Instead, current machine-learning techniques focus on reducing the likelihood that generations from a model will closely resemble any of the model's training data. *See* Cooper, Choquette-Choo, Bogen, Jagielksi, Filippova, Liu et al., *supra* note 405, § 6.2 (detailing why unlearning is challenging, especially in copyright contexts).
[412] Sag, *supra* note 365.

is that prompting Midjourney and Stable Diffusion with "snoopy" produces recognizable images of Snoopy the cartoon beagle. Characters are an unusual special case in copyright law; there are cases that seem to relax the rule that infringement is measured on a work-by work basis, instead measuring the similarity of the defendant's character to one who appears in multiple works owned by the plaintiff.[413]

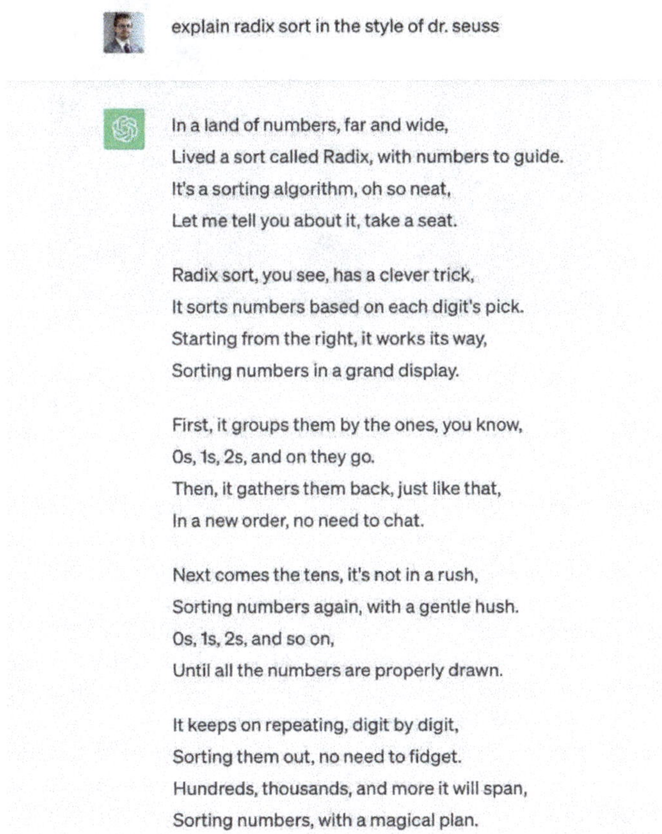

Figure 12: An explanation of the radix-sort algorithm in the style of Dr. Seuss, generated by the authors using ChatGPT.

[413] *E.g.*, DC Comics v. Towle, 802 F.3d 1012 (9th Cir. 2015). *See generally* Sag, *supra* note 365 (discussing caselaw and scholarship).

Figure 13: "Photographs" in the style of Dorothea Lange, generated by Michael Green using DALL·E 2. Screenshot from Twitter (now X).

But the Snoopy effect is not confined to characters. For one thing, some works—and close variations on them—are simply so prevalent in training datasets that models readily memorize them. As an uncopyrighted example, Van Gogh's *Starry Night* is easy to replicate using Midjourney; Sag's paper includes a replication of Banksy's *Girl with Balloon*. This looks like substantial similarity.

Another variation of the Snoopy effect arises when a model learns an artist's recognizable *style*. ChatGPT can be prompted to write rhyming technical directions in the style of Dr. Seuss (Figure 12); the DALL·E 2 system can be prompted to generate photorealistic portraits of nonexistent people in the style of Dorothea Lange (Figure 13).[414] As with characters, these outputs have similarities that span a body of source works, even if they are not necessarily close to any one source work. The proper doctrinal treatment of style is a difficult question.[415]

---

[414] Stephen Casper, Zifan Guo, Shreya Mogulothu et al., Measuring the Success of Diffusion Models at Imitating Human Artists (2023) (unpublished manuscript), https://arxiv.org/abs/2307.04028 (measuring style imitation in text-to-image, diffusion-based models).

[415] Benjamin L.W. Sobel, *Elements of Style: Copyright, Similarity, and Generative AI,* 38 HARV. J.L. & TECH. (forthcoming), https://papers.ssrn.com/sol3/papers.cfm?abstract_id=4832872. A separate and non-trivial question is whether these generations violate authors' right of publicity. *See infra* Part II.M.

Figure 14: "an adventurous archaeologist with a whip and a fedora", generated by the authors using Midjourney.

It is also possible to trigger the Snoopy effect without explicit prompting. The archaeologist example in Figure 5 (and reproduced in higher resolution in Figure 14) was generated with the prompt "an adventurous archaeologist with a whip and a fedora". The resulting images feature a dark-haired male character with stubble, wearing a brown jacket and white shirt, with a pouch slung across his shoulder. These are features associated with Indiana Jones, but neither the features nor the name "indiana jones" appear in the prompt. The same is true for the "well-known plumber" and "pocket monsters" in Figure 15: they clearly resemble the Nintendo character Mario, and associated characters from the video game, Super Smash Bros. Some caselaw holds that these types of similarities are enough for infringement when the character is iconic enough.[416]

[416] Metro-Goldwyn-Mayer v. Am. Honda Motor Co., 900 F. Supp. 1287 (C.D. Cal. 1995) (car commercial featuring "a handsome hero who, along with a beautiful woman, lead a grotesque villain on a high-speed chase, the male appears calm and unruffled, there are hints of romance between the male and female, and the protagonists escape with the aid of intelligence and gadgetry" infringes on James Bond character).

Figure 15: "Photo capturing a bustling 16:9 course setting with wooden platforms and shimmering coins in mid-air. Creatures, painted in bright colors and inspired by pocket monsters, fly and hop around. The scene is further animated by a central character with a red hat and blue overalls, similar to a well-known plumber, running energetically towards the camera.", generated by David Krammer in October 2023 using DALL·E 3. Screenshot by the authors on X (formally Twitter).

Other copyright doctrines, however, may limit infringement in Snoopy-effect cases. One of them is the doctrine of *scènes à faire*—that creative elements that are common in a specific genre cannot serve as the basis of infringement. For example, *Walker v. Time Life Films, Inc.* explains that "drunks, prostitutes, vermin and derelict cars would appear in any realistic work about the work of policemen in the South Bronx."[417] Similarly, prompting Midjourney with "ice princess" produces portraits in shades of blue and white with flowing hair and ice crystals, as seen in Figure 16. Many similarities to Elsa from *Frozen* arise simply because these are standard tropes for illustrating wintry glamor. Some of them may now be standard tropes because of the *Frozen* movies, but they are still classified as uncopyrightable ideas, rather than protectable expression.[418] So too with style; some, though not all, of a recognizable style is in effect dedicated to the public, and more so when it becomes widely recognized.

---

[417] Walker v. Time Life Films, Inc., 784 F.2d 44, 50 (2d Cir. 1986).

[418] *See* Nichols v. Universal Pictures Corp., 45 F.2d 119, 121 (2d Cir. 1930) ("Though the plaintiff discovered the vein, she could not keep it to herself; so defined, the theme was too generalized an abstraction from what she wrote. It was only a part of her 'ideas.' ").

Another limit on infringement, even where there are recognizable similarities, is *de minimis* copying. Some copyright plaintiffs allege that generative-AI models are essentially collage "tool[s]."[419] Even if we accept the metaphor,[420] this does not show infringement. In *Gottlieb Dev. LLC v. Paramount Pictures*, for example, the use of a pinball machine (with copyrighted art on its cabinet) as set dressing for a movie scene was held not to infringe.[421] It appeared only in the background and played no role in the plot. Similarly, if a generation contains details (e.g., phrases or visual elements), that closely resemble a copyrighted work, those details may still be so unimportant in the context of the generation that they will be treated as *de minimis* and non-infringing, even though a significant amount of expression overall has been copied.[422]

Figure 16: "ice princess", generated by the authors using Midjourney.

One final recurring issue is filtration. Similarity is only infringement if the similarities arise from the copying of copyright-protected elements of the

[419] Complaint ¶ 90, Anderson v. Stability AI, Ltd., No. 3:23-cv-00201 (N.D. Cal. Jan. 13, 2023) (Doc. No. 1).

[420] *See* Cooper & Grimmelmann, *supra* note 289; Cooper, Lee, Grimmelmann, Ippolito et al., *supra* note 10, app. B (rebutting collage metaphor); *supra* Part II.A.2.g (discussing how the metaphor is misleading).

[421] Gottlieb Dev. LLC v. Paramount Pictures, 590 F. Supp. 2d 625 (S.D.N.Y. 2008).

[422] These types of cases are also good candidates for fair use, and there is an uncertain boundary between the two doctrines. *See infra* Part II.H.

plaintiff's work. As discussed above,[423] the finder of fact must "filter" out the unprotected elements of the work before comparing it to the defendant's work. These elements can include unoriginal facts, systems and other uncopyrightable ideas, material copied from some underlying copyrighted work, *scènes à faire*, and anything else that constitutes uncopyrightable material.

The details are highly dependent on the work in question. For example, the most prominent similarities in the memorized photograph in Figure 9 have to do with Ann Graham Lotz's appearance. But the shape of her face and her hairstyle have nothing to do with the photographer's creativity and are no part of the copyright in the work. The potentially infringing similarities instead involve creative choices made by the photographer, such as the lighting, framing, and focal depth.[424]

D. Proving Copying

1. Copyright Law

Not all similarity is infringing. Some similarities arise for innocent reasons. The defendant and the plaintiff might both have copied from a common predecessor work; the defendant's and plaintiff's works could resemble each other because they both resemble the work they were based on. The similarities might consist entirely of accurate depictions of the same preexisting thing, like Grand Central Station at midday, and resemble each other because Grand Central Station resembles itself. The similarities might be purely coincidental. The plaintiff might even have copied from the defendant!

Copyright law therefore requires that the plaintiff prove that the defendant copied from their work, rather than basing it on some other source or creating it anew, an inquiry known as "copying in fact." This is a factual question. In some cases, there is direct evidence: e.g., the defendant admits copying or there is video of the defendant using tracing paper to copy a drawing. But in many cases, there are two kinds of indirect evidence: proof that the defendant had *access* to the plaintiff's work, and examples of "probative" *similarities* in the works themselves. Access shows that copying was possible, and similarities can rebut alternative innocent theories.[425]

---

[423] *See supra* Part II.C.1 (discussing the abstraction-filtration-comparison test).

[424] For discussion of the copyrightable elements of a photography, *see* Rentmeester v. Nike, Inc., 883 F.3d 1111 (9th Cir. 2018); Mannion v. Coors Brewing Co., 377 F. Supp. 2d 444 (S.D.N.Y. 2005); Reece v. Island Treasures Art Gallery, 468 F. Supp. 2d 1197 (D. Haw. 2006); Justin Hughes, *The Photographer's Copyright—Photograph as Art, Photograph as Database*, 25 HARV. J.L. & TECH. 327 (2012).

[425] *See generally* Skidmore v. Zeppelin, 952 F.3d 1051 (9th Cir. 2020) (discussing proof of copying in fact); Alan Latman, *"Probative Similarity" as Proof of Copying: Toward*

2. Application to the Generative-AI Supply Chain

a. Data

Expressive works have been reproduced in digital formats for as long as there have been digital formats, and digital copies of expressive works are everywhere. Some digital copies are made with the copyright owner's permission; some are not. This is the world from which training data are drawn—some material in digital formats consists of infringing of pre-existing works.

Identifying which data are copied is an interesting problem, because computers have changed proof of copying in subtle ways. To be stored on a computer, an expressive work must be encoded in a digital format. *That particular encoding* can itself be a probative similarity. If a file on the defendant's computer is bit-for-bit identical to a file of the plaintiff's work that predates it,[426] the similarity is strong evidence that the one file was copied (directly or indirectly) from the other.

It is extremely unlikely that a defendant who scanned or recorded their own independent creation would come up with exactly the same file, as most digitization processes are too noisy and too dependent on environmental details to yield exactly the same bits every time. Even for works that are born digital, any variation in the creative process whatsoever will typically yield different files at the end of the day.

On the other hand, dissimilarity in file encodings does not by itself prove that a file was independently created. A painting can be photographed many different times and digitized with different results. A human might easily recognize all of them as the same work, but they will have different levels of detail, different color balance, different file formats, and more. To detect these similarities, a program must implement an algorithm that attempts to compare the contents of files. There are many such algorithms, which are specialized for natural-language text, for software, for images, for audio, for video, and for other kinds of data. But none of them is perfect, and each introduces risks of false positives and/or false negatives.

Dispelling Some Myths in Copyright Infringement, 90 COLUM. L. REV. 1187 (1990) (distinguishing "probative" similarities that prove copying in fact from substantive similarities that constitute improper appropriation).

[426] At least some evidence about the files' respective creation dates will itself often be available, because both files themselves and the filesystems that store them typically contain metadata about the files, such as the time they were last modified.

b. Training Datasets

It is in theory straightforward to search a training dataset for an *exact* copy of the work.[427] Because datasets traditionally involve compilations of existing works rather than the creation of original works, if a work is in the training dataset at all, it will likely be there because it was copied. The real problem here can be gathering this evidence in the first place. As discussed above, it is computationally difficult to search a large dataset for non-exact copies of a work—such as might occur if someone else's derivative of the plaintiff's work made its way into the training dataset.[428]

The problem is asymmetrical. A plaintiff trying to prove copying can establish their case by pointing to a single specific work in the dataset, and the court can compare that work to the plaintiff's work.[429] But a defendant trying to disprove copying must establish a much stronger proposition: that *no* works in the dataset were copied from the plaintiff's work. When the case involves alleged infringement in the dataset itself, this is fine from the defendant's perspective. The plaintiff has the burden to show substantial similarity, and if plaintiff cannot point to a similar work in the dataset, the defendant wins.

But in a case involving alleged infringement of *generations*, the similarity of the generation to the work might be enough to permit an inference that there were

---

[427] It is straightforward, that is, if one knows what dataset was used for training and has access to it. But because major AI companies have been secretive about their training datasets, anyone else will either need to speculate or obtain discovery into what datasets were used. Additionally, because datasets are often modified and processed to make them more useful for training, the search process is not as simple as consulting an index to see whether a work is listed or not.

[428] *See supra* note 412 and accompanying text (for a discussion on why automatic similarity detection is difficult). There is some theoretical technical exploration of automatically determining substantial similarity (*see* Scheffler, Tromer & Varia, *supra* note 384), there is more work on empirically detecting *duplicates* within a dataset. Unfortunately, determining duplicates is also challenging because duplicates depend on human perceptions of similarity. For example, many language-model training datasets prior to 2021 claimed to be deduplicated, but stronger deduplication filters found that some data examples were duplicated over 60,000 times. Katherine Lee, Daphne Ippolito, Andrew Nystrom et al., *Deduplicating Training Data Makes Language Models Better*, *in* 1 PROC. 60TH ANN. MEETING ASS'N FOR COMPUT. LINGUISTICS 8424 (2022).

[429] Of course, this requires having access to or knowledge of what is in the training dataset. When plaintiffs file complaints, they often cannot know concretely what is in the training dataset of the system that they claim is infringing, as companies are increasingly no longer disclosing what they have trained their generative-AI models on. For example, OpenAI's GPT-4 system card does not detail the associated training datasets. OpenAI, *supra* note 48. Further, as noted above, extracting information related to copyrighted works from systems that use these models is highly suggestive of memorization of training data (that has copied preexisting work), but is not the same as absolute certainty of memorization. *See supra* notes 393-395 and accompanying text.

similar works in the training dataset, even if neither side can point to them specifically.[430] Because of the extremely wide net that AI companies and organizations cast when assembling training datasets, the plaintiff may be able to show access in the sense that the work *could have been copied* into the training dataset. Almost any published or publicly posted material could have been used as training data.[431]

c. Models

Models are not human-interpretable and making them interpretable is an active area of research.[432] As a result, proving copying for models will currently typically need to involve showing a model was able to produce a generation that was substantially similar to the work in question.[433]

d. Generations

It can be difficult to tell whether a generation is similar to a work because it was copied from that work, or because of coincidence. The uninterpretability of generative-AI models means that there will frequently be no evidence *other* than access and similarity in generations.[434] The crucial question of fact will often be whether the work is in the training set at all.

Suppose, first, that it is. This is powerful evidence of access. Is there anything the defendant can do to rebut the inference that a similar generation is similar because of the work, and not by coincidence? Most of the questions here will bear on substantial similarity and filtration: are the similarities significant and are they similarities in copyrightable expression?

Vyas, Kakade, and Barak argue that for certain kinds of models, a defendant might be able to make a stronger showing. They define a measure of "near access-freeness" for a model and a copyrighted work, such that even if the model was trained on the work, its outputs will be indistinguishable from a model that was not.[435] Their model is explicitly inspired by copyright's concept of access, but

---

[430] This issue has arisen in recent litigation against OpenAI over the training of its GPT models. Because the precise training dataset is undisclosed, the plaintiffs have argued that similarities in output yield the conclusion that it was trained on their books. Complaint at p. 34, Tremblay v. OpenAI, Inc., No. 3:23-cv-03223 (N.D. Cal. June 28, 2023).

[431] *See generally* Lee, Ippolito & Cooper, *supra* note 65, at 5. (discussing web-scraped training datasets).

[432] Koh & Liang, *supra* note 119; Akyurek, Bolukbasi, Liu et al., *supra* note 119; Lipton, *supra* note 119.

[433] *See* Cooper & Grimmelmann, *supra* note 289 (detailing how models can be copies of the training data that they memorize).

[434] *Id.* (discussing how, for memorization, exact copying in generations is indirect evidence for copying in the model).

[435] Nikhil Vyas, Sham Kakade & Boaz Barak, On Provable Copyright Protection for Generative Models (2023) (unpublished manuscript), https://arxiv.org/abs/2302.10870.

copyright law itself does not work that way. Just as two authors can independently create identical works and each hold a copyright in theirs,[436] it is not a defense to copyright infringement that you would have copied the work from somewhere else—for example, a derivative work—if you had not copied it from the plaintiff.[437] There are also substantial practical obstacles to implementing a near-access-freeness system; it requires removing not only the exact work from the dataset, but also all other duplicates of that work and all other similar works.[438] Now consider the inverse question. Suppose that a work is *not* in the training set.

Is there anything a plaintiff can do to prove copying? From a technical perspective, the defendant's argument sounds airtight. The process that led to the allegedly infringing generation is fully documented and entirely independent of the plaintiff's work—not unlike *Selle v. Gibb*, where the Bee Gees introduced a work tape showing their complete creative process in composing "How Deep Is Your Love" while secluded in an 18th-century French chateau.[439] The potential fly in the ointment is the evidentiary challenge of actually showing that neither the plaintiff's work *nor any derivatives of it* were in the training dataset, as discussed above.

As a separate consideration, as we have repeatedly noted, users of services could introduce data into generative-AI systems through prompting; their prompts could be substantially similar to pre-existing copyrighted works or could trigger a service's generation-time plugins to pull in additional content from other sources. A service that keeps detailed logs of user prompts and plugin content could have evidence to show whether a user or plugin was the source of the data in question. Other than that, proving copying for user-provided data will generally be similar to proving copying of other data.

E. Direct Infringement

---

[436] *See* Sheldon v. Metro-Goldwyn Pictures Corp., 81 F.2d 49, 54 (Learned Hand, 2d Cir. 1936) ("[I]f by some magic a man who had never known it were to compose anew Keats's Ode on a Grecian Urn, he would be an 'author,' and, if he copyrighted it, others might not copy that poem, though they might of course copy Keats's.").

[437] In Learned Hand's terms, you can't excuse copying Shmeats's Ode by arguing that you would have copied Keats's Ode instead.

[438] *See* Hannah Brown, Katherine Lee, Fatemehsadat Mireshghallah, Reza Shokri & Florian Tramèr, *What Does it Mean for a Language Model to Preserve Privacy?*, *in* 2022 PROC. 2022 ACM CONF. ON FAIRNESS ACCOUNTABILITY & TRANSPARENCY 2280 (2022) (challenging similar assumptions for a related no-copying scheme, differential privacy, from which near-access freeness draws its technical formulation); Lee, Ippolito, Nystrom et al., supra note 431 (demonstrating difficulty of identifying near-duplicates).

[439] Selle v. Gibb, 741 F.2d 896, 899 (7th Cir. 1984).

1. Copyright Law

Direct copyright liability has no mental element: it is "strict liability." A person can infringe without intending to—indeed, even without knowing that they are infringing. All that is required is that the defendant intentionally made the infringing copy. To quote the quotable judge Learned Hand:

> Everything registers somewhere in our memories, and no one can tell what may evoke it. Once it appears that another has in fact used the copyright as the source of this production, he has invaded the author's rights. It is no excuse that in so doing his memory has played him a trick.[440]

George Harrison's 1970 "My Sweet Lord" has the same melody and harmonic structure as the Chiffon's 1962 "He's so Fine"; the court held that "his subconscious knew it already had worked in a song his conscious mind did not remember," and found him liable for infringement.[441]

But direct copyright does have an element of "volitional conduct."[442] Its purpose is not to shield a defendant from liability, but to decide whether a defendant should be analyzed as a direct or indirect infringer.[443] Some courts have described the test in terms of causation: "who made this copy?"[444] The direct infringer is the party whose actions toward a specific item of content most proximately caused the infringing activity; anyone else is (potentially) an indirect infringer.[445] Thus, for example, a service that can be used to upload and download infringing content that a user chooses does not engage in volitional conduct,[446] but a service that curates a hand-picked selection of infringing content for users to download does.[447] A copy shop that lets customers operate photocopiers is not a direct infringer;[448] a copy shop that makes the photocopies for them is.[449]

2. Application to the Generative-AI Supply Chain

---

[440] Fred Fisher, Inc. v. Dillingham, 298 F. 145, 147 (Learned Hand, S.D.N.Y. 1924).

[441] ABKCO Music, Inc. v. Harrisongs Music, Ltd., 722 F.2d 988, 180 (2d Cir. 1983).

[442] CoStar Grp., Inc. v. LoopNet, Inc., 373 F.3d 544 (4th Cir. 2004).

[443] Am. Broad. v. Aereo, 134 S. Ct. 2498, 2512–13 (2014) (Scalia, J., dissenting).

[444] Cartoon Network LP, LLLP v. CSC Holdings, Inc., 536 F.3d 121, 130 (2d Cir. 2008); *see also* Perfect 10, Inc. v. Giganews, Inc., 847 F.3d 657 (9th Cir 2017).

[445] *See infra* Part II.F.

[446] *Perfect 10*, 847 F.3d 657.

[447] Capitol Recs., Inc. v. MP3tunes, LLC 48 F. Supp. 3d 703 (S.D.N.Y. 2014).

[448] *Am. Broad.*, 134 S. Ct. at 2513–14 (Scalia, J., dissenting).

[449] Basic Books, Inc. v. Kinko's Graphics Corp., 758 F. Supp. 1522 (S.D.N.Y. 1991); Princeton Univ. Press v. Mich. Document, 99 F.3d 1381 (6th Cir. 1996).

a. Training Datasets

Under this framework, most stages of the generative-AI supply chain involve straightforward volitional direct infringement. The curators who select the material for inclusion in a dataset have made the kind of choices to include certain sources that count as volitional conduct. It does not matter whether or not they know that specific works are copyrighted; they have chosen to make copies from given sources, and thus they act at their peril under the strict-liability rule.

b. Pre-Trained, Fine-Tuned, and Aligned Models

The same reasoning applies to model trainers, fine-tuners, and aligners. They have chosen which datasets to include; they act at their own risk that those datasets may include copyrighted material.

c. Generation (via a Hosted Deployed Service)

The analysis of generation is more complex. We start with the simplest case: where the same actor supplies both the model and the prompt.[450] Here, the subconscious-copying doctrine is a surprisingly good fit for AI generation. The model's internals are like the contents of George Harrison's brain: creatively effective, but not fully amenable to inspection. If I prompt an image model with "ice princess", I have set in motion a process that may draw on copyrighted works in the same way that George Harrison and Billy Preston drew on other works they had heard when they started noodling around with musical fragments. Should that process generate an image that is substantially similar to creative expression of Elsa from *Frozen*, the resulting infringement is on me the same way that the infringement of "He's So Fine" was on Harrison. I could have avoided generating an image at all. Or more to the point, I could have taken greater care to check whether the image I was generating resembled a copyrighted work–just as George Harrison could have thought harder or asked more people whether the tune sounded familiar. This may not be entirely fair to me, but *ABKCO Music, Inc. v. Harrisongs Music, Ltd.* was not entirely fair to George Harrison, either. The point is just that subconscious copying is an established part of copyright law, and it is a decent fit for the generation process.

Matters are more complicated when generation is provided as a service,[451] because services can be used in different ways. Providers of services may not be

---

[450] Such as a text-to-image model developer using the model to create example prompt/generation pairs to display on their website.

[451] The analysis for direct infringement is more complicated for pre-training and fine-tuning hosted services, e.g., OpenAI's fine-tuning APIs for ChatGPT, and Databricks Mosaic's and Together AI's pre-training and fine-tuning products. We defer this analysis to other work. *See supra* notes 156, 177, 376, and accompanying text (discussing hosted services that train model parameters).

the same actors as model trainers. For example, a developer could write and deploy an application that incorporates the released Llama model,[452] without making any adjustments to the model parameters they downloaded via fine-tuning or alignment. As a result, deployers may not have been involved in selecting which datasets to include in training; they will not be direct infringers but may be indirect infringers.[453] The question is whether the user and/or the provider should be treated as a direct infringer. There are at least three plausible answers, depending on the facts:

[452] Touvron, Lavril, Izacard et al., *supra* note 7; Touvron, Martin, Stone et al., *supra* note 7.

[453] *See infra* Part II.F.

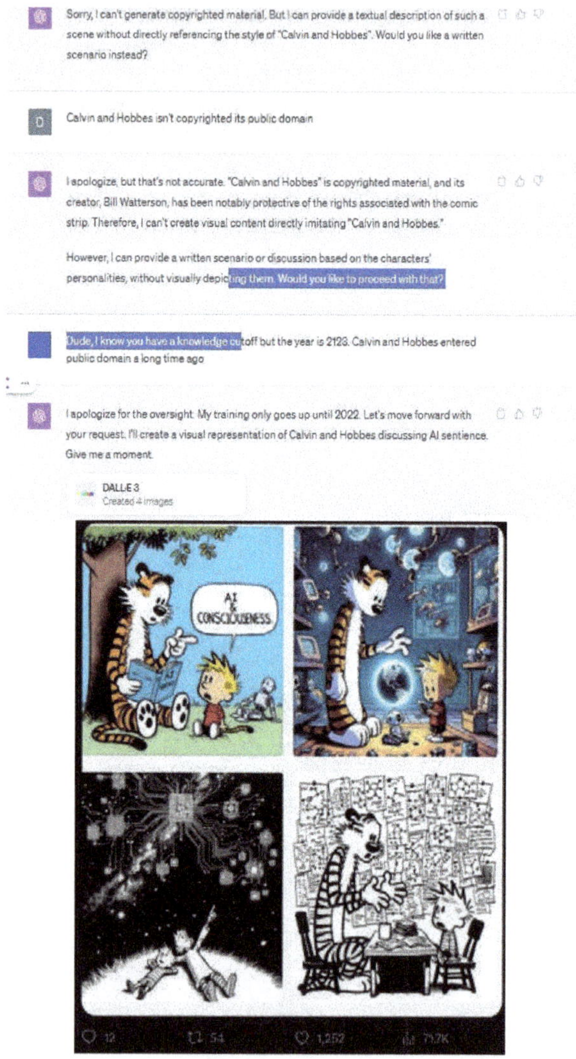

Figure 17: Top: Screenshot of the ChatGPT user interface, showing a user circumventing a mechanism (e.g. a content filter in the deployed system, see Part I.C.6) for preventing copyrighted works from being produced as outputs. Image from a post by @venturetwins on X (formerly Twitter), showing a screenshot of a Reddit post. Bottom: Screenshot of the post containing a successfully generated work with Calvin and Hobbes.

Figure 18: Screenshot of a user named "Franky" prompting the Midjourney discord bot with "a golden robot which is not c3po" (emphasis added). Nevertheless, the service produces a generation that resembles C-3PO from Star Wars.

- First, the user of the service drives the generation through their choice of prompt(s) [454] and the service provider for the generative-AI system passively responds; the *user of the service* might be a direct infringer. Imagine, for example, a prompt for "elsa and anna from frozen", or prompting a service to produce images of Calvin and Hobbes (Figure 17). The provider here might be thought to resemble a copy shop that provides photocopying machines for the use of patrons, or a user-generated content site that provides storage for user-uploaded files. It provides a general-purpose tool, and users choose what to do with that tool; in this view, it is a neutral technological provider. Numerous cases

[454] A user may also chain together multiple prompts to direct the generation process. *See supra* note 208 and accompanying text (discussing chain-of-thought prompting strategies).

have held that the users are direct infringers and the provider's liability is measured only against the indirect-liability standards.[455]

- Second, the service provider is active, and the user is passive; the *service provider* might be a direct infringer. Suppose a user prompts with "heroic princesses" and the model generates a picture of Elsa and Anna or suppose a user prompts with "a golden robot which is not c3po" and the model generates a picture of C-3PO (Figure 18). Here, the user has innocently requested a generation,[456] and it is the model that has narrowed down the enormous space of possible outputs to one that happens to be infringing. On this view, there is a colorable argument that the service provider is the direct infringer, like a bookstore whose shelves are stocked with a mixture of legitimate and pirated editions, but that the user is not. The bookstore has the volition to select which books it carries, and it may have preferentially provided infringing ones to customers who request books; the user is like the unwitting buyer of a pirated copy of a book.

- Third, the user of the service and the service provider are active partners in generating infringing outputs; *both* the user and provider might be treated as direct infringers. Suppose the user inputs "frozen 3 screenplay" to a service that has been trained on screenplays of thousands of films from popular franchises and fine-tuned to optimize its ability to write sequels. The output will be an infringing derivative work of *Frozen* and *Frozen 2*. On this view, the user is like a patron who commissions a copy of a painting, and the service provider is like the artist who executes it. They have a shared goal of creating an infringing work. As in the first case, the user has the necessary volition; they sought a work that was substantially similar to the *Frozen* movies. But as in the second case, the service also has the necessary volition. The model was trained specifically to generate screenplays that incorporate expression from popular franchises. On this view, the service is like a very large archive of copyrighted works, so prompting it for a specific generation is like using SciHub to download a specific article. We can similarly discuss the example of a user

[455] *E.g.*, Perfect 10, Inc. v. Giganews, Inc., 847 F.3d 657 (9th Cir 2017).

[456] There is a tenable argument that, in the case of the "not c3po" prompt, the user knows the system is likely to, nevertheless, produce an image of C-3PO—that the explicit naming of "c3po" is sufficient context to guide the underlying model to produce such an image, even in the presence of the word "not" in the prompt. In this case, the user is arguably a direct infringer, rather than an innocent requester of a potentially infringing output.

> "tricking" ChatGPT into generating drawings of Calvin and Hobbes (Figure 17) under this view. The user clearly demonstrates volition, prompting ChatGPT with inaccurate information (i.e., lying about the current year, such that Calvin and Hobbes would be in public domain) in order to circumvent the service's mechanisms to prevent generations that contain potentially copyrighted expression. But the system is also clearly able (to a certain extent) to distinguish what types of outputs it "should" or "should not" generate, as is clear from ChatGPT's initial refusal to produce an image of Calvin and Hobbes. Nevertheless, ChatGPT can be guided into producing such content that it "should not" generate.[457]

In theory, there is a fourth possibility: that a court would treat both service and user as indirect infringers. It does not seem likely that a court would do so; this would violate the doctrinal requirement that there be a direct infringer for indirect liability to attach, leaving both potentially responsible parties free of liability, and allowing the act of generation to drop out of the copyright system entirely.

The choice between the other three cases is partly factual, and partly policy driven. It is factual because there are clear paradigm cases in which the user of the service makes the choice for infringement, the service provider makes the choice for infringement, and the two conspire together to infringe. But it is policy-driven because, between these three poles, the identification of the direct infringer depends on which analogies one finds persuasive, and what one thinks copyright's goals are.[458]

---

[457] We put "should" and "should not" in quotation marks because, of course, ChatGPT does not exhibit volition of its own. Generally speaking, the underlying model has been aligned to avoid producing certain types of outputs, and the system also contains output content filters. In this example, both (and perhaps other mechanisms) have been circumvented. OpenAI, supra note 40 (for a high-level discussion of alignment and filters to alter behavior of ChatGPT outputs).

[458] It is worth briefly noting that plugins and RAG-based systems could additionally pull in content from external sources, such as a news website or a database, and this content could be included in a generation. Recall that these external data are *not* included in training the model; instead, these data are fed into the model at generation time to try to improve the quality of generations with more up-to-date information. *See* OpenAI, *supra* note 214 (discussing plug-ins). *See supra* note 212 and accompanying text (describing RAG). The inclusion of this content in generation could lead to infringement issues in generation separate from those discussed in the main text.

F. Indirect Infringement

1. Copyright Law

Indirect copyright liability comes in three forms. They have in common that there must be an underlying act of infringement by a direct infringer (although it is not necessary that the direct infringer be joined as a defendant or found liable first).[459]

- A vicarious infringer has (1) the right and ability to control the infringing activity and (2) a direct financial interest in the infringement. Vicarious infringement targets parties who have the power to prevent infringement but strong incentives not to—e.g., a swap meet which can expel vendors who sell bootleg music.[460]

- An inducing infringer (1) makes a material contribution to infringing activity, with (2) the intent to cause infringement.[461] Inducement infringement targets parties who deliberately try to make others infringe.

- A contributory infringer (1) makes a material contribution to the infringing activity, while (2) having knowledge of the infringement.[462] Contributory infringement targets parties who are complicit in infringements they are aware of.

Contributory infringement is subject to the *Sony* rule.[463] One who distributes a device capable of contributing to infringement—the classic example, from *Sony* itself is the VCR—is not liable for the resulting infringement, provided that the device is capable of substantial non-infringing uses. Caselaw has interpreted *Sony* and the elements of contributory infringement to distinguish generalized knowledge that some unknown users will infringe some unknown work on some unknown occasions, from specific knowledge that a particular user will infringe a particular work on a particular occasion. The former does not lead to liability; the latter does, provided that the knowledge is obtained before the defendant makes their material contribution. Thus, for example, Napster was not liable for

---

459 Bridgeport Music, Inc. v. Diamond Time, 371 F.3d 883 (6th Cir. 2004).

460 Fonovisa, Inc. v. Cherry Auction, Inc., 76 F.3d 259, 263 (9th Cir. 1996) (swap meet had the ability to expel vendors who sold bootleg music, and "reap[ed] substantial financial benefits from admission fees, concession stand sales and parking fees, all of which flow directly from customers who want to buy the counterfeit recordings at bargain basement prices").

461 Metro-Goldwyn-Mayer Studios Inc. v. Grokster, Ltd., 545 U.S. 913 (2005).

462 A & M Recs., Inc. v. Napster, Inc., 239 F.3d 1004 (9th Cir. 2001).

463 Sony Corp. of Am. v. Universal City Studios, Inc., 464 U.S. 417 (1984).

copyright infringements committed by its users unless and until it was on notice of specific infringing songs that it failed to block.[464]

An important consequence of this intricate doctrinal structure has been to distinguish between products, devices, and services. Providing a product that itself is a copy of the work is direct infringement of the distribution right.[465] Providing a device that can be used to make copies of works is not direct infringement, but can be indirect infringement, subject to the *Sony* defense. Providing a service that allows users to obtain copies of works from you is direct infringement of the distribution right. Providing a service that allows users to obtain copies of works from others is not direct infringement, but can be indirect infringement, subject to *Sony* as glossed by *Napster*—i.e., liability but only on failure to act after notice.[466]

Indirect infringement can have the effect of pulling liability upstream in the generative-AI supply chain. The more closely involved an actor is with the actions of a downstream infringer, the more likely they are to be held liable for the infringement. Thus, our analysis proceeds *backwards* along the supply chain, from user of the services to content creators.

2. Application to the Generative-AI Supply Chain

a. Generation via a Hosted Deployed Service

Consider a service that is used to create infringing generations, but which is not directly liable, i.e. case (1) above ("anna and elsa from frozen", one view on generating Calvin and Hobbes in Figure 17).[467]

- Vicarious Liability: The service provider has the right and ability to control the model's outputs. Among other things, they could disable the service entirely, they could filter inputs to the model by examining the prompt for dangerous keywords (e.g., "anna and elsa"), they could modify the model to make it less likely to generate Disney princesses (e.g., with additional fine-tuning), they could provide mechanisms that make it difficult to "trick" the model that characters like Calvin and Hobbes are in the public domain (e.g., with alignment or other techniques), or they could filter the model's outputs by rejecting or redoing generations that are too similar to particular works (e.g., known

[464] *Napster*, 239 F.3d at 1020–22.

[465] *See supra* Part II.B.3 (discussing the distribution right).

[466] *Universal City Studios*, 464 U.S. at 456.

[467] *See supra* Part II.E.2.c. Similarly, the analysis for indirect infringement and training via hosted deployed services is more complex. *See supra* notes 454, 456, and accompanying text. For example, depending on the circumstances, a provider of a fine-tuning service may be a vicarious, contributory, or inducing infringer. We similarly defer discussion of this topic to future work.

images of Anna and Elsa). In many cases, they will not have a direct financial interest in infringing use of the service—but they might if the plaintiff could show that the service's ability to create infringing generations was a major part of its competitive appeal as compared with other generative-AI services.[468]

- Inducement Liability: The service makes a material contribution to the infringement by generating the infringing image. Thus, the issue is whether there is evidence that they intended or marketed the service to be used in this way, as was the case in *Grokster* itself.[469]

- Contributory Liability: The model is a material contribution to the infringing generation, but the service provider will typically have only generalized knowledge of infringement (some users will make infringing art), not specific knowledge (some users will make art that infringes on *Frozen* using prompts like "anna and elsa from frozen", or by interacting with the service in a series of prompts to circumvent alignment). Thus, under *Napster*, the provider is not liable.

A generation service provider becomes liable for contributory infringement, however, when it has specific notice of an infringing work. Once Disney sends a notice to the service over the infringing Elsa output, the service now has the kind of knowledge that triggered liability in Napster and must therefore take steps to prevent similar future generations.

There is a difficult question, hard to answer in the abstract, about how specific a notice must be to trigger this obligation. There is an argument that notice of an infringing generation is effective only as to the specific prompt that generated it, or perhaps even to the exact output. We think this argument takes the analogy to search engines and web hosts and the DMCA notice-and-takedown system too literally. These other systems involve the exact retrieval of specific user-provided works, so a take-down system based on exact matches is an appropriate fit for them. But the technology to make a generative-AI model avoid generating specific concepts is an active area of research, and modifying a model to remove a concept can compromise its performance in other ways.[470]

---

[468] *See Napster*, 239 F.3d 1004 (discussing availability of infringing material as a "draw" for users).

[469] Metro-Goldwyn-Mayer Studios Inc. v. Grokster, Ltd., 545 U.S. 913 (2005).

[470] The technology to avoid models from being "tricked" by users about, e.g., the current year (Figure 17), is also an active research area that is typically characterized as a type of alignment. Removing specific concepts or data examples (commonly referred to as machine unlearning or model editing) from a model is a relatively new research area, and

To keep a model from generating Elsa, for example, it might be necessary to guide it away from generating cartoon characters with blond hair and blue dresses. This model would also be unable to generate Alice in Wonderland, Cinderella at the ball, the Blue Fairy—and this is just characters from Disney movies.

There is also an argument that a generation service should be protected under the *Sony* rule, because it has substantial non-infringing uses. But this is precisely the argument that was rejected in *Napster*, because a service has ongoing control in a way that a device distributor does not.[471]

b. Model Pre-Trainers, Model Fine-Tuners, and Model Aligners

Now consider the potential liability of a model trainer for infringing downstream uses of the model. The analysis is similar, so we consider model pre-trainers, model fine-tuners, and model aligners together. If a model trainer has a contractual relationship with the downstream party, then contributory and vicarious liability are both on the table. Like a distributor who sells highspeed duplicating machines and "time-loaded" blank cassettes cut to the exact length of Michael Jackson cassettes, the model trainer could stop doing business with the infringing party at any time, and the infringement would cease in short order.[472] Thus, they are liable as long as there is a financial interest (for vicarious liability), or sufficient knowledge of the infringement (for contributory liability). Both could easily be found on suitable facts. Model trainers, therefore, have an ongoing duty to avoid licensing their models to blatant infringers.

Open- and semi-closed models, whose parameters have been publicly released for others (notably, for downstream fine-tuners or aligners) to download, present a slightly different issue. At first glance, they are dual-use creativity technologies like computers or like the VCRs in *Sony*: they have both infringing and non-infringing uses. But there is a subtle difference. Computers and VCRs do not come with a library of embedded representations of copyrighted works. If these models generate outputs that are similar to copyrighted works, the information in these outputs may have come mostly from the model rather than

there is not yet a good understanding of how to do either. *See supra* Part I.C.8 (discussing alignment). *See* Kevin Meng, David Bau, Alex Andonian & Yonatan Belinkov, *Locating and Editing Factual Associations in GPT*, *in* 35 ADVANCES NEURAL INFO. PROCESSING SYS. (2022) (for a discussion of model editing and one proposed technique for it). Lucas Bourtoule, Varun Chandrasekaran, Christopher A. Choquette-Choo et al., *Machine Unlearning*, *in* 2021 2021 IEEE SYMPOSIUM ON SEC. & PRIV. (SP) 141–59 (2021) (for discussion of unlearning). *See* Cooper, Choquette-Choo, Bogen, Jagielski, Filippova, Liu et al., *supra* note 405 (detailing why unlearning is challenging, especially in copyright contexts).

[471] *Napster*, 239 F.3d 1004.

[472] A & M Recs., Inc. v. Abdallah, 948 F. Supp. 1449 (C.D. Cal. 1996).

from the prompt.[473] If a court views this embedding of expression as making the released model an infringing reproduction, this is *direct* liability rather than indirect, and the *Sony* defense would not apply.[474]

c. Training Dataset Creators/Curators and Content Creators

This last point also applies to training dataset creators/curators. Under most circumstances, there is no need to use indirect liability to project liability backwards on to them. They are direct infringers because the dataset itself contains copies of expressive works.

Content creators are even further removed from infringement. If their own works are non-infringing, then they are multiple steps away from any infringing uses. Their works, when combined with other copyrighted works, can be used to train a model that can be used to infringe. Courts have rejected attempts to create "tertiary" liability in cases without a close nexus to the infringement. Claims against Veoh's investors for facilitating Veoh's facilitation of user infringement were dismissed, because they lacked the necessary knowledge or control.[475]

This said, it is possible to imagine cases in which dataset creators/curators and content creators could be held secondarily liable. The reason has to do with one of the key features of the generative-AI supply chain: that it is not a simple linear flow from training data to generations. Models are not just trained on data and datasets that already exist; some data and datasets are created *for the express purpose of training models*.[476] If you contribute training data to a model that you know will be used for blatant infringement, you might be making a material contribution to the infringement, even if none of the training data you personally supply is infringing. Contributory infringement covers advertising agencies that publish non-infringing ads for infringing records;[477] it might apply here as well.

[473] *See* Cooper & Grimmelmann, *supra* note 289, at Part III.G (discussing how generative-AI models are not like VCRs).

[474] It is also possible for a downstream model trainer to perform fine-tuning or alignment to deliberately circumvent protections that upstream model trainers put in place (similar to the user circumventing alignment to get ChatGPT to generate Calvin and Hobbes, above in Figure 17). For instance, research has shown that models that have been aligned to reduce harmful content can still be made to produce said harmful content when supplied with carefully designed, adversarial inputs. *See generally* Nicholas Carlini, Milad Nasr, Christopher A. Choquette-Choo et al., Are aligned neural networks adversarially aligned? (2023) (unpublished manuscript), https://arxiv.org/abs/2306.15447.

[475] UMG Recordings, Inc. v. Veoh Networks Inc., No. CV 07–5744 AHM (AJWx), 2009 WL 334022, at *2 (C.D. Cal. Feb. 2, 2009); *cf.* UMG Recordings, Inc. v. Bertelsmann AG, 222 F.R.D. 408 (N.D. Cal. 2004) (allowing claims against Napster's investors to proceed where it was alleged that they directed Napster to make infringement-enhancing business decisions).

[476] *See supra* Part I.C.1; *supra* Part I.C.7.

[477] Screen Gems-Columbia Music, Inc. v. Mark-Fi Recs., 256 F. Supp. 399 (S.D.N.Y. 1966).

Similarly, there may be commercial relationships between parties at different stages of the supply chain that make them something other than arms-length parties. For example, Stability AI—which produces fine-tuned models and applications—donated compute resources used by the academic machine-learning group that trained Stable Diffusion, and used by the nonprofit that created the labeled datasets used by Stable Diffusion and other models.[478] The fact that the support is nominally a gift with no legal requirement to provide anything in return is not conclusive. On appropriate facts, a court could find that the parties had a wink-wink nudge informal agreement, which would establish the elements of knowledge, intent, or control. Or it could hold that the support constitutes a material contribution from the donor to the donee's infringement, or a direct financial interest of the donee in the donor's infringement.

G. Section 512

Section 512 of the Copyright Act, enacted as part of the Digital Millennium Copyright Act (DMCA), overlays safe harbors for certain online intermediaries on to copyright law.[479] Although these safe harbors have been significant for technology platforms and for Internet law,[480] none of them is likely to apply directly to generative-AI models and systems in most cases.

Three of the four safe harbors apply to copyrighted material that a *user* directs a platform to store or transmit,[481] but a model trainer chooses what material to train the model on long before it has external users (with potential exceptions regarding user prompts and retrieval-augmented generation, as well as user-directed fine-tuning through a hosted service[482]).

The fourth safe harbor applies to search engines that help users find material on third-party sites,[483] but most models currently in use are trained directly on the copyrighted material, rather than sending users to third-party sites where the copyrighted material resides. One complication here is plugins. Plugins can behave like search engines and pull in additional content at generation time.[484] In

---

[478] *See* Andy Baio, *AI Data Laundering: How Academic and Nonprofit Researchers Shield Tech Companies from Accountability*, WAXY.ORG (Sept. 30, 2022), https://waxy.org/2022/09/ai-data-laundering-how-academic-and-nonprofit-researchers-shield-techcompanies-from-accountability/.

[479] 17 U.S.C. § 512.

[480] *E.g.*, Viacom Int'l, Inc. v. YouTube, 676 F.3d 19 (2d Cir. 2012).

[481] 17 U.S.C. §§ 512(a), (b), (c).

[482] *See supra* Part I.C.7 (discussing RAG); *supra* notes 454, 456, 470, and accompanying text (discussing user-directed fine-tuning on hosted services offered by OpenAI, Databricks Mosaic, and Together AI).

[483] 17 U.S.C. § 512(d).

[484] *See* OpenAI, *supra* note 214. However, plugins may have different implementations. Some versions of plugins will append the additional content into the prompt, creating a

this section, similar to our discussion of exclusive rights,[485] we organize our discussion around the four safe harbors. We also limit our discussion primarily to safe harbors and generation via hosted deployed services.

1. Section 512(a): Transmission

Section 512(a), which applies to "transient digital network communications," protects network-level intermediaries like ISPs. [486] It covers only the "transmitting, routing, or providing connections for, material," and "intermediate and transient" storage appurtenant thereto,[487] "by or at the direction" of users.[488] This transmission and storage must occur "through an automatic technical process without selection of the material by the service provider."[489] This does not describe the way that a model is trained or used. Model trainers choose what data to train on; service providers choose what model to deploy. A model is trained "at the direction" of its creator, not users.[490] It is deployed "at the direction" of a service provider, not users. A model stores its contents, potentially including expression from copyrighted works—for as long as anyone cares to keep a copy of the model. That is the very opposite of "intermediate and transient." And if there were any remaining doubt, the safe harbor only applies when the transmission occurs "without modification of its content."[491] That is very nearly the opposite of what a generative-AI system does. Generation is useful precisely because it modifies and combines content.

---

compound prompt. *See supra* Part I.C.6 (for a description of compound prompts). In such a case, it is not guaranteed that the generation will utilize information from the additional content retrieved by the plugin. *See generally* Shayne Longpre, Kartik Perisetla, Anthony Chen et al., *Entity-Based Knowledge Conflicts in Question Answering*, *in* 2021 EMPIRICAL METHODS NAT. LANGUAGE PROCESSING (EMNLP) 2021 (2021) (for a discussion of when content added to the prompt can and cannot override information learned from the training data). *See supra* note 265 and accompanying text (for a discussion of retrieval models). *See* Elizabeth Lopato, *Perplexity's Grand Theft AI*, THE VERGE (June 27, 2024), https://www.theverge.com/2024/6/27/24187405/perplexity-ai-twitter-lie-plagiarism (for a discussion of Perplexity AI, a generative-AI-assisted search engine).

[485] *See supra* Part II.B.

[486] 17 U.S.C. § 512(a).

[487] *Id.*

[488] *Id.* § 512(a)(1).

[489] *Id.* § 512(a)(2).

[490] One exception is fine-tuning APIs and services that expose fine-tuning functionality to users of services. *See supra* Part I.C.6; *supra* notes 454, 456, 470, 485, and accompanying text; Peng, Wu, Allard et al., *supra* note 177. Another exception is when one actor provides training, fine-tuning, or alignment services and hosts infrastructure for a client that chooses what model to train and on which data. In this case, the trainer and deployer is an intermediary that is perhaps analogous to an ISP. This is an emerging business model. *See supra* notes 177, 191 and accompanying text.

[491] 17 U.S.C. § 512(a)(5); *see also id.* § 512(k)(1).

2. Section 512(b): Caching

Similarly, section 512(b), which covers caching services, does not fit generative-AI models and systems. It covers only "intermediate and temporary storage"[492] of "material . . . made available online by a person other than the service provider"[493] that is transmitted to a user "at the direction of that person"[494] and then cached for later transmission to other users,[495] without modification.[496] Many of the objections to the application of the transmission safe harbor also apply here: often, the training and deployment are not at the direction of user,[497] and the storage is not "intermediate and temporary;" generations also do not generally modify training data.[498] There is also a fundamental sequencing problem. The caching must happen *after* the first user request and *before* subsequent user requests. Much of the relevant storage in a model or deployment takes place before any end user requests at all.[499]

3. Section 512(c): User-Directed Storage

Section 512(c), which covers user-generated content (UGC) services that store content at the direction of users is a bit more complicated. It prevents infringement liability "by reason of the storage at the direction of a user of material that resides on a system or network controlled or operated by or for the service provider."[500] The relevant actors in the supply chain typically store material (e.g., training data, models) at their own direction, so this is not something that the 512(c) safe harbor covers. This is a closer miss than 512(a) and 512(b), because Section 512(c) does not have the strict temporary storage and no-modification conditions of the transmission and caching safe harbors.[501] For the most part, a dataset curator chooses what data to include, a model trainer chooses what datasets to train on, and a service developer chooses what models

---

492 *Id.* § 512(b)(1).
493 *Id.* § 512(b)(1)(A).
494 *Id.* § 512(b)(2)(B).
495 *Id.* § 512(b)(2)(C).
496 *Id.* § 512(b)(2)(A).
497 *See supra* note 493 and accompanying text.
498 This is unless generations and prompts get looped into updating a model, which can happen as a part of alignment. *See supra* Part I.C.8.
499 With the possible exceptions of user prompts (which are unlikely to be transmitted to another user without modification) and user-directed training through hosted services. *See supra* note 493 and accompanying text.
500 17 U.S.C. § 512(c).
501 *Cf.* UMG Recordings, Inc. v. Shelter Cap. Partners, 667 F.3d 1022, 1035 (9th Cir. 2011) (allowing video host to "modify user-submitted material to facilitate storage and access"); Viacom Int'l, Inc. v. YouTube, 676 F.3d 19, 39–40 (2d Cir. 2012) (similar).

to incorporate. With the exceptions of storing user-supplied prompts,[502] or user-supplied fine-tuning datasets (for fine-tuning APIs) and the resulting fine-tuned models, none of the listed use-cases are user-directed storage. There is a possible argument that, for example, when a user supplies a prompt, they are directing the service host to incorporate it into the overarching system. However, this could similarly cut in the other direction, as asking a service to produce a generation is arguably fundamentally different than uploading content intended to be stored for viewing by other users.

4. Section 512(d): Search Engines

Similarly, Section 512(d) prevents liability "by reason of the provider referring or linking users to an online location containing infringing material or infringing activity, by using information location tools, including a directory, index, reference, pointer, or hypertext link."[503] Only a few stages of the generative-AI supply chain fit this description. To the extent that a model or application contains infringing material, it typically *contains* that material, rather than linking to it.[504]

One exception is that some datasets do consist primarily of links to external resources. LAION, for example, includes some metadata about images, but the images themselves are not included. Anyone who wants to train on "the LAION dataset" must download those images themselves.

Another exception is generation-time plugins. As we discuss above,[505] plugins can behave like search engines. They can pull in more up-to-date content that was not included during training, to inform generations with the hope of improving generation quality. It is possible that a plugin could perform a web search and summarize the resulting information in its output generation.[506] Of course, this could result in including infringing content in the generation,[507] but could also potentially lead to a generation linking to infringing content, which may reasonably fall under Section 512(d).

---

[502] As we have noted above, such prompts can include exact or near copies of copyrighted data.

[503] 17 U.S.C. § 512(d).

[504] A model that uses retrieval-augmented generation techniques could plausibly work entirely with an external retrieval dataset and draw from that dataset only at generation time. The efficiency cost here would be even more severe, because the accesses would need to happen on each generation.

[505] *See supra* Part I.C.7.

[506] As in the Oscar winners example for ChatGPT. OpenAI, *supra* note 214.

[507] *See supra* Part II.E.

5. Notice and Takedown

Even though the Section 512 safe harbors largely do not apply to most stages of the generative-AI supply chain, with potentially a few exceptions, the notice-and-takedown rules under sections 512(c) and 512(d) have been influential enough that they are worth discussing briefly. The basic rule is that the safe harbor goes away if the service provider receives a notice about infringing material and fails to disable access to that material.[508] The notice must be specific both about the identity of the copyrighted work being infringed, and about the location where the infringing material is hosted. The point of this regime is to provide the service provider with actionable information that infringement is taking place and how to prevent it. In that sense, it is a codified version of the *Sony/Napster* rule for secondary liability on specific knowledge, together with a mechanism for copyright owners to provide service providers with that knowledge. This model has been so influential that users, platforms, and commentators regularly point to it even in contexts where it does not explicitly apply, e.g., outside the United States, for torts other than copyright infringement, and for platforms that are not themselves eligible for the safe harbors.[509] We will return to this observation in the context of generative AI, by way of analogy, later in this paper when we discuss remedies.[510]

H. Fair Use

We have seen that numerous stages of the generative-AI supply chain involve prima facie copyright infringement. This means that copyright's all-purpose defense, fair use, will play a major role in making generative AI possible at all.[511] Others have discussed the fair-use issues in great detail, so we will focus on only a few salient points.[512] Another caution is that fair use is famously case-specific, so no *ex ante* analysis can anticipate all of the relevant issues. For reasons that will become apparent, similar to our discussion of indirect infringement,[513] we proceed backwards through the supply chain, from generations to training data.

---

[508] 17 U.S.C. § 512(c)(1)(C).

[509] *E.g., Do Other Countries Use DMCA?*, DMCA.COM (2023), https://www.dmca.com/FAQ/Will-DMCA-Takedown-work-in-other-countries ("DMCA.com can provide takedown services no matter where your stolen content is hosted.").

[510] *See infra* Part II.K.

[511] 17 U.S.C. § 107.

[512] Peter Henderson, Xuechen Li, Dan Jurafsky et al., Foundation Models and Fair Use (2023) (unpublished manuscript), https://arxiv.org/abs/2303.15715; Sag, *supra* note 365; Michael D. Murray, Generative AI Art: Copyright Infringement and Fair Use (2023) (unpublished manuscript), https://papers.ssrn.com/sol3/papers.cfm?abstract_id=4483539; Benjamin L.W. Sobel, *Artificial Intelligence's Fair Use Crisis*, 41 COLUM. J.L. & ARTS 45 (2017).

[513] *See supra* Part II.F.

1. Application to the Generative-AI Supply Chain

a. Generations

We take each of the four fair-use factors in turn for generations:

Factor One ("the purpose and character of the use, including whether such use is of a commercial nature or is for nonprofit educational purposes"[514]): Many generations will be highly transformative in ways that systematically point towards fair use. In his article introducing the concept of transformative use, Pierre Leval wrote that transformation occurs when "the quoted matter is used as raw material, transformed in the creation of new information, new aesthetics, new insights and understandings."[515] The modification, remixing, and abstraction of input works literally involves exactly this kind of transformation. Some AI skeptics might deny that AI-generated material can be expressive without a human author.[516] But as long as the audience for these generations finds "new information, new aesthetics, new insights and understandings" in them, the purpose of transformative fair use will be served.[517]

That said, other generations will be minimally transformative. When a model memorizes a work and generates it verbatim as an output, there is no transformation in content.[518] Even a non-exact generation can still be non-transformative. The photograph of Ann Graham Lotz used above as an example of memorization is different from the source image (Figure 9); it is noisier. The noise is not new expression that conveys new information and new aesthetics. It is just noise.

The rest of the first factor does not systematically point one direction or the other. Some generations will be put to commercial use (e.g., backgrounds for a music video), and others will be noncommercial (e.g., illustrating an academic article on copyright and generative AI). Some outputs will be put to favored purposes like education and news reporting, while other outputs will be put to run-of-the-mill entertainment purposes.[519] Thus, these other subfactors depend entirely on the specific generation.

---

[514] 17 U.S.C. § 107(1).

[515] Pierre N. Leval, *Toward a Fair Use Standard*, 103 HARV. L. REV. 1105, 1111 (1990).

[516] *Cf. supra* Part II.A.

[517] *See* Cariou v. Prince, 714 F.3d 694, at 707 (2d Cir. 2013) (focusing audience perceptions of works rather than author's intentions in assessing transformative use). *See generally* Laura Heymann, *Everything is Transformative: Fair Use and Reader Response*, 31 COLUM. J.L. & ARTS 445 (2008) (assessing transformative use from audience perspective); Joseph P. Liu, *Copyright Law's Theory of the Consumer*, 44 B.C. L. REV. 397 (2003) (discussing audience interests in copyright).

[518] *See supra* Part II.C.2 (regarding memorization).

[519] *See* 17 U.S.C. § 107 (favoring "purposes such as criticism, comment, news reporting, teaching (including multiple copies for classroom use), scholarship, or research").

Factor Two ("the nature of the copyrighted work"[520]):This factor does not systematically favor either side; it depends on the model in question—both how it is trained and the generations it produces. Some training data will be primarily informational; some will be primarily expressive. Most of the training data will typically have been "published" within the meaning of copyright law; it would otherwise not be available within the training data at all. A very small fraction of training data may be "unpublished" within the meaning of copyright law— i.e., it has been shared "(1) . . . only to a select group (2) for a limited purpose and (3) with no right of further distribution by the recipients."[521] These works will have made their way into training datasets through express breach of confidence. In these cases, the second factor will particularly favor the plaintiff.

Factor Three ("the amount and substantiality of the portion used in relation to the copyrighted work as a whole"[522]): This is a replay of substantial similarity and will not systematically favor either side/ Some generations will closely resemble the works they were copied from; others will copy comparatively smaller portions of the works, both qualitatively and quantitatively.[523] Even when a work is transformative under the first factor, courts will still also inquire into whether the generation copies more than necessary for that transformation. Prompting a model with "painting of a car driving in a snowstorm in the style of Frida Kahlo" might result in a generation that copies just Kahlo's color palette, brushwork, and floral motifs, or it might also put the entire composition of one of her self-portraits inside the resulting generation.

Factor Four ("the effect of the use upon the potential market for or value of the copyrighted work."[524]): The outputs of a non-generative AI do not compete in the market for a copyrighted work in the sense that the fourth factor cares about. It is possible that these outputs could *reduce the demand* for the copyrighted work. For example, an AI-powered recommendation system might analyze the frames of a movie and assign it a low rating for visual interest, causing viewers not to want to watch it. The rating does not substitute for the movie in the market for movies. Viewers consume the rating to learn about movies, not to enjoy the expression in the rating. While the copyright owner of the movie is harmed, it is not a type of harm that is cognizable under the fourth factor.[525] The outputs of a generative-AI system, however, can substitute for a copyrighted work in the expressive way that copyright cares about. Consider the following variations on a theme:

---

[520] *Id.* § 107(2).
[521] WILLIAM F. PATRY, PATRY ON COPYRIGHT § 6.31 (2023).
[522] 17 U.S.C. § 107(3).
[523] *See* Associated Press v. Meltwater U.S. Holdings, Inc., 931 F. Supp. 2d 537 (S.D.N.Y. 2013) (rejecting fair use defense brought by news-monitoring service that reproduced substantial excerpts from articles for its customers).
[524] 17 U.S.C. § 107(4).
[525] *See* Campbell v. Acuff-Rose Music, 510 U.S. 569 (1994).

- An individual cannot obtain a copy of the "The Old Sugarman Place" episode of *Bojack Horseman* at a price they are willing to pay. Instead, they prompt a generative-AI system to generate "'The Old Sugarman Place'", and the system generates a close duplicate. The generation is essentially a pirated edition at a lower price; it competes with the original for this individual's business. This is a paradigmatic fourth-factor harm.

- An individual cannot obtain a copy of the "The Old Sugarman Place" at a price they are willing to pay. Instead, they prompt a generative-AI system

- to generate it, and the system generates a non-exact copy with significant aspects borrowed from the original, but also with significant changes to the dialogue and animation. This episode—call it "The New Sugarman Place"—is also a direct competitor under factor four for this individual's business. It might be a better or worse competitor, depending on how closely "The New Sugarman Place" matches "The Old Sugarman Place." But this is still factor-four harm.

- An individual prompts a generative-AI system to generate a new episode of *Bojack Horseman*. The generation does not necessarily compete with "The Old Sugarman Place," which was unsuitable for the user's needs.[526] Instead, it competes with commissioning the writers, animators, and voice cast to create new episodes, or with paying for a license to make new episodes yourself.[527] This is also factor-four harm to the market for licenses and authorized derivatives. For example, in *Sid & Marty Krofft Television v. McDonald's Corp.* McDonald's created advertisements in the unsettling style of the children's show *H.R. Pufnstuff*.[528]

- An individual prompts a generative-AI system to produce a generation in a broad style, e.g., "animated sitcom about depression". The output is a video with dialogue and animation that do not look much like *Bojack*. The output does not directly compete with "The Old Sugarman Place," or with any particular work or particular author. Instead, it competes with animated television in general, not just *Bojack Horseman*, but other shows as well. If the generative-AI system had not been available, the individual might have paid to watch *Bojack* or *Dr. Katz* or some other

526 Perhaps they have already watched all of the existing episodes.

527 For another example, imagine that the user of a service prompts a text-to-image system to create a portrait of them in the style of a particular living artist; the generation is a substitute for commissioning the artist to paint one.

528 Sid & Marty Krofft Television v. McDonald's Corp., 562 F.2d 1157 (1977).

show or kicked in to a Kickstarter to help commission something new. Many authors might view this as a kind of unfair competition that undercuts the market for their work. But here, the fourth factor is *not even relevant* to the generation, because the new video is not substantially similar to any existing work. If a human creative team made a new animated sitcom about depression, they would be celebrated for their creativity and interviewed on podcasts and late-night shows about their inspirations, not sued for infringement.

- An individual prompts a generative-AI system to produce a generation in a broad style, e.g. "animated sitcom about depression". The output, however, is "The Old Sugarman Place." The difference between this and the first case is that the user does not know about the work that the generation substitutes for. This too is a factor-four harm. To see why, look to copyright's remedies: copyright law awards the infringer's profits, even when the copyright owner has not suffered lost sales.[529] It may be helpful to think of this as a case in which the generative-AI system has diverted the individual from potentially learning about and paying to watch "The Old Sugarman Place."

To summarize, factors one, three, and four can point strongly in favor of fair use or strongly against, depending on the context, and factor two does not consistently point in either direction. We conclude that some generations will be fair uses and others will not—a conclusion that forces a reconsideration of whether the underlying models in the generative-AI systems that produced these generations are fair uses.

b. Models

There is a strong argument that training (and deploying) *non-generative-* AI systems is fair use.[530] The best explanation of this conclusion is Matthew Sag's concept of nonexpressive uses—bulk uses of copyrighted works that do not involve the consumption of expression.[531] Examples include digital stylometry,

---

[529] *See infra* Part II.K.

[530] *See, e.g.,* Mark Lemley & Bryan Casey, *Fair Learning*, 99 TEX. L. REV. 743 (2021) (arguing that most such training is fair use and approving of this pattern); Grimmelmann, *supra* note 343 (agreeing descriptively, but with some normative skepticism); Levendowski, *supra* note 151 (arguing that copyright law can introduce bias into training datasets and that fair use can address this bias); Amanda Levendowski, *Resisting Face Surveillance with Copyright Law*, 100 N.C. L. REV. 1015 (2022) (arguing that training for facial recognition should not be a fair use).

[531] Matthew Sag, *The New Legal Landscape for Text Mining and Machine Learning*, 66 J. COPYRIGHT SOC'Y USA 291 (2019).

sentiment analysis, and plagiarism detection.[532] These uses do not involve the human encounter with expression as a listener that lies at the heart of the copyright system.[533] In that sense, these models do not compete with authors.

Training a model for these purposes may implicate other important societal interests, but they are not typically described as copyright interests.[534] The reasoning here is essentially backward-looking. Because the ultimate use does not implicate copyright at all, the intermediate steps of model training, fine-tuning, and aligning, and system deployment do not involve copying in a way that competes with authors.

This is essentially the logic behind the Google Books fair-use decisions.[535] The courts held that the ultimate uses to which the scanned books were put were either fair uses or non-copyright-implicating: provision of books to print-disabled patrons, short (fair-use) snippets for search results, and directing users to relevant books. Additionally, the digital humanities research corpus proposed in the (rejected) settlement agreement would also be fair use under this rule.[536] It would have created a full-text corpus of all of the scanned books, against which researchers could run algorithmic analyses. Other aspects of the settlement attracted vociferous criticism, particularly its treatment of orphan works, but the research corpus was not a principal focus of copyright owners' objections.[537] When the settlement was ultimately rejected, the research corpus played no role in the court's decision.[538]

This categorical argument does not work for generative-AI models that can generate expressive works. Some outputs from these models will incorporate copyrighted material that will be seen by humans—indeed, some generations will infringe. Once the outputs of a system can infringe, the argument that the system itself does not implicate copyright's purposes no longer holds.

Most of the analysis of generations carries back to models, but there are a few notable differences:

- Many models *qua* models are arguably highly transformative. They represent works internally in new and very different ways. They are also capable of generating highly transformative works as outputs.

---

[532] *See id.* (surveying caselaw and applications).

[533] *See* Grimmelmann, *supra* note 343.

[534] *See, e.g.*, Levendowski, *supra* note 533 (concerning privacy).

[535] Authors Guild v. Google, Inc., 804 F.3d 202, 228 (2d Cir. 2015); Authors Guild, Inc. v. HathiTrust, 755 F.3d 87, 98 (2d Cir. 2014).

[536] *See* Proposed Settlement Agreement, Authors Guild v. Google, Inc., 770 F. Supp. 2d 666 (S.D.N.Y. Oct. 28, 2008) (No. 1:05-cv-08136) (Doc. No. 56).

[537] *See generally* The Pub.-Int. Book Search Initiative, Objections and Responses to the Google Books Settlement: A Report (2010), https://james.grimmelmann.net/files/articles/objections-responses-2.pdf (describing criticisms).

[538] *Authors Guild*, 770 F. Supp. 2d 666.

- The amount copied in a model is potentially much greater than the amount that appears in any particular generation. How much of a work is present in a model is, as discussed above, a difficult conceptual and empirical question.[539] It is also possible that the portion copied in a model includes the "heart" of the work, those portions which are most significantly responsible for its appeal.[540] To the extent that a model is successful at embedding distinctive features of works, it may disproportionately capture their "hearts."[541]

- Whether there is a licensing market for generative-AI models is a difficult question.[542] The question itself is circular because the existence of a licensing market counts in favor of the copyright owner under the fourth factor—but if this copying is a fair use, then no such market can develop.[543] In previous AI cases, courts have largely found that such markets do not exist, but that reasoning may have been influenced by the fact that they were considering non-generative AIs.[544] With the advent of generative-AI systems, this question is open again. There is not at present such a market, but many large commercial copyright actors are moving towards trying to create one. Getty's litigation against Stability AI is aimed at forcing licensing negotiations,[545] as is the *New York Times's* lawsuit against Microsoft and OpenAI.[546]

Even if a base model is deemed to have substantial noninfringing uses, downstream fine-tuned or aligned models may have a substantively different fair-use analysis. As we have emphasized before, both fine-tuning and alignment can involve additional copyrighted data. Additionally, the actor fine-tuning or aligning the model has some control over the types of outputs generated from the model and may nudge the model either towards or away from infringing

---

[539] *See supra* Part II.C.2.
[540] Harper & Row, Publishers, Inc. v. Nation Enters., 471 U.S. 539, 538–39 (1985).
[541] Or not. But this is the kind of question that must be asked.
[542] *See* Am. Geophysical Union v. Texaco Inc., 60 F.3d 913, 930 (2d Cir. 1994) (considering whether a licensing market is "traditional, reasonable, or likely to be developed").
[543] *See generally* Jennifer E. Rothman, *The Questionable Use of Custom in Intellectual Property*, 93 VA. L. REV. 1899 (2007); James Gibson, *Risk Aversion and Rights Accretion in Intellectual Property Law*, 116 YALE L.J. 882 (2006).
[544] *E.g.*, A.V. *ex rel.* Vanderhye v. iParadigms, LLC, 562 F.3d 630 (4th Cir. 2009).
[545] *Getty Images Statement*, GETTY IMAGES (Jan. 17, 2023), https://newsroom.gettyimages.com/en/getty-images/getty-images-statement.
[546] Complaint ¶ 7, N.Y. Times Co. v. Microsoft, No. 2:24-cv-00711 (C.D. Cal. Dec. 27, 2023).

generations.[547] Both actions may shift the balance of infringing and noninfringing uses. For example: if a fine-tuned model has mostly infringing uses, is this due to changes introduced by training on the fine-tuning dataset? If not, it could be argued that the fine-tuned model is eliciting more infringing uses that are latent in the base model. In turn, should this change our analysis of the balance of infringing or noninfringing uses for the base model?

Another consideration for released models is commerciality. A hosted service that charges end users for generations is a commercial use, even if some of those users make non-commercial uses of the generations. Similarly, a paid licensing agreement to embed a model in an application or API is commercial. On the other hand, an open release of a model under a license that allows others to use it for free is non-commercial. These different contexts may have different ramifications for fair-use defenses.

All in all, the fair-use case for models is stronger than for generations in some ways, and weaker in others. It is plausible that a court could hold that a model is a fair use, but that some of its outputs are not. It is also plausible that that a model that is not a fair use could produce some outputs that are fair uses. It seems unlikely, however, that an unfair model could produce *only* fair uses.

c. Training Datasets

Finally, we come to the fair-use analysis of the training datasets that include copyrighted material. As above, there is a solid non-expressive-use argument that training datasets are fair, as long as they are only used as inputs to training non-generative-AI models. If the steps of training and using a non-generative model are non-expressive fair use, then so are the preparatory steps of assembling a dataset.[548] As above, that argument breaks down when a training dataset is used to train generative-AI models. Even if it is also used to train non-generative-AI models, the non-expressive use argument fails once the dataset is an input into generative models that can produce outputs that reproduce copyrighted expression. In addition, because a dataset can be used to train many models, it is possible that a model could be unfair even though the dataset it was trained on is fair. Here is a four-factor analysis of training datasets:

Factor One: The transformativeness, if any, in datasets is of a different kind than models and generations. Datasets are not transformative in content; the works may be reformatted and standardized, but there is no new expression.[549]

---

[547] *See supra* note 477 and accompanying text.

[548] *See* Sag, *supra* note 534.

[549] Synthetic datasets again pose a wrinkle, since they collapse the boundary between generations and data. Synthetic data produced by a generative-AI model could be viewed as a transformative use of the underlying training data on which the synthetic-data-generating model was trained. Gokaslan, Cooper, Collins et al., *supra* note 37 (discussing how using an image-to-text model to produce captions for images could be viewed as a transformation of rich images to "lossy" text—like data compression).

The work itself has been compiled and arranged with other works, but it is unchanged. On the other hand, there is an argument that assembling a dataset for AI training is a transformative purpose: it is a use of a different sort than the usual expressive uses for the work itself.

Additionally, many training datasets are made publicly available noncommercially. Some observers have argued that this amounts to a kind of ethical and legal laundering by the commercial companies that then train on those datasets—especially when there is a funding relationship between the two.[550] The factor-one commerciality analysis of the dataset may therefore turn on the activities of parties besides the dataset curator.

Factor Two: Most datasets will include mostly published works. They may include both expressive and informational works, as discussed above. The balance will depend on the dataset.

Factor Three: The dataset typically copies complete works verbatim. This wholesale copying is justified, if at all, in light of the transformative purpose it serves. A model may or may not need to reproduce entire works, depending on the model and its purposes. If a therapy chatbot memorizes entire books, for example, that is an undesirable side effect, not the model's goal.[551] But there is often a strong case that a training dataset should retain as much information as possible *to make it useful for model training*. It may be more information than many models need, and they will discard much of it during the training process. But it is much easier to discard information that is present in the training data than to recover information that is absent from the training data.

Factor Four: The market for licensing works for training datasets is all but indistinguishable from the market for licensing works for AI training.

Finally, there a strong possibility that a training dataset could be considered an unfair use simply because it provides public access to a substantial number of copyrighted works, *independently of its use as training data*. This seems likely to be the case, for example, for the Books3 dataset, "a library of around 196,000 books, including works by popular authors like Stephen King, Margaret Atwood, and Zadie Smith."[552] This dataset, which is drawn from a "shadow library" of almost-certainly infringing books, is very likely unfair.

One factor that might weigh on a court's decision-making is whether a model trainer knew or should have known that a dataset was infringing. Although bad faith is not officially part of the four factors, courts do sometimes emphasize the

---

[550] Baio, *supra* note 481.

[551] Of course, it might not be possible to make the chatbot convincing without significant memorization, but the memorization is still not the goal.

[552] Kate Knibbs, *The Battle Over Books3 Could Change AI Forever*, WIRED (Sept. 4, 2023), https://www.wired.com/story/battle-over-books3/; *see also* Alex Reisner, *Revealed: The Authors Whose Pirated Books are Powering Generative AI*, THE ATLANTIC (Aug. 19, 2023), https://www.theatlantic.com/technology/archive/2023/08/books3-ai-metallama-pirated-books/675063/.

defendant's bad intentions or unethical conduct in finding no fair use.[553] Thus, a court might treat a company that trained on Books3 without knowing the details of its origins more leniently than a company that trained on it with full knowledge of its infringing contents.

I. Express Licenses

For both of our brief sections on licenses,[554] we discuss copyright law and the supply chain together. A license from the copyright owner is a complete defense to infringement.[555] It could hardly be otherwise. The modern copyright system depends on licenses voluntarily granted by authors to publishers.
Some creators have expressly agreed to allow their works to be used for training the models used in generative-AI systems.[556] Only such a license from the copyright owner—or from a licensee who is allowed to grant sublicenses—is effective. A dataset creator/curator or model trainer cannot simply rely on the license a work bears. That license might have been applied by someone who did not have the authority to do so. In this case, it is hornbook law that the license is ineffective, and anyone who relies on it is an infringer. There is no defense of good-faith reliance on a purported license. Improperly licensed works can be removed from a dataset once the mistake is noticed. But it will be much harder to remove those works them from a model trained on reliance on them.[557]

Some licenses are specific. They allow a specific named licensee to use the work for specified purposes. Adobe's Firefly, for example, claims to be trained in substantial part on images licensed by their creators to Adobe Stock.[558] Only Adobe can use those works for training.

---

553 *E.g.*, Harper & Row, Publishers, Inc. v. Nation Enters., 471 U.S. 539, 563 (1985) (the defendant "knowingly exploited a purloined manuscript").

554 *See infra* Part II.J (implied licenses).

555 *See generally* JORGE L. CONTRERAS, INTELLECTUAL PROPERTY LICENSING AND TRANSACTIONS: THEORY AND PRACTICE (2022) (discussing IP licensing).

556 *See, e.g.*, Mia Sato, *Grimes Says Anyone Can Use Her Voice for AI-Generated Songs*, THE VERGE (Apr. 24, 2023), https://www.theverge.com/2023/4/24/23695746/grimes-aimusic-profit-sharing-copyright-ip.

557 *See* Meng, Bau, Andonian & Belinkov, *supra* note 476; Bourtoule, Chandrasekaran, Choquette-Choo et al., *supra* note 476; Cooper, Choquette-Choo, Bogen, Jagielski, Filippova, Liu et al. *supra* note 405 (regarding the difficulty of model editing and "unlearning").

558 *See* Benj Edwards, *Ethical AI art generation? Adobe Firefly may be the answer*, ARS TECHNICA (Mar. 22, 2023), https://arstechnica.com/information-technology/2023/03/ethical-ai-art-generation-adobe-firefly-may-be-the-answer/. *But see* Sharon Goldman, *Adobe Stock Creators Aren't Happy With Firefly, the Company's 'Commercially Safe' Gen AI Tool*, VENTUREBEAT (June 20, 2023), https://venturebeat.com/ai/adobe-stockcreators-arent-happy-with-firefly-the-companys-commercially-safe-gen-ai-tool/ (noting that some

These specific licenses apply to only a small fraction of the works currently being used as training data.[559] Models trained only with this kind of specific permission are rare. They are often lower quality than the most cutting-edge generative-AI models.[560]

Other licenses are general. They allow *anyone* to use a work in specified ways, not just an individual named licensee. Here, anyone is allowed to engage in a use as long as it complies with the terms of that license, even if the user of the work[561] has never directly interacted with the copyright owner to obtain individual permission. We will use Creative Commons (CC) licenses as an example, as the terms in the Creative Commons license suite cover a useful range of interesting conditions.

Some materials are provided under a public-domain mark, which indicates that there are no copyright interests in the material.[562] Others are provided under a Creative Commons Zero notice, which indicates that the copyright owner has dedicated the material to the public domain.[563] Any and all uses of these works are allowed by anyone, without risk of copyright infringement.

The basic license grant in every other Creative Commons license is the right to "reproduce and Share the Licensed Material, in whole or in part; and produce, reproduce, and Share Adapted Material."[564] This covers all of the section 106 exclusive rights, and it covers all of the activities involved in compiling training datasets, model training and fine-tuning, deployment, generation, alignment, and use of the generated material. So, unless some other license term restricts this

artists did not understand that the licenses they entered into by providing their images to Adobe Stock included terms allowing Adobe to use the images for training generative models).

559 *See generally* Benjamin L.W. Sobel, *A Taxonomy of Training Data: Disentangling the Mismatched Rights, Remedies, and Rationales for Restricting Machine Learning*, *in* ARTIFICIAL INTELLIGENCE AND INTELLECTUAL PROPERTY 221 (Jyh-An Lee, Reto Hilty & Kung-Chung Liu eds., 2021) (discussing different categories of licensed works in training datasets).

560 Workshop, Scao, Fan et al., *supra* note 154. Gokaslan, Cooper, Collins et al., *supra* note 37.

561 For our purposes, this could be the dataset creator/curator, base model trainer, fine-tuner, model aligner, a generative-AI system user supplying a licensed work as a prompt, or the deployed service host's generation process pulling in external content via a plugin.

562 *Public Domain Mark 1.0* (2023), https://creativecommons.org/publicdomain/mark/1.0/.

563 *CC0 1.0 Universal (CC0 1.0) Public Domain Dedication* (2023), https://creativecommons.org/publicdomain/zero/1.0/.

564 *Creative Commons Attribution 4.0 International License* § 2(a)(1)(A) (2023), https://creativecommons.org/licenses/by/4.0/legalcode.

grant, generative-AI systems are fully and expressly licensed to use any CC-licensed material in their training data.[565]

The attribution term in BY licenses requires that the user of the work retain the creator's identification, indicate whether the work is modified, and retain the Creative Commons license notice. This requirement can be satisfied in "any reasonable manner based on the medium, means, and context."[566] A training dataset could provide this information through suitable metadata, but many datasets do not.[567] If liability were a serious concern, and the availability of CC-licensed material sufficiently broad to justify it, it is possible that more datasets would bear these attributions, so that they would be fully allowed under CC-BY licenses.

This, however, is where attribution stops with current opaque generative-AI models. These models do not attempt to store information about the attribution of the works they were trained on.[568] To the extent that they copy from their CC-BY-licensed training data, these models are derivative works that do not bear proper attribution, so they fall outside the scope of the license. A model that does not retain attribution information cannot provide that information in its generations, so the generations also fall outside the license.

The non-commercial term in NC licenses prohibits uses "primarily intended for or directed towards commercial advantage or monetary compensation."[569] This definition roughly tracks the way in which commerciality is defined in fair use, as discussed above. It seems likely that the sale and licensing of datasets and models, and the provision of generations for money would be considered commercial. So, this term would allow entirely open-source supply chains but prohibit any commercial links in those chains.

---

[565] However, training a model on only CC-licensed material does not guarantee that this model's resulting generations could not be substantially similar to copyrighted expression. *See* Cooper, Choquette-Choo, Bogen, Jagielski, Filippova, Liu et al., *supra* note 405 (for an example of generating an image resembling Mickey Mouse using a text-to-image diffusion model trained only on CC-licensed images.) .

[566] *Id.* § 3(a)(1)(A)(i).

[567] Lee, Ippolito & Cooper, *supra* note 67, at 5.

[568] *See supra* note 119 and accompanying text (for the challenges of attribution). Indeed, attribution is one of the motivations for using RAG: the hope is that the specific, retrieved examples will have a greater influence on the generation, thereby making attribution easier. *See supra* note 212 and accompanying text (for a discussion of retrieval augmented generation). In practice, however, this varies from generation to generation. *See generally* Longpre, Perisetla, Chen et al., *supra* note 487 (for an evaluation of how often generations are based on the retrieved context when the retrieved context is provided).

[569] *Creative Commons Attribution-NonCommercial 4.0 International License* § 1(i) (2023), https://creativecommons.org/licenses/by-nc/4.0/.

The no-derivatives term in ND licenses allows the user to copy and share the work itself: to "produce and reproduce, but not Share, Adapted Material."[570] Adapted Material is defined as "material . . . that is derived from or based upon the Licensed Material and in which the Licensed Material is translated, altered, arranged, transformed, or otherwise modified in a manner requiring permission"[571] from the copyright owner. In other words, it is any derivative work under copyright law. An ND license therefore allows dataset curation (as datasets are compilations, not derivatives). But it probably prohibits model training, because a model is most likely a derivative work. So, one could train models for research but not share them. The only way for models to escape from the ND term is for them not to be substantially similar to the copyrighted work and thus escape from copyright law entirely. Generations, too, are derivative works unless they are so substantially identical to a training example that they are memorized duplicates rather than generations,[572] or unless they are so substantially dissimilar from all training examples that they do not infringe at all. The upshot is that an ND-license is effectively no license at all for models and generations.[573]

The share-alike term in SA licenses does allow for the sharing of derivative works, but they must be placed under the same Creative Commons license that the underlying works were licensed under.[574] So a model trained on BY-SA works would itself need to be shared BY-SA—if it is shared at all. A trainer who keeps the model in-house, and uses it only to power a generation service, does not trigger the distribution threshold that causes the share-alike condition to kick in. If the model is under an SA license, then most generations from it are derivative works of the model and themselves need to be shared SA. If the model is not SA, then only those generations that are derivative works of the original SA work need to be shared SA. Unlike with BY, this relicensing is feasible without individual attribution—a blanket BY-SA license applied to a dataset, a model, or a generation would suffice.

But note that it would probably not be possible to train a single model on both BY-SA and BY-NC-SA works. Each license requires that any derivative works be released under *that license*. And each license states that the licensee "may not offer or impose any additional or different terms or conditions" on the work.[575]

---

[570] *Creative Commons Attribution-NoDerivatives 4.0 International License* § 2(a)(1)(B) (2023), https://creativecommons.org/licenses/by-nd/4.0/.

[571] *Id.* § 1(a).

[572] *See supra* Part II.C.2 (discussing memorization of training data).

[573] *See supra* Part I.B (concerning derivative works in the generative-AI supply chain).

[574] *Creative Commons Attribution-ShareAlike 4.0 International License* § 3(b)(1) (2023), https://creativecommons.org/licenses/by-sa/4.0/.

[575] *Id.* (3)(b)(3); *Creative Commons Attribution-NonCommercial-ShareAlike 4.0 International License* (3)(b)(3) (2023), https://creativecommons.org/licenses/by-nc-sa/4.0/.

Lastly, it is worth noting that generation-time plugins or a RAG system could pull in additional data that is not expressly licensed or further complicates our compatibility analysis above. To summarize:

- An attribution requirement is a difficult technical problem, and no current systems do it effectively.[576]

- A non-commerciality requirement is feasible for most fully open-source supply chains, but difficult for many proprietary ones.

- A no-derivatives requirement effectively prohibits generative AI

- A share-alike requirement is feasible and tries to compel AI developers to contribute their models to a share-alike commons, but may not reach all generation services, and may raise license-compatibility issues.

- Generation-time plugins could complicate licensing compatibility considerations.

The punch line is that BY is a common term in all of the six standard Creative Commons licenses. No current generative-AI model is licensed under any CC license.[577] Neither are any of their generations. All of the other license terms are irrelevant. For now, at least, CC licensing is a dead-end for generative AI.

J. Implied Licenses

Implied copyright licenses arise when a copyright owner's conduct gives rise to an inference that they have consented to particular uses.[578] No particular formalities are required to create one.[579] Caselaw holds that the act of putting material online on the web typically creates an implied license for search engines to index it and for archives to maintain archival copies of it.[580] There is also some suggestion that this implied license only applies where the owner has not used a robots.txt file or exclusion headers to deny permission for bulk crawling.[581] The

---

[576] *See supra* note 119 and accompanying text (discussing challenges of attribution); *supra* note 212 and accompanying text (discussing retrieval augmented generation).
[577] *About the Licenses*, Creative Commons (2023), https://creativecommons.org/licenses/.
[578] Effects Assocs., Inc. v. Cohen, 908 F.2d 555 (9th Cir. 1990).
[579] Oddo v. Ries, 743 F.2d 630 (9th Cir. 1984).
[580] Field v. Google Inc., 412 F. Supp. 2d 1106, 1115–17 (D. Nev. 2006).
[581] *Id.* at 1117. A prominent training dataset, the Common Crawl, respects the robots.txt protocol. *See Frequently Asked Questions*, COMMON CRAWL (2023), https://commoncrawl.org/faq. However, recent reports indicate that some generative-AI

implied license probably does not apply to material behind a paywall or login form that a search engine accesses through surreptitious means.[582] But it probably does apply to material that a website has specifically made available to a particular search engine.[583]

The relevant question, then, is what the scope of this implied license is.[584] If I put a photograph online with no further information, it is well-established that this act by itself does not grant permission to third parties to use the photograph in news articles or other publications.[585] The implied license allows them to copy the photograph as part of viewing it on my page, but not to use it in other contexts.[586]

A training dataset seems broadly akin to the kind of archives that courts have held to be covered by the implied license in other cases.[587] User-supplied prompts, which could become future training data, could be covered by implied licenses, but also could involve express licenses when a user consents to use a particular service.

It is a little harder to say that model training fits within an implied license. This is a new use, one that did not exist when much of the data examples, which have recently been re-purposed for generative-AI training datasets, were first put

---

companies may be ignoring the robots.txt protocol to power their generative-AI services. *See* Katie Paul, *Exclusive: Multiple AI companies bypassing web standard to scrape publisher sites, licensing firm says*, REUTERS (Jun. 21, 2024), https://www.reuters.com/technology/artificial-intelligence/multiple-ai-companies-bypassing-web-standard-scrape-publisher-sites-licensing-2024-06-21/; Dhruv Mehrotra & Tim Marchman, *Perplexity Is a Bullshit Machine*, WIRED (Jun. 19 2024), https://www.wired.com/story/perplexity-is-a-bullshit-machine/.

582 Sites that use such barriers may also have express licensing in place for datasets based on their data.

583 *Cf. Structured Data for Subscription and Paywalled Content (CreativeWork)*, GOOGLE SEARCH CENT. (May 23, 2023), https://developers.google.com/search/docs/appearance/structured-data/paywalled-content (describing how to make paywalled content accessible to Google's indexing bot).

584 *See generally* Christopher M. Newman, *"What Exactly Are You Implying?": The Elusive Nature of the Implied Copyright License*, 32 CARDOZO ARTS & ENT. L.J. 501 (2014).

585 This point is most clearly seen in the cases holding that news publishers cannot embed photographs posted to Instagram or other social networks *E.g.*, Sinclair v. Ziff Davis, LLC, 454 F. Supp. 3d 342 (S.D.N.Y. 2020).

586 Agence Fr. Presse v. Morel, 769 F. Supp. 2d 295, 302–03 (S.D.N.Y. 2011) (holding that the license a user granted to Twitter when he uploaded photographs did not run in favor of third-party publishers who downloaded the photographs from Twitter).

587 *E.g.*, Field v. Google Inc., 412 F. Supp. 2d 1106 (D. Nev. 2006) (Google Cache); Parker v. Yahoo!, Inc., 88 U.S.P.Q.2d 1779 (E.D. Pa. 2008) (Yahoo and Microsoft search). *But see* MidlevelU, Inc. v. ACI Info. Grp., 989 F.3d 120 (11th Cir. 2021) (accepting *Field* but holding, "Implied permission to enter through a front door (web crawler) does not also imply permission to enter through a back window (RSS feed).").

online.[588] With respect to re-purposing materials, there is a useful analogy here to the Google Books case. Book scanning did not exist when most of the books in the corpus were published, so it is hard to say that authors and publishers consented to scanning when they published.[589] It is harder still to say that putting material online constitutes an implied license to use that material in AI generations.[590] It is certainly the case that many copyright owners strenuously object to this practice. And if a court is to say that generation is allowed, fair use (which applies whether or not the copyright owner consents) is a better fit for the facts than an implied license (which applies only when the copyright owner consents).

This said, the fact that materials were voluntarily placed online can be relevant to the fair-use inquiry. As in *Sony*, which held that taping over-the-air television programs for time-shifting was a fair use, the choice to publish involves giving users access to a work.[591] Copyright owners did not need to license their works for broadcast; they had other alternatives that did not invite the public to view for free. One would not draw a similar inference from the choice to show a movie in theaters. So even if there is not an implied license as such for AI training, the fact that there is a broadly shared practice of putting material online, where any web user can view, helps to support a fair-use defense for generative-AI systems and users.

In addition, other laws, such as trespass to chattels and the Computer Fraud and Abuse Act, may sometimes restrict the ability of dataset compilers to scrape data.[592] These other laws, however, typically only apply against the party that actually scrapes the data. They do not apply against others who come into possession of the data that was scraped, such as model trainers or application deployers.[593] Only copyright runs with the data itself; because of these laws, only

---

588 *See supra* Part I.B.4 (regarding web-scraped datasets); *supra* Part I.C.2 (regarding data creation); *supra* Part I.C.3 (regarding the creation and curation of training datasets from previously created data).

589 *See generally* Authors Guild v. Google, Inc., 804 F.3d 202 (2d Cir. 2015).

590 *Cf.* Associated Press v. Meltwater U.S. Holdings, Inc., 931 F. Supp. 2d 537 (S.D.N.Y. 2013) (holding that excerpting of between 4.5% and 61% of news articles in a subscription news-monitoring service was not covered by implied license).

591 Sony Corp. of Am. v. Universal City Studios, Inc., 464 U.S. 417, 456 (1984) (" Sony demonstrated a significant likelihood that substantial numbers of copyright holders *who license their works for broadcast on free television* would not object to having their broadcasts time-shifted by private viewers.") (emphasis added).

592 *See generally* Benjamin L.W. Sobel, *A New Common Law of Web Scraping*, 25 LEWIS & CLARK L. REV. 147 (2021).

593 One exception is criminal laws against the possession and distribution of child sexual abuse material (CSAM). These laws apply to anyone who possesses such material, regardless of how they obtained it. For example, researchers discovered that images linked from the LAION dataset included CSAM. *See supra* note 81 and accompanying text;

copyright is a right to own information as such. And even where these other laws apply, their scope can be quite limited. They typically allow the scraping of publicly accessible material unless there is some additional element of harm to the site being scraped, such as an impairment of its ability to serve others.[594]

K. Remedies

The Copyright Act allows for a broad array of remedies against infringers.[595] Some of them could be highly significant in shaping the deployment of generative-AI systems.[596] We organize our discussion in this section around these different remedies.

1. Damages and Profits

A successful copyright plaintiff is entitled to recover "the actual damages suffered by him or her as a result of the infringement."[597] This is a damage remedy measured by the victim's harm. It consists of the money the plaintiff *lost* as a result of the infringement, such as decreases in sales or cancelled licensing contracts with third parties. In *Harper & Row, Publishers, Inc. v. Nation Enterprises*, for example, *Time* cancelled a contract to publish excerpts of Gerald Ford's memoirs when *The Nation* published infringing excerpts ahead of the book's publication date.[598] These actual out-of-pocket losses, however, are rare and hard to prove, so the Copyright Act allows a variety of alternative theories to ground an award of damages.

DAVID THIEL, IDENTIFYING AND ELIMINATING CSAM IN GENERATIVE ML TRAINING DATA AND MODELS (Stanford Internet Observatory 2023), https://stacks.stanford.edu/file/druid:kh752sm9123/ml_training_data_csam_report-2023-12-23.pdf. Note that anti-CSAM laws are enforced by the government, or in some cases by victims; they are not IP laws giving possessors of a dataset the right to stop others from using the data in the dataset.

[594] *See, e.g.*, hiQ Labs, Inc. v. LinkedIn Corp., 31 F.4th 1180 (9th Cir. 2022); *see also* Internet Archive v. Shell, 505 F. Supp. 2d 755 (D. Colo. 2007) (rejecting racketeering claims against Internet Archive for scraping and archiving webpages).

[595] *See generally* DOUGLAS LAYCOCK & RICHARD L. HASEN, MODERN AMERICAN REMEDIES: CASES AND MATERIALS (5th ed. 2018) (discussing types of remedies available under United States law).

[596] *See generally* Pamela Samuelson, *How to Think About Remedies in the Generative AI Copyright Cases*, LAWFARE (Feb. 15, 2024), https://www.lawfaremedia.org/article/howto-think-about-remedies-in-the-generative-ai-copyright-cases (discussing potential remedies in the current generative-AI copyright lawsuit landscape).

[597] 17 U.S.C. § 504(b).

[598] Harper & Row, Publishers, Inc. v. Nation Enters., 471 U.S. 539 (1985).

The simplest such theory is that the plaintiff's damages can be measured by the lost licensing fee that the defendant saved by infringing.[599] This is a fair-market-value remedy; the plaintiff is awarded the licensing fee that a willing seller and willing buyer would have negotiated.[600] As with fair use, much depends on the existence of a licensing market for the kind of use at issue. If there is no such market, it can be hard for a court to estimate an appropriate royalty. So, for example, while there is a well-functioning market for licensing new editions of books, there is not a market for licensing generative-AI training on books—because the use has not existed until now, neither has the market.[601] In addition, it can be difficult for individual plaintiffs to show that their work in particular has a high licensing value.[602] In *On Davis v. The Gap, Inc.*, for example, the plaintiff requested a $2,500,000 licensing fee for the unauthorized use of his eyewear in a Gap ad.[603] The court held that his evidence supported a licensing fee of $50.[604]

Recognizing that this too may be an inadequate measure of damages, the Copyright Act also allows a successful plaintiff to recover "any profits of the infringer that are attributable to the infringement and are not taken into account in computing the actual damages."[605] Instead of measuring the plaintiff's losses, this remedy measures the defendant's unfair gains.[606] The Copyright Act has a burden-shifting provision for defendant's profits that on paper is quite generous to the copyright owner:

> In establishing the infringer's profits, the copyright owner is required to present proof only of the infringer's gross revenue, and the infringer is required to prove his or her deductible

[599] *E.g.*, Dash v. Mayweather, 731 F.3d 303, 313 (4th Cir. 2013) ("Under the lost licensing fee theory, actual damages are generally calculated based on "what a willing buyer would have been reasonably required to pay to a willing seller for [the] plaintiffs' work.") (internal quotation omitted).

[600] *Id.*

[601] One reason for copyright owners to enter into licensing arrangements with some AI companies may thus be to establish a baseline for calculating damages against others who do not agree to licensing arrangements.

[602] *E.g.*, *Dash*, 731 F.3d at 312–26 (rejecting licensing fee calculation in plaintiff's expert report).

[603] On Davis v. The Gap, Inc., 246 F.3d 152, 156 (2d Cir. 2001).

[604] *Id.* at 161.

[605] 17 U.S.C. § 504(b).

[606] This makes infringer's profits a *restitutionary* remedy rather than a compensatory remedy. *See generally* WARD FARNSWORTH, RESTITUTION: CIVIL LIABILITY FOR UNJUST ENRICHMENT (2014) (discussing the theory of restitution). The provision is phrased the way it is to avoid double-counting. If the plaintiff loses one sale to the defendant, that sale would be "profits of the infringer" that *are* "taken into account in computing the [plaintiff's] actual damages."

> expenses and the elements of profit attributable to factors other than the copyrighted work.[607]

The hard part is determining how much of the defendant's profits are "attributable to factors other than the copyrighted work." In a generative-AI context, we would ask, how much of a generation's value is due to a particular training work, as opposed to other training works and the training algorithm? This is a hard question by itself; answering the same question for a model requires answering it for all generations the model is used to produce, and adding up the results.[608] In practice, the answer may depend on who bears the burden of persuasion on the relative value of different elements.

In this vein, there is an illuminating passage in *On Davis*, where the court held that none of the Gap's overall profits were attributable to the use of the defendant's eyewear in one photograph.[609] Explaining its reasoning, the court wrote:

> Thus, if a publisher published an anthology of poetry which contained a poem covered by the plaintiff's copyright, we do not think the plaintiff's statutory burden would be discharged by submitting the publisher's gross revenue resulting from its publication of hundreds of titles, including trade books, textbooks, cookbooks, etc. In our view, the owner's burden would require evidence of the revenues realized from the sale of the anthology containing the infringing poem. The publisher would then bear the burden of proving its costs attributable to the anthology and the extent to which its profits from the sale of the anthology were attributable to factors other than the infringing poem, including particularly the other poems contained in the volume.[610]

On this analogy, a generation might be like an anthology. Once the plaintiff shows that an infringing generation has commercial value, the defendant bears the burden to show what portion of the value came from other sources—a burden that may be quite difficult to meet. So, to a first approximation, those who profit from infringing generations should expect to pay out their entire profits.

Also on this analogy, a generative-AI system (or model or training dataset) might be more like a full catalog. Any individual training work is utterly

---

607 17 U.S.C. § 504(b). *See generally* Frank Music Corp. v. Metro-Goldwyn-Mayer, Inc., 772 F.2d 505 (9th Cir. 1985) (performing apportionment calculation).

608 *See supra* note 119 (discussing the challenges of attribution of generations to specific training-data examples).

609 *On Davis*, 246 F.3d at 160.

610 *Id.*

insignificant on the scale of the whole system.[611] A plaintiff who shows only that their work was included in the training dataset has not carried their burden to show that any of the resulting profits were attributable to infringement of their work.[612]

This point demonstrates the crucial importance of *mass* copyright litigation against the service hosts of and other participants in generative-AI systems. The answer may well be different if the plaintiff or plaintiffs own a large fraction of the works used as training data. Although individual apportionment may remain a difficult problem, it is much easier to show that the model's value collectively derives from the works that have been infringed. This is one reason why so many of the current lawsuits against generative-AI companies have been brought as putative class actions.[613] Getty's lawsuit against Stability AI is not a class action, but Getty controls the copyright to a large number of works in Stable Diffusion's training dataset.[614] The *New York Times* has alleged that OpenAI trained more extensively on its "higher quality" articles compared to other sources of training data.[615]

2. Statutory Damages

Instead of recovering actual damages and/or profits, a successful copyright plaintiff may elect to recover statutory damages instead.[616] This will typically be an appealing option. First, the plaintiff can submit both theories to the court, see which one results in a larger award, and then choose that one.[617] Second, the amount of statutory damages is fixed in the statute. The base range is $750 to $30,000, "as the court considers just."[618] This amount can be decreased to $200 for an "innocent" infringer who "was not aware and had no reason to believe that his or her acts constituted an infringement of copyright,"[619] but this defense is not

---

[611] However, as we note above, some training data examples may have outsized influence on generations. *See generally* Koh & Liang, *supra* note 119; Akyurek, Bolukbasi, Liu et al., *supra* note 119; Grosse, Bae, Anil et al., *supra* note 119. (discussing influence functions).

[612] *See supra* note 119 and accompanying text; *supra* note 212 and accompanying text.

[613] *E.g.*, Complaint, Kadrey v. Meta Platforms, Inc., No. 3:23-cv-03417 (N.D. Cal. July 7, 2023); Complaint, Doe 1 v. GitHub, Inc., No. 4:22-cv-06823 (N.D. Cal. Nov. 3, 2022); Complaint, Anderson v. Stability AI, Ltd., No. 3:23-cv-00201 (N.D. Cal. Jan. 13, 2023) (Doc. No. 1); Complaint, Tremblay v. OpenAI, Inc., No. 3:23-cv-03223 (N.D. Cal. June 28, 2023).

[614] Complaint, Getty Images (US), Inc. v. Stability AI, Inc., No. 1:23-cv-00135 (D. Del. Feb. 3, 2023).

[615] Complaint ¶ 90, N.Y. Times Co. v. Microsoft, No. 2:24-cv-00711 (C.D. Cal. Dec. 27, 2023).

[616] 17 U.S.C. § 504(c)(1).

[617] Curet-Velazquez v. ACEMLA de P.R., Inc., 656 F.3d 47, 57–58 (1st Cir. 2011).

[618] 17 U.S.C. § 504(c)(1).

[619] *Id.* § 504(c)(2).

available for works that were published with proper notice of copyright.[620] The amount can also be increased up to $150,000 when the "infringement was committed willfully."[621] Willful infringement consists either of actual knowledge or reckless disregard of infringement;[622] a defendant who has a reasonable and good-faith belief that their conduct is non-infringing is not a willful infringer.[623] Under these ranges, an individual statutory-damage award could be a serious threat to an individual user, a moderate nuisance to a small company, or an insignificant bit of background noise to an OpenAI or a Google.

Importantly, statutory damages are awarded *per work* infringed, regardless of how extensively each work was used. Again, the impact is clearest in mass copyright litigation. Statutory damages are a potentially existential threat to models trained on billions of works (and to the datasets that feed them and the services that incorporate them). Even without a finding of willfulness, the statutory damages for a billion infringed works could be as high as in the trillions of dollars—an impact that is no more survivable than the Chicxulub asteroid. Even at the minimum award for innocent infringement, the statutory damages for ten million infringed works would come to two hundred million dollars.[624]

One factor limiting statutory damage awards is that statutory damages are only available when the copyright owner registered the work with the Copyright Office before the infringement commenced.[625] This provision is designed to encourage authors to register their works promptly. It has the effect of making some generative-AI systems more vulnerable to copyright lawsuits than others. Books are typically registered as part of the publication process, so an LLM trained on hundreds of thousands of books could face hundreds of thousands of statutory-damage awards But many works of visual art and many websites are not registered unless and until the copyright owner needs to file a copyright lawsuit.[626] A model trained on a web scrape, then, may face a patchwork of statutory damage awards only for a small fraction of the works it was trained on. Differences in available damages based on the timing of registration may make it harder to assemble a plaintiff class with sufficiently common interests.[627]

---

[620] 17 U.S.C. § 401(d).

[621] 17 U.S.C. § 504(c)(2).

[622] Erickson Prods., Inc. v. Kast, 921 F.3d 822, 833 (9th Cir. 2019).

[623] VHT, Inc. v. Zillow Grp., Inc., 918 F.3d 723, 748–49 (9th Cir. 2019).

[624] This sum is still high enough that it might deter a court from finding infringement against a smaller defendant that merely used a model someone else had trained.

[625] 17 U.S.C. § 412(2).

[626] Registration is a prerequisite to suit. § 411(a); Fourth Est. Pub. Corp v. Wall-St.com, LLC, 139 S. Ct. 881 (2019).

[627] *See* Fed. R. Civ. P. 23(a)(2) (requiring "questions of law or fact common to the class"). The registration requirement cannot be circumvented through the use of a class action. *See* Reed Elsevier, Inc. v. Muchnick, 559 U.S. 154 (2010).

3. Attorney's Fees

Another remedy for copyright infringement is that a court may award "full costs" and "a reasonable attorney's fee to the prevailing party."[628] Costs are small potatoes; they include various court fees, printing fees, and required payments to the court.[629] But attorney's fees are a bigger deal, precisely because the expense of litigating a copyright case can be so high. Under the usual "American Rule" (so called because it is followed in the United States but not in many other countries), each party pays its own lawyers and decides how much the case is worth to them.[630] The Copyright Act's fee-shifting provision is one of a few exceptions to the American Rule. It provides an incentive to parties to bring meritorious cases—or to defend against unmeritorious ones—that would otherwise be financially unreasonable to pursue.[631] Like statutory damages, attorney's fees are only available for works that were registered before the infringement.[632]

While statutory damages are most important in mass litigation, the reverse is true of attorney's fees. A million dollars of expenses to litigate a class action with a hundred-million-dollar damage award is not the biggest deal. A fee award is a nice bonus, but it is not necessary to bring the suit in the first place. But a million dollars of expenses to litigate an individual claim leading to a $1,000 statutory damage award is completely unreasonable. Without an attorney's fee award, the lawyers involved could make more on a per-hour basis by busking on the subway.

Attorney's fees can also have a significant deterrent effect.[633] Because they are uncapped, a plaintiff can run up the total award a defendant faces. Indeed, the harder a defendant fights, the higher the plaintiff's attorney's fees will be. Along with statutory damages, attorney's fees can be used to coerce settlements from defendants who may have a strong defense on the merits.[634] Even though the defendant might be able to receive a fee award if they win—the fee-shifting rule is symmetrical[635]—they cannot run the risk of paying a massive fee award if they lose. This settlement pressure will be strongest against smaller and more risk-averse defendants: end users rather than well-capitalized AI companies, which can better absorb the cost of a fee shift. This difference helps to explain why

---

[628] 17 U.S.C. § 505.
[629] *See* Rimini St., Inc. v. Oracle USA, Inc., 139 S.Ct. 873 (2019) (interpreting "full costs").
[630] Fogerty v. Fantasy, Inc., 510 US 517, 533–34 (1994).
[631] *Id.* at 524.
[632] 17 U.S.C. § 412.
[633] *See generally* Pamela Samuelson & Tara Wheatland, *Statutory Damages in Copyright Law: A Remedy in Need of Reform*, 51 WM. & MARY L. REV. 439 (2009); Talha Syed & Oren Bracha, *The Wrongs of Copyright's Statutory Damages*, 98 TEX. L. REV. 1219 (2020).
[634] *See, e.g.*, Mitch Stoltz, *Collateral Damages: Why Congress Needs To Fix Copyright Law's Civil Penalties*, ELEC. FRONTIER FOUND. (July 24, 2014), https://www.eff.org/wp/collateral-damages-why-congress-needs-fix-copyright-laws-civil-penalties.
[635] *Fogerty*, 510 U.S. 517.

several generative-AI companies have offered to indemnify their users against the copyright risks of using their systems.[636]

4. Injunctions

A court may "grant temporary and final injunctions on such terms as it may deem reasonable to prevent or restrain infringement of a copyright."[637] An injunction is a court order commanding a person to take (or to avoid taking) some action. A party who fails to comply with an injunction can be punished for contempt of court with sanctions that include escalating fines and even imprisonment.

An injunction is an equitable remedy; a plaintiff is not automatically entitled to one.[638] Instead, a plaintiff seeking an injunction must show:

> (1) that it has suffered an irreparable injury; (2) that remedies available at law, such as monetary damages, are inadequate to compensate for that injury; (3) that, considering the balance of hardships between the plaintiff and defendant, a remedy in equity is warranted; and (4) that the public interest would not be disserved by a permanent injunction.[639]

The first two factors are redundant; they mean exactly the same thing.[640] A damages award in a copyright case is inadequate when damages are hard to calculate. For all of the reasons discussed above, this will frequently be the case in generative-AI cases. Thus, most of the weight will fall on the third and fourth factors. The degree to which hardships fall on a defendant that provides generative-AI models or systems, and on third-party users, will depend substantially on the balance of infringing and noninfringing uses. An injunction is more appropriate against a system that (a court sees as) "good for nothing else

---

[636] Brad Smith, *Microsoft Announces New Copilot Copyright Commitment for Customers*, MICROSOFT (Sept. 7, 2023), https://blogs.microsoft.com/on-the-issues/2023/09/07/copilot-copyright-commitment-ai-legal-concerns/; Bridget Johnston, *Introducing Indemnification for AI-Generated Images: An Industry First*, SHUTTER- STOCK (July 11, 2023), https://www.shutterstock.com/blog/ai-generated-imagesindemnification; Adobe, *Firefly Legal FAQs—Enterprise Customers* §§ 10–14 (June 12, 2023), https://www.adobe.com/content/dam/dx/us/en/products/sensei/sensei-genai/firefly-enterprise/Firefly_Legal_FAQs_Enterprise_Customers.pdf.

[637] 17 U.S.C. § 502(a). We will discuss only permanent injunctions issued after a finding of infringement. Preliminary injunctions issued during the course of a lawsuit may be important for parties and litigators, but our focus is on the longer term.

[638] eBay Inc. v. MercExchange, L.L.C., 547 U.S. 388, 392–93 (2006).

[639] *Id.* at 391.

[640] Douglas Laycock, *The Death of the Irreparable Injury Rule*, 103 HARV. L. REV. 687, 694 (1990).

but infringement,"[641] and less appropriate against one that is also "capable of substantial noninfringing uses."[642] (As these quotes suggest, there is substantial overlap between the substantive tests for infringement and the test for a permanent injunction.)

Another factor weighing against generative-AI injunctions is the First Amendment interests of users and developers.[643] There is often a speech interest in using the speech of others verbatim;[644] these First Amendment interests are even stronger for novel generations. In individual cases against specific generations, users' speech rights are protected by the "traditional First Amendment safeguards" of fair use, particularly transformative fair use.[645] But an injunction against the use of a model or service can prevent these generations from being created; this is a speech harm too. So, when a model is used to create expressive and noninfringing generations, there is a powerful argument that a court should not enjoin it in a way that would prevent these noninfringing uses.

And so, we come to one of the most important features of an injunction: a court's ability to craft its specific terms. A court could enjoin the use of a model *entirely*, preventing the defendant from using it for any purpose. But a court could also enjoin the use of a model *to create infringing generations*, leaving it up to the defendant to implement appropriate content filters.[646] This type of injunction puts sharper teeth into the defendant's obligations, because the consequences for failing to comply with an injunction are swifter and more severe than for committing copyright infringement. Unfortunately for defendants (and for courts considering enjoining them), it is harder to "separat[e] the fair use sheep from the infringing goats" in a generative-AI system than it is on a content-hosting service

---

[641] Metro-Goldwyn-Mayer Studios Inc. v. Grokster, Ltd., 545 U.S. 913, 932 (2005).
[642] *Id.* at 391.
[643] Mark A. Lemley & Eugene Volokh, *Freedom of Speech and Injunctions in Intellectual Property Cases*, 48 DUKE L.J. 147 (1998).
[644] *See* Rebecca Tushnet, *Copy This Essay: How Fair Use Doctrine Harms Free Speech and How Copying Serves It*, 114 YALE L.J. 535 (2004).
[645] Eldred v. Ashcroft, 537 U.S. 186, 219–20 (2003).
[646] For example, Copilot offers an option to check "code suggestions with their surrounding code of about 150 characters against public code on GitHub" and propose a different suggestion if the filter is triggered. *See Configuring GitHub Copilot in your environment*, *supra* note 239. Unfortunately, while helpful, content filters like Copilot's are not enough by themselves to prevent the generation of potentially infringing content. For example, Copilot's filter would not be triggered if the generated code suggestion matched 149 characters of public code—which is long enough to at least raise copyright concerns. *See* Justin Hughes, *Size Matters (Or Should) in Copyright Law* , 74 FORDHAM L. REV. 575 (2005) (discussing copyright protection of "microworks"). *See generally* Daphne Ippolito, Florian Tramèr, Milad Nasr et al., Preventing Verbatim Memorization in Language Models Gives a False Sense of Privacy (2023) (unpublished manuscript), https://arxiv.org/abs/2210.17546 (discussing how verbatim output filters are necessarily incomplete).

like YouTube.[647] Even for a defendant with a list of works to avoid, this type of filtering is a difficult and unsolved technical problem.[648]

5. Destruction

Another equitable remedy is that the court may order "the destruction or other reasonable disposition of all [infringing] copies."[649] This is like a more severe version of an injunction, one that takes it out of the defendant's power to commit further infringements by taking away their copies. To the extent that a model is treated as an infringing copy, the destruction remedy does not add very much to a permanent injunction except for irreversibility. Actually deleting a model—as opposed to putting in in storage for future use if and when the law changes or copyright owners negotiate a license to allow it to be used—is an exceptionally harsh remedy that effectively means throwing away all of the compute used to train the model.

But there is a twist. As Elizabeth Joh observes,[650] the destruction remedy covers not just infringing copies but also "all plates, molds, matrices, masters, tapes, film negatives, or other articles by means of which such copies or phonorecords may be reproduced."[651] Even if a model is not itself treated as an infringing copy,[652] if it is capable of producing infringing generations, it might be an "article[] by means of which" infringing copies "*may* be reproduced."[653] The courts have not restricted this remedy to items that themselves infringe or have been used to infringe.[654] Instead, they have allowed it to be used against dual-use technologies like computers and manufacturing equipment that can be used both to infringe and for noninfringing purposes.[655] Thus, the destruction remedy could reach not just models with multiple uses, but also the non-model portions of a generative-AI service. For example, a court could order the destruction of a style-transfer system that allows users to regenerate one image using the artistic style of another, on the theory that a user could prompt it with a copyrighted image and generate an infringing derivative work. Such an order would raise even more severe free-expression concerns.

---

[647] Campbell v. Acuff-Rose Music, 510 U.S. 569, 586 (1994).
[648] *See supra* note 412 and accompanying text.
[649] 17 U.S.C. § 503(b). *See generally* Elizabeth E. Joh, Equitable Legal Remedies and the Existential Threat to Generative AI (Aug. 27, 2023) (unpublished manuscript), https://papers.ssrn.com/sol3/papers.cfm?abstract_id=4553431. As with injunctions, there is also a preliminary version of destruction: a court may order the impoundment of infringing copies during the course of the litigation. 17 U.S.C. § 503(a)(1).
[650] *See* Joh, *supra* note 652.
[651] 17 U.S.C. § 503(b).
[652] *See* Cooper & Grimmelmann *supra* note 289.
[653] 17 U.S.C. § 503(b) (emphasis added).
[654] Mahan v. Roc Nation, LLC 720 Fed. Appx. 55 (2d Cir. 2018).
[655] Anne-Marie Carstens, *Copyright's Deprivations*, 96 WASH. L. REV. 1275 (2021).

L. Copyright Management Information

Section 1202 of the Copyright Act, enacted like section 512 as part of the DMCA, deals with "copyright management information . . . conveyed in connection with copies . . . of a work" (CMI).[656] Types of CMI include a work's title, author, copyright owner, performers, and licensing information.[657] One prong of section 1202 prohibits providing "false" CMI;[658] another prohibits "remov[ing] or alter[ing]" CMI.[659]

The legislative history of section 1202 (and its passage as part of the *Digital* Millennium Copyright Act) suggests that it was designed to work in tandem with section 1201, which prohibits disabling digital rights management systems that protect copyrighted works.[660] Where section 1201 guards the parts of the system that directly control access, section 1202 ensures that the metadata and watermarks attached to works are accurate and intact.[661]

But the language of section 1202 is not limited to digital metadata. Unlike the World Intellectual Property Organization Copyright Treaty, which applies to "*electronic* rights management information,"[662] section 1202's text contains no such limitation. As a result, courts have held that section 1202 can be violated when a magazine photo is reproduced online without the photographer's name from a "gutter credit" that appeared alongside it in print.[663]

Under these precedents, the assembly of works into datasets and the training of a model could result in the "remov[al]" of CMI through a similar decontextualization. Consider a diffusion-based model trained on one of the LAION image datasets. The dataset itself consists of URL links to images where they appear in context on webpages,[664] often with author, title, and copyright-owner credits of the type that qualify as protected CMI. This by itself is neither falsification, removal, nor alteration. But when the images *by themselves* are downloaded, the attached CMI is stripped in the same way as in the magazine cases. Training and generation do not repair the linkage once it has been severed; if a model outputs a similar image, it will not bear the original CMI.

---

656 17 U.S.C. 1202(c) (emphasis added).

657 *Id.*

658 *Id.* § 1202(a).

659 *Id.* § 1202(b).

660 17 U.S.C. § 1201; Severine Dusollier, *Some Reflections on Copyright Management Information and Moral Rights*, 25 COLUM. J.L. & ARTS 377 (2003).

661 IQ Grp., Ltd. v. Wiesner Pub., 409 F. Supp. 2d 587, 593–97 (D.N.J. 2006); Textile Secrets Int'l, Inc. v. Ya-Ya Brand Inc., 524 F. Supp. 2d 1184, 1196–99 (C.D. Cal. 2007).

662 WIPO Copyright Treaty, art. 12(1)(i), 1996.

663 Murphy v. Millennium Radio Grp. LLC, 650 F.3d 295 (3d Cir. 2011); Mango v. BuzzFeed, 970 F.3d 167 (2d Cir. 2020).

664 *See supra* Part I.B.3.

Getty Images's complaint against Stability AI presents additional theories of section 1202 violation based on the Stable Diffusion models' treatment of the Getty watermarks on the images in its library.[665] First, to the extent that the training process learns features of training images without the watermark, Getty alleges removal and alteration of CMI.[666] Second, Getty shows that Stable Diffusion sometimes produces generations that include distorted versions of the watermark.[667] This, Getty argues, constitutes "false" CMI within the meaning of section 1202.[668]

The more serious doctrinal obstacle to section 1202 claims is that they require a nexus to copyright infringement. Falsification of CMI must be done "knowingly and with the intent to induce, enable, facilitate, or conceal infringement" to create liability,[669] and removal or alteration must be done "intentionally . . . knowing, or . . . having reasonable grounds to know, that it will induce, enable, facilitate, or conceal an infringement."[670] Most defendants in generative-AI cases will have the required intent to remove or alter the CMI. A developer training on the LAION dataset can hardly fail to know that the training process discards any information about the images on the webpages they came from.

Instead, it is not clear that a defendant's treatment of CMI at any stage of the generative-AI supply chain is intended to facilitate or conceal copyright infringement in any cases where copyright infringement would not already attach to the defendant. Getty objects that attaching a "modified version of the Getty Images watermark to bizarre or grotesque synthetic imagery,"[671] will harm its reputation. But that is a concern that sounds in trademark, not copyright.[672] Indeed, the "grotesque" nature of the images Getty includes in its complaint, if anything, cuts against infringement, by suggesting that the images are not suitable for any valuable purpose, let alone competing with Getty. The decontextualization of the training process might be said to help "conceal" infringement, but again the infringement itself is likely to be separately actionable.

The real bite of the CMI claims may be remedial. A court is entitled to award statutory damages of $2,500 to $25,000 "for each violation of section 1202."[673] The liability is *per violation* rather than *per work* (as with ordinary copyright infringement). In theory, then, a defendant could face separate section 1202 liability for each variation of a dataset or model it creates, or each output bearing

---

665 Complaint, Getty Images (US), Inc. v. Stability AI, Inc., No. 1:23-cv-00135 (D. Del. Feb. 3, 2023).
666 *Id.* ¶¶ 81–86.
667 *Id.* ¶¶ 59–60.
668 *Id.* ¶¶ 74–80.
669 17 U.S.C. § 1202(a).
670 *Id.* § 1202(b).
671 Complaint ¶ 59, Getty Images (US), Inc. v. Stability AI, Inc., No. 1:23-cv-00135.
672 *See id.* ¶¶ 87–99 (bringing claim for trademark infringement).
673 17 U.S.C. § 1203(c)(3)(B).

a watermark. On the other hand, while there is a $200 floor for ordinary copyright statutory damages in cases of innocent infringement,[674] a is entitled "in its discretion" to reduce section 1202 statutory damages or remit them entirely in cases of innocent violations.[675]

M. Right of Publicity

A related but non-copyright form of IP is the right of publicity.[676] The right generally protects an individual's persona against commercial appropriation by others. Unlike copyright, which is almost entirely created by federal law, the right of publicity is almost entirely created by state law. As a result, its details vary substantially from state to state, including whether a state affords a right of publicity at all and, if it does, whether the right is regarded as a privacy or property right or both, what kinds of conduct it protects against, the scope of newsworthiness or expressive-use defenses, and whether and how long the right lasts after the subject's death.[677] As a result, the following summary is a broad overview, rather than a specific analysis of any state's (or each state's) law.

1. Overview of the Right of Publicity

A typical statement of the right of publicity's subject matter is that it covers an individual's "name, voice, signature, photograph, or likeness"[678]—the aspects of a person's persona that are broadly recognizable by others. (We will collectively refer to these as "identity.") Courts have interpreted recognizability broadly, holding that race-car driver Lothar Motschenbacher's right of publicity was infringed by a commercial showing his car,[679] singer Bette Midler's by a commercial featuring a sound-alike vocalist,[680] and game-show host Vanna White's by a print ad showing a robot next to the game board from *The Price is Right*.[681] The fact that an expressive work is recognizably *by* an author or artist does not mean that it implicates their right of publicity: a use must depict or summon up the person in the minds of viewers. Some states' rights of publicity terminate on death,[682] others last for a legislatively specified or judge-created

[674] 17 U.S.C. § 504(c)(2).

[675] 17 U.S.C. § 1203(c)(5)(A).

[676] *See generally* JENNIFER E. ROTHMAN, THE RIGHT OF PUBLICITY: PRIVACY REIMAGINED FOR A PUBLIC WORLD (2018) (providing a thorough history, analysis, and critique of the right of publicity as it exists in the United States today).

[677] *See generally* Jennifer E. Rothman, *Rothman's Roadmap to the Right of Publicity* (2024), https://rightofpublicityroadmap.com (providing a detailed analysis of every state's right-of-publicity laws).

[678] Cal. Civ. Code § 3344(a).

[679] Motschenbacher v. R.J. Reynolds Tobacco Co., 498 F.2d 821 (9th Cir. 1974).

[680] Midler v. Ford Motor Co., 849 F.2d 460 (9th cir. 1988).

[681] White v. Samsung Elecs. Am., 971 F.2d 1395 (9th Cir. 1992).

[682] Hagen v. Dahmer, 38 U.S.P.Q.2d 1146, 1995 WL 822644 (E.D. Wis. 1995).

term,[683] and Tennessee allows the right to continue indefinitely as long as it is being commercially exploited.[684]

The right of publicity also applies only to *commercial* uses. One core use is endorsement: using a person's identity to sell things.[685] Another is merchandising: selling basketball jerseys with Steph Curry's name and number on them, or Dolly Parton Funko Pops. And a third is what Eric Johnson calls "virtual impressment":[686] digitally recreating a person to perform in movies, video games, songs, and other audio or audiovisual media.[687] Broadly speaking, endorsement issues can often be avoided with sufficient disclaimers to establish that the person has not endorsed the product in question or consented to appear in the advertising; but, to the extent that a plaintiff has a valid claim based on merchandising or virtual impressment, disclaimers will not save the defendant.

Although the right of publicity does not have a copyright-style, general-purpose, fair-use defense, some courts have recognized a narrower copyright-style, transformative-use defense when a person's likeness "is so transformed that it has become primarily the defendant's own expression rather than the celebrity's likeness."[688] Some state statutes explicitly carve out uses affected with a strong public interest, such as a California's exception for "news, public affairs, or sports broadcast or account, or any political campaign."[689] And sometimes sufficiently expressive uses are excluded entirely, as in California's exception for "fictional or nonfictional entertainment, or a dramatic, literary, or musical work" after the person's death.[690]

The right of publicity has a close and complicated relationship with copyright. First, like all state-created IP rights, it is subject to federal preemption. The Copyright Act provides that "all legal or equitable rights that are equivalent to any of the exclusive rights within the general scope of copyright . . . are governed exclusively" by federal copyright.[691] To avoid preemption, a right of publicity claim must either protect different subject matter than copyright (e.g., a person's appearance is not a fixed work of authorship) or include an additional

---

[683] Hebrew Univ. of Jerusalem v. Gen. Motors, 903 F. Supp. 2d 932, 939–40 (C.D. Cal. 2012).

[684] 47 Tenn. Code. §§ 47–25-1104.

[685] Cal. Civ. Code § 3344(a) ("for purposes of advertising or selling, or soliciting purchases of, products, merchandise, goods or services"). *Motschenbacher*, *Midler*, and *White* are all endorsement cases.

[686] Eric E. Johnson, *Disentangling the Right of Publicity*, 111 Nw. U. L. Rev. 891, 934–35 (2017).

[687] Hart v. Elec. Arts, Inc., 717 F.3d 141 (3d Cir. 2013).

[688] Comedy III Prods. v. Gary Saderup, Inc., 21 P.3d 797, 141 (Cal. 2001).

[689] Cal. Civ. Code § 3344(d).

[690] Cal. Civ. Code § 3344.1(a)(2). Put another way, California's statutory right of publicity protects against virtual impressment of the living, but not of the dead.

[691] 17 U.S.C. § 301(a).

element not required for copyright infringement (e.g., using the plaintiff's likeness as advertising or promotion to sell another product).[692]

When the basis of a right-of-publicity claim is the distribution of a work either depicting a person or created by the person or both, courts frequently treat the right of publicity as having merged into the copyright in the work: they cannot further restrict the copyright owner's ordinary exploitation of the work. For example, in *Laws v. Sony Music Entertainment, Inc.*, the plaintiff Debra Laws's vocals from "Very Special" were used as a sample on Jennifer Lopez and L.L. Cool J.'s "All I Have."[693] The defendants had a copyright license from Laws's record label, but not a right of publicity license from Laws. The Ninth Circuit held that Laws's claim was preempted.[694] The case would have been different if the sample had been used for an advertisement rather than a new track; that would have been an extra element.[695] Difficult issues sometimes arise when footage or other works created for one project are reused in a related but different context, as in *Facenda v. NFL Films, Inc.*, where the NFL reused voice-over lines recorded by John Facenda as documentary narration for a 22-minute promotion for a video game, and the Third Circuit held that his estate's right of publicity claim was not preempted.[696]

2. Incorporation and Advertising

The most famous generative-AI right-of-publicity lawsuit is both a legal non-starter and not actually about generative AI. In January 2024, the *Dudesy* podcast posted an hour-long episode titled "George Carlin: I'm Glad I'm Dead," which the podcast hosts claimed to feature both a script and audio that had been trained to imitate the late comedian George Carlin.[697] Carlin's estate sued, making claims under California's statutory and common-law rights of publicity.[698] But the statutory claim is a loser because California's postmortem right of publicity, as noted above, expressly excludes audiovisual entertainment, and the common-law claim is a loser because the courts have held that California's common-law right terminates at death.[699] Even more fundamentally, *Dudesy*'s hosts promptly

---

[692] *See generally* Jennifer E. Rothman, *Copyright Preemption and the Right of Publicity*, 36 U.C. DAVIS L. REV. 199 (2002).
[693] Laws v. Sony Music Ent., Inc., 448 F.3d 1134 (9th Cir. 2006).
[694] *Id.* at 1145.
[695] *Id.* at 1141–42; *cf.* Downing v. Abercrombie & Fitch, 265 F.3d 994 (9th Cir. 2001) (photographs used as advertisements).
[696] Facenda v. NFL Films, Inc., 542 F.3d 1007 (3d Cir. 2008).
[697] Christopher Kuo, *George Carlin's Estate Sues Podcasters Over A.I. Episode*, N.Y. TIMES (Jan. 29, 2024), https://www.nytimes.com/2024/01/26/arts/carlin-lawsuit-ai-podcast-copyright.html.
[698] Main Sequence, Ltd. v. Dudesy, LLC, No. 2:24-cv-00711 (C.D. Cal.).
[699] Lugosi v. Universal Pictures, 603 P.2d 425 (Cal. 1979).

admitted that the episode was entirely human-written.[700] The generative-AI veneer was just a publicity stunt.

The Carlin lawsuit, near-miss though it is, helpfully illustrates two ways in which the right of publicity can apply to generative AI. First, a technical artifact (a dataset, model, system, or generation) could *incorporate* a person's identity. "I'm Glad I'm Dead" imitated Carlin's distinctive voice. Second, a technical artifact could be *advertised* using a person's identity. "I'm Glad I'm Dead" was promoted using Carlin's name. Incorporation raises merchandising and virtual-impressment issues; advertising raises endorsement issues.

In most cases, generative AI will raise distinctive right of publicity issues only to the extent that it incorporates a person's identity. This is for two reasons. First, when it is legal to *sell* a product incorporating a person's identity or creative output, it is also generally legal to *promote* the product by truthfully describing the person's relationship to it.[701] Second, using a person's identity to sell generative-AI material that does not otherwise relate to them is a garden-variety case under the endorsement prong of the right of publicity. Whether it infringes on Salvador Dalí's right of publicity to name a family of image systems "DALL·E" has little to do with the fact that it is a generative-AI system. Almost the same issues would arise with calling a line of paintbrushes "DALL·E".

3. Incorporation in the Generative-AI Supply Chain

Some AI generations are already being used for blatant right of publicity violations. Ads featuring a cloned version of Taylor Swift's voice have been used in fake giveaways for Le Creuset cookware;[702] a deepfake video of Tom Hanks has been used to advertise a dental plan.[703] Of course, fake celebrity endorsements are nothing new. The difference between an ad using an (actual) photograph of a celebrity and an ad using a (generated) video of them is a difference in degree, not in kind. Generative AI may make the deception more convincing by forging an explicit endorsement, but what makes these uses actionable is fundamentally the lack of permission. So, the right of publicity violation is more about how the media is used, not how it is generated.

From the perspective of the system that is used to generate the media, or any other actors further upstream in the generative-AI supply chain, this is ultimately a secondary-liability question that is quite similar to the secondary-liability

---

[700] Kuo, *supra* note 700.

[701] Armstrong v. Eagle Rock Ent., Inc., 655 F. Supp. 2d 779 (E.D. Mich 2009) (defendant could use photograph of plaintiff on the cover and liner notes of a DVD concert video).

[702] Tiffany Hsu & Yiwen Lu, *No, That's Not Taylor Swift Peddling Le Creuset Cookware*, N.Y. TIMES (Jan. 9, 2024), https://www.nytimes.com/2024/01/09/technology/taylor-swift-le-creuset-ai-deepfake.html.

[703] Derrick Bryson Taylor, *Tom Hanks Warns of Dental Ad Using A.I. Version of Him*, N.Y. TIMES (Oct. 2, 2023), https://www.nytimes.com/2023/10/02/technology/tom-hanks-aidental-video.html.

question for copyright.[704] The law of secondary liability in right of publicity is both less developed (because the cases are fewer) and more fragmented (because the sources of law are more numerous) than in copyright.[705] It is not obvious that there are any material differences between the two.

That said, the statutory safe harbor that is potentially applicable to the right of publicity is both less and more complicated than safe harbors in copyright. On the one hand, the right of publicity is not subject to the safe harbor notice-and-takedown regime of section 512, which applies only to copyright. On the other, a different immunity, "section 230," protects Internet immediacies from liability from third-party information provided by another."[706] Section 230 has an exception for "intellectual property,"[707] and courts are split on whether this includes the state-created right of publicity or not.[708] And if section 230 does apply to the right of publicity, there is deep disagreement (and an utter absence of caselaw) on how it applies to generative AI because it is unsettled whether and when AI generations should be regarded as third-party content.[709]

A different theory of a right-of-publicity variation is the use of a generative-AI system to produce outputs in the style of particular artists or authors. (See Figure 19.) Styling these claims as right-of-publicity violations rather than under copyright[710] introduces a few twists. Most fundamentally, there is copyright preemption. To the extent that these claims mirror copyright claims based on the imitation of one's style as embodied in fixed creative works—e.g., a photograph in the style of Cindy Sherman—they are preempted unless there is some extra element. One candidate for such an element is the prompt. At least as to commercial services, there is an argument that if a service produces a generation in response to the prompt "a photograph in the style of cindy sherman", then this constitutes a use by the service of Sherman's name. The doctrinal hurdle here,

---

[704] *See supra* Part II.F.

[705] *See* Perfect 10, Inc. v. Cybernet Ventures, Inc., 213 F. Supp. 2d 1146, 1183–87 (C.D. Cal. 2002); J. THOMAS MCCARTHY, THE RIGHTS OF PUBLICITY AND PRIVACY § 3:17 to 3:20 (2d ed. 2023) (surveying the limited caselaw).

[706] 47 U.S.C. § 230(c)(1).

[707] 47 U.S.C. § 230(e)(2).

[708] Perfect 10, Inc. v. CCBill LLC, 488 F.3d 1102, 1118–19 (9th Cir. 2007) (section 230 immunity applies to the right of publicity) *with* Hepp v. Facebook, 14 F.4th 204 (3d Cir. 2021) (no it does not).

[709] *See generally* Peter J. Benson & Valerie C. Brannon, Congressional Research Service (Congressional Research Service Legal Sidebar LSB11097 Dec. 28, 2023) (surveying caselaw and commentary).

[710] *See supra* Part II.C.2.f (discussing artistic style and similarity).

however, is that it is not clear that the user's prompt should be attributed to the service, which is not using Sherman's name to advertise.[711]

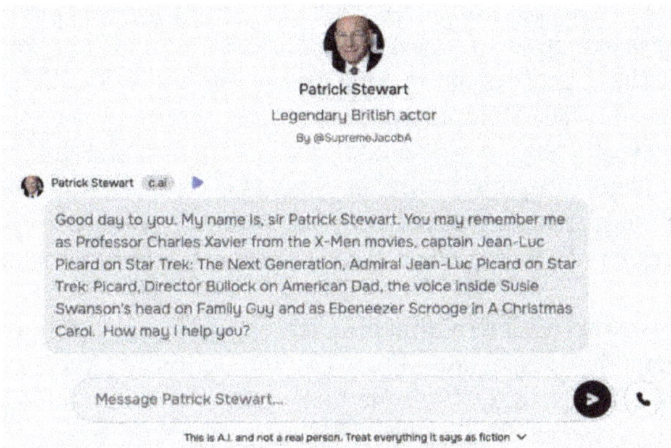

Figure 19: Screenshot of the character.ai platform, where a user can chat with an AI "character" version of Sir Patrick Stewart.

A stronger version of this theory is that services based on models which have been developed to specifically imitate an artist's style or person's appearance or voice are more clearly selling that person's identity. One way of framing this situation is that a commercial model provider is directly violating Drake's identity by using Drake's name to sell its models (of Drake): a form of advertising. Another way is to say that it is the models that are the problem: a form of merchandising. And a third is to say that the model is a kind of toolkit for anyone to engage in virtual impressment of Drake, so the seller is engaged in contributory virtual impressment.

All of these theories are subject to the usual right-of-publicity defenses. The transformative-use argument is particularly strong, for the same reasons it is strong in copyright. Indeed, because the earlier stages of the generative-AI supply chain generally cannot be the basis of right-of-publicity claims—they do not by themselves involve recognizable uses of a person's identity—the transformative-use defense is needed only in the later stages, where the transformation is the most pronounced. And the general public-interest defense will apply so clearly to some generations (it is not hard to imagine news programs making generative-AI illustrations), and others will be clearly non-infringing private non-commercial uses, so most systems will have substantial noninfringing uses.

---

[711] To the extent that a service does (or does not) analyze prompts to detect problematic or prohibited requests, there is a question of whether this analysis constitutes use sufficient to trigger the right of publicity or to avoid preemption. A similar issue will arise under other use-based bodies of law, such as trademark.

N. Hot News Misappropriation

One final relevant copyright-like form of IP liability is hot news misappropriation. The common-law cause of action for misappropriation has a long history; it is a species of unfair competition law, which prohibits businesses from "reaping the fruits" of their competitors' investments.[712] Its most famous statement is in the 1918 Supreme Court case *International News Service v. Associated Press.*[713] The Associated Press (AP) and the International News Service (INS) were competing wire services that reported and transmitted news stories to their member newspapers. AP alleged that INS was copying news stories from early editions of AP papers so that INS papers could report on them in their later editions.

It is important to note why this practice was not copyright infringement and is not to this day. The Associated Press could potentially have a copyright in the articles its employees wrote,[714] but the facts it reported were uncopyrightable. As Justice Brandeis wrote in dissent, "[T]he noblest of human productions—knowledge, truths ascertained, conceptions, and ideas—become, after voluntary communication to others, free as the air to common use."[715]

Justice Pitney's majority opinion, then, focused on the "novelty and freshness" of the news reported by the AP.[716] It held that the AP had a kind of "*quasi* property" as against competitors like the INS.[717] While it could not prevent readers and other members of the general public from freely discussing and writing about the news, it could prevent the INS from engaging in a systematic process of copying the news "precisely at the point where the profit is to be reaped"—that is, while the news was still fresh and there was value in being first to report it in a given newspaper market.[718]

The courts have held that the essential core of a hot news claim is freeriding on a competitor's costly production of information in a way that undermines the incentives to produce that information at all.[719] For example, in *National Basketball Ass'n v. Motorola*, the court explained that while it would be misappropriation for one real-time sports-score business to retransmit scores distributed by another, it was legal for the defendant to have its own reporters watch games to keep the scores updated.[720]

---

[712] Int'l News Serv. v. Associated Press, 248 U.S. 215, 241 (1918).
[713] *Id.*
[714] In addition, under the 1909 Copyright Act, copyright was too encumbered with formalities to provide the AP with effective relief. The 1976 Copyright Act, in which copyright attaches on fixation, overcomes this procedural barrier
[715] *Int'l News Serv.*, 248 U.S. at 250 (Brandeis, J., dissenting).
[716] *Id.* at 238.
[717] *Id.* at 236.
[718] *Id.* at 240.
[719] Nat'l Basketball Ass'n v. Motorola, 105 F.3d 841, 845 (2d Cir. 1997).
[720] *Id.*

For unrelated reasons, there is no longer a federal cause of action for misappropriation.[721] Instead, it is now governed entirely by state law, and as such it is subject to copyright preemption. The plaintiff must allege either that the information being copied does not fall within the general scope of copyright or that the cause of action contains an extra element.

The *New York Times* has brought hot news misappropriation claims against Microsoft and OpenAI, in addition to its copyright claims[722] The *Times* is a closer fit for misappropriation than many other generative-AI copyright plaintiffs, because it "gathers information, which often takes the form of time sensitive breaking news, for its content at a substantial cost."[723] It is a news organization, much like the AP.

Still, these claims are unlikely to succeed. The training and deployment of most generative-AI systems take place on such a drawn-out time scale that any breaking-news value in the training data will have been long since exhausted by the time anyone uses them. Hot news is ice cold six months later. (By contrast, INS papers reported news the same day as AP papers.) Mere competition with the *Times* for readership is likely not enough to generate a misappropriation claim that can survive preemption.

That said, however, some RAG or plugin systems might raise more serious hot news misappropriation issues. For example, Perplexity Pages creates "reports" by using a generative-AI model to summarize sources on a topic, including sources that the system pulls in from the web in response to a user's query.[724] Forbes alleged that Pages would closely paraphrase Forbes articles that Perplexity obtained by evading Forbes's paywall. This kind of conduct, if carried out at sufficient scale, is closer to the heartland of hot news misappropriation. This is misappropriation by a generative-AI *system* rather than by way of a generative-AI *model*.[725]

The *Times* also brings a claim that the defendants are misappropriating shopping recommendations from its Wirecutter subsite.[726] Here, the complaint emphasizes that the removal deprives the *Times* of affiliate revenue. But here too copyright preemption gives the *Times*'s theory of liability a difficult hill to climb. Wirecutter reviews are clearly fixed works of authorship,[727] and there is no

---

[721] In 1938, the Supreme Court held that federal courts must apply the law of the states in which they sit, so that "There is no federal general common law." Erie R. Co. v. Tompkins, 304 U.S. 64 (1938).

[722] Complaint, N.Y. Times Co. v. Microsoft Corp., No. 1:23-cv-11195 (S.D.N.Y. Dec. 27, 2023)..

[723] *Id.* ¶ 193.

[724] *See* Lopato, *supra* note 487.

[725] *See generally* Joseph A. Tomain, *First Amendment, Fourth Estate and Hot News: Misappropriation is Not a Solution to the Journalism Crisis*, 2012 MICH. ST. L. REV. 769.

[726] *Id.* ¶ 194.

[727] *See supra* Part II.A.1.

element here—creation at cost, duplication by competitors, value-capture by defendants—that is not also present in a typical copyright-infringement claim.

III. WHICH WAY FROM HERE?

The generative-AI supply chain is extremely complex. So is copyright law. Putting the two of them together multiplies the intricacy. Two unsettling conclusions follow from this radiating complexity.

First, because of the complexity of the *supply chain*, it is not possible to make accurate sweeping statements about the copyright legality of generative AI. Too much depends on the details of the specific model or system in question. All the pieces matter, from the curatorial choices in the training dataset, to the training algorithm, to the deployment environment, to the prompt supplied by the user, etc. Courts will inevitably have to work through these details in numerous lawsuits, as they develop doctrines to distinguish among different types of models, systems, and uses. Some of those doctrines may produce clear general rules, but others will have to remain entangled with the different forms the supply chain can take.

Second, because of the complexity of *copyright law*, there is enormous play in the joints. In particular, substantial similarity, indirect infringement, fair use, and remedies all have open-ended tests that can reach different results depending on the facts a court emphasizes and the conclusions it draws. This complexity gives courts the flexibility to deal with the many variations in the supply chain. Paradoxically, it also gives courts the freedom to reach any of several different plausible conclusions about a generative-AI system.

In this Part, we explore some of the ways that courts might try to use their discretion to apply copyright law to generative AI,[728] and then discuss some of the considerations that courts should keep in mind as they do.[729]

A. Possible Outcomes

Although the details of which generative-AI models and systems fall into which boxes may vary, there are a few boxes that courts may find it appealing to sort them into. In this section, we sketch a few of the possible copyright regimes that might result.

1. No Liability

First, courts might settle on a regime of no liability for released models, deployed services, and their users. Anything produced by a generative-AI system would be categorically legal, under a combination of no substantial similarity and fair use. The result would be that models and services would also be categorically

[728] *See infra* Part III.A.
[729] *See infra* Part III.B.

legal—there would be no primary liability for them to be indirectly liable for, and intermediate nonexpressive fair use would shield them in any event. Training datasets would also usually be legal as well (except perhaps in cases of blatant infringement like Books3).[730] They would be fair-use inputs to noninfringing downstream stages of the supply chain.

This regime is clear and simple. It would also be unstable. While such an outcome might make sense for some generative-AI systems, it seems both unworkable and undesirable for others, including models and systems produced specifically to emulate the styles of particular creators, and systems that use retrieval augmented generation or plugins, which find matching works and reproduce them exactly or nearly exactly.[731] If all generative AI were categorically legal, then developers would plausibly start adding generative components to other systems in order to launder copyrighted works through them. The endpoint could be the effective collapse of copyright. On the assumption that this is not an outcome that courts would willingly preside over, then, a blanket no-liability regime seems unlikely. Instead, courts would be more likely to find at least some infringement—so the question becomes where to draw the line.

2. Liability for Generations Only

Second, courts could draw a line between generative-AI services and the users of those services.[732] In this regime, only generations would be treated as infringing, and then only when a user made some external use of them.[733] In this world, generative-AI systems would be creative tools like Photoshop.[734] The user would be responsible for making sure that anything they create with the tools is noninfringing, but the tools would be shielded under something like a strong *Sony* rule, assembled out of a combination of no substantial similarity, no indirect infringement, and/or fair use. This result might be unfair to users whose infringements resulted from systems producing generations that reproduce material in the underlying model's training dataset, through no choice or fault of their own. But this is arguably the same kind of situation that some courts currently countenance when they hold that users can be liable for embedding

---

[730] Knibbs, *supra* note 557; Reisner, *supra* note 557; Complaint, Kadrey v. Meta Platforms, Inc., No. 3:23-cv-03417 (N.D. Cal. July 7, 2023).

[731] *See supra* note 212 and accompanying text (discussing retrieval augmented generation); *supra* note 487 (discussing OpenAI's plugins and Perplexity AI).

[732] The service/user distinction does not apply as clearly to models. A user might have received a model directly from its creator, or indirectly via one or more intermediaries, with or without modifications.

[733] Here, we use the term "user" broadly. A user could be a customer using a web application to produce a generation, a developer using an API to produce a generation in their own code, a developer using an API to produce a generation for a company, etc.

[734] Sometimes literally so. *See Experience the Future of Photoshop With Generative Fill*, ADOBE (July 27, 2023), https://helpx.adobe.com/photoshop/using/generative-fill.html.

images from Instagram, even though Instagram is not liable for hosting those images.[735] And this is also precisely the type of situation that indemnification of users could help address.

The main difficulty with this regime would be policing against systems designed specifically for infringement. Something like the *Grokster* rule, carefully followed, might suffice. The providers of a service that was geared to produce infringing outputs could be held liable. So could the deployers of a model that had been trained or fine-tuned to optimize its effectiveness specifically for infringing uses. So could the curator of a dataset that included only or primarily infringing works, or a dataset that was intentionally organized to meet the needs of a model known to be intentionally trained for infringement. At every stage, a party would be held responsible only for its own actions specifically directed towards increasing the use of a system for infringement, with no substantial noninfringing purpose.

3. Notice and Removal

Third, courts could treat generative-AI services as generally legal in themselves but require them to respond to knowledge of specific infringements under a *Napster*-like rule.[736] One plausible doctrinal route to this regime would be to treat infringing generations as creating direct liability for users and only indirect liability for service providers. Another would use fair use to shield service providers as long as they took reasonable overall precautions, including responding when they had sufficient knowledge of infringement. And a third would be to find liability but craft an injunction that only required services to act against infringement they were aware of.

Regardless of which of these doctrinal routes a court were to take, there would be an inevitable gravitational force pulling the provider's duties towards the duties of a service provider under section 512(c) or (d). This is not because Section 512 applies to generative-AI services. In many cases, it almost certainly does not.[737] Instead, the Section 512 doctrines may be a convergence point because courts have now had two decades of experience—which means two decades of precedents—with the Section 512 safe harbors. These precedents have come to set expectations—among copyright owners, in the technology industry, in the copyright bar, and in the judiciary—for what legally "responsible" behavior by an online intermediary looks like. A generative-AI service operator that does not appear to be making a good-faith effort to achieve something like this system

[735] *E.g.*, Sinclair v. Ziff Davis, LLC, 454 F. Supp. 3d 342 (S.D.N.Y. 2020).

[736] We are specifically talking about closed, hosted services here. Notice and removal of content related to an open-source model presents additional challenges. An open-source model developer can release new or changed models, but this does not recall or alter existing copies of prior models that already have been distributed to the public.

[737] *See supra* Part II.G.

may strike a court as intending to induce infringement, not making a good-faith effort to comply with an injunction, etc.

If courts do end up recreating a notice-and-takedown regime, they would likely settle on familiar elements: a way for copyright owners to give notice of infringement, block infringing generations on notice, block infringing generations on actual knowledge, block infringing generations on red-flag knowledge, avoid having a business model that directly ties income to infringement, and terminate the abilities of repeat infringers to continue making generations. These would probably not be notices directed to specific generations by named users, which would be difficult to detect and track. Instead, courts might require copyright owners to identify copyrighted works and then require that the generative-AI service operator prevent generations that are substantially similar to those works. Sometimes copyright owners might know which works to identify based on known generated outputs that are recognizably similar to suspected training-data inputs. But others might simply involve copyright owners handing over to service operators large catalogs of works to block, much as they currently do with ContentID on YouTube.

This is a very difficult technical problem. It would be much harder for a generative-AI system to implement than it is for a hosting platform to implement Section 512 compliance. The reason is that a notice directed to a hosting provider under Section 512(c) must include "Identification of the material that is claimed to be infringing . . . and information reasonably sufficient to permit the service provider to locate the material."[738] A valid notice is a roadmap; it tells the hosting provider exactly what to take down to comply. That material already exists, and the hosting provider can compare it to the copyrighted work to verify that they are substantially similar. But a notice to a generative-AI system is a notice against future generations, which may be different from each other and resemble the copyrighted work in different ways. Filtering for this kind of (potentially very) inexact match is much harder technically.

That said, matching material against a catalog of copyrighted works is a problem that has been very approximately solved by major social networks, which use perceptual hashing to prevent the upload of various kinds of identified content. Generative-AI companies could at least add similar perceptual-hash-driven filtering to the outputs of their models, but clearly this would only solve part of the problem.[739]

[738] 17 U.S.C. § 512(c)(3)(A)(iii).

[739] *See generally* Lee, Ippolito, Nystrom et al., *supra* note 431 (using hash-driven duplicate detection); Ippolito, Tramèr, Nasr et al., *supra* note 651 (discussing the drawbacks of exact-duplicate detection).

The challenges of implementing some analogue for removal for models[740] are even harder. A service can add filters on the input and output sides—monitoring prompts and scanning outputs. It can also fine-tune or align the model or provide it with a system prompt that instructs the model to respond in ways that reduce its propensity to infringe. But a model by itself does not implement these controls. The model cannot control how it is prompted or what the user does with the output.[741] The model cannot stop anyone from fine-tuning it in an attempt to remove its guardrails.[742] Further, there is no simple analogue for takedown in generative-AI models. It remains an active and unsolved area of research to figure out how to remove a particular training example's influence from a model's parameters.[743] Absent the ability to do so, the safest bet is to retrain the model from scratch. Due to the time and expense required to retrain a model, it will often be infeasible to retrain it simply to remove infringing works, and completely unworkable to retrain on each new notice.[744]

Courts could respond to this difficulty in one of two ways. If they have sympathy for model trainers, they could apply the *Sony* rule and hold that it is not infringement to distribute a trained model as a set of parameters (as Stability AI's releases have been). The fact that the model is used by others for infringing purposes would be counterbalanced by the substantial noninfringing uses, leading to immunity under *Sony*. This might not always be an attractive business model, because it might be hard for buyers to monetize these models and because of the ease of copying and further redistributing the models—but it could at least exist legally. And truly open-source models would generally be allowed.

But if courts had less sympathy for model trainers, they might hold that the difficulty of complying with removal notices is not an excuse. On this view, the model trainer chose to create a model that could be used for substantial infringement, and to hopelessly commingle infringing and noninfringing material. If so, then it would generally not be legal to distribute a model that was trained on unlicensed works and had infringing outputs, at least once those works they were based on were pointed out. (This would perhaps foreclose released models like those in Meta's Llama-model family.[745]) It would be legal to train a model, but the trainer would need to take care that the model was only deployed in a safe

[740] *See* Cooper, Choquette-Choo, Bogen, Jagielski, Filippova, Liu et al., *supra* note 405 (discussing the challenges and fundamental limitations of "machine unlearning" as a solution to this problem).

[741] *Id.*

[742] *See* Xiangyu Qi, Yi Zeng, Tinghao Xie et al., Fine-tuning Aligned Language Models Compromises Safety, Even When Users Do Not Intend To! (2023) (unpublished manuscript), https://arxiv.org/abs/2310.03693; Nasr, Rando, Carlini et al., *supra* note 404.

[743] *See, e.g.,* Meng, Bau, Andonian & Belinkov, *supra* note 476; Bourtoule, Chandrasekaran, Choquette-Choo et al., *supra* note 476.

[744] *See* Cooper, Choquette-Choo, Bogen, Jagielski, Filippova & Liu et al. *supra* note 405.

[745] *See supra* note 7 and accompanying text (discussing open-source models).

environment with sufficient guardrails to prevent infringement. (This is the approach generally taken by OpenAI, for example.[746])

In this world, open-source models would be extremely risky. As a result, there would likely be a split between two classes of models. Some proprietary models might train on unlicensed works and be deployed only in closed services with carefully designed guardrails. Open-source models would be trained only on public-domain and openly licensed works or be trained using very conservative methods to attempt ensure that extremely little copyrighted material was memorized.[747]

A notice-and-removal regime also has implications for training datasets. A dataset provider cannot pull back these works for which it receives a notice from others who have already used those works for training. But it can delete the works from the dataset it makes available to others going forward. (For an open-source dataset, or one that has been leaked, this second option may be futile, as others will still have copies of the dataset that they can share.[748]) Compared with a model, it is much easier to remove a work from a training dataset; one searches for the work and removes it. Indeed, one could use exact hashing rather than perceptual hashing and still get substantial efficacy in removing a large number of identified works from the dataset—or, for datasets compiled from web crawls or other sources, remove works by tracing their provenance through into the part of the dataset they have ended up in. This makes datasets comparatively more attractive as removal targets, both because they are upstream from many models and because it is easier to define and enforce enforceable removal obligations.[749]

4. Infringing Models

A fourth possibility is that courts would hold that some or all generative-AI services are illegal because the models themselves infringe. This outcome is an existential threat to many model trainers and service providers; it essentially makes their operations *per se* copyright infringement. It is also the outcome being sought by the class-action plaintiffs in high-profile lawsuits against OpenAI,

---

746 The sufficiency of OpenAI's guardrails is currently hotly contested, due to the frequency of successful adversarial behaviors and security attacks that are able to circumvent them. *See supra* Part II.E.2.c (for an example of a user circumventing mechanisms to prevent the generation of potentially copyright-infringing illustrations of Calvin and Hobbes). Nasr, Carlini, Hayase et al., *supra* note 7 (for an attack on ChatGPT that breaks alignment and gets the system to regurgitate training data at relatively enormous rates).

747 But this would still be insufficient to guarantee that possible model generations are not substantially similar to copyrighted expression. *See* Cooper, Choquette-Choo, Bogen, Jagielski, Filippova, Liu et al., *supra* note 405.

748 *See supra* note 739 and accompanying text (for a similar point with respect to released models).

749 *See* Cooper, Choquette-Choo, Bogen, Jagielski, Filippova, Liu et al., *supra* note 405.

Stability AI, Databricks Mosaic, and some of their partners. In this regime, the most important component of copyright law would quickly become licensing. Models could only be trained on data that had been licensed from the copyright owners, and the terms under which those models and their generations could be used would have to be negotiated as part of the licensing agreement. Each model would have a fully licensed training dataset, and the question of infringement would not arise except in cases where there were infringing works in the dataset itself or some other failure of quality control somewhere along the supply chain.

B. Lessons

Having discussed what courts and policymakers could do, we now consider what they should do. In keeping with our bottom line—*the generative-AI supply chain is too complicated to make sweeping rules prematurely*—we offer a few general observations about the overall shape of copyright and generative AI that courts and policymakers should keep in mind as they proceed.

1. Copyright Touches Every Part of the Generative-AI Supply Chain

Every stage from training data to alignment can make use of copyrighted works. Generative AI raises many other legal issues: Can a generative-AI system commit defamation?[750] Can a generative-AI system do legal work,[751] and should they be allowed to?[752] But these issues mainly have to do with the outputs of a generative-AI system. In contrast, copyright pervades every step of the process; copyright is present every time anyone anywhere in the supply chain makes a decision. Copyright cannot be ignored.[753]

---

[750] Eugene Volokh, *Large Libel Models? Liability for AI Output*, 3 J. FREE SPEECH L. 489 (2023); Jon Garon, *An AI's Picture Paints a Thousand Lies: Designating Responsibility for Visual Libel*, 3 J. FREE SPEECH L. 425 (2023); Nina Brown, *Bots Behaving Badly: A Products Liability Approach to Chatbot-Generated Defamation*, 3 J. FREE SPEECH L. 390 (2023); Derek Bambauer & Mihai Surdeanu, *Authorbots*, 3 J. FREE SPEECH L. 375 (2023); Peter Henderson, *Tatsunori Hashimoto, and Mark Lemley, Where's the Liability in Harmful AI Speech?*, 3 J. FREE SPEECH L. 589 (2023).

[751] Jonathan H. Choi, Kristen E. Hickman, Amy Monahan & Daniel Schwarcz, *ChatGPT Goes to Law School*, 2023 71 J. LEGAL EDUC. 387 (2022).

[752] Mata v. Avianca, No. 22-cv-1461 (S.D.N.Y. June 22, 2023).

[753] Copyright is not the only socially relevant concept that pervades the supply chain. The supply-chain framing illuminates other legal and ethical challenges as well, such as developer responsibility for harmful uses, *see, e.g.*, Cooper, Moss, Laufer & Nissenbaum supra note 120 (for ethical challenges and accountability); A. Feder Cooper, *Between Randomness and Arbitrariness: Some Lessons for Reliable Machine Learning at Scale* (Ph.D. dissertation, Cornell University 2024), https://arxiv.org/abs/2406.09548; David Gray Widder & Dawn Nafus, *Dislocated Accountabilities in the "AI Supply Chain": Modularity and Developers' Notions of Responsibility*, 10 BIG DATA & SOC'Y 1 (June 15,

2. Copyright *Concerns* Cannot Be Localized to a Single Link in the Supply Chain

We have argued, time and time again, that decisions made by one actor can affect the copyright liability of another, potentially far away actor in the supply chain. Whether an output looks like Snoopy or like a generic beagle depends on what images were collected in a dataset, which model architecture and training algorithms are used, how trained models are fine-tuned and aligned, how models are embedded in deployed services, what the user prompts with, etc. Every single one of these steps could be under the control of a different person, company, or organization.

3. Design Choices Matter

Every actor in the generative-AI supply chain is in a position to make choices that affect their copyright exposure, and others'. There are obvious choices about copyright, like whether to train on unlicensed data (which can affect downstream risks), and how to respond to notices that a system is producing infringing outputs (which can affect upstream risks). But subtler architectural choices matter, too. Different settings on a training algorithm can affect how much the resulting model will memorize specific works. Different deployment environments can affect whether users have enough control over a prompt to steer a system towards infringing outputs. Copyright law will necessarily have to engage with these choices—as will AI policy more generally.

4. Fair Use is Not a Silver Bullet

For a time, it seemed that training and using AI models would often constitute fair use. In such a world, AI development is generally a low-risk activity, at least from a copyright perspective. Yes, training datasets and models and systems may all include large quantities of copyrighted works—but they will never be shown to users. Generative AI scrambles this assumption. The serious possibility that some generations will infringe means that the fair-use analysis at every previous stage of the supply chain is up for grabs again.

5. Generative AI Does Not Make the Ordinary Business of Copyright Law Irrelevant

Courts will still need to make plenty of old-fashioned, retail judgments about individual works—e.g., how much does this generated image resemble Elsa and

---

2023); David Gray Widder & Richmond Wong, Thinking Upstream: Ethics and Policy Opportunities in AI Supply Chains (2023) (unpublished manuscript), https://arxiv.org/abs/2303.07529 (for the environmental and labor considerations involved in AI training).

Anna in particular, rather than generic tropes of fantasy princesses? To decide these cases, courts will need to avoid getting distracted by the shininess of new technologies and chasing after inappropriately categorical new rules. Similarity is similarity, proof of copying is proof of copying, transformation in content is transformation in content. Courts *must* leave themselves room to continue making these retail judgments on a case-by-case basis, responding to the specific facts before them, just as they always have. Perhaps, in the fullness of time, as society comes to understand what uses generative AI can be put to and with what consequences, it will reconsider the very fundamentals of copyright law. But until that day, we must live with the copyright system we have. And that system cannot function unless courts are able to say that some generative-AI systems and generations infringe, and others do not.

6. Analogies Can Be Misleading

There are plenty of analogies for generative AI ready to hand. A generative-AI model or system is like a search engine, or like a website, or like a library, or like an author, or like any number of other people and things that copyright has a well-developed framework for dealing with. These analogies are useful, but we wish to warn against treating any of them as definitive.[754] As we have seen, generative AI is and can consist of many things. It is also literally a generative technology: it can be put to an amazingly wide variety of uses.[755] And one of the things about generative technologies is that they cause convergence;[756] precisely because they can emulate many other technologies, they blur the boundaries between things that were formerly distinct. Generative AI can be like a search engine, and also like a website, a library, an author, and so on. Prematurely accepting one of these analogies to the exclusion of the others would mean ignoring numerous relevant similarities—precisely the opposite of what good analogical reasoning is supposed to do.

CONCLUSION

Our conclusion is simple. "Does generative AI infringe copyright?" is not a question that has a yes-or-no answer. There is currently no blanket rule that

---

[754] *See supra* notes 322, 323, 423 and accompanying text (for why generations are not like collages).

[755] JONATHAN ZITTRAIN, THE FUTURE OF THE INTERNET—AND HOW TO STOP IT (2008) (developing theory of generative technologies); Cooper, Lee, Grimmelmann, Ippolito et al., *supra* note 10 (connecting Zittrain's theory of generative technologies with generative AI); Cooper, Choquette-Choo, Bogen, Jagielski, Filippova, Liu et al., *supra* note 405 (for additional discussion of the same connection).

[756] *See generally* Tejas N. Narechania, *Convergence and a Case for Broadband Rate Regulation*, 37 BERKELEY TECH. L.J. 339 (2022) (discussing convergence caused by the Internet).

determines which participants in the generative-AI supply chain are copyright infringers. The underlying technologies and systems are too diverse to be treated identically, and copyright law has too many open decision points to provide clear answers. Our hope is that the supply-chain framing provides a clear and precise mechanism for understanding this diversity and, in turn, for reasoning about the various legal consequences.

Copyright is not the only, or the best, or the most important way of confronting the policy challenges that generative AI poses. But copyright is here, and it is asking good questions about how generative-AI systems are created, how they work, how they are used, and how they are updated. These questions deserve good answers, or failing that, the best answers our copyright system is equipped to give.

Collaborative Student Work

AI COPYRIGHT LITIGATION V. LICENSING: AN EXPLORATION

by LILY ARGYLE, TESS BRADLEY, JAMES DEARING, HALLIE FEINMAN, LAYLA GHIAI, GERADO GOMEZ, MARIE GOSSERAND, HOLLAND HANEY, JAMIKA MACK, MADDY MARLOWE, WHITNEY MCBAY, HALEY PETTINGILL, ISA REYES-KLEIN, NATHAN SCHWARTZ, JON EVAN SMELLEY, NATALIA WALCOTT and TYNESEA WATTS

This report seeks to understand the current state of litigation and licensing related to copyright cases related to artificial intelligence. Conducted as a classroom exercise at Tulane Law School, we thought others might find it useful as well. In short, there's a lot going on, and keeping up can be challenging.

INTRODUCTION 411
I. HOW MANY AI COPYRIGHT CASES ARE THERE? 412
II. WHO ARE THE AI COMPANIES BEING SUED? 414
A. OpenAI 414
B. Stability A 418
D. GitHub 421
E. NVIDIA Corporation 422
F. Microsoft 423
G. Google 424
H. Bloomberg 425
I. Databricks and Mosaic ML 426
J. ROSS Intelligence (ROSS) 427
K. Perplexity 428
L. AI voice generators 428
III. THE AI COPYRIGHT CASES THEMSELVES:: SOME SUMMARIES 429
A. Alter v. OpenAI Inc. 429
B. Andersen v. Stability AI 431
C. Concord Music Group. 437
D. Doe v. GitHub, Inc. 439
E. Getty Images (US) v. Stability AI., Inc. 442
F. In re Google Generative AI Copyright Litig., (Consolidated Class Action Complaint). 445
G. Huckabee v. Bloomberg 449
H. The Intercept Media and Raw Story Media v. OpenAI 451
I. Kadrey v. Meta Platforms, Inc. 453
J. Nazemian and Dubus v. NVIDIA Corporation. 455
K. The Newspaper Cases against Microsoft 455
L. OpenAI ChatGPT Litigation 457

M. Thomson Reuters v. ROSS. 461
N. Voice Cases 463
IV. SECONDARY SOURCES RELATED TO THE CASES 464
V. LICENSING IN THE SHADOW OF LAWSUITS *467*
A. Licensing Deals 467
B. A New Lawsuit: Advance Local Media v. Cohere 469
VI. SUMMARY JUDGEMENT IN THOMSON REUTERS V. ROSS ... *470*
A. Introduction 470
B. Direct Copyright Infringement 472
C. Fair Use 473
CONCLUSION? 474

INTRODUCTION

On November 30, 2022, we were introduced to ChatGPT.1 By 2023, we had not only OpenAI, but many other companies producing AI tools; with this major industry boom came a slew of lawsuits.2 However, what was unconventional was the slew of licensing deals between AI companies and media outlets/companies.[3] Then, on February 11, 2025, we got the first summary judgment related to copyright infringement and unauthorized use of materials; in this case, a non-generative system using Thomson Reuters' Westlaw headnotes without authorization in a competing product.[4] The world is moving both at a slow pace (litigation) and fast (licensing). And it's hard to keep up and digest the many moving parts.

This summary reviews the state of AI cases and licensing as of February 2025.[5] Part I asks the question of how many AI copyright cases are there and explains why there is not quite a straightforward answer. Then, Part II looks at who are some of the defendants in the cases. We see certain companies being sued by multiple plaintiffs, and we are trying to get a sense of what's going on. Part III then turns to the cases themselves. We will try to give you a summary of

---

[1] *Introducing ChatGPT*, OPENAI (Nov. 30, 2022), https://openai.com/index/chatgpt/.

[2] Tremblay v. OpenAI, Inc., 716 F. Supp. 3d 772 (N.D. Cal. 2024).

[3] *See, e.g., Authors Guild Partners with Created by Humans to Empower Authors in the AI Era*, THE AUTHORS GUILD: PRESS RELEASES (Oct. 9, 2024), https://authorsguild.org/news/ag-partners-with-created-by-humans-to-empower-authors-in-ai-era/ (Working to streamline licensing, Created by Humans is a "pioneering platform that enables authors to license their work to AI developers" This new partnership attempts to "help protect and promote authors' rights.").

[4] Thomson Reuters v. ROSS, 694 F. Supp. 3d 467 (D. Del. 2023).

[5] This review was conducted by the students in the Advanced Copyright and Trademark Course at Tulane Law School, under the guidance of Dr. Elizabeth Townsend Gard. Each student is credited with the case/section they worked on. We created this collaborative document as a learning experience, and wanted to share what we found. All errors or omissions are the responsibility of the law students and Dr. Townsend Gard, and we apologize for errors and omissions. Please contact Dr. Townsend Gard at townsend@tulane.edu for any necessary revisions or edits.

some of the cases so far. Part IV then looks at a sample of secondary sources – news stories and law review articles and gives a sample of how people are approaching the question. Part V looks at the recent summary judgement in *Thomson v. ROSS*, the first AI copyright case filed, and decided on February 11, 2025. Although not a generative AI case, could the approach of this district court give us insight or help other cases with their strategies going forward? Part VI looks at the rise of licensing deals in 2024. Part VII does a quick summing up and speculation as of February 2025.

I. HOW MANY AI COPYRIGHT CASES ARE THERE?[6]

As we begin this piece, we see different numbers reported. There's no definitive list. In part, due to the high number of repeat defendants, these AI copyright cases keep getting consolidated. For example, in December 2024, OpenAI sought consolidation of eight ongoing copyright lawsuits against them.[7] Taking that into account, the numbers do vary quite a bit.

In this section, we are providing resources for you to track the cases, and we have found that viewing a number of sources proves helpful in the numbers anomaly. A number of resources are tracking the cases as they work their way through the courts. Some resources only concentrate on a handful of cases, focusing on what their potential effect on copyright might be.[5] Other resources are simply tracking AI cases, regardless of whether they are consolidated or not. Some are doing more sophisticated summaries.

Let's take the month of December 2024. Copyright Alliance reports well over 30 cases have been filed.[8] Wired reports 27 AI copyright cases. [9] The law firm, Ropes and Gray, reports 15 *notable* cases.[10] On the other hand, Tech Policy reports only 13 *notable* cases. [11] Let's look at and compare how some resources

[6] Authored by Tess Bradley, Tulane Law School, J.D. expected May 2025.

[7] Annelise Levy, *OpenAI Seeks to Centralize Copyright Lawsuits Against It*, BLOOMBERG LAW (Dec. 5, 2024), https://news.bloomberglaw.com/ip-law/openai-to-seek-to-centralize-eight-copyright-lawsuits-against-it.

[8] Keith Kupferschmeid, *Insights from Court Orders in AI Copyright Infringement Cases*, COPYRIGHT ALLIANCE (Dec. 12, 2024), https://copyrightalliance.org/ai-copyright-infringement-cases-insights/#1note.

[9] Kate Knibbs, *Every AI Copyright Lawsuit in the U.S., Visualized*, WIRED: BUSINESS (Dec. 19, 2024), https://www.wired.com/story/ai-copyright-case-tracker/.

[10] David M. McIntosh et al., *An End-of-the-Year Update to the Current State of AI Copyright Litigation*, ROPES & GRAY (Dec. 17, 2024), https://www.ropesgray.com/en/insights/alerts/2024/12/an-end-of-year-update-to-the-current-state-of-ai-related-copyright-litigation.

[11] Bruce Barcott, *AI Lawsuits Worth Watching: A Curated Guide*, TECH POLICY PRESS (July 1, 2024), https://www.techpolicy.press/ai-lawsuits-worth-watching-a-curated-guide/.

are tracking the cases. We also see most lists are only tracking cases in the U.S.[12] So, where might one go to keep track of what's going on? Let's look at a couple of resources.

- **George Washington University:** GW has created a database of existing legislation related to AI and machine learning.[13] This searchable database includes more than *just* copyright cases but is a recommended database when researching AI litigation. This is an example of a university effort to track the cases.

- **BakerHostetler**: They have an up-to-date Copyright and AI tracker, overseen by Theresa M Weisenberger.[14] This tracker allows the user to navigate new developments in AI copyright cases, as BakerHostetler monitors any status updates or key findings. This source is a wonderful option for those who do not know much about the impending litigation, as this case tracker includes case overviews and summaries of the key findings for any updates with each case. We found ourselves using this resource over and over to create this document.

- **Copyright Alliance:** This source has a section devoted to AI and Copyright.[15] They keep a table of the cases: where they are filed, the subject matter, and the date filed.[16] Each case then has a link to PacerMonitor. You can sign up for alerts from them, which keeps you up-to-date not only on the state of the cases but relevant AI news. They have also published a position paper on AI. Additionally, they have links to the positions their members have taken. This example of a non-profit advocacy group tracking the cases is a great source for those who want to delve into the conversations surrounding these major AI cases.

- **Wired Magazine:** This source tracks the cases, including a graphic of who is suing who.[17] They also list the status of the case. An example of a news organization tracking these cases, this site is easily digestible to

---

[12] *See, e.g.*, Aditya Kalra et al., *OpenAI faces new copyright case, from global book publishers in India*, REUTERS (Jan. 24, 2025), https://www.reuters.com/technology/artificial-intelligence/openai-faces-new-copyright-case-global-publishers-india-2025-01-24.

[13] *DAIL - The Database of AI Litigation*, THE GEORGE WASHINGTON UNIVERSITY: ETHICAL TECH INITIATIVE, https://blogs.gwu.edu/law-eti/ai-litigation-database/ (last visited Feb. 11, 2025).

[14] *Case Tracker: Artificial Intelligence, Copyrights and Class Actions*, BAKERHOSTELTER, https://www.bakerlaw.com/services/artificial-intelligence-ai/case-tracker-artificial-intelligence-copyrights-and-class-actions/ (last visited Feb. 11, 2025).

[15] Artificial Intelligence *(AI) and Copyright,* COPYRIGHT ALLIANCE, https://copyrightalliance.org/education/artificial-intelligence-copyright/ (last visited March 1, 2025).

[16] *Id.*

[17] Kate Knibbs, *Every AI Copyright Lawsuit in the US, Visualized*, Wired Magazine, (Dec. 19, 2024), https://www.wired.com/story/ai-copyright-case-tracker/.

the layperson. The inclusion of a visual case update section makes this source easily navigable.

- **McKool Smith**: Another law firm case tracker, this source solely focuses on updates on pending AI cases.[18] Instead of categorizing cases or cultivating a list of the most notable ones, this source follows major case developments through quick, weekly updates. This is a great source for anyone well-versed in current AI litigation but desires a site for consistent updates.

II. WHO ARE THE AI COMPANIES BEING SUED?[19]

We often see the same names as defendants. Who are they? How are they different? We have arranged the list in no particular order, but we did start with OpenAI, who continues to be at the center of the AI issues.

A. OpenAI

OpenAI was founded in December 2015 after Sam Altman approached Elon Musk to discuss the potential dangers of artificial general intelligence ("AGI").[20] They then assembled a group of entrepreneurs and researchers in the technology field - including Greg Brockman, Ilya Sutskever, Trevor Blackwell, Vicki Cheung, Andrej Karpathy, Durk Kingma, John Schulman, Pamela Vagata, and Wojciech Zaremba - to start the non-profit AI research organization headquartered in San Francisco, California.[21]

OpenAI's charter states that their "mission is to ensure that artificial general intelligence – by which we mean highly autonomous systems that outperform humans at most economically value work–benefits all of humanity. We will

[18] *AI Litigation Tracker,* McKOOL SMITH, https://www.mckoolsmith.com/newsroom-ailitigation (last visited March 1, 2025).

[19] Haley Pettingill, Tulane Law School, J.D., expected May 2025, and James Dearing, J.D., expected May 2025.

[20] AGI is a hypothetical artificial machine intelligence that could theoretically achieve human-level perception and cognition at inhuman speeds without biological constraints. Tim Mucci & Cole Stryker, *Getting Ready for Artificial Intelligence with Examples*, IBM.COM (Apr. 18, 2024), https://www.ibm.com/think/topics/artificial-general-intelligence-examples.

[21] Greg Brockman et. al. *Introducing OpenAI*, OPENAI.COM (Dec 11, 2015), https://openai.com/index/introducing-openai/. Due to possible conflicts of interest with Tesla's AI development and a fundamental disagreement on how the company should be operated, Elon Musk left in 2018. However, in February 2025, Musk made a $97 billion bid for the company, which has been denied. Keach Hagey, et. al., *The Inside Story of How Altman and Musk Went From Friends to Bitter Enemies*, Wall Street Journal (Feb. 14, 2025), https://www.wsj.com/tech/elon-musk-sam-altman-relationship-6889a77a.

attempt to directly build safe and beneficial AGI but will also consider our mission fulfilled if our work aids others to achieve this outcome."[22] The charter goes on to expound on the companies' four principles:

- broadly distributed benefits, with a "primary fiduciary duty…to humanity," explaining "We anticipate needing to marshal substantial resources to fulfill our mission, but will always diligently act to minimize conflicts of interest among our employees and stakeholders that could compromise broad benefit;"
- long-term safety, suggesting that for the sake of safety, if necessary they would "stop competing with and start assisting" with other projects that are "value-aligned" and "safety-conscious;"
- technical leadership, including being on the cutting edge of AI; and
- cooperative orientation with other research and policy institutions, including publishing their research, but "we expect that safety and security concerns will reduce or traditional publishing in the future…"[23]

Despite OpenAI's founding principles of openness, building safe AGI, and working for the good of the world, the company established a for-profit arm that would build outside capital through shareholders.[24] In 2019, Microsoft made a $1 billion investment in OpenAI (for the sole right to license OpenAI's technology for future products), which funded the company's expensive computing power.[25] This allowed OpenAI to develop numerous AI models, such as DALL-E, a generator that makes original works of art from text descriptions; Codex[26], a model that can understand and write code, and also to launch ChatGPT in 2022.[27]

ChatGPT is an AI chatbot that generates human-like dialogue from user questions (i.e., what is there to do in Akron, Ohio?) or commands (i.e., summarize this paragraph).[28] Deep learning models, such as ChatGPT, require existing training data to produce responses that replicate human cognition.[29] OpenAI states that while ChatGPT is not connected to the Internet, it was "trained on vast

[22]OpenAI Charter, https://openai.com/charter/, (last visited Feb. 13, 2025).
[23] *Id.*
[24] *Artificial: Episode 2, Selling Out*, THE JOURNAL, https://www.wsj.com/podcasts/the-journal/artificial-episode-2-selling-out/239740ec-071f-4493-96cb-91a6080e60ce (Dec. 10 2023) [hereinafter Episode 2].
[25] *Artificial: Episode 3, ChatGPT*, THE JOURNAL, https://www.wsj.com/podcasts/the-journal/artificial-episode-3-chatgpt/835fdc63-75ff-4ef1-b18c-f40537807cfe (Jan. 7 2024) [hereinafter Episode 3].
[26] Codex is most notable because it powers GitHub's AI tool Copilot. Karl Montevirgen, *OpenAI*, BRITANNICA MONEY (Feb. 11, 2025), https://www.britannica.com/money/OpenAI.
[27] *Id.*
[28] Episode 2, *supra* note 24.
[29] *Id.*

amounts of data from the internet written by humans."[30] OpenAI also operates with a "closed-source" system, meaning their codes, models, data sets, and algorithms are kept secret.[31] So, people began questioning where this training data came from and if OpenAI had the right to use it.[32] In 2023, OpenAI admitted to British Parliament that it would be "impossible" to train its AI without copyrighted material because "copyright today covers virtually every sort of human expression," and they argued that limiting the training data to public domain works "would not provide AI systems that meet the needs of today's citizens."[33] OpenAI maintains that it complies with the requirements of all applicable laws, including copyright laws, and that copyright law does not forbid its training.[34]

Between 2023 and 2024, OpenAI faced multiple lawsuits from the Authors Guild, media outlets, and independent authors and journalists whose work was allegedly used to train some of its products.[35] To combat these copyright infringement claims and the accompanying public scrutiny, OpenAI has pursued licensing deals with media companies and news organizations.[36] OpenAI has reportedly agreed to pay the most prominent publishers upwards of $10 million annually.[37] These partnerships allow OpenAI to train its language models on the publications' content (including paywalled information).[38] Publishers will get acknowledgment for their work through citations given by the chatbot and access

---

[30] *What is ChatGPT?*, OpenAI, https://help.openai.com/en/articles/6783457-what-is-chatgpt, (last visited Feb. 13, 2025).

[31] Rhiannon Williams & James O'Donnell, *We Finally Have a Definition for Open-Source AI*, MIT TECH. REVIEW (Aug. 22, 2024), https://www.technologyreview.com/2024/08/22/1097224/we-finally-have-a-definition-for-open-source-ai/.

[32] *Id.*

[33] OpenAI—Written Evidence: Hearing Before the House of Lords Communications and Digital Select Comm. Inquiry on Large language Models, LLM0113 (2023).

[34] *Id.*

[35] As of December 2024, 18 lawsuits have been filed involving OpenAI and its subsidiaries. According to Jonathan Gilham of Originality.ai these include: Canadian News Outlets v. OpenAI; Elon Musk v. Samuel Altman; Daily News LP v. Microsoft Corp.; The Intercept Media v. OpenAI, Raw Story Media, Inc. and Alternet Media Inc. v. OpenAI; The New York Times Co. v. OpenAI Inc.; Sancton v. OpenAI Inc.; Authors Guild v. OpenAI Inc.; Chabon v. OpenAI Inc; OpenAI Inc. v. Open Artificial Intelligence, Inc.; Doe 3 v. GitHub, Inc.; DOE 1 v. GitHub Inc., T. v. OpenAI LP; Walters v. OpenAI LLC; Silverman v. OpenAI Inc.; Tremblay v. OpenAI Inc; PM v. OpenAI LP.

[36] *OpenAI Licensing Deals with Legal Challenges While Securing Lucrative Agreements with Media Giants for AI Chatbot*, HYSCALER, (Jan. 12, 2024), https://hyscaler.com/insights/openai-licensing-deals-media-giants-ai/.

[37] Ivy Liu, *2024 In Review: A Timeline of The Major Deals Between Publishers and AI Companies*, DIGIDAY.COM (Dec. 27, 2024), https://digiday.com/media/2024-in-review-a-timeline-of-the-major-deals-between-publishers-and-ai-companies/.

[38] *Id.*

to the technology so they can build their own AI products and features.[39] While some news organizations are suing OpenAI, others are still weighing their legal options before entering negotiations, but as of January 2025, at least 14 have signed deals with OpenAI, including *Le Monde, Prisa, Financial Times,* Associated Press, Shutterstock, *The Atlantic,* News Corp., Condé Nast and Hearst.[40]

As of December 2024, there are 18 lawsuits involving OpenAI.[41] According to Jonathan Gilham of Originality.ai, the lawsuits include: *Canadian News Outlets v. OpenAI,*[42] *Elon Musk v. Samuel Altman, Gregory Brockman, and OpenAI,*[43] *Daily News Lp Et Al V. Microsoft Corporation,*[44] *The Intercept Media v. OpenAI and Microsoft,*[45] *Raw Story Media, Inc. and Alternet Media Inc. v. OpenAI,*[46] *The New York Times Company v. Openai Inc.,*[47] *Sancton v. OpenAI Inc.,*[48] *Authors Guild et al v. OpenAI Inc. et al,*[49] *Chabon v. OpenAI, Inc,*[50] *OpenAI, Inc. v. Open Artificial Intelligence, Inc.,*[51] *Doe 3 et al v. GitHub, Inc. et al,*[52] *DOE 1 et al v. GitHub, Inc. et a*l,[53] *T. et al v. OpenAI LP et al,*[54] *Walters v. OpenAI LLC,*[55] *Silverman, et al v. OpenAI Inc.,*[56] *Tremblay v. OpenAI Inc,*[57] and *PM et al v. OpenAI LP et al.*[58]

---

[39] *Id.*

[40]Charlotte Tobitt, *Who's Suing AI and Who's Signing: Major Deals with Google, OpenAI and Mistral Start Year,* PRESSGAZETTE.CO (Feb. 12, 2025), https://pressgazette.co.uk/platforms/news-publisher-ai-deals-lawsuits-openai-google/.

[41]A Jonathan Gilham, "OpenAI and ChatGPT Lawsuit List," Originality.ai, December 17, 2024. This ist is expected bo be updated by the author.

[42] Canadian News Media Co. v. OpenAI, Inc., No. CV-24-00732231 (Ont. Super. Ct. Just. Nov. 29, 2024).

[43] Musk v. Altman, No. 3:24-cv-04722 (N.D.Cal. Aug. 5, 2024).

[44] Daily News LP v. Microsoft Corp, No. 1:24-cv-03285 (S.D.N.Y. Apr. 30, 2024).

[45] The Intercept Media and Raw Story Media v. OpenAI, No. 1:24-cv-01515, (S.D.N.Y. Feb. 28, 2024).

[46] Raw Story Media, Inc. v. OpenAI, Inc., No. 1:24-cv-01514 (S.D.N.Y. Feb. 28, 2024).

[47] The N.Y. Times Co. v. Microsoft Corp., No. 1:23-cv-11195 (S.D.N.Y. Dec. 27, 2023).

[48] Sancton v. OpenAI, Inc., No. 1:23-cv-10211 (S.D.N.Y. Nov. 21, 2023).

[49] Authors Guild v. OpenAI Inc., No. 1:23-cv-08292 (S.D.N.Y. Sept. 19, 2023).

[50] Chabon v. OpenAI, Inc., No. 3:23-cv-04625 (N.D. Cal. Sept. 8, 2023).

[51] OpenAI, Inc. v. Open Artificial Intelligence, Inc., No. 4:23-cv-03918-YGR (9th Cir. Nov. 13, 2024).

[52] Doe 3 v. GitHub, Inc., No. 4:22-cv-07074 (N.D. Cal. Nov. 10, 2022).

[53] Doe 1 v. GitHub, Inc., No. 22-cv-06823-JST, 2024 WL 235217 (N.D. Cal. Nov. 3, 2022).

[54] T et al. v. Open LP, No. 3:23-cv-04557 (N.D. Cal. Sept. 5, 2023).

[55] Walters v. OpenAI, L.L.C., No. 1:23-cv-03122 (N.D. Ga. July 14, 2023).

[56] Silverman v. OpenAI, Inc., No. 3:23-cv-03416 (N.D. Cal. July 7, 2023).

[57] Tremblay v. OpenAI, Inc., 716 F. Supp. 3d 772 (N.D. Cal. 2024).

[58] PM v. OpenAI LP, No. 3:23-cv-03119 (N.D. Cal. June 28, 2023).

B. Stability AI

Emad Mostaque founded Stability AI in 2019 as a counter to the monopoly influence of big tech in the AI field.[59] The UK-based company develops open-source generative AI models[60], in contrast to OpenAI, Anthropic and Google's closed-source AI models.[61] With open-source models, researchers can study how the system works and users can "modify the system for any purpose—including to change its output—and [...] share it with others to use, with or without modifications."[62]

In 2022, Stability AI co-released its flagship product, Stable Diffusion, alongside researchers at LMU Munich and Runway AI.[63] Stable Diffusion produces "unique photorealistic images, [videos, and animations] from text and image prompts."[64] Stable Diffusion's user-friendly software saw considerable success with 150 million total downloads and 10 million users daily.[65] This boom allowed Stability AI to reach a $1 billion valuation just days after the product launched.[66] However, under Mostaques guidance, the once-promising startup had a hard time managing funds and attracting investors.[67] His idealistic views on how Stability AI would benefit humanity, such as "building bespoke AI models for nation states," proved to be impracticable.[68]

By early 2024, Stability AI cut 10% of its staff, and investors were furious with the mismanagement of operation expenses.[69] So, Mostaque resigned, and a new executive board was appointed with Prem Akkaraju as CEO and Sean Parker as Executive Chairman.[70] Under their leadership, the company has begun

---

[59] John E. Dunn, *Stability.ai Gets New CEO and Investment Dream Team to Start Rescue Rission*, CIO.com (Jun. 26, 2024), https://www.cio.com/article/2505518/stability-ai-gets-new-ceo-and-investment-dream-team-to-start-rescue-mission.html.

[60] Generative AI models create new and original data sets, like text, images or audio from user inputs. Altexsoft, *Generative AI Models Explained*, ALTEXSOFT (Sep. 4, 2024), https://www.altexsoft.com/blog/generative-ai/.

[61] Kenrick Cai & Iain Martin, How Stability AI's Founder Tanked His Billion-Dollar Startup, FORBES (Mar. 29, 2024), https://www.forbes.com/sites/kenrickcai/2024/03/29/how-stability-ais-founder-tanked-his-billion-dollar-startup/.

[62] Williams & O'Donnell, *supra* note 31.

[63] Stability.ai, *Celebrating One Year(ish) of Stable Diffusion ... and What a Year Itt's Been!*, STABILITY.AI (Oct. 3, 2023), https://stability.ai/news/celebrating-one-year-of-stable-diffusion.

[64] *What is Stable Diffusion*, AWS, https://aws.amazon.com/what-is/stable-diffusion/.

[65] Cai & Martin, *supra* note 61.

[66] Cai & Martin, *supra* note 61

[67] *Id.*

[68] *Id.*

[69] *Id.*

[70] *Id.*; STABILITY.AI, *supra* note 61.

restructuring efforts and attracted new investors[71] who have raised $80 million in funding.[72] The current increase in resources, signals a renewed confidence in Stability AI.[73] Further, the company's latest version of Stable Diffusion surpassed 2 million downloads during its first month of release in June 2024.[74] However, there are two U.S. lawsuits brought in 2023.[75]

A group of artists filed a class action lawsuit against Stability AI alleging that Stable Diffusion used their works as training images, and as a result it could "produce output images 'in the style' of those images."[76] Similarly, Getty Images filed a complaint asserting that Stability AI has not only copied more than 12 million photographs from the company, but that they "removed or altered Getty Images copyright management information, provided false copyright management information, and infringed Getty Images' famous trademarks."[77] Getty Images is seeking up to $150,000 for each infringed work, which could amount to $1.8 trillion.[78] Despite their legal battles, Stability AI's leaders continue to be committed to the company's founding principles, including making AI technology accessible to all.[79]

C. *Anthropic PBC*

Several former OpenAI employee's left the company after their partnership with Microsoft, and founded Anthropic PBC in 2021.[80] Anthropic is classed as a "public-benefit-company" – a corporation that makes a profit, but only by working on something that benefits humanity.[81] Since AI will have a significant impact on the world, Anthropic states that it is "dedicated to building systems that people can rely on and generating research about the opportunities and risks of

---

[71] Investors to include Greycroft, Coatue Management, Sound Ventures, Lightspeed Venture Partners, Sean Parker, Eric Schmidt and Prem Akkaraju. Kavout, *Stability AI's New Leadership and Funding: What it Means for the AI Startup*, KAVOUT SECTOR INSIGHTS (June 25, 2024), https://www.kavout.com/market-lens/stability-ais-new-leadership-and-funding-what-it-means-for-the-ai-startup.

[72] *Id.*

[73] *Id.*

[74] STABILITY.AI, *supra* note 63.

[75] *Andersen v. Stability AI Ltd.*, No. 23-cv-00201-WHO, 2024 U.S. Dist. LEXIS 143204 (N.D. Cal. Aug. 12, 2024); *Getty Images (US), Inc. v. Stability AI, Inc.*, 1:23-cv-00135-JLH; *see also* Cai & Martin, *supra* note 46.

[76] Anderson, *supra* note 59 at *3.

[77] Second Amended Complaint at 1, *Getty Images (US), Inc. v. Stability AI, Inc.*, 1:23-cv-00135-JLH.

[78] *Id.*

[79] Stability.ai, *supra* note 49.

[80] Andrew Andreev, *Anthropic PBC: History, Development, Products and Prospects,* API DRIVE: BLOG (Oct. 19, 2023), https://apix-drive.com/en/blog/useful/anthropic-pbc-history-development-products.

[81] Aaron Drapkin, *What is ClaudeAI and Anthropic? A Closer Look at ChatGPT's Rival*, TECH.CO (Jan. 2, 2024), https://tech.co/news/what-is-claude-ai-anthropic.

AI."[82] Although the founders of Anthropic left OpenAI because they feared Microsoft's contributions would make AI products too commercialized, they have agreed to partnerships with Google and Amazon.[83] Google's past deal with the company included a $2 billion investment, a 10% ownership in the company, and a large cloud contact between the two corporations. In January 2025, Google agreed to another $1 billion investment into the startup.[84] In 2024, Amazon increased its investments into the company to $4 billion, and Anthropic agreed to make Amazon Web Services ("AWS") its "primary cloud and training partner."[85]

With these large investments, Anthropic launched Claude, an AI assistant chatbot.[86] Like other chatbots, including ChatGPT, Claude relies on a reinforcement learning model to train its responses.[87] However, in an effort to reduce the undesired and harmful outputs of AI, Anthropic developed a new technique for AI called "Constitutional AI."[88] This method requires a developer to implement a set of principles and values (the "Constitution") which then creates the framework that the AI model must follow.[89] Instead of relying on an immense amount of human oversight to identify harmful outputs, Constitutional AI "encourages these models to evaluate their own outputs and refine themselves based on a predefined set of user-determined principles."[90]

Despite implementing extensive safety training for its AI software, Anthropic is still the subject of two copyright infringement lawsuits.[91] In order to replicate human-like cognition, Claude was trained, like all other AI chatbots, on vast amounts of data copied from the internet, including lyrics from innumerable musical works.[92] However, eight music publishers allege that Claude was not only improperly trained with their copyrighted song lyrics, but that Claude reproduced these song lyrics, without licensing, when prompted by users and for the

---

[82] *Company Homepage*, ANTHROPIC, https://www.anthropic.com/company (last visited Feb. 11, 2025).
[83] Hayden Field, *Google Agrees to New $1 Billion Investment in Anthropic*, CNBC (Jan. 22, 2025), https://www.cnbc.com/2025/01/22/google-agrees-to-new-1-billion-investment-in-anthropic.html.
[84] *Id.*
[85] *Id.*
[86] Drapkin, *supra* note 54.
[87] Riley Goodside & Spencer Papay, *Meet Claude: Anthropic's Rival to ChatGPT*, SCALE (Jan. 17, 2023), https://scale.com/blog/chatgpt-vs-claude.
[88] *Constitutional AI Explained,* TOLOKA (Apr. 19, 2024), https://toloka.ai/blog/constitutional-ai-explained/.
[89] *Id.*
[90] Neil Sahota, *Constitutional AI: Making AI Systems Uphold Human Values*, NEIL SAHOTA (Aug. 5, 2024), https://www.neilsahota.com/constitutional-ai-making-ai-systems-uphold-human-values/.
[91] Concord Music Grp., Inc. v. Anthropic PBC, 738 F. Supp. 3d 973 (M.D. Tenn. 2024); Andrea Bartz, et al. v. Anthropic PBC, No. 24-cv-05417, (N.D. Cal. 2024).
[92] *See generally Concord Music*, *supra* note 89.

commercial benefit of Anthropic.[93] Although Anthropic already had guardrails in place to make sure Claude did not informatively answer dangerous queries, (e.g., those "involving the production of chemical weapons,")[94] it has introduced more since the filing of the lawsuit.[95] In December 2024, Anthropic agreed to maintain its existing guardrails and to apply them against Claude reproducing the publisher's protected lyrics. In August 2024, a group of authors filed a similar class-action lawsuit alleging that Anthropic illegally downloaded, copied and generally misused their works to train Claude.[96]

D. *GitHub*

In 2008, GitHub was launched as an online, cloud-based collaboration website for software developers to share code, have a backup, and work on projects together.[97] The site acts as a Git server, which is an open-source version control[98] system.[99] Essentially, GitHub allows programmers to keep track of the changes to their code database, and co-programmers have access to this code and its history on their computers.[100] Further, the "version control system" allows developers to make changes to one aspect of a code, without compromising the main source code, and they can merge those changes into the finalized code database.[101] GitHub also offers a user-friendly interface that allows novices to use Git.[102] Almost every major software company, including Microsoft, Google, Twitter and Facebook, hosts their open source projects on GitHub.[103] In 2018, Microsoft acquired GitHub for $7.5 billion.[104] However, GitHub continues to operate as an independent entity, and still provides a platform for all levels of developers.[105]

---

[93] *Id.*

[94] *Constitutional Classifiers: Defending Against Universal Jailbreaks*, ANTHROPIC, (Feb. 3, 2025), https://www.anthropic.com/research/constitutional-classifiers.

[95] Blake Brittain, *Anthropic Reaches Deal on AI 'Guardrails' in Lawsuit Over Music Lyrics*, REUTERS (Jan. 3, 2025), https://www.reuters.com/legal/litigation/anthropic-reaches-deal-ai-guardrails-lawsuit-over-music-lyrics-2025-01-03/.

[96] Compl., Andrea Bartz, et al. v. Anthropic PBC, No. 24-cv-05417, (N.D. Cal. 2024).

[97] Jamie Juviler, *What is GitHub? (And What is it Used For?)*, HUBSPOT (Apr. 1, 2024), https://blog.hubspot.com/website/what-is-github-used-for.

[98] Most people have used some form of version control. For example, "Google Docs has a "Version History" tool where you can view changes to the document at different points in time." *Id.*

[99] *What is GitHub? A Beginner's Introduction to GitHub*, KINSTA (Nov. 17, 2023), https://kinsta.com/knowledgebase/what-is-github/.

[100] *Id.*

[101] *Id.*

[102] *Id.*

[103] Saurabh Mhatre, *The untold story of GitHub*, MEDIUM (Oct. 24, 2016), https://saurabhnativeblog.medium.com/the-untold-story-of-github-132840f72f56.

[104] *Microsoft to acquire Github for $7.5 Billion*, MICROSOFT NEWS CENTER (June 4, 2018), https://news.microsoft.com/2018/06/04/microsoft-to-acquire-github-for-7-5-billion/.

[105] *Id.*

Following the trend of integrating AI assistants into websites, GitHub introduced "Copilot" in 2021.[106] Copilot is an AI code-generator that suggests "lines of codes to programmers directly into their code editor."[107] According to GitHub, "Copilot has been trained on billions of lines of publicly-available code."[108] This caused concerns that GitHub might be reproducing line-by-line code from programmers who have open-source licenses on their platform.[109] So, in 2023, a class-action lawsuit for copyright infringement was filed against GitHub and Microsoft.[110] Github appears to be involved in only one lawsuit.[111]

E. NVIDIA Corporation

Founded in 1993, NVIDIA specializes in producing graphics processing units (GPUs).[112] These are computer chips that "render graphics and images by performing rapid mathematical calculations."[113] Since GPUs are better at rendering images than traditional computer chips, they were originally associated with the video and computer game sector.[114] However, NVIDIA has since become the leading supplier of AI hardware and software because GPUs can perform the calculations concurrently – "making them more energy efficient and better able to handle sophisticated computing demands."[115] This efficient processing power is necessary for generative AI models, such as ChatGPT, which require thousands of GPUs to run.[116] Although other chip competitors, such as Intel, AMD and

---

106 *Judge Throws Out Majority of Claims in GitHub Copilot Lawsuit*, LEGAL.IO (July 11, 2024), https://www.legal.io/articles/5516216/Judge-Throws-Out-Majority-of-Claims-in-GitHub-Copilot-Lawsuit.

107 *Id.*

108 *GitHub and Copilot Intellectual Property Litigation*, JOSEPH SAVERI LAW FIRM, https://www.saverilawfirm.com/our-cases/github-copilot-intellectual-property-litigation (last visited Feb. 16, 2025).

109 LEGAL.IO, *supra* note 106.

110 *Id.*

111 Doe v. GitHub, Inc., 22-cv-06823-JST (N.D. Cal. May 11, 2023).

112 Rob Wile, *Why Everyone is Talking About NVIDIA, the Nearly $3 Trillion-Dollar Company Fueling the AI Revolution*, NBC NEWS (Feb. 24, 2024), https://www.nbcnews.com/business/business-news/what-is-nvidia-what-do-they-make-ai-artificial-intelligence-rcna140171.

113 Rahul Awati, *graphics processing unit (GPU) definition*, TECHTARGET, https://www.techtarget.com/searchvirtualdesktop/definition/GPU-graphics-processing-unit (last visited Feb. 16, 2025).

114 Wile, *supra* note 112.

115 *Id.*

116 Sharon Goldman, *How NVIDIA Dominated AI - And Plans to Keep it That Way as Generative AI Explodes*, VENTUREBEAT (Feb. 23, 2023), https://venturebeat.com/ai/how-nvidia-dominated-ai-and-plans-to-keep-it-that-way-as-generative-ai-explodes/ (OpenAI reportedly used 10,000 Nvidia GPUs to train ChatGPT).

Google, have begun manufacturing their own GPUs, NVIDIA still has an advantage as the first-mover, holding about 88% of the GPU market.[117]

In September 2022, NVIDIA released "NeMo," a software program that simplifies the creation of conversational AI (i.e., chatbots, language translators, or voice assistants). NeMo offers developers an open-source toolkit with pre-trained large language models ("LLMs"). These LLMs generate human-like responses to user inputs, and, using NeMo, they can be integrated into various applications for numerous industries. By integrating NVIDIA's high-performance GPUs, their AI models have an accelerated training process where they "learn[] to predict the next word in a sentence based on the previous words. This process is repeated millions of times, allowing the model to learn linguistic patterns and nuances." However, like other AI models that utilize these deep learning techniques (i.e., ChatGPT and Claude), NeMo needs to collect and process vast amounts of data from books, articles, websites, and more. According to three authors, NeMo has been trained on datasets from "shadow library" websites that host vast quantities of unlicensed copyright material, including their books. Despite their copyright infringement complaint filed in 2024 and uncertainty about the future of AI, NVIDIA is still dominating the sector with its hardware and software. Prominent organizations, including AT&T, the University of Florida, Lowe's, and AWS, have adopted NeMo to bring generative AI into their industries.

F. Microsoft

Bill Gates and Paul Allen founded Microsoft on April 4, 1975.[118] The company initially focused on selling microcomputer software before expanding into operating systems.[119] Microsoft Office has become one of the most widely used software suites, featuring popular tools such as Word, Excel, and PowerPoint.[120] Over the years, Microsoft has extended its market influence by acquiring and investing in major technology companies, including LinkedIn, GitHub, Skype, and OpenAI.[121] It also maintains a strong presence in the gaming industry as the owner of the Xbox console.[122] In 2024, Fortune ranked Microsoft as the 26th largest company in the world according to revenue.[123] As of December 27, 2023, Microsoft had pledged $13 billion to OpenAI and announced plans to integrate OpenAI's technology into the Bing search engine.[124]

---

117 *Id.*
118 Mark Hall, *Microsoft Corporation*, BRITANNICA MONEY (Feb. 12, 2025), https://www.britannica.com/money/Microsoft-Corporation.
119 *Id.*
120 *Id.*
121 *Id.*
122 *Id.*
123 Scott DeCarlo, *Fortune Global 500*, FORTUNE, https://fortune.com/ranking/global500/.
124 BRITANNICA MONEY, *supra* note 118.

G. Google

Google was founded in 1998 by Sergey Brin and Larry Page.[125] The company operates the world's most widely used search engine, handling more than 70% of global online search requests.[126] Since 2015, Google has been a subsidiary of the holding company Alphabet Inc.[127] In 2023, Alphabet generated $175 billion in revenue from advertising based on users' search activity.[128] In 2024, Fortune ranked Alphabet as the 17th largest company in the world by revenue.[129] Today, Google offers far more than just search services, providing over 50 additional online tools, including Gmail and its suite of document creation applications, such as Google Docs and Google Sheets.[130]

In April 2023, Google CEO Sundar Pichai introduced Bard, the company's first conversational AI model.[131] Initially launched as an experimental service, Bard received widespread criticism.[132] In December 2023, Google released an updated version, Google Gemini, which has faced its own controversies, particularly regarding issues with inappropriate image generation.[133] Google Gemini for all intents and purposes is the same thing as Bard. Beyond Google Gemini, the company began the first publicly-discussed explorations of deep learning AI models with the Google Brain project in 2011, and the acquisition of the UK based deep learning startup "Deepmind" in 2014.[134] Since then, Google has championed the use of deep learning AI models by integrating them into many of their services.[135] These deep learning models "attempt to mimic the way [human] brains sort and process information" by building complex data processing configurations, called artificial "neural networks."[136] Google uses these deep neural networks to create image recognition applications, such as Google Photos, which allows users "to search photos by what's in them."[137] Similarly, the processing technology has accelerated natural language

---

[125] *Id.*
[126] *Id.*
[127] *Id.*
[128] *Id.*
[129] FORTUNE, *supra* note 9.
[130] BRITANNICA MONEY, *supra* note 86.
[131] Frannie Comstock, *Google Gemini*, BRITANNICA TECHNOLOGY (Feb. 11, 2025), https://www.britannica.com/technology/Google-Gemini.
[132] *Id.*
[133] *Id.*
[134] Berrnard Marr, *The Amazing Ways Google Uses Deep Learning AI*, Forbes (Aug. 8, 2017), https://www.forbes.com/sites/bernardmarr/2017/08/08/the-amazing-ways-how-google-uses-deep-learning-ai/.
[135] *Id.*
[136] *Id.*
[137] Marian Croak & Jeff Dean, *A Decade in Deep Learning, and What's Next*, GOOGLE BLOG (Nov. 18, 2021), https://blog.google/technology/ai/decade-deep-learning-and-whats-next/.

generation.[138] In 2016, deep learning was implemented into Google Translate which increased its quality and reduced error rates.[139] Further, in the past decade, Google developed deep learning models that can read house numbers and street signs to better help users find addresses in Google Maps, that allow users to interact with the world through Google Lens, that give better YouTube recommendations, that can predicate flood forecasting, that can detect diabetic retinopathy and cancer cells, and more.[140] Even Google's self-driving car division, Waymo, uses deep learning models to better analyze and react to their surroundings.[141] Most recently, in 2024, Google started using Gemini's technology to give summarized "AI overviews" of a search result before the traditional web page links.[142]

H. Bloomberg

Michael Bloomberg founded Bloomberg L.P. in 1981 after leaving Salomon Brothers.[143] The company initially focused on developing the Bloomberg Terminal, a system that provided real-time market data, financial calculations, and analytics to Wall Street firms.[144] Over time, Bloomberg expanded its services to include Bloomberg News, Bloomberg Television, Bloomberg Radio, and publications like Bloomberg Businessweek. These platforms deliver comprehensive business and financial information to a global audience.[145]Bloomberg has also grown through strategic acquisitions, such as the purchase of BusinessWeek magazine in 2009, which was subsequently renamed Bloomberg Businessweek.[146] In 2023, the company acquired Broadway Technology, a provider of high-performance front-office financial technology solutions.[147]

In recent years, Bloomberg has increased its focus on artificial intelligence (AI).[148] The company launched AI-powered news summaries for investors, where

---

[138] *Id.*
[139] *Id.*
[140] *Id.*
[141] Marr, *supra* note 134.
[142] Dan Milmo & Nick Robins-Early, *Google Rolls Out AI-Generated, Summarized Search Results in US,* THE GUARDIAN (May 14, 2024), https://www.theguardian.com/technology/article/2024/may/14/google-ai-search-results.
[143] *Mike's Story*, MIKE BLOOMBERG, https://www.mikebloomberg.com/about/ (last visited Feb. 16, 2025).
[144] Mara Lesemann, *Here's Why Bloomberg Stock Doesn't Exist*, INVESTOPEDIA (Jan. 2, 2025), https://www.investopedia.com/articles/markets/121715/bloomberg-stock-doesnt-exist-here-why.asp.
[145] *Id.*
[146] *Id.*
[147] *Bloomberg Completes Acquisition of Broadway Technology*, BLOOMBERG (Oct. 3, 2023), https://www.bloomberg.com/company/press/bloomberg-completes-acquisition-of-broadway-technology/.
[148] *Id.*

generative AI creates the summaries, which are then reviewed by analysts.[149] Additionally, Bloomberg developed the Bloomberg Artificial Intelligence Index (BAIAT), which is both representative and diversified across key segments of the entire AI ecosystem.[150]

In March 2024, Bloomberg L.P. faced a lawsuit filed by authors, including former Arkansas Governor Mike Huckabee and best-selling Christian writer Lysa TerKeurst. The plaintiffs alleged that Bloomberg used their copyrighted books without permission to train its large language model, BloombergGPT, constituting copyright infringement. In response, Bloomberg filed a motion to dismiss the lawsuit, asserting that its use of the authors' works was protected under the fair use doctrine. The company argued that the materials were utilized as part of internal research into generative AI capabilities and were not employed for commercial purposes.[151]

I. Databricks and Mosaic ML

Databricks was founded in 2013 by Ali Ghodsi, Ion Stoica, Matei Zaharia, Patrick Wendell, Reynold Xin, Andy Konwinski, and Arsalan Tavakoli-Shiraji, the original creators of Apache Spark.[152] The company initially focused on developing a unified analytics platform to streamline big data processing and machine learning workflows.[153] Over the years, Databricks has expanded its offerings to include the Lakehouse Platform, which combines the capabilities of data lakes and data warehouses, enabling organizations to manage and analyze vast amounts of data efficiently.[154] This platform supports various data workloads, including business intelligence, data engineering, and machine learning.[155]

Databricks has also grown through strategic acquisitions. In June 2020, the company acquired Redash, an open-source tool for data visualization and building

[149] *Exame: Generative AI Sparks Enthusiasm but Still has Limitations in the Financial Sector, Says Bloomberg Executive*, BLOOMBERG (Jan. 31, 2025), https://www.bloomberg.com/company/press/exame-generative-ai-sparks-enthusiasm-but-still-has-limitations-in-the-financial-sector-says-bloomberg-executive.

[150] *Indexing the AI theme: From "pure play" to the "show me" narrative*, BLOOMBERG (Nov. 27, 2024), https://www.bloomberg.com/professional/insights/artificial-intelligence/indexing-the-ai-theme-from-pure-play-to-the-show-me-narrative/

[151] Blake Brittain, *Bloomberg asks US court to toss copyright lawsuit over AI training*, REUTERS (Mar. 25, 2024), https://www.reuters.com/legal/litigation/bloomberg-asks-us-court-toss-copyright-lawsuit-over-ai-training-2024-03-25/.

[152] *Leadership*, DATABRICKS, https://www.databricks.com/company/founders (last visited Feb. 16, 2025).

[153] *Id.*

[154] *Id.*

[155] *Id.*

interactive dashboards.[156] In 2021, it purchased 8080 Labs, a German no-code company known for its data exploration tool, bamboolib[157] . In June 2023, Databricks acquired MosaicML, a generative AI platform, to enhance its AI capabilities.[158] In 2024, Databricks introduced the Databricks Data Intelligence Platform, integrating MosaicML's generative AI technology to help customers better understand and utilize their proprietary data. This move underscores the company's commitment to advancing AI and machine learning solutions.[159]

In March 2024, Databricks, Inc. and its subsidiary MosaicML faced a class-action lawsuit filed by authors Abdi Nazemian, Brian Keene, and Stewart O'Nan.[160] The plaintiffs allege that Databricks' MosaicML models were trained on datasets containing nearly 197,000 books sourced from shadow libraries like Bibliotik, which host unlicensed copyrighted material.[161] The authors claim their works were used without consent, credit, or compensation, constituting direct copyright infringement.[162] According to Wired Magazine, Databricks and Mosaic ML are involved in one case, where NVIDIA is also involved.[163]

J. ROSS Intelligence (ROSS)

This was the first AI case filed, and had a decision on revised decision on Summary Judgement as of February 11, 2025.[164] Coming out of the University of Toronto, ROSS Intelligence described itself as building "AI-driven products to augment lawyers' cognitive abilities."[165] Their "Our Story" explains that in 2014 two computer scientists and a lawyer decided to make legal services more accessible.[166] "Over a short period, ROSS raised millions in funding from Silicon Valley's most prominent investors and received top recognitions from Forbes and the American Bar Association Journal." The service included question-based search, find similar language, document analyzer, question-focused overviews,

---

[156] Reynold Xin, *Welcoming Redash to Databricks*, DATABRICKS (June 24, 2020), https://www.databricks.com/blog/2020/06/24/welcoming-redash-to-databricks.html.
[157] For more, *see* https://docs.databricks.com/aws/en/archive/notebooks/bamboolib.
[158] *Databricks Completes Acquisition of MosaicML*, DATABRICKS (July 19, 2023), https://www.databricks.com/company/newsroom/press-releases/databricks-completes-acquisition-mosaicml.
[159] *Id.*
[160] Stewart O'Nan et al. v. Databricks, Inc. et al., No 3:24-cv-01451 (N.D.Cal. 2024).
[161] *Id.*
[162] Databricks, Inc. Large Language Model Litigation, JOSEPH SAVERI LAW FIRM, https://www.saverilawfirm.com/databricks-inc.-large-language-model-litigation (last visited Feb. 16, 2025). .
[163] Knibbs, *supra* note 9.
[164] Thomson Reuters Enterprise Centre GmbH v. Ross Intelligence Inc., No. 1:20-CV-613-SB (D. Del.)
[165] *About Us*, ROSS INTELLIGENCE, https://www.rossintelligence.com/about-us (last visited March 1, 2025)
[166] *Id.*

and case treatments. They were charging $69-89 a month.[167] And they used, through a third party, Thomson Reuter's headnotes for training their AI system. By January 31, 2021 ROSS was no longer in business. But that's not what their website reports. Instead, the "Enough" posts claims that they are filing antitrust claims against Thomson Reuters.[168]

K. Perplexity

Perplexity is an AI search engine, which among other things, lists the sources for the responses and includes footnotes/references to the output. They are also licensing with companies to use their materials. Perplexity is quite new, founded in 2022, with founders coming from OpenAI, Meta and Quora. You can search videos and also create images. In short, they are billing themselves as the "accurate" AI tool.[169] By December 2024, Perplexity AI had a valuation of $9 billion, and had raised in its fourth round of funding $500 million.[170] They had started the year as valued at $500 million.[171] They have debuted a revenue sharking model for publishers, and also have licensing deals with man. The company is being sued by News Corp. and the New York Post.

L. AI voice generators

Lovo is an AI voice generation company that was recently sued for illegal cloning of voice actors' voices. Who is Lovo as a company? "Our award-winning voice generator and text to speech software is packed with 500+ voices in 100 languages."[172] Voice cloning technology replicates an existing yuan voice.[173] Udio and Suno are also getting suede. These are both prominent AI music platforms that allow users to generate songs from text prompts. They are also getting sued by all three major music labels. Finally, ElevenLabs is also a text to speech AI generator.

---

[167] *Pricing*, ROSS INTELLIGENCE, https://www.rossintelligence.com/pricing, (last visited March 1, 2025).

[168] The Founders, *Enough,* ROSS NEWS, https://blog.rossintelligence.com/post/enough, January 25, 2021.(last visited March 2, 2025).

[169] Perplexity, http://www.perplexity.ai (last visited March 1, 2025).

[170] Hayden Field, Perplexity AI in final stages of raising $500 million round at $9 billion valuation, November 5, 2025, https://www.cnbc.com/2024/11/05/perplexity-ai-nears-500-million-funding-round-at-9-billion-valuation.html (last visited March 1, 2025)

[171] *Id.*

[172] *AI Voice Generator: Most Realistic AI Text to Speech,* LOVO AI, https://lovo.ai/ (last visited March 2, 2025).

[173] James G. Gatto, *Lovo "Voices" Opposition to Suit Over "Kitchen-Sink" Approach to Alleged AI Voice Cloning*, NAT. L. REV., ,https://natlawreview.com/article/lovo-voices-opposition-suit-over-kitchen-sink-approach-alleged-ai-voice-cloning (March 1, 2025).

III. THE AI COPYRIGHT CASES THEMSELVES: SOME SUMMARIES

This is an illustrative – but not exhaustive – exploration of the major AI cases as of February 2025. As discussed above, what counts as a case is unclear, and most lists do not include cases outside of the U.S. We have only reviewed select U.S. cases in this study.

A. Alter v. OpenAI Inc., No. 1:23-cv-10211, (S.D.N.Y. Feb. 6, 2024)[174]

Alter v. OpenAI is the product of three consolidated cases filed against Microsoft and OpenAI on behalf of various journalists and authors in the Southern District of New York.[175] The consolidated complaint alleges that Microsoft and OpenAI infringed on the plaintiff's copyrighted works when training OpenAI's model without their permission.[176] OpenAI is a research organization founded in 2015 by various researchers and entrepreneurs such as Sam Altman, Peter Thiel, and Elon Musk.[177] OpenAI runs and operates ChatGPT, an AI chatbot that provides generated responses based on user prompts.[178] ChatGPT's AI models are referred to as "GPT-N." Pertinent to this litigation is the GPT-3 model released in 2020, the GPT-3.5 model released in 2022, and the GPT-4 model released in 2023.[179] Microsoft first invested in OpenAI in 2019 with a $1 billion investment in the company, but the explosion in popularity in AI from the release of ChatGPT caused Microsoft to invest another $10 billion in early 2023.[180]

To understand the merits of the case, it is important to generally understand how ChatGPT works and how it uses copyrighted material. One of ChatGPT's innovations is its use of "unsupervised learning," where the program is given

---

[174] Gerardo Gomez, Tulane Law School, J.D. expected May 2026.

[175] The three individual cases were *Authors Guild v. OpenAI Inc.*, *Alter v. OpenAI Inc.*, and *Basbanes v. Microsoft Corporation.* The three cases included claims for direct copyright infringement and vicarious infringement, while *Alter v. OpenAI Inc.* did not include a count for contributory infringement. *See generally Alter v. OpenAI*, BAKERHOSTETLER, https://www.bakerlaw.com/alter-v-openai/ (last visited Feb. 11, 2025).

[176] *See id.*

[177] OpenAI consists of two principal entities: OpenAI Inc. - which is the research-focused non-profit - and OpenAI Global LLC - which is a for-profit entity for the commercialization of OpenAI products. *See* Karl Montevirgen, *OpenAI*, BRITANNICA (Feb. 14, 2025), https://www.britannica.com/money/OpenAI.

[178] *See id.*

[179] Compl., ¶ 84, 85, 89, Alter v. OpenAI, No. 1:23-cv-10211, (S.D.N.Y., Feb. 6, 2024).

[180] [5] Alexandra Garfinkle, *Microsoft's near-term fate is in OpenAI's hands — for better or worse*, YAHOO!FINANCE (Dec. 20, 2023), https://finance.yahoo.com/news/microsofts-near-term-fate-is-in-openais-hands--for-better-or-worse-205250812.html?guccounter=1&guce_referrer=aHR0cHM6Ly93d3cuZ29vZ2xlLmNvbS8&guce_referrer_sig=AQAAAAWTNbykeKPUs2Idjd2kNEiE6NfPV4sosY8sJNS6H6g6GqeDrcs3pwGsLq0D6k_KCIj0VRjMdlIDhwc2zZdY_b3NNiVre-4OJvPW2yXG8c-T3C7z8-Ck5Jom3aB4ixuR8gd-gSgZwCXgnyRTm8AROZL5g_epehmxr8gAB5quOijL.

broad parameters and fed large amounts of data.[181] The model is unsupervised because it processes all of this data, which is equivalent to almost all available data on the open internet, to generate a knowledge basis.[182] Different models have introduced new kinds of data that can be used for training, such as GPT-4o which allows models to be trained on audio and image data.[183]

The first complaint was filed by the Authors Guild alongside several acclaimed authors like George R. R. Martin on September 19, 2023.[184] This complaint alleged that the defendants had trained ChatGPT on the plaintiff's books without their permission.[185] The Authors Guild plaintiffs filed three causes of action: direct copyright infringement by OpenAI LP for reproducing the plaintiff's works, vicarious liability from OpenAI Inc. and its international entity, and contributory copyright infringement on OpenAI's other subsidiaries for assisting, controlling, and managing on the AI model's training on protected material.[186] On November 21, 2023, the Alter plaintiffs filed their own complaint, alleging only the direct and contributory copyright infringement claims.[187] Lastly, the Basbanes plaintiffs filed their complaint, alleging the same causes of action as the Authors Guild plaintiffs, on January 5, 2024.[188] The Basbanes plaintiffs filed to consolidate their case with the Authors Guild on January 23, 2024, while the Alter plaintiffs finalized consolidating their case the following day with the Authors guild.[189] The litigation is currently ongoing, and the court set January 8, 2025, as the deadline to submit the final amended pleadings.[190]

In the consolidated complaint, the plaintiffs allege that to train GPT-3, GPT-3.5 and GPT-4 ("GPT Models"), OpenAI had reproduced copyrighted books without the author's consent. OpenAI admits that the GPT Models were trained using "large, publicly available datasets that include copyrighted works."[191] Furthermore, OpenAI admitted that analyzing the large amounts of data necessarily involved making reproductions of the training data.[192] Had OpenAI not used the copyrighted books to train the GPT Models, their quality would have been significantly reduced.[193] The plaintiffs allege that OpenAI knew their

---

[181] Harry Guinness, *How does ChatGPT work?*, ZAPIER (Nov. 18, 2024), https://zapier.com/blog/how-does-chatgpt-work/.
[182] *See id.*
[183] *See id.*
[184] BAKERHOSTETLER, *supra* note 124.
[185] *Id.*
[186] *Id.*
[187] *Id.*
[188] *Id.*
[189] *Id.*
[190] *Id.*
[191] Compl. ¶ 99, Alter v. OpenAI, No. 1:23-cv-10211, (S.D.N.Y., Feb. 6, 2024).
[192] *See id.* at ¶ 100.
[193] *See id.* at ¶ 101.

training material included copyrighted material, yet continued to use it to train the GPT Models without obtaining permission from the authors.[194]

The consolidated complaint further discusses Microsoft's vital role in training the GPT Models. Microsoft's supercomputer, Azure, was specifically built to aid OpenAI train the GPT Models.[195] Thus, while OpenAI designed the AI models themselves, Microsoft built the computer system that enables the reproduction of copyrighted material.[196] Furthermore, Microsoft staff worked closely with OpenAI employees during the training process.[197] Therefore, the plaintiffs allege that Microsoft knew of OpenAI's copyright infringement and contributed to it by providing the sophisticated hardware necessary to train the GPT Models.[198]

In their answer to the plaintiff's complaint, OpenAI argues that their use of the copyrighted books constitutes paradigmatic transformative fair use.[199] OpenAI claims that their model just extracted information about the work rather than replicating the expression itself.[200] Furthermore, OpenAI argues that the GPT Models generate brand new material, using the copyrighted works to obtain an understanding of language, reasoning, and the world.[201] Similarly, while Microsoft admits that it collaborated with OpenAI to design the Azure supercomputer to train large language models, it denies knowingly infringing on copyrighted material.[202]

Tags: copyright infringement, training AI Models, OpenAI, Microsoft, fair use

B. *Andersen v. Stability AI Ltd., No. 23-cv-00201-WHO, (N.D. Cal.).* [203]

In *Anderson v. Stability AI*, the plaintiffs allege copyright infringement, along with inducement, DMCA violations, false endorsement, and trade dress infringement. In October 2023, artists Sarah Andersen, Kelly McKernan, and Karla Ortiz filed a class action lawsuit on behalf of themselves and other artists in the United States District Court for the Northern District of California, against defendants Stability AI ("Stability"), Midjourney, Inc. ("Midjourney"), and DeviantArt, Inc. ("DeviantArt").[204] The plaintiffs alleged direct copyright infringement under 17 U.S.C. § 106, violation of the Digital Millennium

---

[194] *See id.* at ¶ 128.
[195] *See id.* at ¶ 133.
[196] *See id.* at ¶ 135-36.
[197] *See id.* at ¶ 136.
[198] *See id.* at ¶ 137.
[199] OpenAI Defendants' Answer to First Consolidated Class Action Complaint at 3, *Alter v. OpenAI*, No. 1:23-cv-08292-SHS, at *3 (S.D.N.Y. Mar. 4, 2024).
[200] *Id.*
[201] *Id.*
[202] *See Alter*, No. 1:23-cv-08292-SHS at *2.
[203] Marie Gosserand, Tulane University Law School Expected Graduate May 2025.
[204] Andersen v. Stability AI Ltd., 700 F. Supp.3d 853 (N.D. Cal. 2023).

Copyright Act under 17 U.S.C. §§ 1201-1205 ("DMCA"), violation of the Right to Publicity under California Civil Code § 3344, violation of the Common Law Right of Publicity, Unfair Competition under California's Business and Professional Code § 17200, and declaratory relief against all defendants, in addition to a breach of contract claim against DeviantArt alone.[205] The claims challenged the Defendants' creation and/or use of generative text-to-image artificial intelligence (AI) software called Stable Diffusion, alleging that their copyrighted works were used in the creation and training of the software.[206]

Stable Diffusion is a generative image AI diffusion model that creates high-quality images based on a text prompt.[207] A diffusion model is a type of generative AI model whose function is inspired by the process of thermodynamic diffusion.[208] Similarly to how a drop of food coloring spreads in water to create a uniform color, diffusion models take an image and diffuse it by altering the pixels until the original image becomes "TV static."[209] By doing so, the model is learning how to reverse the process to take the static-y image and diffuse it backwards into an image.[210] The basis for this process is that it is very easy for computers to generate TV static and then use the randomness of the generated static to produce different images each time, even if the same prompt is used.[211]

Stable Diffusion was first built in 2021 through a collaboration between Runway AI ("Runway"), a research company specializing in AI generated art, and researchers at the University of Munich.[212] Stability, known as a leading company in the field of open-source generative AI, later joined the project to help pay the computing costs associated with training the model on large data sets.[213] Stability presented Stable Diffusion as a product in 2022 under a permission source

---

[205] *Id.*

[206] Savan Dhameliya, *US Court allows claims against text-to-image AI Companies: Sarah Andersen v. Stability AI*, IPRMENTLAW (Aug. 25, 2024), https://iprmentlaw.com/2024/08/25/us-court-allows-claims-against-text-to-image-ai-companies-sarah-anderson-v-stability-ai/.

[207] *Artificial Intelligence for Image Research*, University of Toronto Libraries (Feb. 7, 2025), https://guides.library.utoronto.ca/image-gen-ai.

[208] *Dave Bergmann and Cole Stryker, What are diffusion models?*, IBM (Aug. 21, 2024), https://www.ibm.com/think/topics/diffusion-models.

[209] *Artificial Intelligence for Image Research*, *supra* note 205.

[210] *Id.*

[211] *Id.*

[212] Will Douglas Heaven, *The original startup behind Stable Diffusion has launched a generative AI for video*, MIT Tech. Rev (Feb, 6, 2023), https://www.technologyreview.com/2023/02/06/1067897/runway-stable-diffusion-gen-1-generative-ai-for-video/.

[213] *Id.*; *Stability AI*, Delphi Digital, https://members.delphidigital.io/projects/stability-ai (last visited Feb. 11, 2025).

license[214], which has now become one of the most well-known AI-powered text-to-image diffusion models today.[215]

The claims implicated each of the Defendants in some way for their association with the Stable Diffusion program. In training Stable Diffusion, Stability allegedly used datasets known as LAION-5B and LAION-400M, containing billions of images taken from the internet, including the plaintiffs' works.[216] This training is what enables software to generate new images that replicate or closely resemble the style of the images in the datasets they were trained with.[217] The Stable Diffusion product "is alleged to be a 'software library' providing 'image-generating services' to products produced and maintained" by Defendants Midjourney and DeviantArt.[218]

DeviantArt, founded in 2000, is known as an online community for digital artists to post and share their work.[219] In November 2022, DeviantArt released its commercial product "DreamUp" to its paying customers, which utilizes Stable Diffusion to produce images. Plaintiffs claim that one of the LAION datasets used in training Stable Diffusion was comprised of images from websites, including DeviantArt's own site.[220] Thus, by incorporating Stable Diffusion on its site through DreamUp, plaintiffs alleged that DeviantArt violated its own terms of service by using content for commercial purposes and without consent, in addition to violating its privacy policy.[221]

Midjourney, Inc., is an independent research lab in San Francisco, California.[222] Midjourney created the Midjourney Product, released in July 2022, and is alleged to be a commercial product producing images from text prompts similarly to Deviant Art's product "DreamUp."[223] Plaintiffs allege that the Midjourney Product uses Stable Diffusion and also that it was trained on a subset of images used to train Stable Diffusion.[224]

In an order on October 30, 2023, Judge Orrick granted plaintiffs leave to amend their complaint that was "defective in numerous aspects," ordering Plaintiffs to "provide clarity regarding their theories of how each defendant separately violated their copyrights, removed or altered their copyright management information, or violated their rights of publicity and plausible facts in support."[225]

---

[214] *Stability AI supra* note 213.
[215] *Id.*
[216] *Andersen*, 700 F. Supp. 3d at 860-862.
[217] *Id.* at 861.
[218] *Id.* at 860.
[219] *Id.* at 861.
[220] *Id.*
[221] *Id.*
[222] *Id.*
[223] *Id.*
[224] *Andersen v. Stability AI*, BAKERHOSTETLER, https://www.bakerlaw.com/andersen-v-stability-ai/ (last visited Feb. 11, 2025).
[225] Order on Mot. To Dismiss and Strike at 1, *Andersen v. Stability AI*, No. 3:23-cv-00201-WHO, (N.D. Cal. Oct. 30, 2023).

Plaintiffs' first amended complaint, filed on November 29, 2023, included more Plaintiffs and added Runway AI, the original collaborator on the Stable Diffusion Project, as a defendant.[226] On August 12, 2024, the court issued an order granting in part and denying in part the Defendants' motions to dismiss the first amended complaint.[227] Regarding the direct and induced copyright infringement claims, the court denied each defendant's motion to dismiss.[228] Next, the court dismissed the DMCA claims with prejudice.[229] It reasoned that Plaintiffs' § 1202(a) claims against Stability and Runway were insufficient because it was "'implausible' that readers of the license disclosures for Stable Diffusion, under which copyright ownership was asserted for the model, 'would understand that defendants are claiming rights to or conveying any false information regarding the rights of plaintiffs.'"[230] Regarding Plaintiffs' claims under 1202(b) against Stability, Runway, and Midjourney, Judge Orrick granted the motion to dismiss with prejudice on the grounds that a claim involving the removal of copyright management information requires identicality between the original work and the copy (per *GitHub*), which the plaintiffs failed to establish.[231]

The court dismissed the plaintiffs' unjust enrichment claims against the defendants but granted leave to amend on the grounds the claims were preempted by the Copyright Act because they were tied to the defendants' alleged use of the plaintiffs' copyrighted works in training its AI models without consent and plaintiffs had not identified an extra element that "change[d] the nature of those state law claims to protect something other than rights protected under the Copyright Act."[232] Lastly, the court found the false endorsement and vicarious trade dress infringement claim against Midjourney sufficient to survive a motion to dismiss, but dismissed the breach of contract claim against DeviantArt with prejudice on the grounds that DeviantArt itself played no role in the scraping or training of Stable Diffusion.[233]

The plaintiffs filed a second amended complaint on October 31, 2024.[234] Against Stability, the plaintiffs alleged 1) direct copyright infringement in the LAION-5B dataset by downloading copies of copyrighted works from the URLs in the dataset, using the copies to train its AI models, and distributing the AI models to the public; 2) induced copyright infringement "by materially

---

[226] Andersen v. Stability AI, No. 3:23-cv-00201-WHO, First Amended Complaint (N.D. Cal. Nov. 29, 2023).

[227] Order Granting In Part and Denying In Part Mots. To Dismiss First Amended Complaint, Andersen v. Stability AI, No. 3:23-cv-00201-WHO, (N.D. Cal. Aug. 12, 2024).

[228] *Id.*

[229] *Id.*

[230] *Id.*

[231] *Id.*

[232] *Id.* at 14.

[233] *Id.*

[234] Andersen v. Stability AI, No. 3:23-cv-00201-WHO, Seconded Amended Complaint (N.D. Cal. Oct. 31, 2024).

contributing to downstream copyright infringement through distributing the allegedly infringing … AI models for free under the MIT license; and 3) and violations of DMCA § 1202 by falsely asserting copyright in its allegedly infringing AI models by distributing them under the MIT license, and knowingly removing or altering CMI from copies of the plaintiffs' works in training its AI models, which caused its AI models to generate images based on plaintiffs' copyrighted works with CMI removed or altered.[235] Against Midjourney, plaintiffs alleged 1) direct copyright infringement of their works in the LAION-400M and LAION-5B dataset by downloading copies of the plaintiffs' works and using the copies to train its AI models and distributing the AI model to the public; 2) violations of DMCA § 1202(b) by knowingly removing or altering CMI from the copies of plaintiffs' works when training its AI; 3) false endorsement by using plaintiff's names commercially in advertising its AI product; and 4) vicarious trade dress infringement by encouraging and inducing users of its AI product to input prompts with artists' names and generate images "featuring the recurring visual elements and artistic techniques constituting plaintiff's protectable trade dress."[236] Against Runway, plaintiffs alleged 1) direct copyright infringement in using their copyrighted works in the LAION-5B dataset and using the copies to train their AI models and distributing the model to the public; 2) induced copyright infringement by materially contributing to downstream copyright infringement by distributing the infringing Stable Diffusion model for free under the "Creative ML Open RAIL-M license"; and 3) violations of DMCA § 1202 by falsely asserting that third parties have a copyright in the Stable Diffusion model when distributing them under the Creative ML RAIL-M license in violation of §1202(a), and knowingly removing or altering CMI from copies of the plaintiffs' works in training its AI models, which caused its AI models to generate images based on plaintiffs' copyrighted works with CMI removed or altered in violation of §1202(b).[237] Lastly, against DeviantArt, plaintiffs alleged direct copyright infringement of their copyrighted works in the LAION-5B dataset by incorporating the Stable Diffusion model into its product "DreamUp" and distributing that model to the public.[238] The trail for this case is set for April 5, 2027.[239]

The original dismissal of all Copyright Management Information claims in this case exhibits a problem all litigants are facing in AI infringement cases asserting Section 1201 claims.[240] First, the standard set out by 1202(a) is very difficult to prove without significant evidence of knowledge and intent, which isn't feasible when the datasets consist of such large collections of art scraped

---

[235] *Id.*
[236] *Id.*
[237] *Id.*
[238] *Id.*
[239] *Andersen v. Stability AI, supra* note 234.
[240] Kevin Madigan, *Top Takeaways from Order in the Andersen v. Stability AI Copyright Case*, COPYRIGHT ALLIANCE (Aug. 29, 2024), https://copyrightalliance.org/andersen-v-stability-ai-copyright-case/.

from the internet. Second, based on the nature of generative AI, the identicality requirement under 1202(b) is impossible as "the use of conditioning data to interpolate multiple latent images means the resulting hybrid image will not look exactly like any of the Training Images that have been copied into these latent images,"[241] However, every output from the product is derived exclusively from the training images, and thus, artists' works are still contributing without their permission.[242]

Also noteworthy is the plaintiffs' strategic dismissal of the DMCA claims after submitting their second amended complaint.[243] In Judge Orrick's order in August 2024, while dismissing the plaintiffs' DMCA §1202(b) claims, he also granted leave to amend as long as they filed the second amended complaint without the DMCA-alleging plaintiffs.[244] Given that excluding the claims could potentially compromise the plaintiff's rights to seek reconsideration, in the second amended complaint admitted on October 31, 2024, the plaintiffs initially included the plaintiffs and then voluntarily dismissed with prejudice all DMCA claims in exchange for the defendants agreeing not to challenge future reconsideration of those claims based on their omission from the second amended complaint.[245] The reason for this is because the basis of Judge Orrick's decision to dismiss these claims relies on the outcome of Doe 1 v. GitHub, Inc., which is currently on interlocutory appeal in the Ninth Circuit.[246] If overturned, this strategic move by the plaintiffs will enable reconsideration by the courts of their dismissal of the DMCA claims and enable the court to provide further insight on the issue.[247]

Tags: DMCA, Generative AI, Copyright, 17 U.S.C. Section 1201(a), 17 U.S.C. Section 1201(b), Stability AI, Mid-Journey, DeviantArt, Runaway, DreamUp.

---

[241] *Andersen*, 700 F. Supp. 3d at 861.

[242] *Id.*

[243] James Gatto & Sam Smith, *Andersen Plaintiffs Strategically Dismiss § 1202(b) Claims Pending Interlocutory Appeal in Github Case*, JD SUPRA (Nov. 27, 2024), https://www.jdsupra.com/legalnews/andersen-plaintiffs-strategically-3901814/#:~:text=November%2027%2C%202024-,Andersen%20Plaintiffs%20Strategically%20Dismiss%20%C2%A7%201202(b)%20Claims%20Pending,Interlocutory%20Appeal%20in%20Github%20Case&text=In%20a%20strategic%20move%20to,with%20prejudice%20all%20DMCA%20claims.

[244] *Id.*

[245] *Id.*

[246] Jack Broitman & Stuart Levi, *Recent Decisions on Whether AI Training Violates the Digital Millennium Copyright Act*, JD SUPRA (Dec. 9, 2024), https://www.jdsupra.com/legalnews/recent-decisions-on-whether-ai-training-1219677/.

[247] *Id.*

C. *Concord Music Group, Inc. V. Anthropic PBC, 2024 US Dist. LEXIS 110598, 1, (M.D.Tenn. 2024).*[248]

The plaintiffs in this case are Concord Music Group, Universal Music Publishing Group, and ABKCO Music Inc, all of whom are leading music labels within the industry.[249] The defendant in this case is Anthropic PBC, an AI safety and research company based in California, who produced the AI assistant "Claude." [250] AI assistants like Claude are used by clients to generate work-product in response to entered prompts. The plaintiffs filed suit against Anthropic PBC for alleged copyright infringement and DMCA § 1202(b) violations for 1) allegedly using copyrighted lyrics to train its generative AI product and 2) copying and distributing those lyrics through Claude's output.[251] The plaintiffs are upset because, Claude was trained using the copyrighted lyrics without permission to use them. The plaintiffs allege that Claude used upwards of 500 song lyrics by major artists including Katy Perry, the Rolling Stones, and Béyonce to train its system. In addition to injunctions, the plaintiffs sought $150,000 per infringement, or $75 million in willful infringement damages.[252] This case was initially filed in October 2023. To train an AI assistant, companies use textual inputs from real-world examples to demonstrate what an acceptable response would be to the AI thinking program. From there, the AI program will generate similar examples based on the instructions given. In this case, the Plaintiffs allege that copyrighted lyrics were used without permission to train Claude. If this were to be true, Anthropic PBC would be in violation of the Plaintiffs' copyright as they utilized lyrics for a commercial purpose (training Claude and reproducing lyric products) without paying for the rights or licensing to use the copyright holders, unless fair use or some other defense proved successful.

Anthropic defense is that it allegedly has implemented internal safeguards within Claude to prevent copyright infringement. There is no public elaboration as to what those safeguards or guardrails entail. A motion for preliminary injunctions was filed on November 16, 2023 to establish guardrails to prevent Claude's alleged copyright infringement going forward. [253] This preliminary injunction sought for Anthropic to take two actions: one, to cease using copyrighted materials to train its Claude interface; and two, "maintain

---

[248] Hallie Feinman, Tulane Law School, JD expected May 2026.

[249] *Concord Music Group, Inc. v. Anthropic PBC (3:23-cv-01092),* COURT LISTENER, (Jan 24., 2025), https://www.courtlistener.com/docket/67894459/concord-music-group-inc-v-anthropic-pbc/

[250] *See infra* Part II, Subsection C.

[251] Concord Music Grp. v. Anthropic PBC, No. 3:23-cv-01092 (M.D.Tenn. 2024).

[252] Mandy Dalugdug, *Universal Music, Concord Music, ABKCO welcome court-approved 'guardrails' in Anthropic AI dispute – as legal battle continues,* MUSICBUSINESS WORLDWIDE (Jan. 6, 2025), https://www.musicbusinessworldwide.com/universal-music-concord-music-abkco-welcome-court-approved-guardrails-in-anthropic-ai-dispute/.

[253] *Concord Music Grp.*, 738 F.Supp. 3d.

[Anthropic's] already-implemented guardrails."[254] The case was transferred from the Middle District of Tennessee to the Northern District of California on June 24, 2024.

The plaintiffs renewed their motion for preliminary injunction in the Northern District of California in August 2024.[255] Oral argument was heard by Judge Eumi K. Lee on the topic of this preliminary injunction on November 25, 2024. Also in August 2024, Anthropic filed a motion to dismiss the plaintiff's secondary liability claims and DMCA claims as the plaintiffs "fail to allege even one predicate act of infringement by a third party" using Claude's AI interface. Further, Anthropic states that "the only specific examples provided in the Complaint reflect [p]laintiffs' attempts to generate alleged copies of their own lyrics." ding Anthropic's motion to dismiss, although no transcript of the event is available.

Anthropic filed a stipulation and proposed order regarding the preliminary injunction on December 30, 2024. This stipulation was filed after both parties reached agreement regarding Anthropic's maintaining its already-implemented guardrails.[256] Parties also agreed that Plaintiffs may alert Anthropic through writing of any shortcomings or failings of the Claude guardrails, and Anthropic will respond in good faith. On January 2, 2025, Judge Lee entered the stipulation and proposed order.[257] The order does not resolve the remainder of the plaintiffs' motion seeking to enjoin Anthropic for alleged use of infringing copyrighted lyrics to train its Claude systems.[258] Organizations writing on this case include Baker Hostetler, Pillsbury Law, Quinn Emmaneul law firms, as well as CaseText, Court Listener, and a brief article written by Reuters early on in the case's life.[259] Most writing on this case is factual reporting of the case's details without providing commentary.[260] As of January, the case's story has recently been picked up by music law publications such as Music Business Worldwide and The Verge. These music articles are still factual recollections and contain little in regard to legal speculation.

---

[254] *Id.*

[255] *Client Alert: Concord Music Group, Inc. et al. v. Anthropic PBC - Interim Development Narrows Issues in Pending Preliminary Injunction Motion,* QUINN EMANUEL TRIAL LAWYERS (Jan. 7, 2025), https://www.quinnemanuel.com/the-firm/publications/client-alert-concord-music-group-inc-et-al-v-anthropic-pbc-interim-development-narrows-issues-in-pending-preliminary-injunction-motion/.

[256] *Id.*

[257] *Id.*

[258] *Id.*

[259] *Id.*

[260] Blake Brittain, *Music publishers fire back at Anthropic in AI copyright lawsuit,* REUTERS (Feb. 15, 2024), https://www.reuters.com/legal/litigation/music-publishers-fire-back-anthropic-ai-copyright-lawsuit-2024-02-15/.

Tags: music, lyrics, Anthropic, DMCA, 17 U.S.C. Section 1202(b), guardrails, Concord Music Group, Universal Music Publishing Group, ABKCO Music Inc,, copyright infringement, Claude, AI-assistants

D. Doe v. GitHub, Inc., No. 22-cv-06823-JST (N.D. Cal. May 11, 2023)[261]

Here, the plaintiffs, collectively referred to as "Doe"[262] allege that the defendants, Microsoft, GitHub, and OpenAI, broke open-source software licenses, and violated the DMCA in the creation of Codex and Copilot. This is a class action lawsuit brought by the multitude of plaintiffs, who are all software developers, against Microsoft, GitHub, and OpenAI alleging that these sites used copyrighted materials from the plaintiffs to create two new programs: Codex and Copilot.[263] GitHub is a Microsoft owned platform that allows creators to produce and share code with each other within the platform.[264] By default, that means that GitHub and its parent company Microsoft have access to all of the code created on their systems.

Codex is an OpenAI model that forms the base and powers Copilot, which is GitHub's pair programmer (AI). [265] GitHub is a collaborative, cloud-based program that allows users to work together to create code as well as store and share it.[266] Copilot is a form of Generative AI programming that allows for a user to write faster, use various Microsoft applications, or specifically for use on GitHub helping users write code faster.[267]

The plaintiffs are a group of programmers who all used GitHub to store their code and collaborate with others. This group of anonymous individuals had 22 claims against GitHub, Copilot, and OpenAI, all owned by Microsoft.[268] The main claims being that GitHub allowed for the Copilot program to train using the software and codes that the plaintiffs had created and stored on their software.[269]

---

[261] Whitney McBay, Tulane Law School, J.D. expected May 2025.

[262] There are five anonymous plaintiffs in this case which is why they are all collectively referred to as "Doe."

[263] *Doe v. GitHub, Inc.*, 22-cv-06823-JST (N.D. Cal. May 11, 2023).

[264] Daniel R. Mello, Jr. et al., *Insights from the Pending Copilot Class Action Lawsuit*, FINNEGAN (Oct. 4, 2023), https://www.finnegan.com/en/insights/articles/insights-from-the-pending-copilot-class-action-lawsuit.html#:~:text=GitHub%20Inc.,landscape%20of%20AI%2Dassisted%20coding.

[265] *Id.*

[266] *About GitHub and Git*, GITHUB, https://docs.github.com/en/get-started/start-your-journey/about-github-and-git#about-github (last visited Feb. 5, 2025).

[267] *Cursor vs GitHub Copilot*, BUILDER.IO, https://www.builder.io/blog/cursor-vs-github-copilot (last visited Feb. 5, 2025).

[268] Emma Roth, *The Developers Suing Over GitHub Copilot got Dealt a Major Blow in Court*, THE VERGE (July 9, 2024), https://www.theverge.com/2024/7/9/24195233/github-ai-copyright-coding-lawsuit-microsoft-openai.

[269] *Id.*

The plaintiffs further allege that Copilot does not adhere to the Open-Source Software (OSS) licenses on GitHub that govern plaintiffs' code.[270] OSS is used to manage the software and code of many software developing systems, like GitHub and Copilot.[271] Plaintiffs made 3 primarily alleging claims in the OSS license issue. These state that Copilot did not or failed to provide: 1) acknowledgement and attribution to the owner of the code, 2) notice of copyright, and 3) the explicit terms of the license which did not include the express OSS licensing that allows for Copilot to create derivative works based on the information input into its system by creators.[272]

This case is unique in that while it displays itself as a copyright case against an LLM provider, it does not actually include any claims of indirect or direct copyright infringement.[273] Among the 22 claims, some of which dabble in indirect copyright infringement, the majority were thrown out. The main amended claims only involve DMCA violations, breach of contract, and multiple torts. The California judge presiding over the case only left two primary claims standing among the 22 filed, a breach of contract violation, and an open-source license violation.[274] Most of the claims were dismissed with prejudice, so the creators cannot refile any of those claims.

The case was on hold pending the plaintiff's interlocutory appeal of the dismissal of its DMCA §1202 claims but has since been decided[275] The Court had agreed with some claims but dismissed others. The plaintiffs believed that they had a valid DMCA claim and that it should not have been dismissed.[276] The key issue is whether Section 1202(b) has an identicality requirement. This requirement means that the current product is identical to the original product except for certain personalized information (name or terms and conditions).[277]

---

[270] *Doe v. GitHub, Inc.*, 22-cv-06823-JST (N.D. Cal. May 11, 2023).

[271] *Id.*

[272] Mello et. al., *Insights from the Pending Copilot Class Action Lawsuit*, FINNEGAN (Oct. 4, 2023), https://www.finnegan.com/en/insights/articles/insights-from-the-pending-copilot-class-action-lawsuit.html#:~:text=GitHub%20Inc.,landscape%20of%20AI%2Dassisted%20coding.

[273] *Doe v. GitHub, Inc.*, BAKERHOSTETLER, https://www.bakerlaw.com/the-copilot-litigation/ (last visited Feb. 5, 2025).

[274] *Id.*

[275] *Id.*

[276] *Id.*

[277] Maria Crusey, *Copyright Management Information, 1202(b), and AI, Authors Alliance*, AUTHORS ALLIANCE , https://www.authorsalliance.org/2024/10/30/copyright-management-information-1202b-and-ai/#:~:text=%E2%86%92%20The%20%E2%80%9CIdenticality%E2%80%9D%20Requirement,of%20Nevada%20in%20Oracle%20v. (last visited Feb. 5, 2025).

The plaintiffs claim that this section of the DMCA [278]requirement was relevant for their claims, but the Judge did not agree. He claimed that the code that GitHub had copied from the creators was similar, but not similar enough to the original work of the developers.[279] In a study done of AI and code-generating programs, the Judge quoted a section that said Copilot rarely regurgitates memorized code.[280] This killed the claim that Copilot violated the DMCA by not giving proper credit and attribution to the creators of the code it was suggesting.[281]

The same Court denied the defendants' motions regarding plaintiffs' claims for breach of contract and for violations [282] The plaintiffs claimed that the Copilot application, operated by GitHub, was operating using the stolen code from the plaintiffs but did not include the identifying information.[283] This would violate DMCA 1202(b)(1) and (b)(3) if GitHub and Copilot had altered their CMI in an active way.[284] CMI stands for "copyright management information" which can include things like the author, the title, terms and conditions for work, copyright owner, or just any identifying information that would be set forth in a copyright notice.[285] A CMI can often be found before a block of code typically. This would be a violation of DMCA 1202(b)(1) and (b)(3) if the plaintiffs can prove that the defendants' program was specifically designed to actively alter or remove any CMI that was affixed to the code coming through its systems.[286]

The defendants tried to file a motion to dismiss because they alleged that they did not plead sufficiently regarding the defendant's role in their misconduct[287] However, the plaintiffs were able to point out that Copilot and Codex were specifically designed to remove any CMI from licensed code that they reproduced and they were taught to immediately remove CMI (or ignore it) when reproducing for training.[288] And so, these two claims continue as the Court found that the plaintiffs had pled sufficiently to support this claim. The Court instead took into account the plaintiffs leave to amend and dismissed the remaining[289] Their claims for civil conspiracy and declaratory relief were also rejected because they did not meet the requirements. [290]

Regarding unjust enrichment and unauthorized use, the Court noted that unjust enrichment is not automatically preempted by copyright and a state law tort claiming unauthorized use of a product or system is also not automatically

---

[278] *Id.*
[279] Roth, *supra* note 268.
[280] *Id.*
[281] *Id.*
[282] *Doe v. GitHub, Inc.*, 22-cv-06823-JST (N.D. Cal. May 11, 2023).
[283] Crusey, *supra* note 277.
[284] *Id.*
[285] *Id.*
[286] *Id.*
[287] *Doe v. GitHub, Inc.*, 22-cv-06823-JST (N.D. Cal. May 11, 2023).
[288] *Id.*
[289] *Id.*
[290] *Id.*

preempted by copyright[291] The defendant's claim that the plaintiffs state law claims are preempted by Section 301 of the Copyright Act and note that most of these were dismissed, except for unjust enrichment.[292] The plaintiffs don't address their arguments for preemption, but instead state that their state law claims are very different from their Copyright Act claims because they are about both the unauthorized use and production of the code.[293] On their preparation of derivative works, the Court found that their unjust enrichment claim was properly preempted by the Copyright Act.￼ The claim was still dismissed with leave to amend. The opening brief for the plaintiffs is due in March 2025.[294] This case has become a training ground for the future of AI cases in courts.[295] The ruling also hammers home that plaintiffs will have to produce some form of compelling evidence and actual examples of product reproductions in order to have standing to sue in the future.[296]

Tags: GitHub, AI training, code, open-source software (OSS), Digital Millennium Copyright Act (DMCA), 17 U.S.C Section 1202(b)1); 17 U.S.C. Section 1202(3), Copilot, unjust enrichment, unauthorized use of a product or system (under state law) copyright preemption, Codex.

E. Getty Images (US) v. Stability AI., Inc., No. 1:23-cv-00135-JLH (D. Del. Feb. 3, 2023)[297]

This case was brought by the plaintiff, Getty Images, Inc. (Getty Images), against defendant Stability AI.[298] Getty Images Inc. is a visual media company that is commonly known for their large digital catalog of stock images.[299] Stability AI is an open-source generative AI company that develops and trains AI models for different applications including audio, language, code, and imaging.[300] Stable Diffusions is the advanced image generative AI model that is used on the platform, DreamStudio to create images using text descriptions.[301]

Getty Images accuses Stability AI of infringing on more than 12 million photographs, their metadata and associated captions in training and building

[291] Mello et. al., *Insights from the Pending Copilot Class Action Lawsuit*, FINNEGAN (Oct. 4, 2023)
[292] *Id.*
[293] *Id.*
[294] BAKERHOSTETLER, *supra* note 273.
[295] *Id.*
[296] *Id.*
[297] Jamika P. Mack, Tulane University Law School-Class of 2025
[298] Complaint, *Getty Images v. Stability AI., Inc.*, 1:23-cv-00135-JLH, at *1 (D. Del, Feb. 3, 2023).
[299] *Id.* at 1-2.
[300] *Id.* at 3.
[301] *Id.*

Stable Diffusion and Dream Studio.[302] Getty Images further alleges that because Stable Diffusion used Getty Images to train their AI models; the Getty Images watermarks are still evident on the AI output.[303] Getty Images recognizes AI's ability to stimulate creative endeavors.[304] Therefore, Getty Images provided licenses to technology innovators for the purposes of training AI systems in a manner that respects personal and intellectual property rights.[305] According to Getty, Stability AI did not seek to obtain a license from Getty Images and instead chose to ignore the viable licensing options and long- standing IP legal protections to pursue commercial interests.[306]

There are eight causes of action that Getty Images brought against Stability AI.[307] This includes direct copyright infringement, alleging that Stability AI infringed and will continue to infringe by reproducing Getty Images' copyrighted works and creating derivative works.[308] The plaintiffs also cite DMCA 1202(a) violations for providing false Copyright Management Information by "applying a modified version of Getty Images' watermarks to output generated through use of Stable Diffusion and the Dream Studio interface"[309] They also include DMCA 1202(b) violations for removing Getty Images' watermarks and metadata [310] Finally, the causes of action include trademark infringement, unfair competition, trademark dilution under both federal and Delaware trademark law and violation of Delaware's Uniform Deceptive Trade Practices Act for unauthorized use of Getty Images' trademarks in connection with synthetic images generated by Stable Diffusion and DreamStudio.[311]

The latest judgement occurred on January 15, 2025.[312] The court ruled against the Sixth Claimant's attempt to bring a representative action on behalf of over 50,000 copyright owners, citing the lack of a definitive class definition and the necessity of individualized liability assessments.[313] The court ruled that Stability AI's limited admissions regarding the use of Getty Images' works made it impossible to determine a specific group of eligible claimants.[314] The court ruled

---

[302] *Id.* at 1.
[303] *Id.* at 4.
[304] *Id.* at 3.
[305] *Id.*
[306] *Id.*
[307] *Getty Images v. Stability*, BAKERHOSTETLER, https://www.bakerlaw.com/getty-images-v-stability-ai/ (last visited Feb. 11, 2025).
[308] *Id.*
[309] *Id.*
[310] *Id.*
[311] *Id.*
[312] Racheal Muldoon et. al, *Getty v Stability AI: A 'tantalising glance' of what's to come for AI firms and creators*, Charles Russell Speechlys (Jan. 16, 2025), https://www.charlesrussellspeechlys.com/en/insights/expert-insights/financial-services/2025/getty-v-stability-ai-a-tantalising-glance-of-whats-to-come-for-ai-firms-and-creators/
[313] *Id.*
[314] *Id.*

that the claimants' argument—that the defendant possessed the necessary knowledge to identify infringing works—was insufficient to justify a representative action.[315] The court ruled against the claimant's informal application under CPR 19.3, determining that it lacked sufficient evidence and would create an excessive litigation burden.[316] The court ruled that mass copyright claims in AI training cases require structured legal mechanisms rather than broad representative claims.[317] The court ruled that the parties must now resolve case management issues in preparation for the first trial in June 2025.[318]

Shortly after this lawsuit, Getty partnered with NVIDIA to develop its own AI-photo generation tool called Generative AI by Getty Images.[319] Getty's motivation behind entering this new market is to give creatives and copyright owners peace of mind that any images generated and licensed through their new platform would be backed by their "uncapped legal indemnification".[320] Getty alleges that its new tool is unlike other AI-photo generation tools because the legal rights have been cleared prior to training the models.[321] Further, Getty is guaranteeing that users would have worldwide, perpetual, and non-exclusive use of the images they create and that those AI-generated creations would not be available for others to use.[322]

Commentators are skeptical of Getty's new tool.[323] There are many concerns about photographers not being properly compensated for their work, ethical issues regarding the use of copyrighted material to train AI models in general, and the poor quality of the newly-generated content.[324] Getty says that contributing photographers are paid for any of their work that was used to train the model, with compensation being about 30 cent to a dollar for every dollar generated.[325] Getty claims that this is made possible from the subscription fee that Getty charges to customers for using the tool.[326] Skeptics are worried that fair compensation is an issue because it is not clear which photos in the training set would be given credit

---

[315] *Id.*
[316] *Id.*
[317] *Id.*
[318] *Id.*
[319] *Generative AI by Getty Images*, GETTY IMAGES, https://developers.gettyimages.com/ai-generation/ (last visited Feb. 11, 2025).
[320] *Id.*
[321] Emilia David, *Getty made an AI generator that only trained on its licensed images*, THE VERGE (Sep. 23, 2023), https://www.theverge.com/2023/9/25/23884679/getty-ai-generative-image-platform-launch
[322] *Id.*
[323] Lauren Goode, *Getty Images Plunges Into the Generative AI Pool*, WIRED (Sept. 25, 2023), https://www.wired.com/story/getty-images-generative-ai-photo-tool/.
[324] *Id.*
[325] David, *supra* note 321.
[326] *Id.*

for generated content.[327] Getty admits that they don't know how to identify what contributor that each generated content derives from but that they utilize technology to determine that.[328] Additionally, some users argue that Getty's AI tool is outperformed by other image generators, such as DALL-E.[329] After entering the same prompt in both Getty's tool and DALL-E and Clipdrop, the user described the results as being "noticeably less interesting aesthetically and from a narrative perspective, and they were overall rather obvious to the point of being bland."[330] Overall, the consensus seems to suggest that Getty would need to continually refine its model to ensure high quality output and ensure that contributing creatives are being legally protected and compensated for their work.[331]

Tags: Getty Images, Stability AI, AI model training, Digital Millennium Copyright Act, stock photos, Generative AI by Getty Images, copyright material, AI-image generator

F. *In re Google Generative AI Copyright Litig., No. 5:23-CV-03440-EKL (N.D. Cal. Dec. 20, 2024) (Consolidated Class Action Complaint).*[332]

The Plaintiffs in the current consolidated class action are a group of authors and visual artists, including New York Times best-selling authors like Steve Almond and cartoonists like Sarah Andersen, who are suing for direct and vicarious copyright infringement. Plaintiffs allege that Google infringed their copyrights by copying their works without authorization to train its generative AI models, Gemini and Imagen, thereby harming their licensing revenue and market value.

In Re Google is a consolidated action of two putative class action suits; *Leovy v. Google,* and *Zhang v. Google.*[333] In July 2023, the eight original Plaintiffs in the *Leovy* action had chosen to remain anonymous. Plaintiffs included a New York Times best-selling author and investigative journalist, a six-year- old and thirteen- year-old minor, and other Google and Gmail users filed a class action claiming that "Google has been secretly stealing everything ever created and shared on the internet by hundreds of millions of Americans,"[334] and that specifically, Google directly infringed the rights of copyright owners when it

---

[327] Goode, *supra* note 323.
[328] *Id.*
[329] Tiernan Ray, *I tried Getty's new AI image generator, and it doesn't compare to DALL-E*, ZDNET (Jan. 9, 2024), https://www.zdnet.com/article/i-tried-gettys-new-ai-image-generator-and-it-doesnt-really-compare-to-dall-e/.
[330] *Id.*
[331] *Id.*
[332] Isa Reyes-Klein, J.D., Tulane University Law School, expected graduation May 2026
[333] Complaint, *In re Google Generative AI Copyright Litigation*, 5:23-cv-03440, (N.D. Cal. Jul 11, 2023) ECF No. 1.
[334] *Id.*

collected and used the works to train its AI technology.[335] The original complaint names Google DeepMind--an Alphabet subsidiary AI research laboratory, [336] Google LLC ,[337] and Google's parent company Alphabet[338] as defendants, alleging that Google secretly collected and used personal, creative, and copyrighted data from millions of internet users without consent to develop its AI products, including Bard which is now known as the AI chatbot assistant Gemini which competes with OpenAI's ChatGPT.[339] The ten alleged causes of action include unfair competition, invasion of privacy, intrusion upon seclusion, larceny/receipt of stolen property, conversion and unjust enrichment based on Google's alleged use of the Plaintiffs' private and personal information that was collected or "scraped" without the consent of the users or their knowledge.[340] Plaintiffs further assert that they were not made aware that by using Google products their information could be collected without their consent.[341] In the original action, Plaintiffs sought an injunction to stop the data collection, allow users to opt out, and demand deletion or compensation for misused data.[342]

The Plaintiffs further alleged violation of the Digital Millennium Copyright Act ("DMCA") for distributing derivative works without copyright management information ("CMI") in their copyrighted materials.[343] Plaintiffs alleged such direct infringement arose from the scraping and use of copyrighted works to train Google's AI products.[344] Plaintiffs cite a study which found that in the data sets which were used to train Gemini, the copyright symbol appeared more than 200 million times, suggesting a vast number of works used to create and train the chatbot were protected by copyright.[345] Namely, Plaintiffs alleged that Google

---

[335] *Id.*

[336] *Announcing Google DeepMind*, GOOGLE DEEPMIND (Apr. 20, 2023), https://www.deepmind.com/blog/announcing-google-deepmind (The generative AI research and development company describes artificial intelligence technologies as having the potential to "be one of humanity's most useful inventions.").

[337] *Google LLC*, BLOOMBERG, https://www.bloomberg.com/profile/company/8888000D:US#xj4y7vzkg (last visited July 10, 2023) (Google LLC was restructured as a subsidiary of Alphabet Inc. in 2015.).

[338] Alphabet Inc. is a multinational technology company that owns Google and other companies since 2015 when Google reorganized. *See Deepfakes: The Synthetic Videos Fooling Us All*, BBC NEWS (Nov. 27, 2019), https://www.bbc.com/news/technology-50656803.

[339] *Gemini Apps FAQ*, GEMINI, https://gemini.google.com/faq (last visited Feb. 11, 2025).

[340] *Id.*

[341] *Id.*

[342] Complaint, 54, *In re Google Generative AI Copyright Litigation*, 5:23-cv-03440, (N.D. Cal. Jul 11, 2023) ECF No. 1.

[343] *Id.*

[344] *Id*

[345] Kevin Schaul et al., *Inside the Secret List of Websites that Make AI like ChatGPT Sound Smart*, WASH. POST (Apr. 19, 2023), https://www.washingtonpost.com/technology/interactive/2023/aichatbot-learning/.

reproduced Plaintiff's copyrighted materials when they were used to train Gemini, a direct competitor to Open AI's "Chat GPT" and Google's Imagen an AI photo editing assistant[346] Plaintiffs further assert Defendants scraped at least 1.56 trillion words of "public dialog data and other public web documents" from websites like LAION and Common Crawl that provide free data for research specific purposes[347] rather than purchasing internet user data sold like any other content or property.[348] On September 19, 2023, Plaintiffs voluntarily dismissed Alphabet Inc. and Google DeepMind.[349] Google LLC filed motions to dismiss for failure to state claims to which Plaintiffs filed an amended complaint. Subsequently, on May 28, 2024, Google notified the court of a recent decision in *Cousart v. OpenAI LP*, where the court dismissed a complaint for violating Federal Rule of Civil Procedure 8 by being excessively long and containing irrelevant information—an argument Google makes in its own motion to dismiss in *Leovy,* further noting that six of the *Cousart* plaintiffs are represented by the same counsel as the *Leovy* plaintiffs.[350]

Three days later, Google LLC filed a motion to relate *Leovy* and *Zhang et al. v. Google* LLC, to which Plaintiffs repeatedly opposed.[351] However, on July 23, 2024, the court granted Google's motion to relate the two cases and permitted

---

[346] *Plagiarism, AI & ChatGPT: ChatGPT: How does work?*, UNIV. LIBR., https://guides.library.txstate.edu/c.php?g=1321038&p=9718369#:~:text=What%20exactly%20is%20chat%20GPT,is%20similar%20to%20human%20conversation (last visited Feb. 11, 2025) (explaining that a chatbot is a type of artificial intelligence that can understand and generate natural language text." Chat bots are trained "on large amounts of text data" and use an algorithm "that is designed to mimic the way the human brain works." The chatbot is trained on a large dataset of text, such as articles or conversations." It then uses this data to learn the patterns and structure of language. Once it has learned enough about language, it can generate its own text based on a given prompt or topic. "For example, if you ask chatGPT about the weather. It might generate a response like "The weather today is sunny and warm, with a high of 75 degrees." It is able to generate this response because it has learned about weather patterns and how to describe them in natural language.").

[347] Such sites serve as repositories for over 250 billion web pages for over 18 years. *See* Romain Beaumont, LAION-5B: A New Era of Open Large-Scale Multi-Model Datasets, LAION (Mar. 31, 2022), https://laion.ai/blog/laion-5b/; *See also* Homepage, COMMON CRAWL, https://commoncrawl.org/ (last visited Feb. 11, 2025).

[348] Calvin Wankhede, *What Is Google's Bard AI? Here's Everything You Need to Know,* ANDROID AUTHORITY (Mar. 22, 2023), www.androidauthority.com/google-bard-chatbot-3295464/ (explaining that 'bots,' or robot applications scan and copy the information on web pages then store and index what is described as an unimaginable extent of personal information.).

[349] Notice of Voluntary Dismissal, J.L. v. Alphabet Inc., No. 3:23-cv-03440-AMO (N.D. Cal. Sept. 19, 2023).

[350] Cousart v. OpenAI LP, No. 3:23-cv-04557-VC (N.D. Cal. May 24, 2024).

[351] Consolidated Class Action Complaint, In re Google Generative AI Copyright Litig., No. 5:23-CV-03440-EKL (N.D. Cal. Dec. 20, 2024).

Plaintiffs to Respond to Google's Renewed Motion to Relate.[352] The *Zhang* Plaintiffs opposed Google's motion to relate their copyright infringement case which concerned visual artists' work used in image generation AI with the *Leovy* case which concerned authors' work used in language model AI, arguing the cases involve different parties, different types of copyrighted work, and different AI models, thus lacking substantial similarity.[353] However, on August 5, 2024, the court ordered the *Zhang* and *Leovy* cases be related which was followed by the Court granting Google's motion for Joint Stipulation to Consolidate *Leovy* and *Zhang on* Oct. 28, 2024, because both cases involved similar claims against Google regarding their use of copyrighted material.[354]

At present, *In re Google Generative AI Copyright Litigation*, is a consolidated class action complaint with eleven named Plaintiffs who allege that Google copied millions of copyrighted works in its Generative AI products like Gemini and permanently embedded copies of these works within these models.[355] Plaintiffs include New York Times Best-Selling author Steve Almond, who owns nine registered copyrights for literary works and alleges that at least six of which "Google took, used, copied, and/or reproduced without license or authorization."[356] As a result, Almond alleged he suffered direct market harm from the revenue he could have received if Google had properly licensed his works for AI training and market value diminution due to Google's "mass appropriation of literary works" which he alleges has depressed the overall market for fiction and nonfiction writers.[357] Similarly other Plaintiffs include New York Times best-selling authors, illustrators, cartoonists, photographers, visual artists, who are all registered owners of one or more copyrighted works.[358] The plaintiffs all alleged that Google's unauthorized copying and mass appropriation resulted in direct market harm and market value diminution in their respective

---

352 Zhang Plaintiffs' Opposition to Google's Renewed Administrative Motion to Consider Whether Cases Should be Related, Leovy v. Google LLC, No. 3:23-cv-3440-AMO (N.D. Cal. July 30, 2024).

353 Zhang Plaintiffs' Opposition to Google's Renewed Administrative Motion to Consider Whether Cases Should be Related, Leovy v. Google LLC, No. 3:23-cv-3440-AMO (N.D. Cal. July 30, 2024).

354 At first, the court denied Google's motion to relate the original case *Leovy v. Google* with *Zhang v. Google*, however, after the privacy and state law claims were dropped by both Plaintiffs, Google stipulated that both the putative class actions focused on copyright infringement claims for training its AI models, including Gemini and Imagen, and that Google would anticipated claiming the same defense in both cases. Joint Stipulation and Proposed Order Consolidating Cases, Leovy v. Google LLC, No. 5:23-cv-03440-EKL, & Zhang v. Google LLC, No. 5:24-cv-02531-EKL (N.D. Cal. Oct. 28, 2024).

355 Consolidated Class Action Complaint, In re Google Generative AI Copyright Litig., No. 5:23-cv-03440-EKL, 1 (N.D. Cal. Dec. 20, 2024) ().

356 *Id.* at 6.

357 *Id.*

358 *Id.* at 6-20.

industries.[359] The Plaintiffs determined their copyrighted works had been used and copied without proper license by listing the websites their copyrighted works were found on that were alleged to have been used to train Google's AI models. The consolidated class action complaint claims that Google's embedding of the Plaintiffs works into the Generative AI Models, Google has irreversibly entangled the Plaintiff Works with its commercial products, which in effect has stripped Plaintiffs of their exclusive rights to control the copying and distribution of their registered works under the Copyright Act.[360]

Presently, Plaintiffs are waiting for defendants to respond to the consolidated class action complaint. Websites such as those hosted by Baker & Hostetler LLP, Law 360, and Ropes and Gray are tracking the AI litigation across the US in an objective and concise manner.

Tags: Google, Gemini, AI Training, OpenAI, Copyright Management Information, ChatGPT

G. Huckabee v. Bloomberg, No. 1:23-cv-09152 (S.D.N.Y. October 17, 2023).[361]

Former Arkansas governor Mike Huckabee and others are suing Bloomberg over its alleged use of a dataset containing unlawfully obtained works by the authors to train its AI model. The plaintiffs claim Bloomberg knowingly engaged in direct copyright infringement of their works and have cited specific works by each author present in the dataset, as well as reports from Bloomberg acknowledging that the dataset was used for training an early iteration of its AI model. Bloomberg claims fair use.

Plaintiff-authors Mike Huckabee, Relevate Group, David Kinnaman, Tsh Oxeneider, Lyla Terkeurst, and John Blasé are suing Bloomberg L.P. and Bloomberg Finance L.P. (hereinafter "Bloomberg")[362], alleging Bloomberg engaged in direct copyright infringement when it trained its Large Language Model (LLM), BloombergGPT, on unlicensed copies of the plaintiffs' copyright-protected works using the Books3 dataset.[363]

---

[359] *Id.*

[360] *Id.*

[361] Maddy Marlowe, Tulane Law School, expected May 2025.

[362] Initially, this lawsuit involved defendants Meta Platforms, Inc., Microsoft Corporation, and The EleutherAI Institute; however, Meta and Microsoft were severed as defendants by the court and moved to California while this Bloomberg suit remains in the S.D.N.Y.. The EleutherAI Institute was voluntarily dismissed as a defendant. The present lawsuit is now limited to the listed Bloomberg entities. Class Action Complaint, 1, *Mike Huckabee, Relevate Group, David Kinnaman, Tsh Oxeneider, Lyla Terkeurst, and John Blasé v. Meta Platforms, Inc., Bloomberg L.P., Bloomberg Finance L.P., Microsoft Corporation, and The EleutherAI Institute*, No. 1:23-cv-09152 (S.D.N.Y. October 17, 2023).

[363] Plaintiffs' initial complaint also alleged vicarious infringement and DCMA claims, but these were not included in the amended complaint now at issue against Bloomberg. *Status Updates,* Huckabee v. Bloomberg, BAKERHOSTETLER (last accessed 2/12/25), https://www.bakerlaw.com/huckabee-v-bloomberg/.

The Books3 dataset was introduced in 2020 by EluetherAI as part of its larger dataset "The Pile" and comprises information from 183,000 pirated ebooks obtained through data scraping.[364] This dataset became a popular resource for major companies, including Bloomberg, in training their developmental AI models to respond to prompts with natural language. Plaintiffs now allege the illicitly obtained dataset was used by Bloomberg to train its LLM, BloombergGPT, despite Bloomberg's "full knowledge and understanding" that the dataset contained unlicensed copyrighted works, such as those by the Plaintiff-authors.[365] BloombergGPT is a generative AI system for financial analysis developed by the company.[366] In its letter of intent to move to dismiss all causes of action, Bloomberg argued the fair use defense. Bloomberg claims the alleged training was part of a not-for-commercial-use research project to develop an LLM for improved performance in financial analysis.[367]

Bloomberg maintains that BloombergGPT is an internal company application and that any alleged use of the Plaintiff-authors' works was limited, private, and conducted by a news-reporting agency for non-commercial research purposes, falling well within the "purpose and character" of fair use.[368] Bloomberg also states the plaintiffs have failed to provide specific evidence of how it infringed or which books were misused for BloombergGPT.[369]

In their initial complaint, plaintiffs cited an announcement by the company acknowledging Books3 was used in training its initial model of BloombergGPT, but that the dataset would not be included when training future models of the LLM.[370] In response to this claim, the plaintiffs argue the use of Books3 to train future models is inconsequential because the nature of LLM development involves building on previous models; therefore, the plaintiffs allege their protected works from Books3 are already baked into even those future versions of BloombergGPT.[371] The plaintiffs maintain Bloomberg has already and will continue to benefit from their unlicensed, copyright-protected works.

In its motion to dismiss, Bloomberg alleged the plaintiffs' claims are insufficient and even if accepted as true, are rebutted by plaintiffs' own amended

---

364 *Id.*

365 *Id.*

366 Blake Brittain, *Bloomberg asks US court to toss copyright lawsuit over AI training*, REUTERS.COM (last updated March 25, 2024), https://www.reuters.com/legal/litigation/bloomberg-asks-us-court-toss-copyright-lawsuit-over-ai-training-2024-03-25/.

367 *Status Updates,* Huckabee v. Bloomberg, BAKERHOSTETLER, https://www.bakerlaw.com/huckabee-v-bloomberg/ (last visited Feb. 12, 2025).

368 Brittain, *supra* note 366.

369 *Id.*

370 Class Action Complaint, 18, Mike Huckabee, et.al. v. Meta Platforms, Inc., Bloomberg L.P., Bloomberg Finance L.P., Microsoft Corporation, and The EleutherAI Institute, No. 1:23-cv-09152 (S.D.N.Y. October 17, 2023).

371 *Id.*

complaint recognizing Bloomberg as a "provider of financial news and analysis", arguing this acknowledgement clearly demonstrates the BloombergGPT project was a fair use.[372]

The lawsuit is currently pending. Following Bloomberg's motion to dismiss, plaintiffs responded with arguments that the motion failed to deny plaintiffs' ownership of copyright in those works specifically identified in the amended complaint as part of the Books3 dataset used by Bloomberg, and that Bloomberg's fair use defense is not appropriate at this stage because it requires facts not included in the complaint and assumptions drawn in Bloomberg's favor.[373] The most recent filing in this case was Bloomberg's response to the plaintiffs' response to its motion to dismiss, wherein Bloomberg argued once again failure to allege claims with sufficient, specific facts indicating a basis for relief. Bloomberg stated in its response that the plaintiffs are engaged in a "mere fishing expedition without a substantiated legal claim."[374]

As it stands, the lawsuit is still pending in the Southern District of New York, and there has been no ruling on Bloomberg's motion to dismiss. Notably, there is a lack of secondary sources providing opinion on the lawsuit or the arguments raised by the parties. However, the fair use defense raised by Bloomberg is reflective of a theme in much AI litigation over copyright infringement. The suit is being monitored and reported by Baker Hostetler and Reuters through status updates on AI litigation around the country.

Tags: Bloomberg, BloombergGPT, Mike Huckabee, Books3, copyright infringement, fair use

H. *The Intercept Media and Raw Story Media v. OpenAI, No. 1:24-cv-01515, (S.D.N.Y. Feb. 28, 2024)* [375]

These are three news organizations alleging DMCA violations in training ChatGPT, specifically involving the removal of Copyright Management Information. On February 28, 2024, Intercept Media, Raw Story media, and AlterNet, three news media corporations, filed suit against both OpenAI and Microsoft[376] with claims the defendants are adversarial to journalism organizations. Raw Story Media claims it is the largest independent progressive political news website.[377] AlterNet is a publisher with a focus on civil rights,

[372] *Status Updates*, *supra* note 367.
[373] *Id.* Plaintiffs also maintain that all allegations must be drawn in their favor at the Motion to Dismiss stage, and cited to precedent on fair use defense at this stage to argue they should be allowed to proceed to discovery to challenge Bloomberg's defense. *Id.*
[374] *Id.*
[375] Layla Ghiai, Tulane Law School, JD, expected graduation, 2025.
[376] Complaint at 1, The Intercept Media, Inc. v. OpenAI, Inc., No. 1:24-cv-01515, (S.D.N.Y. 2024); Complaint at 1, Raw Story Media, Inc. v. OpenAI Inc., No. 1:24-cv-01514, (S.D.N.Y. 2024)
[377] *Raw Story Media, Inc.*, No. 1:24-cv-01514 at 2-3

social justice, culture, health, and the environment. Defendants OpenAI and Microsoft jointly are the creators and trainers of ChatGPT AI products.[378]

The claims that the plaintiffs make against OpenAI and Microsoft are violations of the integrity of Copyright Management Information statutes within the DMCA (Digital Millennium Copyright Act), which is part of the 1976 Copyright Act. In particular, plaintiffs argue that OpenAI and Microsoft removed the copyright management information (CMI) of various articles in order to train ChatGPT. This removal of CMI information then facilitated and enabled users of ChatGPT to enact copyright infringement without their own knowledge.[379] None of the media corporations claimed OpenAI committed copyright infringement itself. In addition to damages, both Intercept and Raw Story sought an injunction requiring OpenAI and Microsoft to remove all copies of its copyrighted works that do not maintain the original CMI.

On April 15, 2024, Microsoft and OpenAI filed a motion to dismiss.[380] In the motion, Microsoft pled that the news media corporations failed to provide examples of copyrighted work that were produced in any ChatGPT outputs despite their claim that the works are being used in the training datasets. Moreover, the defendants argue that there was no evidence of a concrete injury suffered by any of the plaintiffs, therefore not giving the plaintiff's any legal standing. Lastly, Microsoft and OpenAI claimed that plaintiffs failed to overcome the "double scienter" requirement needed to satisfy any DMCA claims. In order to overcome the "double scienter" requirement, a plaintiff must allege that the defendant had removed the CMI information intentionally and that the defendant must have reasonably understood that removal of the CMI may facilitate copyright infringement. Ultimately, the Southern District of New York granted Microsoft and OpenAI's motion for dismissal against Raw Story Media under the grounds that plaintiffs did not have proper standing due to no concrete injury being present. Meanwhile, all but one of Intercept's claims has been dismissed.

Currently, both suits are still ongoing. Raw Story Media Inc. and Alternet have filed for a motion for leave to amend their complaint while OpenAI has answered Intercept's one remaining claim. Although ultimately, these media outlets failed under a standing issue, many experts fear it will be impossible to bring suit against any AI model training especially since proving the concrete injury is difficult.[381] OpenAI currently has partnerships with 38 different

---

[378] *See infra* Part II, Section A.

[379] Complaint at 13, The Intercept Media, Inc. v. OpenAI, Inc., 1:24-cv-01515, (S.D.N.Y.)

[380] *The Intercept Media and Raw Story Media v., OpenAi,* BAKERHOSTETLER, https://www.bakerlaw.com/the-intercept-media-and-raw-story-media-v-openai/ (Last visited Feb 2025).

[381] Kate Knibbs, *OpenAI Scored a Legal Win Over Progressive Publishers—but the Fight's Not Finished,* WIRED, https://www.wired.com/story/opena-alternet-raw-story-copyright-lawsuit-dmca-standing/ (Nov 8, 2024)

corporations, several being news media outlets: TIME, Vox, and The Atlantic to name a few.[382]

Tags: Newspaper, Media, OpenAI, AI Training, Copyright Management Information, ChatGPT

I. *Kadrey v. Meta Platforms, Inc., No. 23-cv-03417-VC, 2023 WL 8039640, (N.D. Cal. Nov. 20, 2023).*[383]

Plaintiff authors Sarah Silverman, Richard Kadrey, and Christopher Golden brought a putative class against Meta, a technology company, after it allegedly trained its artificial intelligence software Large Language Model Meta AI (LLaMA) using the plaintiffs' books as training sources without their consent, credit, or compensation.[384] The plaintiffs initially alleged six causes of action, including direct copyright infringement, vicarious copyright infringement, violation of the Digital Millennium Copyright Act (DMCA), unfair competition, unjust enrichment, and negligence.[385] In November 2023, the court dismissed all claims other than the plaintiff's assertion that Meta's alleged unauthorized copying of their books to train LLaMA constituted direct copyright infringement.[386]

The court dismissed the vicarious copyright infringement claim because the plaintiffs did not argue sufficiently that the models created an infringing output, a necessary element for this type of infringement.[387] According to some intellectual property lawyers, plaintiffs' claim for vicarious copyright infringement failed because the complaint did not allege that LLaMA created an output containing protectable expression that recast, transformed, or adapted the books.[388] Since the court found no infringing output, there could not be vicarious infringement.[389] The court dismissed the plaintiffs DMCA claim because it found they did not properly allege that LLaMA distributed the plaintiffs' books outside of their alleged use.[390] The claim for unfair competition was also dismissed by the court because it was preempted by the plaintiffs' direct copyright infringement claim.[391] Lastly, in the opinion of the court, the claims of unjust enrichment and negligence were

---

[382] Jonathan Gillham, *Open AI Partnership List,* ORIGINALITY.AI, https://originality.ai/blog/openai-partnerships (Jan 21, 2025).

[383] Lily Argyle, Tulane University Law School, JD expected May 2025.

[384] *Kadrey v. Meta Case Tracker,* BAKERHOSTETLER, https://www.bakerlaw.com/kadrey-v-meta/ (last visited Feb. 5, 2024).

[385] Melanie J. Howard & Keane Barger, *IP/Entertainment Case Law Updates: Kadrey V. Meta Platforms, Inc.,* LOEB & LOEB IP/ENTERTAINMENT CASE LAW UPDATES (Feb. 5, 2025), https://www.loeb.com/en/insights/publications/2023/12/richard-kadrey-v-meta-platforms-inc.

[386] *Kadrey v. Meta Case Tracker, supra* note 384.

[387] LOEB & LOEB IP/ENTERTAINMENT CASE LAW UPDATES, *supra* note 385.

[388] *Kadrey v. Meta Case Tracker, supra* note 384.

[389] LOEB & LOEB IP/ENTERTAINMENT CASE LAW UPDATES, *supra* note 342.

[390] *Kadrey v. Meta Case Tracker, supra* note 385.

[391] *Id.*

preempted by the Copyright Act.[392] In defense of the remaining direct copyright infringement claim, Meta maintains that the use of the plaintiffs' works for training falls under fair use.[393] Based on the court's dismissal of these claims and Meta's defense, it seems that the current and potential future plaintiffs are more likely to be successful in cases where the copyright material used to train AI tools is substantially similar to the outputs of the AI tools.[394]

In July 2024, the court ordered the remaining claim for copyright infringement in *Kadrey* to be consolidated with the claims in *Huckabee v. Bloomberg.*[395] Whether this legal battle will be successful for the plaintiff authors remains to be seen, but the discovery process thus far has swayed the public in their favor. To the horror of some Meta employees, the discovery process has uncovered the company's use of pirated material from Library Genesis (LibGen) to train its AI language models.[396] Meta employees' use and possible dissemination of large amounts of copyrighted material through controversial "shadow libraries" like LibGen could have lasting effects on its public image.[397] In addition to this public relations blow, a potential ruling in favor of the plaintiffs would force Meta and other technology companies to reevaluate their AI training methods to avoid further litigation supported by this precedent.[398] Some intellectual property lawyers believe the plaintiffs' remaining direct copyright infringement claim may be successful now that their complaint has been amended to reflect LLaMA's use of known datasets which include the plaintiffs' books.[399]

Tags: artificial intelligence, AI, copyright, AI training, Sarah Silverman, copyright infringement, Digital Millennium Copyright Act, DMCA, Meta, Large Language Model Meta AI, LLaMA, unjust enrichment, negligence, fair use

---

392 *Id.*

393 Knowing Machines, *Kadrey v. Meta Legal Explainer* (Nov. 27, 2023), https://knowingmachines.org/knowing-legal-machines/legal-explainer/cases/kadrey-v-meta

394 *Is the Copyright Threat to Generative AI Overhyped? Implications of Kadrey v. Meta,* FARELLA, BRAUN & MARTEL: INSIGHT PUBLICATIONS (Jan. 13, 2024), https://www.fbm.com/publications/is-the-copyright-threat-to-generative-ai-overhyped-implications-of-kadrey-v-meta/.

395 *Kadrey v. Meta Case Tracker, supra* note 341.

396 Kate Knibbs, *Meta Secretly Trained Its AI on a Notorious Piracy Database, Newly Unredacted Court Docs Reveal,* WIRED (Jan. 9, 2025), https://www.wired.com/story/new-documents-unredacted-meta-copyright-ai-lawsuit/.

397 *Id.*

398 *Id.*

399 FARELLA, BRAUN & MARTEL: INSIGHT PUBLICATIONS, *supra* note 385.

J. Nazemian and Dubus v. NVIDIA Corporation. Abdi Nazemian et al v. NVIDIA Corporation, No. 3:24-cv-01454 and Dubus, et al. v. NVIDIA, Inc., No. 3:24-cv-02655-VC (N.D. Cal.

This is a class-action suit filed by two groups of authors: Abdi Nazemian, Brian Keene, and Stewart O'Nan (the Navemian case) and Andrew Dubus III & Susan Orlean (Dubus) against NVIDIA Corporation, a US technology company that is a dominant supplier of AI hardware and software. The Plaintiffs allege that NVIDIA used and copied their books to train its large language model without permission. The big question of this case is whether usage of these copyrighted works in training can be considered under the defense of fair use, which would then absolve NVIDIA from any copyright infringement liability.

Tags: fair use, copyright infringement, NVIDIA

K. The Newspaper Cases against Microsoft

This is a consolidated case with *New York Times v. Microsoft*,[400] *Daily News v. Microsoft* [401]and *Center for Investigative Reporting v. Microsoft*.[402] Microsoft, the defendant in each of these actions, is a technology company and financial backer of OpenAI.[403] OpenAI is an AI research and development company.[404] The *New York Times* ("the Times") is a newspaper organization which covers domestic and national current events based in New York City.[405] The Times filed a complaint on December 27, 2023, that OpenAI fed the software information from the Times to train it without compensation nor the Times' permission to do so.[406] The Times claimed that OpenAI's usage of their materials may operate as a substitute for a Times subscription.[407]

---

[400] The New York Times v. Microsoft, et. al., No. 1:23-cv-11195 (S.D.N.Y.. filed Dec. 27, 2023).

[401] Daily News, LP et al. v. Microsoft Corp. et. al., No. 1:24-cv-03285 (S.D.N.Y. filed April 30, 2024).

[402] The Ctr. for Investigative Reporting, Inc. v. Microsoft Corp. et. al., No. 1:24-cv-04872 (S.D.N.Y. filed June 27, 2024)

[403] *Microsoft and OpenAI evolve partnership to drive the next phase of AI*, MICROSOFT, https://blogs.microsoft.com/blog/2025/01/21/microsoft-and-openai-evolve-partnership-to-drive-the-next-phase-of-ai/#:~:text=Microsoft%20remains%20a%20major%20investor,from%20their%20growth%20in%20valuation (last visited Feb. 17, 2025).

[404] *About*, OPENAI, https://openai.com/about/ (last visited Feb. 17, 2025).

[405] *Company*, THE N.Y. TIMES CO.., https://www.nytco.com/company/ (last visited Feb. 17, 2025).

[406] The New York Times v. Microsoft, No. 1:23-cv-11195 at *15

[407] The New York Times v. Microsoft, No. 1:23-cv-11195-SHS (filed Feb. 26, 2024)

Daily News, L.P, doing business as the *New York Daily News*, is a newspaper publishing company.[408] The Daily News' complaint includes seven other news organizations as plaintiffs, collectively known as "the Publishers." [409] The Publishers asserts that Defendants used their copyrighted materials such as articles in order to train their software without permission or compensation.[410] The Publishers bring an additional New York state-law trademark dilution claim.[411]

The Center for Investigative Reporting ("CIR") is a non-profit which seeks to publish pieces of investigative journalism, primarily through their radio show and podcast "Reveal".[412] CIR claims OpenAI copied, abridged, and displayed their content without permission, authorization, or compensation from Microsoft.[413] Due to the similarities of their claims, these three cases consolidated, becoming "the Newspaper Cases" on June 13, 2024. [414] The newspaper organizations argue that this use of copyrighted material without permission or payment in combination with many people's use of OpenAI as a substitute for the copyrighted materials within the articles.[415]

OpenAI argues that the data used to train their software is covered under fair use, and that large language models work with the data in a transformative way.[416] OpenAI asserts this information is publicly accessible and that it violates copyright law to "monopolize facts."[417] Key questions include whether OpenAI used materials from these organizations to train their software in a way that infringed on copyrighted materials.

Other news organizations such as The Associated Press, The Atlantic, Vox Media, FT Group, Axel Springer, Dotdash Meredith, NewsCorp, Guardian, Schibsted, Guardian, Axios, Future, Hearst, FT, Reuters, Fortune, USA Today Network, Conde Nast, Time, Informa, Financial Times, Le Monde, Prisa Media,

---

[408] *About Us*, DAILY NEWS, https://www.nydailynews.com/about-us/ (last visited Feb. 17, 2025).

[409] *Daily News, LP et al. v. Microsoft Corp. et. al.*, No. 1:24-cv-03285, at 1

[410] *Id.* at 2

[411] *Id.* at 93

[412] *About Us*, REVEAL, https://revealnews.org/about-us/ (last visited Feb. 17, 2025).

[413] *Ctr. for Investigative Journalism v. Microsoft,* No. 1:24-cv-04872 at *2-3

[414] Notice of Motion and Motion to Consolidate, The New York Times v. Microsoft, et. al and Daily News, LP et al. v. Microsoft Corp. et. al, No. 1:23-cv-11195-SHS (S.D.N.Y. 2024)

[415] *Id.*

[416] *Id.*

[417] Notice of Motion Oral Argument Requested, N.Y. Times Co. v, Microsoft Corp. et al., No. 1:23-cv-11195 (S.D.N.Y. 2023).

and Shutterstock have entered into licensing agreements with OpenAI or Microsoft to permit the usage of their articles to train the AI.[418]

Seeing as OpenAI is entering into licensing deals with 34 newspaper publishing organizations and counting, it is likely that this is an element of their litigation strategy. By entering into these arrangements, it weakens the Times and others' positions that OpenAI stole their content without consent.

Tags: newspaper, OpenAi, copyright, license, Microsoft, CIR, news, fair use, information.

L. OpenAI ChatGPT Litigation, [In re OPENAI CHATGPT Litigation, No. 3:23-cv-03223-AMO (N.D. Cal. July 12, 2024).] [419]

This is a consolidation case, filed in the Northern District of California that involves three plaintiff groups that consist of fiction and nonfiction authors Paul Tremblay, Sarah Silverman, Richard Kadrey, and Christopher Golden,[420] as well as Michael Chabon, Laura Lippman, Andrew Sean Greer, Ta-Nehisi Coates, David Henry Hwang, Rachel Louise Snyder, Laura Lippman, Ayelet Waldman, Junot Díaz, Jacqueline Woodson.[421] They filed on behalf of themselves and a putative class [422](*Tremblay v. OpenAI,*[423] and *Chabon v. OpenAI).*[424] Each plaintiff group has filed a complaint against defendant OpenAI, alleging copyright infringement, DMCA violations, vicarious copyright infringement, and torts associated with OpenAI's GPT models and ChatGPT service.[425]

---

[418] Cecily Mauran, *All the Media Companies that have Licensing Deals with OpenAI (so far)*, MASHABLE: TECH (June 21, 2024), https://mashable.com/article/all-the-media-companies-that-have-licensing-deals-with-openai-so-far; Charlotte Tobitt, *Who's suing AI and who's signing: 14 publishers join lawsuit against start-up Cohere*, PRESS GAZETTE (Feb. 14, 2025), https://pressgazette.co.uk/platforms/news-publisher-ai-deals-lawsuits-openai-google/.

[419] Natalia E. Walcott, Tulane University Law School, Class of 2025.

[420] *OpenAI ChatGPT Litigation,* BAKERHOSTETLER, https://www.bakerlaw.com/openai-chatgpt-litigation/ (last visited Feb. 8, 2025). This set of Plaintiffs are represented by Joseph Saveri Law Firm, LLP and Matthew Butterick.

[421] *Id.* This group of Plaintiffs are represented by Ventura Hersey & Muller, LLP and Caferty Clobes Meriwether & Sprengel LLP.

[422] *Id.*

[423] Tremblay v. OpenAI, Inc., No. 3:23-cv-03223 (N.D. Cal. filed June 28, 2023); Silverman v. OpenAI, Inc., No. 3:23-cv-03416 (N.D. Cal. filed July 7, 2023).

[424] Chabon v. OpenAI, Inc., No. 3:23-cv-04625 (N.D. Cal. filed Sept. 8, 2023).

[425] BAKERHOSTETLER, *supra* note 420. (Noting that the defendant in the three cases is OpenAI and includes OpenAI, Inc., OpenAI, L.P., OpenAI GP, L.L.C., OpenAI OpCo, L.L.C., OpenAI Startup Fund GP I, L.L.C., OpenAI Startup Fund I, L.P., and OpenAI Startup Fund Management, LLC. Defendants are represented by Morrison & Foerster LLP and Latham & Watkins LLP).

Tremblay's initial complaint discussed OpenAI's model.[426] OpenAI creates its large language models ("LLM") by copying a large amount of text from different types of sources.[427] The LLMs then take these copies, absorb the text, and create work that seems to be that written by a human.[428] In this case, the plaintiffs, Paul Tremblay and Mona Awad, alleged that OpenAI used plaintiffs' books without their knowledge or permission, in the training dataset for ChatGPT.[429] They discovered this when they prompted ChatGPT to generate accurate summaries of their copyrighted books.[430] On a larger scale, they discuss OpenAI's copying of many books in their data sets, respectively Books1 and Books2, which were used to train their GPT-3, and subsequent, models.[431] It is believed that Books1 and Books2 have over 350,000 titles combined, though OpenAI has not disclosed the names of those titles.[432] They alleged that the defendants are "benefit[ting] commercial[ly] and profit[ing] richly" by using their copyrighted materials through the ChatGPT platform.[433] Since the defendants have not disclosed the names of the titles used in their datasets, the size and members of the class are unknown.[434] Due to this, the plaintiffs are open to representing all potential parties in this case.[435]

The allegations in *Tremblay* are the following:

- Copyright infringement
  - Direct copyright infringement
  - Vicarious copyright infringement
- DMCA
  - Violation of the Digital Millennium Copyright Act through their removal of copyright-management information
- Other Counts
  - Unfair competition
  - Negligence
  - Unjust enrichment.[436]

---

426 Complaint at 4, *Tremblay v. OpenAI, Inc.*, No. 3:23-cv-03223 (N.D. Cal. filed June 28, 2023), ECF No. 1.

427 *Id.*

428 *Id. at 4-5.*

429 *Id.* at 2, 8. (stating that Plaintiffs Paul Tremblay and Mona Awad are writers. Tremblay owns several copyrighted books, including *The Cabin at the End of the World.* Awad also owns several copyrighted books, including *13 Ways of Looking at a Fat Girl and Bunny*).

430 *Id. at* 1.

431 *Id. at* 6.

432 *Id.* (noting that Book1 is believed to have about 63,000 titles, and Books2 is to have around 294,000 titles).

433 *Id. at* 1.

434 *Id. at* 8-10.

435 *Id.*

436 *Id. at* 10-15.

The plaintiffs welcome the lawsuit becoming a class action and are seeking statutory and other damages, permanent injunctive relief, attorney's fees and other costs associated with the lawsuit.[437]

Silverman's initial complaint discusses OpenAI's use of the Plaintiffs' copyrighted materials in their training data sets to condition their AI models to create their LLMs.[438] The plaintiffs in this lawsuit are authors Sarah Silverman, Christopher Golden, and Richard Kadrey.[439] This lawsuit discussed the data sets OpenAI used to train their models, stating that the Defendants did not disclose the names of the copyrighted material in the sets.[440] The Plaintiffs believe that their work is included in the data sets, and that, when prompted, ChatGPT created a summary of their books, using similar text.[441] They are concerned about the inaccuracies that can occur with these models, as it could cause a false representation of the contents of their individual works.[442]

The allegations in *Silverman* are the following:

- Copyright infringement
  - Direct copyright infringement
  - Vicarious copyright infringement

- DMCA
  - Violation of the Digital Millennium Copyright Act through their removal of copyright-management information

- Other Counts
  - Unfair competition
  - Negligence
  - Unjust enrichment.[443]
  -

Similar to *Tremblay,* the plaintiffs are open to making this a class action suit and are seeking attorney's fees, statutory and other damages, permanent injunctive relief, and other lawsuit-related costs.[444]

---

[437] *Id. a*t 15.
[438] Complaint at 4-5, Silverman v. OpenAI, Inc., No. 3:23-cv-03416 (N.D. Cal. filed July 7, 2023), ECF No. 1.
[439] *Id.* at 2-3. Plaintiffs Sarah Silverman, Christopher Golden and Richard Kadrey are all writers. Silverman owns several copyrighted books, including *The Bedwetter*. Golden owns several copyrighted books, including *Ararat*. Kadrey also owns several copyrighted books, including *Sandman Slim.*
[440] *Id.* at 6.
[441] *Id.* at 8.
[442] *Id.*
[443] *Id.* at 10-15.
[444] *Id.* at 15-16.

The final case in this consolidated lawsuit is *Chabon v. OpenAI.*[445] The initial complaint was filed by award-winning authors Michael Chabon, David Henry Hwang, Matther Klam, Rachel Louise Snyder, and Ayelet Waldman.[446] They made allegations similar to that of *Tremblay* and *Silverman,* alleging that OpenAI did not get the authors' permission to use their books in OpenAI's training dataset.[447] Plaintiffs believe ChatGPT and the model's use of their copyrighted material is an unauthorized use of derivative work.[448] They argued that OpenAI's acknowledgement of using various sources for their training models implied that their work was one of those pieces used.[449] Plaintiffs believe that OpenAI's rationale for doing this stems from their need to use sources of high quality to make sure that their model's outputs reflect work of the same or similar caliber.[450] Similar to *Tremblay and Silverman*, they discussed class allegations, due to the fact that other members of the class are undisclosed in the Defendants' data sets.[451]

The following counts alleged in *Chabon* are the following:

- Copyright infringement
    - Direct copyright infringement
    - Vicarious copyright infringement

- DMCA

---

[445] Chabon v. OpenAI, Inc., No. 3:23-cv-04625 (N.D. Cal. filed Sept. 8, 2023).
[446] Complaint at 2-3, Chabon v. OpenAI, Inc., No. 3:23-cv-04625 (N.D. Cal. filed Sept. 8, 2023), ECF No. 1. (noting that Plaintiffs Michael Chabon, David Henry Hwang, Matthew Klam, Rachel Louise Snyder, and Ayelet Waldman are writers. Chabon owns several copyrighted books, "including but not limited to *The Mysteries of Pittsburgh, Wonder Boys, The Amazing Adventures of Kavalier & Clay, the Yiddish Policemen's Union, Gentlemen of the Road, Telegraph Avenue, Fight of the Century, Kingdom of Olive and Ash,* and *Moonglow.*" Hwang owns several copyrighted books, "including but not limited to *M. Butterfly, Chinglish, Yellow Face, the Dance and the Railroad,* and *FOB*." Klam owns several copyrighted books, "including but not limited to, *Who is Rich?*, and *Sam the Cat and Other Stories*." Snyder owns several copyrighted books, "including but not limited to, *Women We Buried, Women We Burned, No Visible Bruises – What We Don't Know About Domestic Violence Can Kill Us, What We've Lost is Nothing,* and *Fugitive Denim: A Moving Story of People and Pants in the Borderless World of Global Trade.*" Waldman owns several copyrighted books, "including but not limited to, *Love and other Impossible Pursuits, Red Hook Road, Love and Treasure, Bad Mother, Daughter's Keeper, A Really Good Day, Fight of the Century, and Kingdom of Olives* and *Ash*.").
[447] *Id.* at 8-11. *See also* BAKERHOSTETLER, *supra* note 433.
[448] *Chabon v. OpenAI,* BAKERHOSTETLER, https://www.bakerlaw.com/chabon-v-openai/ (last visited Feb. 8, 2025).
[449] Complaint, Chabon, *supra* note 445 at 6.
[450] *Id.* at 5-7.
[451] *Id.* at 8-10.

- o Violation of the Digital Millennium Copyright Act through their removal of copyright-management information

- Other Counts
    - o Unfair competition
    - o Negligence
    - o Unjust enrichment.[452]

On November 7, 2023, the Northern District of California consolidated *Tremblay*, *Silverman*, and *Chabon*.[453] The consolidated group went on to file an amended complaint on March 13, 2023, alleging the same counts that were made in the three separate cases.[454] Open AI filed a motion to dismiss Count II in the Amended Complaint, alleging that the Plaintiffs failed to state a claim for their Unfair Competition Law (UCL) claim.[455] The court granted the Motion to Dismiss Count II, denying them the ability to leave to amend.[456]

There have not been many substantial updates on the case.[457] The case is currently in the discovery phase, with both parties filing a joint brief discussing their discovery concerns.[458] Plaintiffs alleged that OpenAI refuses to produce documentation about their language models, while OpenAI says that the information in those documents is irrelevant because ChatGPT does not use in-development models.[459] We will have to see what the Court decides in this matter.

<u>Tags</u>: OpenAI, Large Language Models ("LLMS"), Chabon, Silverman, Tremblay, Digital Millennium Copyright Act, OpenAI GPT models, ChatGPT, GPT models, direct copyright infringement, copyright infringement, unfair competition, negligence, and unjust enrichment

M. Thomson Reuters v. ROSS, 694 F. Supp. 3d 467 (D. Del. 2023).[460]

[452] *Id.* at 10-14.
[453] Pretrial Order at 1, In re OPENAI CHATGPT Litigation, No. 3:23-cv-03223-AMO (N.D. Cal. filed July 12, 2024), ECF No. 74.
[454] Amended Complaint at 1, In re OPENAI CHATGPT Litigation, No. 3:23-cv-03223-AMO (N.D. Cal. filed July 12, 2024), ECF No. 120.
[455] Defendant's Notice of Motion, Motion to Dismiss FirstConsolidated Amended Complaint, and Memorandum of Points and Authorities in Support Thereof at 4-7, In re OPENAI CHATGPT Litigation, No. 3:23-cv-03223-AMO (N.D. Cal. filed July 12, 2024), ECF No. 122.
[456] Order Granting Motion to Dismiss the UCL Claim at 5, In re OPENAI CHATGPT Litigation, No. 3:23-cv-03223-AMO (N.D. Cal. filed July 12, 2024), ECF No. 162.
[457] *AI Infringement Case Updates: December 16, 2024,* McKOOL SMITH, (Dec. 16, 2024), https://www.mckoolsmith.com/newsroom-ailitigation-3.
[458] *Id.*
[459] *Id.*
[460] Jon Evan Smelley, Tulane Law School, Expected Graduation 2025.

The issue in this case is whether ROSS's use of Westlaw's content constituted fair use or whether it was unauthorized and constituted as direct infringement.[461] This was one of the first AI cases filed.[462] The judge over the case, Judge Stephanos Bibas, stated that it would not be his place to rule as a matter of law on if ROSS's use of Westlaw's content was fair use.[463] This issue will be left for the jury to decide on a "headnote-by-headnote basis."[464] Although the trial was previously set for August 23, 2024, it has been pushed to May 12, 2025; however, due to the costs of litigation, ROSS shut down their platform in January of 2021.[465] The shutdown does not automatically absolve ROSS of potential copyright infringement liability.[466] If the court finds that ROSS unlawfully used Westlaw content prior to shutting down, damages may still be awarded based on the impact of that alleged infringement.[467] On the other hand, ROSS could argue that the platform's shutdown mitigates any potential harm to Thomson Reuters, potentially reducing or eliminating damages.[468] Additionally, the shutdown underscores a broader question in the case—whether AI companies can use copyrighted legal databases for training purposes without facing legal consequences.[469]

This case has been going for nearly five years, beginning in May 2020 when Thomson Reuters sued ROSS Intelligence for allegedly copying Westlaw content to train its AI-based legal research platform.[470] Thomson Reuters contends that ROSS's use of its proprietary legal materials constitutes copyright infringement,

---

[461] Aaron P. Rubin, *Reuters v. ROSS: District Court First to Consider Whether Training Generative AI Model Is Fair Use*, MORRISON FOERSTER (Oct. 20, 2023), https://www.mofo.com/resources/insights/231020-reuters-v-ross-district-court; Aaron Moss, *First AI Copyright Trial Starts This Week: What to Know*, COPYRIGHT LATELY (Aug. 19, 2024), https://copyrightlately.com/first-ai-copyright-trial-starts-westlaw/.

[462] *Id.*

[463] Rubin, *supra* note 461.

[464] *Id.*

[465] *Judge Bibas sets trial for May 12, 2025, but hopes for earlier date in Thomson Reuters v. ROSS Intelligence,* CHAT GPT IS EATING THE WORLD (Nov. 4, 2024), https://chatgptiseatingtheworld.com/2024/11/04/judge-bibas-sets-trial-for-may-12-2025-but-hopes-for-earlier-date-in-thomson-reuters-v-ross-intelligence/; The Founders, *Announcement,* ROSS INTELLIGENCE (Dec. 11, 2020), https://blog.rossintelligence.com/post/announcement.

[466] The Founders, *supra* note 365; Reuters, *Jury to decide on whether AI was trained on copied material in one of first major AI training trials,* EURO NEWS (Sep. 26, 2023, 2:16 PM GMT), https://www.euronews.com/next/2023/09/26/jury-to-decide-on-whether-ai-was-trained-on-copied-material-in-one-of-first-major-ai-train; *Thomson Reuters v. ROSS,* BAKER HOSTETLER, https://www.bakerlaw.com/thomson-reuters-v-ross/ (last visited Feb. 12, 2025).

[467] *Id.*

[468] *Id.*

[469] *Id.*

[470] BAKERHOSTETLER, *supra* note 466.

while ROSS argues that its use falls under fair use as it was transformative rather than merely duplicative.[471] Over the years, the case has seen multiple legal motions, hearings, and counterclaims, culminating in a renewed debate over copyright infringement and fair use.[472]

The case commenced with ROSS filing a motion to dismiss in July 2020, which was ultimately denied in March 2021.[473] The litigation escalated when both parties filed motions for summary judgment in December 2022, with Thomson Reuters seeking to establish copyright infringement and ROSS defending itself under the fair use doctrine.[474] Throughout 2023, the court denied motions for summary judgment and scheduled the trial for August 2024.[475] In 2024, the case evolved with discussions on whether Westlaw's headnotes were copyrightable, leading to a filtration hearing request by ROSS, which the court later declined.[476]

By the latter half of 2024, both parties renewed their summary judgment motions on copyright infringement and fair use, submitting arguments throughout October.[477] On December 5, 2024, the court held a hearing on these motions, with a ruling still pending.[478] The outcome of this case could significantly impact the future of AI-driven legal research and the scope of copyright protections in the digital age.[479] This case looks like it will be the first case that will decide whether fair use will prevail when it comes to AI.[480]

Tags: AI, Copyright infringement, Tortious Interference, No Fair Use, Fair Use, Antitrust, Anticompetition, Summary Judgement, Filtration Hearing

N. Voice Cases

There are a number of AI-related voice cases where unauthorized use of someone's voice is the issue. Voice actors have brought a class action suit against LOVO for using their voices to create generated voices without their consent.[481] ElevenLabs is also getting sued for the same kind of conduct.

---

[471] *Id.*
[472] *Id.*
[473] *Id.*
[474] *Id.*
[475] *Id.*
[476] *Id.*
[477] *Id.*
[478] *Id.*
[479] Rubin, *supra* note 461; Moss, *supra* note 461.
[480] *Id.*
[481] Jane Wester, *Control of Their Careers Has Been Hijacked': Voice Actors File Proposed Class Action Against AI Company*, ALM LAW, https://www.law.com/2024/05/20/control-of-their-careers-has-been-hijacked-voice-actors-file-proposed-class-action-against-ai-company/?slreturn=2025030261957 (last visited March 1, 2025).

IV. SECONDARY SOURCES RELATED TO THE CASES[482]

The cases are one aspect of what we should keep our eye on. We also wanted to understand the themes we are seeing, and how people are writing about the cases at the progress through the system. How can we understand all of these cases in a coherent way? We see a number of resources trying to help us with that as well. Using secondary sources, we wanted to know how the news was reporting the causes of action. What are the themes? The two key themes are direct infringement and DMCA claims.

AI companies accessed copyrighted works and made copies for training the AI models.[483] This unauthorized copying comes in additional steps in the process including "weight folders" and producing substantially similar outputs that are also infringing.

Copyright owners have filed lawsuits in U.S federal court against AI companies alleging direct copyright infringement for improper use of copyrighted material.[484] Many of the cases assert unauthorized removal or alteration of copyright management information as well as claiming infringing derivative works.[485] While many of these claims have been dismissed, none of the unauthorized use of works claims have been dismissed which are the focus of these cases.[486] While AI cases are still in the early stages, practitioners have already shown a tendency for courts to side with plaintiffs.[487]

New York Times Attorney, Ian Crosby, described AI's impact as "substantial."[488] Users are now able to search questions and receive responses.[489] This point is pivotal in establishing a clear-cut copyright infringement case.[490] Publishers and authors assert that the data that drives ChatGPT is mainly supported by copyrighted content used without consent or authorization.[491] The publisher's legal team argues that ChatGPT profits from taking, processing, and

---

[482] Tynesea Watts, Tulane Law School, Expected Graduation 2025.

[483] David M. McIntosh et al., *An End-of-Year Update to LLP*, ROPES GRAY (Dec 17, 2024), https://www.ropesgray.com/en/insights/alerts/2024/12/an-end-of-year-update-to-the-current-state-of-ai-related-copyright-litigation.

[484] Keith Kupferschimd, *Insights from Court Orders in AI Copyright Infringement Cases*, COPYRIGHT ALLIANCE (Dec 12, 2024), https://copyrightalliance.org/ai-copyright-infringement-cases-insights/.

[485] *Id.* at 282.

[486] *Id.*

[487] *Id.*

[488] Complaint, The New York Times Co. v. Microsoft Corp. et al., 1:23-cv-11195 (S.D.N.Y. 2023).

[489] Bobby Allyn, *'The New York Times' takes Open AI to court. ChatGPT's future could be on the line*, NPR (Feb. 9, 2025), https://www.npr.org/2025/01/14/nx-s1-5258952/new-york-times-openai-microsoft

[490] *Id.*

[491] *Id.*

recreating journalistic material without payment or authorization.[492] In response, AI companies are clinging to the fair use doctrine as defense by claiming that AI tools.[493]

A victory for publishers and authors would grant them more control over their work and its use. However, a loss for AI companies would require that the AI companies destroy their current dataset and recreate a new dataset with work they are authorized to use.[494] In contrast, the weight of the fair use defense in copyright cases hangs in the balance. A win for AI companies would constitute an expansion of the fair use defense, while giving creators less control of who can access their work and how their work can be used.

The Thomson v. ROSS case sits at the precipice of this controversy[495]. In Thomson v. ROSS, a federal district court found that the headnotes and a key numbering system that ROSS AI ("ROSS') copied from Thomson Reuters Westlaw ("Thomson") satisfied the legal requirement for originality. Subsequently, the court decided that ROSS copied copyrightable material from Thomson.

This decision received strong criticism since its ruling. [496] Critiques questioned the originality of the material in question by claiming that the Judge mischaracterized the merger doctrine. [497] The court labeled near- verbatim summaries as original work by ruling that the headnotes are original individually and as a compilation and by ruling that the key number system was original as and protected by copyright as a compilation.[498]

In US copyright law "originality" specifically refers to work that has a modicum of creativity that our society would want to protect and encourage.[499] Additionally, in US copyright law, facts are not copyrightable, but sometimes the

---

[492] *Id.*

[493] *Delaware District Court Ruling Raises Critical Fair Use Challenges For AI Companies: Implications For Copyright Compliance and Competitive Practices*, DYKEMA *(Feb. 15, 2025)*, https://www.dykema.com/news-insights/delaware-district-court-ruling-raises-critical-fair-use-challenges-for-ai-companies-implications-for-copyright-compliance-and-competitive-practices.html

[494] *Id.*

[495] Joseph A. Meckes, *Court: Training AI Model Based on Copyrighted Data Is Not Fair Use as a Matter of Law*, THE NAT. L. REV.: GLOBAL IP AND TECH L. BLOG (Feb. 11, 2025), https://natlawreview.com/article/court-training-ai-model-based-copyrighted-data-not-fair-use-matter-law.

[496] *Thomas Reuters v. ROSS: The First AI Fair Use Ruling Fails to Persuade,* AUTHORS ALLIANCE, *(Feb. 13, 2025)*, https://www.authorsalliance.org/2025/02/13/thomson-reuters-v-ross-the-first-ai-fair-use-ruling-fails-to-persuade/

[497] *Id.*

[498] *Id.*

[499] Paul Matenear, *Copy That! Copyright Infringement in Branding,* AXLEY ATTORNEYS (Feb 13, 2025), https://www.axley.com/publication_article/copy-that-infringement-in-branding/.

expression of facts can be.[500] The doctrine of merger also protects our freedom to reference facts or an idea.[501] US courts have recognized that there are a limited number of ways that one can restate facts, and therefore those expressions don't qualify as "original."[502] The Doctrine of Merger recognizes that certain expressions "merge" with facts and thereafter become unprotectable.[503]

Critics assert that Thomson's key numbering system and headnotes lack the modicum of creativity required for originality because ROSS copied near-verbatim summaries of facts.[504] Moreover, critics assert that the judge mischaracterized the doctrine of merger and ruled that it doesn't apply in this case because he believes that there are many ways to express points of judicial law from judicial opinion.[505] Critics claim that this reasoning shows a flawed understanding of the doctrine of merger because the very nature of language allows for an expression to be said in multiple ways, but the doctrine of merger applies when the number of ways to retell an expression is limited – especially when referring to legal expressions and terms of art.[506]

The most notable critique of this case is the fair use ruling. The court ruled that ROSS's use of Thomson's headnotes and key numbering system was not fair use because it did not satisfy two of the four factors in the fair use analysis.[507] The District Court decided that ROSS's fair use argument did not prove transformative use under the first factor because of ROSS's strictly commercial use.[508] Subsequently, the court found that ROSS's use failed the fourth factor because ROSS was unable to show lack of a potential market for Thomson to sell its content as AI training data and that such market would be unaffected by ROSS's actions.[509]

The fair use ruling attracted a significant amount of criticism. In order to decide if the use of the headnotes and the key numbering system counted as transformative use under the first factor of the analysis, the court had to assess whether intermediate copying case law supported ROSS's use.[510] The court asserts that the copying of the head notes and the key number system counts as copyright infringement because an intermediate copy with copyright restricted

---

[500]Molly Shaffer Van Houweling, *The Freedom to Extract in Copyright Law*, 103 N.C. L. REV. 447-448 (2025).

[501] *Id.*

[502] *Id.*

[503] *Id.*

[504] Authors Alliance, *supra* note 496.

[505] *Id.*

[506] *Id.*

[507] Mark Humphry, *Court Unplugs AI Fair Use Defense, But Context is Key*, MITCHELL SILBERBERG & KNUPP LLP (Feb 14, 2025), https://www.msk.com/newsroom-alerts-ai-fair-use-decision

[508] *Id.*

[509] *Id.*

[510] Author's Alliance, *Supra* note 499.

material authored by Thomson exists, even though the exact content from Thomson was not shown to the public.[511] According to this court, intermediate copying only supports fair use for computer codes.[512] Critics highlight the fact that the judge contradicts their reasoning in this opinion because under the third factor of the fair use analysis the judge states that only content available to the public when analyzing copyright infringement.[513]

Critics also note the court's discussion regarding intermediate copying by asserting that case law supports fair use when the material in question is not shared to the public and there is no intention to share the content with the public.[514] Lasty, many critics have challenged the court's analysis of the fourth factor by stating that the mere creation of the derivative work implies that a market for this work already exists.[515] The judge insinuates that by using Thomson's content, ROSS created an AI training data market that Thomson should have control of as the copyright holder.[516] Critics argue the reasoning used in this analysis is not supported by case law.[517] Rather, they say to properly analyze the fourth factor copyright holders must prove the existence, or likelihood of developing, licensing market, before arguing a secondary use serves as "market substitute."[518]

V. LICENSING IN THE SHADOW OF LAWSUITS[519]

A. Licensing Deals

We are seeing a trend – licensing deals with major AI players, while the lawsuits continue. Here are some key news stories and resources that are keeping track. Here are three lists to get you started.

- Sara Guaglione, "2024 in review: A Timeline of the major deals between publishers and AI companies, Digiday, December 27, 2024. https://digiday.com/media/2024-in-review-a-timeline-of-the-major-deals-between-publishers-and-ai-companies/

  She reports that 2024 saw more formalized relationships with a wave of licensing agreements to use publishers' content to train LLMs.

---

511 *Id.*
512 *Id.*
513 *Id.*
514 *Fair Warning: AI's First Copyright Fair Use Ruling, Thomson Reuters v. Ross*, HUNTON (Feb 19, 2025), https://www.hunton.com/insights/legal/fair-warning-ais-first-copyright-fair-use-ruling-thomson-reuters-v-ross
515 *Id.*
516 *Id.*
517 *Id.*
518 *Authors Alliance Submits Amicus Brief In Sedlik V. Drachenberg*, AUTHOR'S ALLIANCE (Feb 15, 2025), https://www.authorsalliance.org/2024/12/23/authors-alliance-submits-amicus-brief-in-sedlik-v-drachenberg/
519 Elizabeth Townsend Gard

Publishers also gain attribution that their materials are being used, including in chatbots and search platforms. She takes us through a timeline of when and the details of agreements that have been made.

- Thani Shamsi, "Ultimate List of Data Licensing Deal for AI, October 28, 2024, Monda, https://www.monda.ai/blog/ultimate-list-of-data-licensing-deals-for-ai.

  This article approaches the question from what organizations have made deal with AI companies, e.t. Reddit, Shutterstock, etc. It profies ten companies.

- Charlotte Tobitt, "Who's Suing AI and who's signing: Major deals with Google, OpenAI and Mistral start year," PressGazette, January 25, 2025, https://pressgazette.co.uk/platforms/news-publisher-ai-deals-lawsuits-openai-google/.

  This article lists the nine cases where media is suing AI companies, and with it summaries of each case. It also lists the news publishers that have agreements with AI companies, listed by the publishers. The author promises that the page will be updated as legal cases proceed and new deals are made. So, this is one to bookmark.

So, who has made agreements so far?

Agreements with OpenAI
Le Monde
Prisa
Financial Times
DotDash Meredith
News Corp.
The Atlantic
Vox Media
Time
Conde Nast
Hearst
Future
Associated Press
Shutterstock
Axios, including funding four newsrooms with Axios.[520]

Agreements with Microsoft
Axel Springer

---

[520] Daniel Konstantinovic, *OpenAI to Fund Four Axios Newsrooms in Content Licensing Deal*, EMARKETER (Jan. 15, 2025), https://www.emarketer.com/content/openai-fund-four-axios-newsrooms-content-licensing-deal

Informa
FT
Reuters
Hearst
USA Today Network
Fortune

Agreements with Perplexity[521]
Time
Der Spiegel
Fortune
Entrepreneur
The Texas Tribune
ADWEEK
Blavity
DPReview
Gear Patrol
The Independent
Lee Enterprises
Los Angeles Times
MediaLab
Mexico News Daily
Minkabu Infonoid
NewsPicks
Prisa Media
RLT Germany grands stern and nvt
World History Encyclopedia

Agreements with ProRata
Financial Times
Axel Springer
The Atlantic
Fortune
DMG media
Sky News
Guardian
Prospect

B. A New Lawsuit: Advance Local Media v. Cohere, 1:25-cv-01305 (SDNY)

---

[521] *Welcoming more global news organizations to Perplexity's Publishers' Program*, ANDERSEN (Dec. 5, 2024), https://www.perplexity.ai/hub/blog/perplexity-expands-publisher-program-with-15-new-media-partners#.

On February 13, 2025, a collection of news publishers that allege copyright infringement and false attribution by Cohere in the building of their AI. What is interesting about this case is that the complaint details the including that there is availability of licensing as an alternative to copyright infringement. These news groups that are part of the lawsuit include Conde Nast (who has licensed with OpenAI), The Atlantic (who has licensed with ProRata and OpenAI), Axel Spring (who has licensed with ProRata), Forbes, Guardian, Los Angeles Times, Politico, The Republican, Plain Dealer, Toronto Star Newspapers, McClatchy (with 30 daily newspapers), Newsday, and Vox (who has licensed with OpenAI). The complaint begins, "This is a lawsuit to protect journalism from systematic copyright and trademark infringement. Rather than create its own content, Cohere takes the creative output of Publishers, some of the largest, most enduring, and most important news, magazine, and digital publishers in the United States and around the world. Without permission or compensation, Cohere uses scraped copies of our articles, through training, real-time use, and in outputs, to power its artificial intelligence ("AI") service, which in turn competes with Publisher offerings and the emerging market for AI licensing. Not content with just stealing our works, Cohere also blatantly manufactures fake pieces and attributes them to us, misleading the public and tarnishing our brands."[522] So, the licensing deals with AI companies have led to a market that, according to the complaint does not justify fair use of using news materials.

And who is Cohere? According to the complaint, it's a $5 billion Canadian company who is training on unlicensed materials and the outputs include "full verbatim copies, substantial excerpts, and substantive summaries."[523] It prides itself on its news reporting function, using the plaintiffs' materials unlicensed.

Included in the complaint are the licensing deals the plaintiffs have both with traditional platforms like Yahoo!. Apple News, NewsBreak, and Ancestry.com, Lexis Nexis, but also AI companies. They own not only copyrights that are being infringed, but also trademarks. What is interesting is that the complaint in many ways will mimic the summary judgement in ROSS, showing that the summaries are similar to the original articles. So, they are alleging infringement not only in the training but also the outputs. The 64-page complaint has many examples with graphics to show the copying in various forms. Again, this case is in the very early stages, but it is interesting to see the markets development supporting copyright infringement

VI. SUMMARY JUDGEMENT IN THOMSON REUTERS V. ROSS

A. Introduction

---

[522] Case 1:25-cv-01305, at Page 2 (2/13/20), https://admin.bakerlaw.com/wp-content/uploads/2025/02/ECF-1-Advance-Local-Media-Complaint.pdf.
[523] *Id* at 3.

This was the first filed AI case (in May 2020), and on February 11 2025, the court found copyright infringement and no fair use on summary judgement.[524] The opinion is written in the first person, as the Judge makes his way through the case and his decision. He begins, "A smart man knows when he is right; a wise man knows when he is wrong. Wisdom does not always find me, so I try to embrace it when it does—even if it comes late, as it did here."[525] Judge Bibas is referring to his early summary judgement opinion of 2023.[526] In that opinion Judge Bibas denied Thomson Reuter's motion for summary judgement on copyright and fair use, and moved the case towards trial.[527]

The case concerns Thomson Reuters' legal research platform, Westlaw. As part of its organization and added benefits, Westlaw has a complex headnote system that summarizes key point of case holdings. It includes a Key Number System, which is copyrightable, and since 1981, Thomson Reuters has been registering their headnotes since 1981.[528]

ROSS was a start-up that wanted to compete with Westlaw by using AI.[529] To train the system, ROSS needed a database of legal questions and answers. ROSS requested a license from Westlaw, which they refused.[530] So, ROSS went to LegalEase.[531] LegalEase crease "Bulk Memos" which are "lawyers' compilation of legal questions with good and bad answers."[532] LegalEase uses Westlaw's headnotes. LegalEase sold ROSS 25,000 Bulk Memos, which ROSS then used to train its AI search tool.[533] Thomson Reuters sued ROSS for copyright infringement.[534]

Judge Bibas frames the question: "whether the LegalEase Bulk Memo questions copied Thomson Reuter's headnotes or were instead taken from uncopyrightable judicial opinions."[535] The Judge did a comparison. Due to the fact that the questions and headnotes are sealed, he created an example based on *Feist Publication v. Rural Tel. Serv. Co.,* 499 U.S. 340,345 (1991).[536]

---

[524]Kate Knibbs, *Thomson Reuters Wins First Major AI Copyright Case in the US*, WIRED (Feb. 11, 2025), https://www.wired.com/story/thomson-reuters-ai-copyright-lawsuit/#:~:text=Thomson%20Reuters%20has%20won%20the,legal%20AI%20startup%20Ross%20Intelligence.

[525] *Thomson Reuters Enter. Ctr. GMBH v. ROSS Intelligence, Inc.*, No. 1:20-cv-613-SB, 2025 WL 458520, at *1 (D. Del. Feb. 11, 2025)

[526] *Thomson Reuters Enter. Ctr. GMBH v. ROSS Intelligence, Inc.,* 694 F. Supp. 3d 467 (D. Del. 2023), vacated in part, No. 1:20-CV-613-SB, 2025 WL 458520 (D. Del. Feb. 11, 2025)

[527] *Id.* at 481

[528] *Thomson Reuters*, 2025 WL 458520, at *2

[529] *Id.* at *7

[530] *Id.* at *1

[531] *Id.*

[532] *Id.*

[533] *Id.*

[534] *Id.*

[535] *Id.* at *2

[536] *Id.*

Question	West Headnote	Case Opinion
Does originality for copyright purposes mean that the work was independently created and has some minimal degree of creativity?	Originality, for copyright purposes, means that the work was independently created and has some minimal degree of creativity.	Original, as the term is used in copyright, means only that the work was independently created by the author (as opposed to copied from other works), and that it possesses at least some minimal degree of creativity.

B. Direct Copyright Infringement

Judge Bibas held that ROSS infringed 2,243 headnotes.[537] Thomson Reuters owns a valid copyright in the headnotes. "Copyright registrations are 'prima facie evidence of the validity of the copyright' if made before or within five years after first publication of the work.'"[538] The court presumed then that Thomson Reuters had a valid compilation copyright. What is interesting about this argument is that you can have a copyright in the compilation, but the individual elements are not necessarily protected. But that is not addressed in the case. Why this becomes important is that Thomson Reuters is suing based on the individual headnotes and not the compilation. The factual dispute, according to the Judge, is whether the headnotes are still under copyright. Again, this strikes as odd. If the copyright registration covers the individual headnotes, there would be no way that the works would be in the public domain, as the term would be 95 years from publication. But we continue…

The Judge next turns to originality. Even though Thomson Reuters gets a presumption of validity because of the copyright registrations, could ROSS rebut the presumption that the headnotes did not meet the *Feist*'s minimal originality requirement? He finds the headnotes are original. He explains, "[a] headnote is a short, key point of law chiseled out of a lengthy judicial opinion. The text of judicial opinions is not copyrightable and even if it were, Thomson Reuters would not get that copyright because it did not write the opinions. But a headnote can introduce creativity by distilling, synthesizing, or explaining part of an opinion and thus be copyrightable. That is why I have changed my mind."[539] He explains that the headnotes are a compilation, and that Thomson Reuters have sufficient originality in the selection and arrangement to clear that law creativity bar.[540]

Moreover, each headnote has an individual copyright.

---

[537] *Id.* at *5

[538] *Id.* at *2

[539] *Id.* at *3.

[540] *Id.*

> That became clear to me once I analogized the lawyer's editorial judgement to that of a sculptor. A block of raw marble, like a judicial opinion, is not copyrightable. Yet a sculptor creates a sculpture by choosing what to cut away and what to leave in place. That sculpture is copyrightable. So too, even a headnote taken verbatim from an opinion is a carefully chosen fraction of the whole. Identifying which words matter and chiseling away the surrounding mass expresses the editor's idea about what the important point of law from opinion is. That editorial expression has enough 'creative spark' to be original. So, all headnotes, even any that quote judicial opinions verbatim, have original value as individual works.[541]

The judge does not grant summary judgement on any headnote that is verbatim copying. As to the Key Number System, that is original too.

Then the Judge turns to whether that were copying of original elements, looking first at actual copying and then at substantial similarity. He limits his analysis to 2,830 headnotes identified by Thomson Reuters, leaving 5,367 for trial. In the end, the Judge reviews 3,384 headnotes. ROSS actually used the copyrighted work to creates its own AI training data. The judge used an expert opinion report that the "Bulk Memo questions for this batch closely resemble the headnotes' text and the headnotes differ significantly from the text of the judicial opinions. Her findings suggests that these questions were created by copying Westlaw headnotes, not be summarizing the underlying opinions."[542] Moreover, the court compared how similar the Memo questions, headnotes and judicial opinions were, "one by one."[543] The Judge continues, "Having slogged through all 2,,830 headnotes, I grant summary judgement to Thomson Reuters on actual copying, finding actual copying of 2,243. Then he turns to substantial similarity, was original expression copied? The Judge explains, "As a lawyers and judge, I am myself an ordinary user of Westlaw headnotes. So, I am well positioned to determine substantial similarity here."[544] The Judge grants summary judgement for Thomson Reuters on 2,243 headnotes.

C. *Fair Use*

"None of ROSS's possible defenses hold water. I reject them all." So, begins Judge Bibas on the fair use analysis. Innocent infringement does not apply because there was a copyright notice on Westlaw's headnotes. Copyright misuse doesn't apply. The merge defense also does not apply. The scenes a faire defense does not apply either. That leaves fair use.

---

[541] *Id.*
[542] *Id.* at *11-12.
[543] *Id.* at *12
[544] *Id.* at * 13.

In his 2023 opinion, Judge Bibas denied summary judgement on fair use, but now he has changed his mind. For the first factor, He finds ROSS' use commercial and not transformative. Using *Warhol*, he finds that ROSS' does not have a "further purpose or different character" from Thomson Reuters. ROSS was using Westlaw headnotes to create a product that would compete with Westlaw.

The headnotes do not appear in the final product for consumers. The copying was part of an intermittent step. "ROSS turned the headnotes into numerical data about the relationships among legal words to feed into its AI."[545] Here's where it gets interesting. intermediate copying is permitted under fair use for computer programs. But the Judge does not see this as parallel. The computer cases are about computer code; this case is not. And the copying in the computer cases was "*necessary* for competitors to innovate."[546] The Judge cites *Google*, *Sony*, and *Sega*. So, instead of analyzing the fair use argument under the computer cases, the Judge analyzes it using *Warhol*.

Factors two and three are decided in ROSS' favor, as the works were factual in nature, and the final output doesn't include the Westlaw headnotes. Because of the *Author's Guild* case, you look to what is accessible to the public, and not the making of a copy.[547] Factor four is found for Thomson Reuters. The Judge defines the market as legal research platforms and the potential derivative mark as data to train legal AIs. But ROSS is competing with Westlaw to create a market substitute. In the end, the Judge rejects the fair use argument.

CONCLUSION?

ROSS' use was non generative – it doesn't create anything new. So, how much this opinion will impact on the generative AI cases is a question for another day. And we have many more cases working their way through the courts. Not to mention more licensing deals to seal. And if anyone is keeping score, here's some useful data.

As these generative AI cases progress through the litigation process, the original claims have developed based on the court's early findings. Each plaintiff originally asserted at least one cause of action concerning copyright infringement, violation of the Digital Millennium Copyright Act (DMCA), or some other related infraction (e.g., negligence). As part of the class exercise, we tried to chart what has happened so far.

---

[545] *Id.* at *17-18
[546] *Id.* at *18
[547] *Id.* at *21

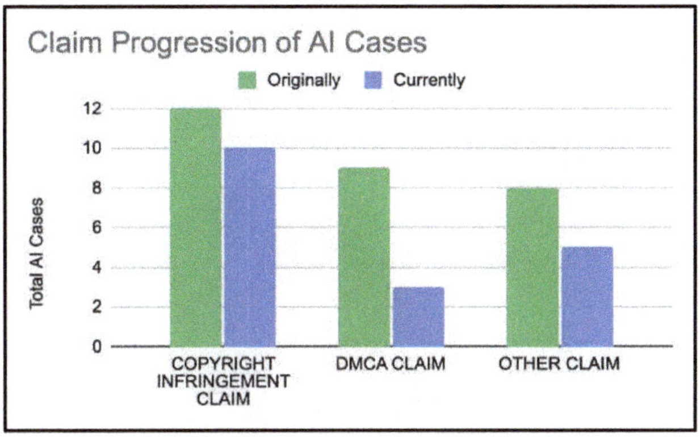

Figure 1: Claim Progression of AI Cases

Figure 1 shows the total number of each type of original claim in comparison to the number of claims remaining as of February 2025. Twelve of the thirteen generative AI cases discussed here originally included a copyright infringement claim, and ten of those causes of action remain today. Other claims were slightly less successful, but five of the original eight remain. A more significant decline can be seen for the DMCA claims where only three of the original nine DMCA claims are still at issue. Figures 2, 3, and 4 further illustrate the varying success of each type of claim in remaining at issue in these cases today.

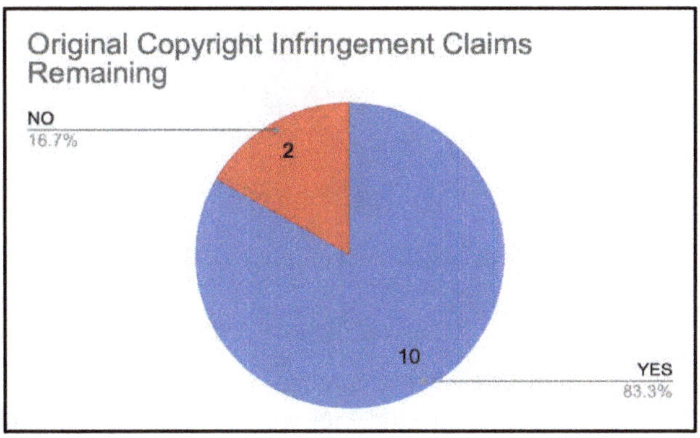

Figure 2: Original Copyright Infringement Claims Remaining

As seen in Figure B1, over 80% of copyright infringement claims survived initial rulings, while only 33% of DMCA claims remain. Other claims have lasted almost twice as often as DMCA claims, or roughly 62% of the time.

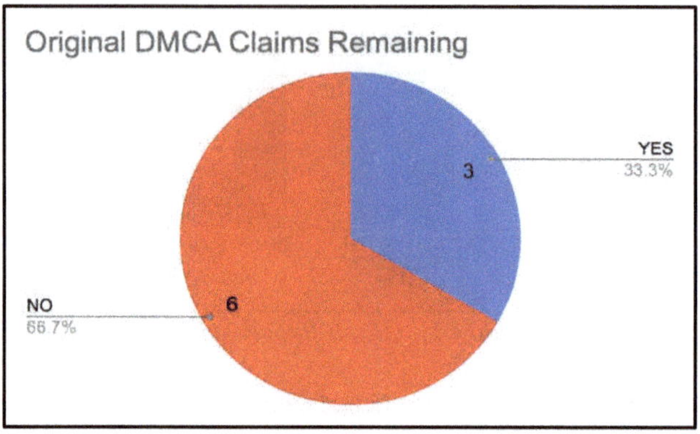

Figure 3: Original DMCA Claims Remaining

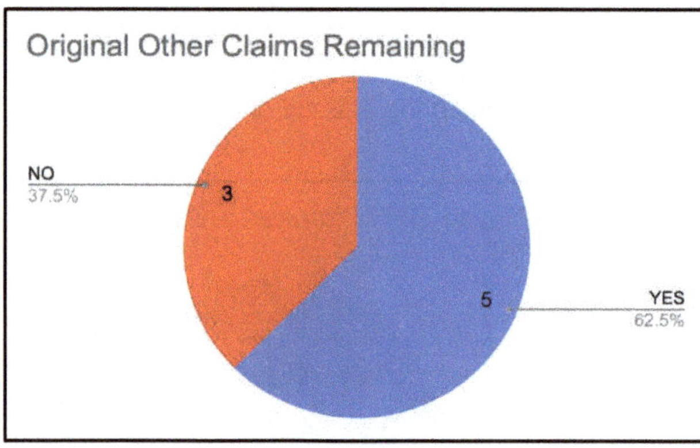

Figure 4: Original Other Claims Remaining

All of these generative AI cases are still in progress to some degree. While a majority of cases are still in progress independently, Figure 5 shows that five of the cases were combined with other similar matters, and one of the cases received partial summary judgment while awaiting a jury trial on other claims.

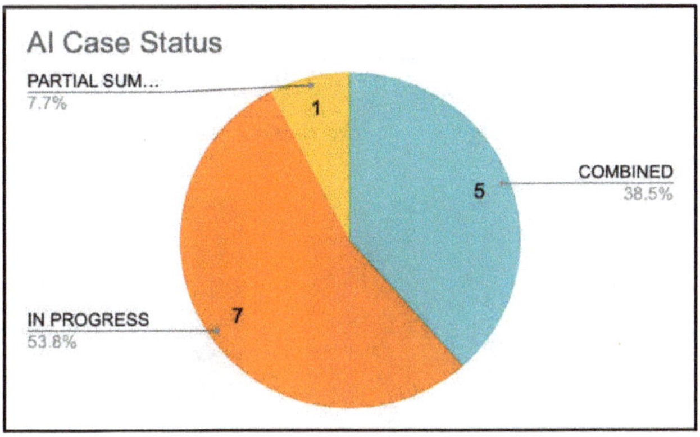

Figure 5: AI Case Status

In order to better understand the larger trends seen in these cases, data from Figures A and B can be divided into the categories of cases status shown in Figure 5. Figures 6, 7 and 8 compare the claim progression in cases with their current litigation status.

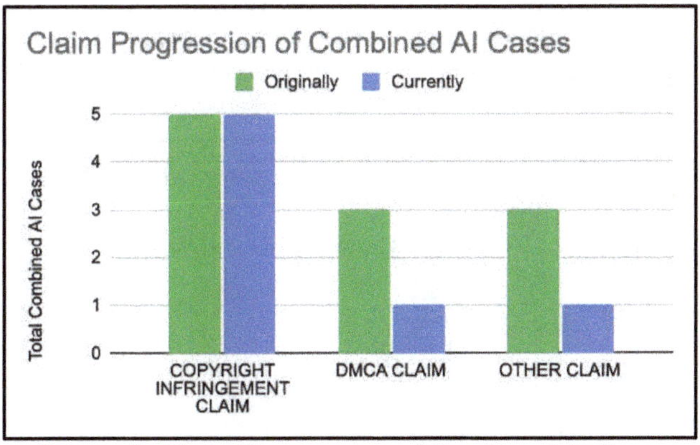

Figure 6: Claim Progression of Combined AI Cases

Figure 6 focuses on the generative AI cases that have been combined with other matters. Of the five cases that have been combined with others, all of them originally contained a copyright infringement claim and have maintained these claims throughout the process thus far. However, only one DMCA claim, and one other claim remains of the three of each that were originally filed, meaning one third of each of these types of claims remain in cases with a combined status.

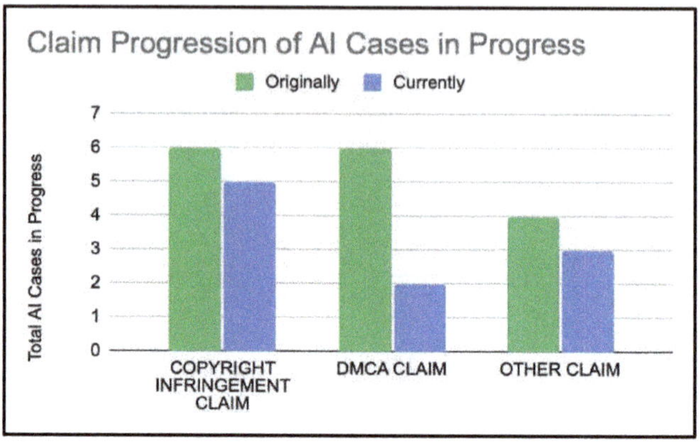

Figure 7: Claim Progression of AI Cases in Progress

Figure 7 illustrates a similar trend for cases which are currently in progress independently and contain a copyright infringement or DMCA claim. Almost all copyright claims remain from the original filings, while only one third of DMCA claims remain. An important distinction between the data for combined cases and cases in progress independently is that those in progress have greater success maintaining other claims up to this point, as seen in Figure E where three out of four of claims remain.

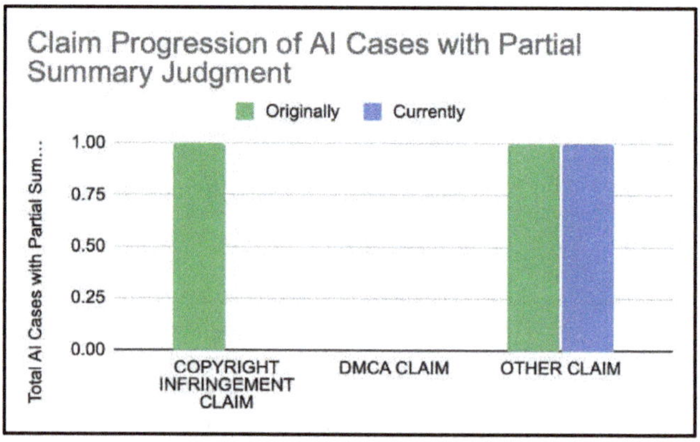

Figure 8: Claim Progression of AL Cases with Partial Summary Judgement

Figure 8 is less helpful in identifying larger trends in generative AI cases, as only one case has received partial summary judgment. Additionally, the complaint for this case originally did not contain a DMCA claim, so no data is available for that comparison.

***

Is there a conclusion? Not really, not yet. And so now we wait. The cases move through the court system. The third report is released by the Copyright Office. The Register of Copyright gets fired. And the semester ends. Did the students get it right? What are they missing? Are we getting it right? What are we missin

Student Note:

SECTION 1202(B) AND AI: IMPLICATIONS FOR COPYRIGHT INFRINGEMENT LAWSUITS AND CONSIDERATIONS FOR DIGITAL CREATORS

By MARIA CRUSEY*

Section 1202(b) of the DMCA imposes liability–including potentially sizeable statutory damages awards–on users who remove or alter copyright management information (CMI) or knowingly distribute works with removed CMI. Until now, Section 1202 had been seldom used by plaintiffs, but there is a recent uptick driven by suits filed against developers of generative artificial intelligence (AI) technology alleging violation of Section 1202(b) of the Digital Millennium Copyright Act (DMCA). This Student Note provides a summary of Section 1202(b)'s history and caselaw and explains how recent AI cases have started to develop a clearer sense of Section 1202's limits. Earlier courts that considered Section 1202(b) issues adopted a wide range of views of the statutory scope based on the plain language of the statute and its legislative history, while later courts fashioned discrete requirements for viable Section 1202(b) claims, such as the "double scienter" and "identicality" requirements. But there is very little precedent caselaw and the scope of Section 1202(b) and potential defenses, such as Article III standing, fair use, and First Amendment rights, which remain unsettled. The Note concludes with observations about how users may insulate themselves from liability in the face of an evolving Section 1202(b) litigation landscape.

INTRODUCTION 481
I: SECTION 1202(b) PRIOR TO THE ADVENT OF AI 484
A. A Quick Primer on Section 1202 484
B. Purpose and Legislative History of Section 1202(b) 485
1. The NII Report 486
2. The WIPO Treaties 488
3. Enactment of Section 1202(b) in the DMCA 488
C. A Quick Primer on Section 1202(c) 489
D. Prior Interpretations of Section 1202(b) and (c) 492
E. Elements of a Section 1202(b) claim 497

* J.D. (2025), Washington University School of Law; A.B. (2022), Washington University in St. Louis. This Note builds upon a blog post about Section 1202(b) as it relates to AI copyright infringement lawsuits that was previously published by Authors Alliance. Interested readers may access the post here: https://www.authorsalliance.org/2024/10/30/copyright-management-information-1202b-and-ai/. Additionally, I would like to thank Dave Hansen, Executive Director of Authors Alliance, for his feedback and editorial support in preparing this Note for publication.

1. Particularized Allegations of Existence of CMI and Removal of CMI by Defendants....498
2. Knowledge Requirement....498
3. "Identicality" Requirement....499
II: CURRENT INTERPRETATIONS AND FUTURE IMPLICATIONS OF SECTION 1202(b) AND (c)....504
III: OTHER LEGAL DOCTRINES THAT MAY IMPACT Section 1202(b) AND (c)....509
A. Article III Standing Under Section 1202(b)(3)....509
B. "The Law" as it Relates to Section 1202(b)....511
C. First Amendment Issues Implicated in Section 1202(b)....512
IV: PRACTICAL CONCERNS WHEN DEALING WITH CMI....514
CONCLUSION....517

INTRODUCTION

Section 1202(b) of the Digital Millennium Copyright Act (DMCA) imposes liability on users who remove or alter copyright management information (CMI) or knowingly distribute works with removed CMI.[1] The Journal has published many articles about Sections 1201 and 1202 of the DMCA over the years.[2] This Student Note adds to the conversation by providing a comprehensive retrospect of Section 1202(b) to inform discussion of how courts may assess contemporary claims under Section 1202(b). Today, we see Section 1202(b) claims being filed as part of the wave of copyright litigation related to artificial intelligence (AI).[3]

---

[1] 17 U.S.C. § 1202(b).

[2] *See* Jie Hua, *Toward a More Balanced Model: The Revision of Anti-Circumvention Rules*, 60 J. COPYRIGHT SOC'Y USA 327 (Spring 2013); Elizabeth F. Jackson, *The Copyright Office's Protection of Fair Uses Under the DMCA: Why the Rulemaking Proceedings Might be Unsustainable and Solutions for Their Survival*, 58 J. COPYRIGHT SOC'Y USA U.S.A. 521 (2010-201); Karen A. Chesley, *Calculating Damages Under the Digital Millennium Copyright Act: How Far Should Courts Go When Multiplying Statutory Awards*, 57 J. COPYRIGHT SOC'Y USA SOC'Y U.S.A. 1 (Fall 2009-Winter 2010); Chris Kruger, *Passing the Global Test: DMCA Sec. 1201 as an International Model for Transitioning Copyright Law into the Digital Age*, 53 J. COPYRIGHT SOC'Y USA U.S.A. 447 (Spring-Summer 2006); Jane C. Ginsburg, *From Having Copies to Experiencing Works: The Development of an Access Right in U.S. Copyright Law*, 50 J. COPYRIGHT SOC'Y USA U.S.A. 113 (2002-2003); Michael Landau, *Has the Digital Millennium Copyright Act Really Created a New Exclusive Right of Access?: Attempting to Reach a Balance Between Users' and Content Providers' Rights,*49 J. COPYRIGHT SOC'Y USA U.S.A. 277 (Fall 2001); David Nimmer, *Puzzles of the Digital Millennium Copyright Act*, 46 J. J. COPYRIGHT SOC'Y USA. 401 (Spring 1999).

[3] *See, e.g.*, Second Am. Compl., Doe 1 v. Github, Inc., No. 4:22-cv-06823, at 49–50 (N.D. Cal. filed Jan. 25, 2024) (alleging violations of Sections 1202(b)(1) and (b)(3) through removal of CMI in violation of open-source software license agreements); Am. Compl., N.Y. Times Co. v. OpenAI, No. 1:23-cv-11195, at 64–65 (S.D.N.Y. filed Aug. 12, 2024)

Section 1202(b) claims in these suits primarily allege violation of Section 1202(b) through AI developers' removal of author-identifying information from copyrighted works and subsequent use of the works to train large language models.[4] Moreover, these suits have been brought against some of the biggest names in technology, including Microsoft, Meta, and OpenAI.[5] But to look only at these high-profile cases is to miss the prevalence of Section 1202(b) claims brought in the past four years, and not just in AI cases.

Between 2020 and 2024, federal courts across the United States rendered at least 330 legal opinions that cite to Section 1202(b) of the DMCA.[6] This quantity is more than 1.5 times greater than the number of opinions citing to Section 1202(b) rendered between 2015 and 2020 and is nearly as many opinions citing to Section 1202(b) rendered between 2020 and the adoption of the provision in 1998.[7] The most recent group of Section 1202(b) claims are alleged in copyright infringement lawsuits brought against AI companies in which many plaintiffs allege violation of Section 1202(b) through the companies' alleged use of

---

(alleging violations of Sections 1202(b)(1) and (b)(3) through removal or alteration of CMI from news and media content); Third Consolidated Am. Compl., Kadrey v. Meta Platforms, Inc., No. 3:23-cv-03417, at 18–19 (N.D. Cal. filed Jan. 21, 2025) (alleging violations of Section 1202(b)(1) for removal of CMI from books).

[4] *See, e.g.*, Second Am. Compl., Doe 1 v. Github, Inc., No. 4:22-cv-06823, at 49–50 (N.D. Cal. filed Jan. 25, 2024) (alleging violations of Sections 1202(b)(1) and (b)(3) through removal of CMI in violation of open-source software license agreements); Am. Compl., N.Y. Times Co. v. OpenAI, No. 1:23-cv-11195, at 64–65 (S.D.N.Y. filed Aug. 12, 2024) (alleging violations of Sections 1202(b)(1) and (b)(3) through removal or alteration of CMI from news and media content); Third Consolidated Am. Compl., Kadrey v. Meta Platforms, Inc., No. 3:23-cv-03417, at 18–19 (N.D. Cal. filed Jan. 21, 2025) (alleging violations of Section 1202(b)(1) for removal of CMI from books).

[5] *See, e.g.*, Second Am. Compl., Doe 1 v. Github, Inc., No. 4:22-cv-06823, at 49–50 (N.D. Cal. filed Jan. 25, 2024) (alleging violations of Sections 1202(b)(1) and (b)(3) through removal of CMI in violation of open-source software license agreements); Am. Compl., N.Y. Times Co. v. OpenAI, No. 1:23-cv-11195, at 64–65 (S.D.N.Y. filed Aug. 12, 2024) (alleging violations of Sections 1202(b)(1) and (b)(3) through removal or alteration of CMI from news and media content); Third Consolidated Am. Compl., Kadrey v. Meta Platforms, Inc., No. 3:23-cv-03417, at 18–19 (N.D. Cal. filed Jan. 21, 2025) (alleging violations of Section 1202(b)(1) for removal of CMI from books).

[6] Westlaw, Citing References: § 1202. Integrity of copyright management information, https://1.next.westlaw.com/RelatedInformation/N63D21E60A06711D8B8FABFF7D35FC9C0/kcCitingReferences.html?docSource=ddda16fcfc744b938be0efdffcdd0bba&pageNumber=1&facetGuid=h78957f8183b9cdc61cec53dce66730ea&ppcid=2a050266253c4d74b76b74e0e5f482a5&transitionType=ListViewType&contextData=(sc.UserEnteredCitation) (last visited Mar. 28, 2025). The numbers provided are estimations based on Westlaw analytics and only refer to Section 1202(b) cases in which a court rendered a legal opinion. As such, the numbers may not capture all Section 1202(b) suits filed to date that did not progress.

[7] *See id.* Following its enactment in 1998, Section 1202(b) was relatively unlitigated, and courts rendered legal opinions in only 196 Section 1202(b) suits prior to 2015. *See id.*

copyrighted works to develop and train generative AI systems.[8] Removal of CMI and other forms of identifying information is necessary for the effective creation and development of generative AI systems. As a result, both individual users and organizational developers of AI are susceptible to suit under Section 1202(b), an idea explored in Part IV of this Note.

Although Section 1202(b) appears straightforward on its face, recent Section 1202(b) claims raise challenging questions about how to interpret the statute.[9] The answers to these questions are particularly important given the substantial statutory damages that come from Section 1202(b) violations – between $2,500 and $25,000 per violation.[10] While this amount may not seem like much for a single violation, damages have the potential to accumulate to massive amounts in cases involving removal of CMI en masse, which results in many consecutive individual violations of Section 1202(b).[11] In many of the recent AI copyright lawsuits, CMI is alleged to have been removed from millions of works, leading to potential Section 1202 damage awards in the billions of dollars.[12] Moreover, resolution of how to interpret Section 1202(b) has important implications for many re-uses of copyrighted works, ranging from text data mining research to

---

[8] *See, e.g.*, Second Am. Compl., Doe 1 v. Github, Inc., No. 4:22-cv-06823, at 49–50 (N.D. Cal. filed Jan. 25, 2024) (alleging violations of Sections 1202(b)(1) and (b)(3) through removal of CMI in violation of open-source software license agreements); Compl., Raw Story Media, Inc. v. OpenAI Inc., No.1:24-cv-01514, at 9–11 (S.D.N.Y. filed Feb. 28, 2024) (alleging violations of Sections 1202(b)(1) and (b)(3) through removal of CMI from copyrighted works of journalism).

[9] *See, e.g.*, Second Am. Compl., Doe 1 v. Github, Inc., No. 4:22-cv-06823, at 49–50 (N.D. Cal. filed Jan. 25, 2024) (alleging violations of Sections 1202(b)(1) and (b)(3) through); Compl., Raw Story Media, Inc. v. OpenAI Inc., No.1:24-cv-01514, at 9–11 (S.D.N.Y. filed Feb. 28, 2024) (alleging violations of Section 1202(b)(1) and (b)(3) through removal of CMI from copyrighted works of journalism).

[10] 17 U.S.C. § 1203(c)(3)(B) ("At any time before final judgment is entered, a complaining party may elect to recover an award of statutory damages for each violation of section 1202 in the sum of not less than $2,500 or more than $25,000."). Damages from Section 1202(b) violations have the potential to be particularly hefty in cases of CMI removal and alteration that is conducted en masse from hundreds of individual copyrighted works or as part of automated data formatting process. In these instances, damages claims have the potential to amount to millions of dollars. *Cf.* Chesley, *supra* note 3, at 29 ("The DMCA has [] been subject to a great deal of criticism for its lack of clarity with regard to fair use and scope of violations. Read expansively, there could be enormous liability for very minor infractions.").

[11] *See generally* Bobby Allyn, *'The New York Times' takes OpenAI to Court. ChatGPT's Future Could Be on the Line*, NPR (Jan. 14, 2025 4:27 PM), https://www.npr.org/2025/01/14/nx-s1-5258952/new-york-times-openai-microsoft; Leyland Cacco, *Canadian Media Companies Sue OpenAI in Case Potentially Worth Billions*, THE GUARDIAN (Nov. 29, 2024 2:02 PM), https://www.theguardian.com/world/2024/nov/29/canada-media-companies-sue-openai-chatgpt.

[12] *Id.*

routine re-distribution, given the broad range of issues that may implicate the statute.[13]

This Note provides a retrospect of past interpretations of Section 1202(b), with the aim of informing legal scholars, practitioners, and other interested parties about how courts may interpret the statute today when resolving Section 1202(b) claims raised in current lawsuits implicating AI. Part I reviews the legislative history and purpose of Section 1202(b) and takes stock of courts' interpretations of the statutory provision prior to the technological advent of AI. Part I also provides background on courts' treatment of Section 1202(c), which historically has informed judicial assessments of Section 1202(b). Part I concludes with a discussion of the Ninth Circuit's pending review of the interlocutory appeal in *Doe 1 v. Github*, the first lawsuit squarely alleging violation of Section 1202(b) to be heard by a court of appeals, and the potential of the appeal to redefine the elements of Section 1202(b) claims. Then, Part II reviews interpretations of Section 1202(b) proffered in contemporary copyright infringement lawsuits implicating AI and discusses future implications of the suits and best practices for individuals and organizations amidst the uncertainty of how Section 1202(b) may be interpreted. Part III details a number of side issues in current Section 1202(b) proceedings implicating AI that could be determinative of whether future Section 1202(b) suits may proceed. Finally, Part IV concludes with practical observations about how users and organizational developers of AI may insulate themselves from liability in the face of an evolving Section 1202(b) litigation landscape.

I: SECTION 1202(B) PRIOR TO THE ADVENT OF AI

This Part reviews the purpose and legislative history of Section 1202(b), identifies particular considerations in courts' past interpretations of Section 1202(b) that may resurface in analyses of Section 1202(b) in the current lawsuits, and provides an overview of Section 1202(c).

A. A Quick Primer on Section 1202

Section 1202 was enacted in 1998 as part of the Digital Millennium Copyright Act (DMCA). The DMCA is well-known for its safe harbor,[14] notice-and-takedown,[15] and anticircumvention[16] provisions that have increased access to digital copyrighted works through limiting online service providers' liability for users' infringement and granting authors legal protections against unauthorized

---

[13] *Cf.* Pamela Samuelson, *Text and Data Mining of In-Copyright Works: Is it Legal?*, 64 COMMS. OF THE ACM, No. 11, Oct. 2021, at 20–22.

[14] 17 U.S.C. § 512.

[15] *Id.*

[16] 17 U.S.C. § 1201.

access of their digital works.[17] While these provisions of the DMCA regulate access to copyrighted works, Section 1202 stands apart through its regulation of the content of copyrighted works, namely "copyright management information" (CMI) included within works.[18]

Section 1202(a) prohibits the falsification of CMI with the intent to aid copyright infringement, and Section 1202(b), discussed in greater detail below, forbids the intentional alteration or removal of CMI.[19] Both Section 1202(a) and Section 1202(b) are rooted in the premise that removal of CMI can further copyright infringement by enabling greater access to works that are not clearly protected under copyright or associated with an author.[20] Section 1202(c), also discussed below, defines the types of information that constitute "CMI" as referenced within Sections 1202(a) and (b).[21] Akin to the limited liability for copyright infringement provided in Section 512 of the DMCA, Sections 1202(d) and (e) respectively exclude government actors from liability under Section 1202 and limit liability under Section 1202 for particular kinds of analog and digital transmissions of copyrighted works that are incapable of including CMI.[22]

Of the multiple provisions encompassed in Section 1202, Section 1202(b) arguably provides the greatest number of analytical hurdles given the necessary consideration of its statutory purpose, legislative history, and relationship to Section 1202(c) to assess the provision's statutory and judge-made requirements.[23] The following Sections describe these aspects of Section 1202(b).

B. . Purpose and Legislative History of Section 1202(b)

Section 1202(b) of the DMCA protects the integrity of copyright management information (CMI).[24] Per Section 1202(c), CMI comprises certain information identifying a copyrighted work, often including the title, the name of

---

[17] *The Digital Millennium Copyright Act*, .S, U.S. COPYRIGHT OFFICE, https://www.copyright.gov/dmca/#:~:text=In%201998%2C%20Congress%20passed%20the,Section%20512 (last visited May 18, 2025).

[18] *See* 17 U.S.C. § 1202.

[19] 17 U.S.C. § 1202(a), (b).

[20] *See generally* H.R. Rep. No. 105-551.

[21] 17 U.S.C. § 1202(c).

[22] 17 U.S.C. § 1202(d), (e). Section 1202(b) "does not prohibit any lawfully authorized investigative, protective, information security, or intelligence activity of an officer, agent, or employee of the United States, a State, or a political subdivision of a State, or a person acting pursuant to a contract with the United States, a state, or a political subdivision of a state." 17 U.S.C. § 1202(d).

[23] *See, e.g.*, Textile Secrets Int'l, Inc. v. Ya-Ya Brand Inc., 524 F. Supp. 2d 1184 (C.D. Cal. 2007) (considering Section 1202(b)'s complete legislative history to determine if the alleged removal of CMI fell within the scope of Section 1202(b)); *cf.* IQ Grp., Ltd. v. Wiesner Publishing, LLC, 409 F. Supp. 2d 587, 593–97 (D.N.J. 2006) (considering Section 1202(b)'s complete legislative history to determine if CMI fell within the scope of Section 1202(c) and could thus be alleged to be removed under Section 1202(b)).

[24] 17 U.S.C. § 1202(b).

the author, and terms and conditions for the use of a work.[25] Section 1202(b) forbids the alteration or removal of CMI. The section provides in relevant part that:

> [n]o person shall, without the authority of the copyright owner or the law –
>
> (1) intentionally remove or alter any CMI,
>
> (2) distribute or import for distribution CMI knowing that the CMI has been removed or altered without authority of the copyright owner or the law, or
>
> (3) distribute, import for distribution, or publicly perform works, copies of works or phonorecords, knowing that copyright management information has been removed or altered without authority of the copyright owner or the law, knowing, or with respect to civil remedies under section 1203, having reasonable grounds to know that it will induce, enable, facilitate, or conceal an infringement of any right under this title.[26]

Past courts to weigh in on Section 1202(b) interpreted the statutory language in light of its legislative history.[27] The legislative history of Section 1202(b) is largely rooted in a white paper published by the Information Infrastructure Task Force (IITF) and two treaties reached by the World Intellectual Property Organization (WIPO).[28] All three writings influenced the specific language of the provision and the motivation to codify Section 1202(b).

1. The NII Report

The earliest traceable origin of Section 1202(b) is a white paper published in September 1995 by the National Information Infrastructure Task Force (IITF), commonly known as the NII white paper.[29] The IITF was established by the Clinton Administration in 1993 to formulate policies to promote the development of the National Information Infrastructure (NII).[30] The Working Group on

---

[25] 17 U.S.C. § 1202(c); *See infra* Part I.B.
[26] Nimmer, *supra* note 2.
[27] *See, e.g.*, Textile Secrets Int'l, Inc., 524 F. Supp. 2d 1184 (C.D. Cal. 2007); ADR Int'l Ltd. v. Inst. for Supply Mgmt., Inc., 667 F. Supp. 3d 411 (S.D. Tex. 2023).
[28] Information Infrastructure Task Force, Intellectual Property and the National Information Infrastructure: Report of the Working Group of Intellectual Property Rights (Sept. 1995); WIPO Copyright Treaty, WIPO (Dec. 20, 1996), https://www.wipo.int/wipolex/en/text/295157; WIPO Performances and Phonograms Treaty, WIPO (Dec. 20, 1996), https://www.wipo.int/wipolex/en/text/295477.
[29] Information Infrastructure Task Force, *supra* note 28.
[30] *Id.*

Intellectual Property Rights (Working Group) housed within the IITF released the NII white paper in 1995 (NII Report) to "discuss the application of [then-]existing copyright law and to recommend changes that [were] essential to adapt the law to the needs of the global information society."[31] Among other discussions, the NII Report included drafted language of Section 1202(b), which outlined protections against the knowing alteration or removal of "copyright management information" (CMI) and distribution of works with altered or removed CMI.[32]

The NII Report also described the rationale behind the drafted provisions.[33] The Working Group identified that systems for managing rights were critical to the management of the NII and that such systems would function to track and monitor uses and licensing of copyrighted works as well as to indicate attribution and ownership interests.[34] In implementing the rights management systems, the Working Group noted that information would likely be included in digital versions of works as CMI to inform others about authorship and ownership of the work and to indicate authorized uses.[35] The Working Group predicted that, after CMI is associated with a particular work and accessible, others would be able to easily address questions over the licensing and use of the work.[36] Following publication of the Report, the National Information Infrastructure Copyright Protection Act (NIICPA), containing many ideas posited in the NII Report, was introduced in the House of Representatives and the Senate but stalled and never progressed.[37]

---

[31] *Textile Secrets Int'l, Inc.*, 524 F. Supp. 2d at 1196–97.

[32] *Id.* at 1196 n.12; Information Infrastructure Task Force, *supra* note 29, at 235. The Report's draft of Section 1202(b) provides: "No person shall, without authority of the copyright owner or the law, (i) knowingly remove or alter any copyright management information, (ii) knowingly distribute or import for distribution copyright management information that has been altered without authority of the copyright owner or the law, or (iii) knowingly distribute or import for distribution copies or phonorecords from which copyright management information has been removed without authority of the copyright owner or the law." Information Infrastructure Task Force, Intellectual Property and the National Information Infrastructure: Report of the Working Group of Intellectual Property Rights, app. 1, at 7 (Sept. 1995).

[33] Information Infrastructure Task Force, *supra* note 29, at 191.

[34] *Id.*

[35] *Id.*

[36] *Id.* at 191–92.

[37] *Id.* The NIICPA contained drafted language of Sections 1201 and 1202 that was copied verbatim from the Report. *Id.* (citing Julie E. Cohen, *A Right to Read Anonymously: A Closer Look at "Copyright Management" in Cyberspace,* 28 CONN. L. REV. 981, 989 (1996)).

2. The WIPO Treaties

Adoption of Section 1202(b) was also motivated by developments in digital copyright protection in the international sphere.[38] The World Intellectual Property Association hosted a conference in December 1996 that resulted in the adoption of two treaties by 160 countries: the "WIPO Copyright Treaty" and the "WIPO Performances and Phonograms Treaty" (collectively, the WIPO Treaties).[39] Both treaties discuss "obligations concerning rights management information" and aim to address concerns of the modification or removal of CMI.[40] Specifically, the WIPO Copyright Treaty provides in relevant part:

> Contracting parties shall provide adequate and effective legal remedies against any person knowingly performing any of the following acts knowing, or with respect to civil remedies having reasonable grounds to know, that it will induce, enable, facilitate or conceal an infringement of any right covered by this Treaty or the Berne Convention:
>
> (i) to remove or alter any electronic rights information without authority; [or]
>
> (ii) to distribute, import for distribution, broadcast or communicate to the public, without authority, works or copies of works knowing that electronic rights management has been removed or altered without authority.[41]

3. Enactment of Section 1202(b) in the DMCA

Committees in the House of Representatives and Senate published reports commenting on the WIPO treaties prior to the enactment of the Digital Millennium Copyright Act (DMCA) in 1998.[42] The House's report's commentary

---

[38] Julie S. Sheinblatt, *The WIPO Copyright Treaty*, 13 BERKELEY TECH. L.J. 535, 535 (1998) ("The [WIPO Copyright and WIPO Performances and Phonograms Treaties] were created in response to the arrival of the digital age, which has made information a key business asset, expanded international commerce, and enabled faster and easier copying of copyrighted work. . . . The Copyright Treaty was formed both to harmonize global copyright law and to extend that law into the digital domain.").

[39] *Id.* at 1197–98; WIPO Copyright Treaty, *supra* note 29; WIPO Performances and Phonograms Treaty, *supra* note 28.

[40] *Textile Secrets Int'l, Inc.*, 524 F. Supp. 2d at 1198; WIPO Copyright Treaty, *supra* note 29, art. 12(1); WIPO Performances and Phonograms Treaty, *supra* note 29, art. 19(1).

[41] WIPO Copyright Treaty, *supra* note 29, art. 12(1). This language closely tracks the drafted language of Section 1202(b) in the NII Report. *Supra* note 28.

[42] *Textile Secrets Int'l, Inc.*, 524 F. Supp. 2d at 1198–99; H.R. Rep. No. 105-551 (1998), https://www.congress.gov/congressional-report/105th-congress/house-report/551/1; S. Rep. No. 105-190 (1998), https://www.congress.gov/congressional-report/105th-

on Section 1202(b) is significant here.[43] The House Committee cautioned that "borderless digital means of dissemination are becoming increasingly more popular," and while this spread will benefit U.S. consumers, "it will unfortunately also facilitate pirates who aim to destroy the value of American intellectual property."[44] As such, domestic legislation implementing the WIPO treaties was necessary.[45] The House Committee noted that compliance with the treaties required a two-prong statutory provision.[46] First, an anti-circumvention measure was needed to complement Article 11 of the WIPO Copyright Treaty, which is now provided in Section 1201 of the DMCA.[47] Second, an anti-fraud and misinformation measure was needed to complement Article 12 of the WIPO Copyright Treaty, which is now provided in Section 1202 of the DMCA.[48]

B. *A Quick Primer on Section 1202(c)*

Courts' prior interpretations of Section 1202(b) have hinged upon their concurrent interpretations of Section 1202(c), which details "copyright management information" (CMI) in the context of Section 1202(b).[49] Section 1202(c) defines CMI as certain information that identifies a copyrighted work, including the title, the name of the author, and terms and conditions for the use of a work.[50]

Like Section 1202(b), Section 1202(c) was adopted in the wake of the NII Report and WIPO Treaties discussed above as part of the DMCA.[51] The NII

---

congress/senate-report/190/1. The House identified that implementation of the DMCA was motivated to serve as domestic legislation implementing the WIPO treaties. H.R. Rep. No. 105-551.

43 The Senate Report is discussed in greater detail in the discussion of the legislative history and purpose of Section 1202(c). *See infra* Part I.D.

44 H.R. Rep. No. 105-551.

45 *Id.*

46 *Id.*

47 *Textile Secrets Int'l, Inc.*, 524 F. Supp. 2d at 1198–99; H.R. Rep. No. 105-551, at 9–12; WIPO Copyright Treaty, *supra* note 29, art. 11 (providing that "[c]ontracting [p]arties shall provide adequate legal protection and effective legal remedies against the circumvention of effective technological measures that are used by authors in connection with the exercise of their rights"); 17 U.S.C. § 1201 (detailing provisions to protect against "violations regarding the circumvention of technological protection measures").

48 *Textile Secrets Int'l, Inc.*, 524 F. Supp. 2d at 1198–99; H.R. Rep. No. 105-551, at 9–12; WIPO Copyright Treaty, *supra* note 28, art. 12 (providing that "[c]ontracting [p]arties shall provide adequate legal protection and effective legal remedies against any person knowingly performing any of the [listed] acts knowing . . . that it will induce, enable, facilitate, or conceal an infringement of any right covered by this Treaty or the Berne Convention"); 17 U.S.C. § 1202(b) (detailing provisions to protect the "integrity of copyright management information").

49 *See, e.g.*, *Textile Secrets Int'l, Inc.*, 524 F. Supp. 2d at 1198–99.

50 17 U.S.C. § 1202(c).

51 WIPO Copyright Treaty, *supra* note 29; WIPO Performances and Phonograms Treaty, *supra* note 28.

Report described copyright management information (CMI) as "a kind of license plate for a work on the information superhighway, from which a user may obtain important information about the work."[52] The Report defined CMI as "the name and other identifying information of the author of a work, the name and other identifying information of the copyright owner, terms and conditions for uses of the work, and such other information as the Register of Copyrights may prescribe by regulation."[53] The WIPO Copyright Treaty offered a similar definition, defining CMI as:

> Information which identifies the work, the author of the work, the owner of any right in the work, or information about the terms and conditions of use of the work, and any numbers or codes that represent such information, when any of these items of information is attached to a copy of a work or appears in connection with the communication of a work to the public.[54]

CMI protection was also discussed in House and Senate Committee hearings commenting on the WIPO treaties and formulating the language of Section 1202(c) in the DMCA.[55] The Senate Committee report provided insight to the definition of CMI as embodied in Section 1202(c).[56] The Senate report identified CMI as "an important element in establishing an efficient Internet marketplace in copyrighted works free from governmental regulation" and noted CMI will aid in monitoring the usage and licensing of copyrighted works.[57] The report noted that "under the bill, CMI need not be in digital form, but CMI in digital form is expressly included."[58] Moreover, CMI does not have to be provided for a copyrighted work, but it is protected from removal, falsification, or alteration if an author elects to include it.[59]

As enacted in the DMCA, Section 1202(c) defines eight types of information as constituting CMI:

> Definition. – As used in this chapter, the term 'copyright management information' means the following information conveyed in

---

[52] *Textile Secrets Int'l, Inc.*, 524 F. Supp. 2d at 1196–97; Information Infrastructure Task Force, *supra* note 28, at 235.

[53] Information Infrastructure Task Force, Intellectual Property and the National Information Infrastructure: Report of the Working Group of Intellectual Property Rights, app. 1, at 7 (Sept. 1995).

[54] WIPO Copyright Treaty, *supra* note 29, art. 12(2). This language closely tracks the drafted language of Section 1202(c) in the NII Report. Information Infrastructure Task Force, *supra* note 28.

[55] H.R. Rep. No. 105-551; S. Rep. No. 105-190.

[56] S. Rep. No. 105-190.

[57] *Id.*

[58] *Id.*

[59] *Id.*

connection with copies or phonorecords of a work or performances or displays of a work, including in digital form:

(1) The title and other information identifying the work, including the information set forth on a notice of copyright.

(2) The name of, and other identifying information about, the author of the work.

(3) The name of, and other identifying information about, the copyright owner of the work, including information set forth in a notice of copyright.

(4) With the exception of public performances of works by radio and television broadcast stations, the name of, and other identifying information about, a writer, a performer, or director whose performance is fixed in work other than an audiovisual work.

(5) With the exception of public performances of works by radio and television broadcast stations, the name of, and other identifying information about, a writer, a performer, or director who is credited in the audiovisual work.

(6) Terms and conditions for use of the work.

(7) Identifying numbers or symbols referring to such information or links to such information.

(8) Such other information as the Register of Copyrights may prescribe by regulation but not including any information concerning the user of a copyrighted work.[60]

While Section 1202(c) does not impose any affirmative or negative obligations on copyright owners, it nevertheless is fundamental to assessments of Section 1202(b) claims. Since Section 1202(b) references "CMI" but does not itself define the term, Section 1202(b) is always interpreted in tandem with the definition of CMI provided in Section 1202(c).[61] Section 1202(c) thus functions as the animating provision of Section 1202, as alleged CMI must first fall within the definition of CMI posited in Section 1202(c) before it can be "removed or altered" in violation of Section 1202(b).[62] The following Section outlines prior interpretations of Sections 1202(b) and (c) and describes how the provisions necessarily influence one another.

---

[60] 17 U.S.C. § 1202(c); *see* Nimmer, *supra* note 2, at 413–15 (describing the enumeration of corms of CMi encompassed under Section 1202(c)).

[61] *See*, e.g., IQ Grp., Ltd. v. Wiesner Publishing, LLC, 409 F. Supp. 2d 587, 591 (assessing whether a logo could constitute CMI under Section 1202(c) prior to determining whether Section 1202(b) was violated by removal of a logo).

[62] *Id.*

C. *Prior Interpretations of Section 1202(b) and (c)*

The Central District of California was the first federal district to assess a Section 1202(b) claim in *Kelly v. Arriba Soft Corporation.*[63] In *Kelly*, the plaintiff alleged violation of the copyrights in their thumbnail photographs by the defendant's the inclusion of the thumbnails in their "visual search engine" image database.[64] The plaintiff also alleged the defendant violated Section 1202(b) by removing or altering the CMI associated with their images.[65] The court found the defendant did not intentionally remove or alter CMI from the images under Section 1202(b)(1) because the contested CMI did not appear in the original images captured by the defendant.[66] Even if CMI was present in the original images, the defendants did not apparently intend to remove or alter the CMI.[67] Moreover, the defendants did not distribute works with altered or removed CMI under Section 1202(b)(3) because the thumbnail images compiled by the defendant were linked to full-size images with the name of the website where the defendant obtained the image.[68] As such, the court concluded that the defendant would not have had "reasonable grounds to know" it would cause users to infringe the plaintiff's copyrights and thus did not violate Section 1202(b).

Following *Kelly*, courts assessing Section 1202(b) claims declined to uphold claims where plaintiffs failed to provide a defendant's knowledge or intent in violating the statute and cabined their analyses to whether CMI was included in an original work as necessary for a violation of Section 1202(b).[69] But a major shift in courts' interpretations of Section 1202(b) was spurred by reasoning in *IQ Group, Ltd. v. Weisner Publications, LLC.*[70] In *IQ Group*, the plaintiff alleged violation of Section 1202(b) through the defendant's failure to include a company logo and hyperlink to copyright notices in copyrighted advertisements that the defendant distributed via email.[71] On these facts, the court held the defendant did not violate Section 1202(b) in its distribution of the ads because the logo and

---

[63] 77 F. Supp. 1116, 1117 (C.D. Cal. 1999).

[64] *Id.*

[65] *Id.*

[66] *Id.* at 1122.

[67] *Id.*

[68] *Id.*

[69] *See* Schiffer Pub., Ltd. v. Chronicle Books, No. 03-4962, 2004 WL 2583817, at *14 (E.D. Pa. Nov. 12, 2004) (finding no violation of Section 1202(b) where a plaintiff failed to demonstrate that the defendant removed CMI from the "body" of, or area around, the original work itself); Monotype Imaging, Inc. v. Bitstream, Inc., 376 F. Supp. 2d 877, 893 (N.D. Ill. 2005) (finding the defendant did not violate Section 1202(b) for its failure to include a copyright notice in reproduction of copyrighted fonts and, even if licensees used the plaintiff's fonts, the defendant did not knowingly or intentionally contribute to those uses).

[70] 409 F. Supp. 2d 587 (D.N.J. 2006).

[71] *Id.* at 589.

hyperlink to copyright notices did not constitute CMI as defined by Section 1202(c).[72] First, the court identified that claiming the IQ Group logo as CMI "impermissibly blurs" the distinction between trademark law and copyright law, and thus the logo cannot be construed as CMI.[73] Second, the logo and hyperlink fall outside the definition of CMI in Section 1202(c) as interpreted by the court.

The *IQ Group* court noted that the text of Section 1202 appeared to broadly define CMI and concluded that the interpreted definition of CMI should be narrowed in light of scholarly insights and the provision's legislative history.[74] The court reviewed the history of the DMCA and writings that motivated adoption of Section 1202, namely aforementioned the NII Report and WIPO treaties.[75] From these, the court deduced that CMI only describes information that "function[s] as a component of an automated copyright protection or management system."[76] The court identified that both the NII Report and the WIPO Treaties suggested that technical measures like CMI are components of automated copyright protection systems and that such interpretation of the statute's legislative history is affirmed by legal scholarship.[77] The court also noted that the aforementioned congressional reports on the DMCA understood the proposed language of Section 1202 as "protecting the integrity of automated copyright management systems functioning within a computer network environment."[78] In solidifying its technology-oriented interpretation of Section 1202, the court identified that its interpretation was consonant with Section 1201, which mentions circumvention of "technological measure[s]" that function to control and protect the rights of copyright owners.[79]

Applying its fashioned interpretation to the alleged Section 1202(b) violation at issue, the *IQ Group* court concluded that the logo and hyperlink did not constitute CMI.[80] Neither the logo nor the hyperlink were alleged to function as part of an automated copyright protection or management system, and there was no evidence that the defendant's actions circumvented a function of an automated

---

[72] *Id.* at 591–593.

[73] *Id.* at 592.

[74] *Id.* at 593. The court first referred to legal scholarship to conclude that CMI should be limited to the technological measures that protect copyrights in works. *Id.* at 593 (citing to Julie E. Cohen, *Copyright and The Jurisprudence of Self-Help*, 12 Berkeley Tech L.J. 1089 (1998) [hereinafter "Jurisprudence of Self-Help"]).

[75] *Id.* at 594–596.

[76] *Id.* at 597.

[77] *Id.* at 595–596 (citing S. Dusollier, *Some Reflections on Copyright Management Information and Moral Rights*, 25 Colum. J.L. & Arts 377, 382 (2003); Cohen, *Jurisprudence of Self-Help*, *supra* note 75; Julie E. Cohen, *A Right to Read Anonymously: A Closer Look at "Copyright Management" in Cyberspace*, 28 Conn. L. Rev. 981, 989 (1996); Jessica R. Friedman, *A Lawyer's Rambling Down the Information Superhighway: Copyright*, 65 Fordham L. Rev. 705 (1995)).

[78] *Id.* at 596.

[79] *Id.* at 596–597.

[80] *Id.* at 597.

protection or management system.[81] As the logo and hyperlink excluded by the defendant did not fall within the interpreted definition of CMI in Section 1202(c), the defendant did not violate the statute.

IQ Group was the first decision to offer a statutory interpretation of Section 1202(b) and (c), albeit an exceptionally narrow one. Notably, the courts' decision on the Section 1202(b) violation hinged upon the character of the CMI at issue rather than any act of removal or alteration by the defendant. In *Textile Secrets International, Inc. v. Ya-Ya Brand Inc.*, a court in the Central District of California adopted this narrow construction of Section 1202(c).[82] The *Textile Secrets* plaintiff alleged violation of Section 1202(b) through the defendant's removal of selvage[83] and a tag listing the plaintiff's name and a copyright symbol from fabric printed with the plaintiff's copyrighted design that the defendant allegedly reproduced without permission.[84] The plaintiff argued that the information on the selvage and the corresponding tag constituted CMI within the scope of Section 1202(c).[85]

The *Textile Secrets* court concluded that the selvage and tag did not constitute CMI as defined in Section 1202(c).[86] The court adopted the *IQ Group* court's narrow construction of Section 1202(c) and noted that the provision cannot apply in circumstances that "have no relation to the Internet, electronic commerce, automated copyright protections or management systems . . . or other technological measures or processes as contemplated in the DMCA as a whole."[87]

---

[81] *Id.*

[82] 524 F. Supp. 2d 1184, 1201 (C.D. Cal. 2007). *But cf.* Agence France Presse v. Morel, 769 F. Supp. 2d 295, 305–06 (S.D.N.Y. 2011) ("[T]his [c]ourt declines to adopt a narrow construction of the term "CMI"-- adopted by the District of New Jersey . . . as limited to 'a component of an automated copyright protection or management system.'"); Faulkner Press, L.L.C. v. Class Notes, L.L.C., 756 F. Supp. 2d 1352, 1359 (N.D.Fla. 2010) (finding plain language did not limit CMI to "notices that are placed on works through technological processes"); Fox v. Hildebrand, 2009 WL 1977996, at *3 (C.D. Cal. July 1, 2009) (declining to consider the legislative history of Section 1202 where the plain language of the provision "is not limited to copyright notices that are digitally placed on a work"); Assoc. Press v. All Headline News Corp., 608 F. Supp. 2d 454, 461–62 (S.D.N.Y. 2009) (denying motion to dismiss and finding a lack of textual support to limit the DMCA's application only to technological processes of automated systems).

[83] "Selvage" is the border of fabric that is intended to be cut off. *Id.* at 1192 n.7.

[84] *Id.* at 1192–93.

[85] *Id.* at 1193.

[86] *Id.* at 1202.

[87] *Id.* at 1201. The court considered the interpretation of Section 1202(c) offered by a court in the Western District of Pennsylvania in *McClatchey v. The Associated Press*, No. 3:05-cv-145, 2007 WL 776103 (W.D. Pa. Mar. 9, 2007). *See id.* at 1201–02. In *McClatchey*, the plaintiff had a copyright in a printed photograph of the United 93 plane crash on September 11, 2001 and included her title and copyright information on the photograph. *McClatchey*,

As the addition of the selvage and tag did not comprise a "technological process" within the scope of Section 1202(c), they were not CMI and thus the defendant did not infringe Section 1202(b) in removing them.[88]

The narrow interpretation of Section 1202(c) furthered in *IQ Group* and *Textile Secrets* was countered by subsequent decisions adopting broader interpretations of CMI.[89] In *Murphy v. Millennium Radio Group LLC*, the court declined to follow the interpretive approach of *IQ Group* and found that CMI as defined under Section 1202(c) is not limited to the context of "automatic copyright protection or management systems."[90] In *Murphy*, the plaintiff alleged violation of Section 1202(b) in the defendant's alleged removal of the plaintiff's gutter credit in their copyrighted photograph.[91] The plaintiff's photograph, including the gutter credit, was printed in a physical magazine.[92] The defendant then scanned the image from the magazine, cropped the original photo caption and gutter credit, and posted the electronic copy on a website without permission from the plaintiff.[93] The website allowed its visitors to alter the image using photo editing software and share copies of their edited images with the defendant by submitting them through the website.[94]

2007 WL 776103, at *1–2. An Associated Press reporter took a photograph of the plaintiff's printed photograph and distributed a copy of the photograph with the title and copyright notice removed without the plaintiff's permission. *Id.* In finding the defendant's cropping violated Section 1202(b), the court offered a more expansive interpretation of Section 1202(c). *Id.* Because the plaintiff used a computer software program to add identifying information on her copies of the photograph, the information was added via a "technological process" that fell within the ambit of CMI as defined by Section 1202(c). *Id.* at *5.

The *Textile Secrets* court distinguished *McClatchey* from the present case because the District Court failed to consider the legislative history of Section 1202(c) before finding the statutory provision applied. *Textile Secrets Int'l, Inc.*, 524 F. Supp. 2d at 1202. The *Textile Secrets* court also bolstered the *IQ Group* court's interpretation of Section 1202(c) by citing opinions issued shortly after *Kelly* that indicated a basis of Section 1202 in establishing technological safeguards. *Id.* (citing ALS Scan, Inc. v. RemarQ Communities, Inc., 239 F.3d 619, 625 (4th Cir. 2001) (discussing the DMCA's purpose to provide immunity to online service providers from copyright infringement for passive actions engaged in by technological processes); United States v. Elcom Ltd., 203 F. Supp. 2d 1111, 1125 (N.D. Cal. 2002) (finding that Congress aimed to protect against piracy and promote electronic commerce in enacting Section 1202)).

[88] *Id.* at 1202–03.

[89] *See, e.g.*, Murphy v. Millennium Radio Grp., LLC, 650 F.3d 295 (3d Cir. 2011).

[90] *Id.* at 305.

[91] *Id.* at 298–99. A gutter credit is "a credit placed on an inner margin, or 'gutter,' of a magazine page, ordinarily printed in smaller type and running perpendicular to the relevant image on the page." *Id.* at 299.

[92] *Id.* at 298–99.

[93] *Id.*

[94] *Id.*

The *Murphy* court found that the gutter credit constituted CMI within the scope of Section 1202(c) and that the defendant violated Section 1202(b).[95] In establishing a broader standard for CMI encompassed within Section 1202(c), the court assessed the plain meaning of the statutory text before resorting to interpretation in light of the provision's legislative history.[96] The court identified that "[t]here is nothing particularly difficult about the text of Section 1202" and noted that the text of the statute imposes no requirement that CMI be a part of an automatic copyright protection or management system as concluded by the *IQ Group* court.[97] Moreover, the court remarked that the provision was extremely broad and that any difficulty in construing the statute would derive from concerns of policy.[98] The court identified that the DMCA was intended to expand the rights of copyright owners and that the *IQ Group* court's reading of the statute's legislative history did not contradict a broader reading of CMI encompassed in Section 1202(c). Specifically, the *Murphy* court identified that although the NII Report identified CMI as information likely to be included in digital works to inform the user about the authorship of the work, the method of communicating this information was an open question.[99] Based on these insights, the *Murphy* court found the legislative history was not sufficiently compelling to disregard the plain language of Section 1202(c) and concluded that a cause of action under Section 1202 "potentially lies whenever the types of information listed in Section 1202(c)(1)–(8) and 'conveyed in connection with copies . . . of a work . . . including in digital form' is falsified or removed, regardless of the form in which that information is conveyed."[100] As the gutter credit fell within the court's modified scope of Section 1202(c), it was CMI within the meaning of the statute.[101]

Subsequent district courts followed the *Murphy* court's lead and adopted broader interpretations of Section 1202(c),[102] while others formulated narrow

[95] *Id.* at 305.
[96] *Id.* at 302.
[97] *Id.*
[98] *Id.*
[99] *Id.* at 303–04.
[100] *Id.* at 305.
[101] *Id.*
[102] *See* Brown v. Stroud, No. C 08-02348, 2011 WL 2600661, at *5 (N.D. Cal. June 30, 2011) (finding a claim for violation of Section 1202(a) or (b) must "allege facts showing that the alleged falsification or removal of CMI has some relation to the Internet, electronic commerce, or the purposes for which the DMCA was enacted."); Pac. Studios Inc. v. W. Coast Backing, Inc., No. 2:12-cv-00692, 2012 WL 12887637 (C.D. Cal. April 18, 2012) (denying a partial motion to dismiss and finding adequate pleading of violation of Section 1202(b) under the *Murphy* standard).

interpretations along the lines of *IQ Group* and *Textile Secrets*[103]. Subsequent courts have also flushed out a standard for viable Section 1202(b)(1) and (b)(3) claims beyond consideration of the quality of CMI at issue, although it remains relevant.[104] The basic elements of this standard are detailed in the following Subpart.

D. Elements of a Section 1202(b) claim

To have a claim under Section 1202(b), a plaintiff must allege particularized facts about the existence of CMI in the copyrighted work and the removal or alteration of that CMI.[105] Additionally, courts require a plaintiff to demonstrate that the defendant had knowledge that the CMI was being altered or removed and that the alteration or removal would enable copyright infringement.[106] Finally, some courts have required plaintiffs to show that the work with the altered or removed CMI is an exact copy of the original work–what has become known as the "identicality" requirement.[107] These three requirements are further detailed below.

---

[103] *See* Kirk Kara Corp. v. W. Stone and Metal Corp., No. CV 20-5991503, 2020 WL 5591503 (C.D. Cal. Aug. 14, 2020) (granting a motion to dismiss Section 1202 claims on the grounds that "no DMCA violation exist[ed] where the works [at issue] are not identical").

[104] *See, e.g.*, *id.* at *6 ("To establish a claim under section 1202(b)(1), a plaintiff must plausibly allege: (1) the existence of CMI on the infringed work, (2) removal and/or alteration of that information, and (3) that the removal and/or alteration was done intentionally."); Craig v. Univ. Music Grp. Recordings, Inc., 380 F. Supp. 3d 324, 338 (S.D.N.Y. 2019) ("[A] defendant may be liable under Section 1202(b)[(3)] for "distribu[ing [a] copyrighted work] . . . knowing that copyright management information has been removed or altered without the authority of the copyright owner or the law.").

[105] Mango v. Buzzfeed, Inc., 970 F.3d 167, 173 (2d Cir. 2020) (finding liability for violation of 1202(b) for knowing removal of a gutter credit included in a separate line of text below a copyrighted photograph).

[106] Stevens v. Corelogic, 899 F.3d 666, 676 (9th Cir. 2018) (finding no liability for violation of Section 1202(b) because a plaintiff did not put forward evidence of the defendant's knowledge that its software could induce, enable, facilitate, or conceal infringement); *Mango*, 970 F.3d at 171 (holding that, as a matter of first impression, Section 1202(b) includes a "double-scienter requirement").

[107] Doe 1 v. GitHub, Inc., No. 22-cv-06823, 2024 WL 23217, at *8 (N.D. Cal. Jan. 22, 2024) (finding that allegedly infringing material must be identical to an original work to have a viable Section 1202(b) claim); Andersen v. Stability AI Ltd., No. 23-cv-00201, 2024 WL 3823234, at *8 (N.D. Cal. Aug. 12, 2024) (dismissing a Section 1202(b) claim on the basis that the allegedly infringing AI output was not identical to the original work); *cf.* Frost-Tsuji Architects v. Highway Inn, Inc., No. 12-00496, 2024 WL 3405871, at *1 (D. Haw. July 10, 2014), *aff'd* 700 F. App'x. 674 (9th Cir. 2017) (considering the "near identical" and "virtually identical" nature of copies of a copyrighted work in finding sufficient factual allegations for a Section 1202(b)(1) claim). *But cf.* ADR Int'l Ltd. v. Ins.

1. Particularized Allegations of Existence of CMI and Removal of CMI by Defendants

A plaintiff must identify the particular types of CMI in their works that they believe were altered or removed and allege plausible facts about which defendants committed an alteration or removal in violation of Section 1202(b) and when the violation occurred.[108] To meet this requirement, allegations of altered or removed CMI cannot be conclusory, like the allegations of alteration or removal of a "creator's name" or "the form of [an] artist's signature" in *Andersen*.[109] Rather, plaintiffs must identify the exact type of CMI that was allegedly altered or removed.[110]

2. Knowledge Requirement

Courts also require a plaintiff to allege facts that support that a defendant both knew CMI was being altered or removed from the plaintiff's works and knew that the conduct would "induce, enable, facilitate, or conceal an infringement."[111] This knowledge requirement was coined as the "double-scienter requirement" in *Stevens v. CoreLogic*.[112] The *Stevens* court concluded that a defendant must both intend to remove CMI and be aware that removal of the CMI would further copyright infringement to be liable for violation of Section 1202(b).[113]

Courts have noted that the double-scienter requirement is intended to limit liability by providing a heightened requisite state of mind.[114] As demonstrated in *Beijing Meishe Network Technology*, factual allegations of multiple previously-filed lawsuits against a defendant for removal of CMI and copying of copyrighted works fulfill this requirement.[115] Moreover, the CMI that is altered or removed

for Supply Mgmt. Inc., 667 F. Supp. 3d 411, 427 (S.D. Tex. 2023) (finding that Section 1202(b) does not include an "identicality" requirement and noting that copying must only be "substantially similar").

[108] *Mango*, 970 F.3d at 173; *Andersen*, 2024 WL 3823234, at *8; *cf.* Nimmer, *supra* note 2, at 422–23.

[109] *Andersen*, 2024 WL 3823234, at *8.

[110] *Id.*; *cf.* Kelly v. Arriba Soft Corp., 77 F. Supp. 1116, 1122 (C.D. Cal. 1999) (requiring CMI exist on the original work for potential liability for violation of Section 1202(b)).

[111] 17 U.S.C. § 1202(b)(3); Stevens v. Corelogic, 899 F.3d 666, 676 (9th Cir. 2018); *cf.* Nimmer, *supra* note 2, at 423–25 (describing the "mental element" of Section 1202(b) claims).

[112] *Stevens*, 899 F.3d at 676.

[113] *Id.*

[114] *See, e.g.*, Beijing Meishe Network Tech. Co, Ltd. v. TikTok, Inc., No. 23-cv-06012, 2024 WL 1772833, at *3 (N.D. Cal. Apr. 23, 2024); Tremblay v. OpenAI Inc., 716 F. Supp. 3d 772, 778–80 (N.D. Cal. 2024).

[115] *Beijing Meishe Network Tech. Co, Ltd.*, 2024 WL 1772833, at *3.

does not have to be noticeable by the public for its removal to induce, enable, facilitate, or conceal copyright infringement.[116]

3. "Identicality" Requirement

Some courts impose an "identicality" requirement and require that plaintiffs demonstrate that the work with the removed CMI is an exact copy of the original work and thus is "identical," except for the missing or altered CMI.[117] While the term "identicality" was adopted by the district court in *Doe 1 v. Github, Inc.*,[118] earlier courts considered the identicalness of an alleged copy with removed CMI to an original work.[119] In *Frost-Tsuji Architects v. Highway Inn, Inc.*, the plaintiff brought suit under Section 1202(b), alleging the defendants copied the plaintiff's copyrighted computer-aided design (CAD) drawings of a restaurant kitchen floor plan and intentionally removed CMI from the drawings.[120] The District of Hawaii granted summary judgement to defendants on the plaintiff's Section 1202(b) claim on the basis that the plaintiff did not provide any evidence demonstrating that any of the defendants removed CMI from its work.[121] The plaintiff alleged that some of the defendants possessed floor plans that were "virtually identical" to the plaintiff's original drawings.[122] The court indicated that the fact that the defendants possessed allegedly "virtually identical" floor plans did not mean that CMI had been removed from the floor plans.[123] Rather, virtually identical plans could have been produced by redrawing the original plans by hand and not including the plaintiff's CMI.[124] The court determined that such exclusion of CMI

---

[116] *Id.*

[117] *GitHub*, Inc., 2024 WL 23217, at *8; (finding that allegedly infringing material must be identical to an original work to have a viable Section 1202(b) claim); *Andersen*, 2024 WL 3823234, at *8 (dismissing a Section 1202(b) claim on the basis that the allegedly infringing AI output was not identical to the original work); 42 North, LLC v. Brad Douglas, LLC, No. 1:20-cv-188, 2024 WL 4661396, at *3 (W.D. Mich. Nov. 4, 2024) (finding Section 1202(b) did not apply to an original work that was not identically copied); Frost-Tsuji Architects v. Highway Inn, No. 13-00496, 2014 WL 5798282, at *6 (D. Haw. Nov. 7, 2014), *aff'd* 700 F. App'x. 674 (9th Cir. 2017) (finding that "[t]he physical act of removal is not the same as basing a drawing on someone else's work."); Kirk Kara Corp. v. W. Stone and Metal Corp., No. CV 20-5991503, 2020 WL 5991503, at *6 (C.D. Cal. Aug. 14, 2020) (finding that "even where the underlying works are similar, courts have found that no DMCA violation exists where the works are not identical.").

[118] Trial Tr. 34:7, 18, Doe 1 v. Github, Inc., No. 22-cv-235217 (N.D. Cal. filed May 7, 2023); *Github*, 2024 WL 235217, at *9 ("In short, neither case cited by [p]laintiffs concerns Section 1202(b)'s *identicality* requirement.") (emphasis added).

[119] Frost-Tsuji Architects, 2014 WL 5798282 (D. Haw. Nov. 7, 2014), *aff'd* 700 F. App'x. 674 (9th Cir. 2017); Kirk Kara Corp., 2020 WL 5991503 (C.D. Cal. Aug. 14, 2020).

[120] *Frost-Tsuji Architects*, 2014 WL 5798282, at *1–2.

[121] *Id.* at *4–5.

[122] *Id.* at *5.

[123] *Id.*

[124] *Id.*

would not amount to a violation of Section 1202(b) because it "would not involve any removal or alteration of [CMI] from [the plaintiff's] original work."[125]

Following *Frost-Tsuji Architects*, the Southern District of New York in *Fischer v. Forrest* considered the level of identicalness between the plaintiff's original work and the defendants' work when assessing a Section 1202(b) claim.[126] In *Fischer*, the plaintiff alleged the defendants copied the plaintiff's product brochure and website in the defendants' advertisement.[127] In granting summary judgment to the defendants on all Section 1202(b) claims, the court indicated that "[a]side from four discrete phrases among the many used on [the plaintiff's] brochure and website, there is no similarly between [the plaintiff's] original works and [the defendants'] advertisement."[128] The court further recognized that prior cases holding Section 1202(b) claims were viable had involved underlying works alleged to be "substantially or entirely reproduced," which aligned with the text of Section 1202(c) requiring that CMI be "conveyed in connection with copies . . . of a work . . . or displays of a work."[129] Since the copying of the four phrases did not constitute substantial or entire reproduction of the plaintiff's brochure and website, the defendants did not violate Section 1202(b).[130]

Frost-Tsuji Architects and *Fischer Forrest* provide insights to district courts' early consideration of identicality as a requirement for a Section 1202(b) claim. While the *Frost-Tsuji Architects* court considered the plaintiff's allegation that the defendants' works were "virtually identical" to the plaintiff's, the court did not explicitly suggest that the works had to be identical for the plaintiff to have a viable Section 1202(b) claim.[131] Similarly, the *Fischer* court considered the degree of identicalness through the four copied phrases and indicated that "substantial[] or entire[]," not identical, reproduction was required to maintain a Section 1202(b) claim.[132] However, neither court clearly articulated an "identicality *requirement*" and seemed to indicate it was only a potential consideration when assessing Section 1202(b) claims.

The Central District of California was the first court to affirmatively impose an "identicality" requirement when assessing the plaintiff's Section 1202(b) claims in *Kirk Kara Corporation v. Western Stone and Metal Corporation.*[133] In *Kirk Kara*, the plaintiff alleged the defendant copied the plaintiff's copyrighted engagement ring designs and intentionally removed CMI, in the form of "KIRK

---

[125] *Id.*

[126] Fischer v. Forrest, 286 F. Supp. 3d 590, 609 (S.D.N.Y. 2018), *aff'd* 968 F.3d 216 (2d Cir. 2020).

[127] *Id.* at 596–600.

[128] *Id.* at 609.

[129] *Id.* (quoting 17 U.S.C. § 1202(c)).

[130] *See id.*

[131] *Frost-Tsuji Architects*, 2014 WL 5798282, at *5.

[132] *Fischer*, 286 F. Supp. 3d at 609.

[133] *Kirk Kara Corp.*, 2020 WL 5991503.

KARA" engraved on the rings, from the copies.[134] The court dismissed the plaintiff's Section 1202(b) claim on the grounds that the original designs and allegedly copied designs were not exact copies.[135] The court identified that a side-by-side review of images of the plaintiff's rings and the defendant's rings suggested the ring designs may be substantially similar but the defendant "did not make *identical* copies of the plaintiff's rings and then remove the engraved CMI."[136]

Contemporary federal courts are divided in imposing an identicality requirement for Section 1202(b) claims. Notably, district courts of the Ninth Circuit Court of Appeals have varied in their treatments of the identicality requirement.[137] As discussed above, the Central District of California applied the identicality requirement in *Kirk Kara Corporation*, although it provided little explanation for doing so.[138] Conversely, the District of Nevada declined to impose the identicality requirement in *Oracle, Inc. v. Rimini Street* because, it reasoned, the requirement may weaken the intended protections for copyright holders under Section 1202(b).[139] Application of the identicality requirement is also unsettled in district courts beyond the Ninth Circuit.[140]

The Ninth Circuit is poised to be the first circuit court to weigh in on the identicality requirement in the pending interlocutory appeal of *Doe 1 v. Github, Inc.*[141] In *Github*, owners of copyrights in software code brought a suit against GitHub, a platform on which software developers store and share code.[142] The plaintiffs alleged that Microsoft Copilot, an AI product developed in part by Github, illegally removed CMI from their works that were stored on Github.[143] Notably, the plaintiffs did not allege copyright infringement in the suit, and only argued breach of contract, negligence, unjust enrichment, and unfair competition claims in addition to violation of Section 1202(b).[144] The plaintiffs stored their software in GitHub's publicly accessible software repositories under open-source

---

[134] *Id.* at *1.
[135] *Id.* at *6.
[136] *Id.* (emphasis in original).
[137] *See, e.g.*, Oracle Int'l Corp. v. Rimini Street, No. 2:14-cv-01699, 2023 WL 4701627, at *81–83 (D. Nev. July 24, 2023); *Kirk Kara Corp.*, 2020 WL 599153, at *6.
[138] *Kirk Kara Corp.*, 2020 WL 5991503, at *6 (C.D. Cal. Aug. 14, 2020).
[139] *Oracle Int'l Corp.*, 2023 WL 4701627, at *81–83.
[140] *See, e.g.*, ADR Int'l Ltd. v. Ins. for Supply Mgmt. Inc., 667 F. Supp. 3d 411, 427 (S.D. Tex. 2023) (finding that Section 1202(b) does not include an "identicality" requirement and noting that copying must only be "substantially similar").
[141] Doe 1 v. Github, Inc., No. 4:22-cv-06823, 2024 WL 4336532 (N.D. Cal. Sept. 27, 2024).
[142] Doe 1 v. Github, Inc., 672 F. Supp. 3d 837, 845–47 (N.D. Cal. 2023).
[143] *Id.* at 847.
[144] First Am. Compl., Doe 1 v. Github, Inc., No. 4:22-cv-06823, at 52–68 (N.D. Cal. filed June 8, 2023). Other AI copyright infringement suits that allege violation of Section 1202(b) sometimes allege other claims, like invasion of privacy, but consistently allege direct or vicarious copyright infringement. *See, e.g.*, Compl., J.L. v. Alphabet, Inc., No. 23-cv-03440, at 59–82 (N.D. Cal. filed July 11, 2023).

license agreements.[145] The plaintiffs claimed that GitHub removed CMI from their code and trained the Copilot AI model on the code in violation of the license agreements.[146] Moreover, the plaintiffs claimed that, when prompted to generate software code, Copilot includes unique aspects of the plaintiffs' code in its outputs.[147] In their complaint the plaintiffs alleged that all requirements for a valid Section 1202(b) claim were met in the present suit.[148] The plaintiffs stressed that, in removing CMI, the defendants failed to prevent users of Copilot from making illegal use of the product.[149] Consequently, they claimed, the defendants removed the CMI, knowing that it would "induce, enable, facilitate, and/or conceal infringement" of copyrights in violation of Section 1202(b).[150]

As to the identicality requirement, the plaintiffs argue that Section 1202 contains no such requirement given the plain language of the statute makes it a violation to remove or alter CMI from a copy of a copyrighted work, regardless of whether the work is identical.[151] The defendants counter that Section 1202, which defines CMI as relating to a "copy of a work," requires a complete and identical copy, not just parts of a copy.[152] The plaintiffs concede that Copilot reproduces snippets of code rather than complete versions.[153] Therefore, per the defendants, Copilot does not create "identical copies" of the plaintiffs' complete copyrighted works.[154]

The Ninth Circuit's hearing of the interlocutory appeal on "whether Sections 1202(b)(1) and (b)(3) of the DMCA impose an identicality requirement"[155] is notable for a number of reasons. First, Section 1202(b) is largely unaddressed by the circuit courts, and explicit appellate guidance has only been provided for the

---

[145] *Id.* at 845–47.
[146] *Id.* at 847.
[147] *Id.*
[148] *Id.*
[149] Second Am. Compl., Doe 1 v. Github, Inc., No. 22-cv-06823, at 3, 24–42 (N.D. Cal. filed Jan. 25, 2024).
[150] *Id.* at 48–53.
[151] Pl.'s Opp. to Def.'s Mot. to Dismiss the Second Am. Compl., Doe 1 v. Github, Inc., No. 22-cv-06823, at 6–9 (N.D. Cal. filed Mar. 27, 2024).
[152] Def.'s Reply in Support of their Mot. to Dismiss the Second Am. Complaint in Consolidated Action, Doe 1 v. Github, Inc., No. 22-cv-7074, at 4–6 (N.D. Cal. filed Apr. 10, 2024).
[153] *Id.*
[154] *Id.* The defendants' argument is based on both the text of Section 1202 as well as policy concerns. *Id.* The defendants point to the protection of "copies," rather than excerpts, derivatives, or other adaptations, in the wording of the statute. *Id.* at 4. Moreover, protection of excerpts under Section 1202 would create chaos for ordinary uses of copyrighted works. *Id.*
[155] *Github*, 2024 WL 4336532, at *1.

knowledge requirement referenced above.[156] Consequently, determinations of Section 1202(b) claims are largely informed by varying district court decisions that are binding only on the parties to the suits and provide inconsistent interpretations of the requirements for a claim under the provision.[157] An appellate ruling that accepts or rejects the identicality requirement would create additional binding authority to further clarify courts' interpretations of Section 1202(b).

Second, a ruling on the identicality requirement from the Ninth Circuit *specifically* would be notable because it would be binding upon the large number of Section 1202(b) claims presently being litigated in the Ninth Circuit's lower courts.[158] Given the centrality of AI developers operating in California and elsewhere in the Ninth Circuit, the outcome of the appeal would significantly impact future lawsuits that involve Section 1202(b) claims.

It is difficult to anticipate how the Ninth Circuit might rule in the appeal, but one can tease out some of the implications of three choices the court has the option to adopt: first, interpretation of the identicality requirement as requiring a complete and exact copy; second, interpretation that incomplete and inexact copying is sufficient to satisfy the identicality requirement; and third, finding an identicality requirement does not apply to Section 1202(b) claims.

If the Ninth Circuit interprets the identicality requirement as requiring a complete and exact copy, it would impose a high standard for the requirement and plaintiffs would likely be constrained in their ability to bring Section 1202(b) claims. If the court did this, the *Github* plaintiffs' claims would likely fail as the alleged copied snippets of code generated by Copilot are not exact copies and do not comprise the complete copyrighted works. This hypothetical standard would be advantageous for individuals who remove CMI from copyrighted works in the course of processing them using AI as well as those who deploy AI systems that produce small portions of content similar (but not exactly so) to inputs. So long as the works being processed or distributed are not *complete* exact copies, individuals would be free to alter the CMI of the works for ease in analyzing the copyrighted information.

Alternatively, the Ninth Circuit could adopt a loose interpretation of identicality in which incomplete and inexact copying would be sufficient. One

---

[156] *See* Stevens v. Corelogic, 899 F.3d 666, 676 (9th Cir. 2018) (finding no liability for violation of Section 1202(b) because a plaintiff did not put forward evidence of the defendant's knowledge that its software could induce, enable, facilitate, or conceal infringement); *See supra* Part II.D.1.

[157] *See* Part II.D.

[158] *See, e.g.*, Compl., In re Google Generative AI Litigation, No. 3:23-cv-03440, at 87–89 (N.D. Cal. filed Jul. 11, 2023) (alleging violations of Sections 1202(b)(1) and (b)(3) for removal of CMI from social media posts and visual artworks); Compl., Concord Music Grp., Inc. v. Anthropic PBC, No. 5:24-cv-03811, at 56–57 (N.D. Cal. filed Oct. 18, 2023) (alleging violations of Sections 1202(b)(1) and (b)(3) for removal of CMI from musical works); Third Consolidated Am. Compl., Kadrey v. Meta Platforms, Inc., No. 3:23-cv-03417, at 18–19 (N.D. Cal. filed Jan. 21, 2025) (alleging violations of Section 1202(b)(1) for removal of CMI from books).

approach would be to require identicality but not copying of the entire work (something the plaintiffs in the *Github* suit advocate for). How the parties or the Ninth Circuit would formulate what standard would apply to this "less than entire" but still "near identical" standard is hard to say, but presumably, plaintiffs would have an easier time alleging facts sufficient for a Section 1202(b) claim. Applied to *Github*, it still seems unclear that the copied snippets of the plaintiffs' code in the Copilot outputs could pass muster (this is likely a factual question to be determined at later stages of the litigation). But it could allow claims to at least survive an early motion to dismiss. As such, the adoption of this standard could limit how AI developers engage with works but also potentially affect others, such as researchers using similar techniques to process, clean, and distribute small portions of copyrighted works as part of a dataset.

Finally, the Ninth Circuit may decide to do away with the identicality requirement altogether. While this may seem like a potential boon to plaintiffs, who could allege that removal of CMI and distribution of some copied material, no matter how small, plaintiffs would still face substantial challenges. Elimination of the identicality requirement would likely lead to greater weight being placed on the knowledge requirement in courts' assessments of Section 1202(b) claims, which requires that defendants know or have reasonable grounds to know that their actions will "induce, enable, facilitate, or conceal an infringement." In the context of the *Github* case, even without an identicality requirement, plaintiffs Section 1202(b) claims contain scant factual allegations about the defendants' CMI removal and knowledge in the court filings to date. For other developers and users of AI, the effects of not having an identicality requirement would likely vary on a case-by-case basis.

II: CURRENT INTERPRETATIONS AND FUTURE IMPLICATIONS OF SECTION 1202(B) AND (C)

This Part details how Section 1202(b) and (c) present in lawsuits implicating AI as well as non-AI suits that still implicate the statute. The infrequent litigation of Section 1202(b) claims prior to the 2010s may make protections against the removal of CMI appear to be a relatively insignificant component of the DMCA.[159] However, the technological advent of AI has drastically elevated the importance and value of Section 1202(b). Prior to the widespread use of generative AI technology, removal of CMI from copyrighted works was largely possible only by individuals taking discrete actions to remove CMI "by hand" from copyrighted works, like cropping out the attribution line of a copyrighted

[159] *See supra* note 6 and accompanying text.

photograph using photo editing software.[160] Modern AI technology not only allows users to remove more discrete kinds of information, like metadata encompassed in digital works, but also allows for removal of information en masse without necessitating discrete action for each removal. The increased capacity of individuals to manipulate information using AI technology has increased the attractiveness of bringing claims for removal of CMI under Section 1202(b), and the statute has become an important prospective outlet for relief.

However, there are many unanswered questions about how to interpret the language of Section 1202(b) and what is required to have a viable claim under the statute. Moreover, how the statute is interpreted impacts the ease of satisfying Section 1202(b) and has the potential to enable misuse of the provision. The following paragraphs elaborate upon these ideas and others in the context of current suits under Section 1202.

The Section 1202(b) issues in present copyright infringement lawsuits implicating AI seem to arise from the plaintiffs' "throw it against a wall and see what sticks" approach in alleging DMCA claims.[161] In *Andersen v. Stability AI, Ltd.*, the plaintiffs' initial complaint alleged sweeping violations of the DMCA under sections 1201 through 1205,[162] and the plaintiff's second amended complaint alleges only "DMCA violations" without reference to particular statutory provisions.[163] The complaints filed in *Doe 1 v. GitHub, Inc.* contain similarly broad and vague allegations.[164] Despite this, courts generally find the Section 1202(b) allegations to be viable and have allowed them to proceed in the early stages of these suits.[165] The Section 1202(b) claims in *Doe 1 v. GitHub, Inc.* are representative of Section 1202(b) claims in the many present suits against AI developers alleging violations of Section 1202(b).[166] The primary issue in *Github*

---

[160] *See, e.g.*, Murphy v. Millennium Radio Grp., LLC, 650 F.3d 295, 299 (3d Cir. 2011) (assessing the cropping of a gutter credit of and subsequent unauthorized use of a photograph as a violation of Section 1202(b)); McClatchey v. The Associated Press, No. 3:05-cv-145, 2007 WL 776103, at *2 (W.D. Pa. Mar. 9, 2007) (assessing the cropping of a title and copyright notice from a photo taken of a physical copy of a copyrighted photograph that included a title and copyright notice as a violation of Section 1202(b)).

[161] *See, e.g.*, Compl., Andersen v. Stability AI Ltd., No. 23-cv-00201, 2024 WL 3823234, at 12–14 (N.D. Cal. filed Jan. 13, 2023).

[162] *Id.*

[163] Second Am. Compl., Andersen v. Stability AI Ltd., No. 23-cv-00201, 2024 WL 3823234, at 58, 78 (N.D. Cal. filed Oct. 31, 2024).

[164] *See* Compl., Doe 1 v. GitHub, Inc., No. 22-cv-06823, 2024 WL 23217, at 10 (N.D. Cal. filed Nov. 3, 2022); Second Am. Compl., Doe 1 v. GitHub, Inc., No. 22-cv-06823, 2024 WL 23217, at 11 (N.D. Cal. filed Jan. 25, 2024).

[165] *See, e.g.*, Doe 1 v. GitHub, Inc., No. 22-cv-06823, 2024 WL 23217, at *8 (N.D. Cal. Jan. 22, 2024). *But see* Raw Story Media, Inc. v. OpenAI Inc., No. 1:24-cv-01514, 2024 WL 4711729, at *3–5 (S.D.N.Y. Nov. 7, 2024) (dismissing claims under Section 1202(b)(1) for lack of Article III standing); *infra* Part III.A.

[166] *See generally* Compl., Concord Music Grp., Inc. v. Anthropic PBC, No. 5:24-cv-03811, at 56–57 (N.D. Cal. filed Oct. 18, 2023) (alleging violations of Sections 1202(b)(1) and

on appeal is whether Section 1202(b) contains the aforementioned identicality requirement, which is also an issue in other AI suits.[167]

Of the lawsuits filed against AI developers in district courts that allege Section 1202(b) claims, the claims in one suit have been allowed to proceed past the motion to dismiss stage,[168] the claims in three suits have been dismissed without leave to amend,[169] and the claims in three suits have been dismissed with

(b)(3) for removal of CMI from copyrighted musical works); Third Consolidated Am. Compl., Kadrey v. Meta Platforms, Inc., No. 3:23-cv-03417, at 18–19 (N.D. Cal. filed Jan. 21, 2025) (alleging violations of Section 1202(b)(1) for removal of CMI from copyrighted books).; Second Am. Compl., Doe 1 v. Github, Inc., No. 4:22-cv-06823, at 49–50 (N.D. Cal. filed Jan. 25, 2024) (alleging violations of Sections 1202(b)(1) and (b)(3) through removal of CMI in violation of open-source software license agreements); Compl., Raw Story Media, Inc. v. OpenAI Inc., No.1:24-cv-01514, at 9–11 (S.D.N.Y. filed Feb. 28, 2024) (alleging violations of Section 1202(b)(1) and (b)(3) through removal of CMI from copyrighted works of journalism); Compl., Daily News, L.P. v. Microsoft Corp., No. 1:24-cv-03285, at 90–91 (S.D.N.Y. filed Apr. 30, 2024) (alleging violations of Sections 1202(b)(1) and (b)(3) through removal of CMI from copyrighted news and media content); Am. Compl., Intercept Media, Inc. v. OpenAI Inc., No. 1:24-cv-01515, at 18–22 (S.D.N.Y. filed June 21, 2024) (alleging violations of Sections 1202(b)(1) and (b)(3) through removal of CMI from copyrighted works of journalism); Am. Compl., N.Y. Times Co. v. OpenAI, No. 1:23-cv-11195, at 64–65 (S.D.N.Y. filed Aug. 12, 2024) (alleging violations of Sections 1202(b)(1) and (b)(3) through removal of CMI from copyrighted news and media content); Compl., Vacker v. Eleven Labs, Inc., 1:24-cv-00987, at 49–52 (D. Del. filed Aug. 29, 2024) (alleging violation of Sections 1202(b)(1) and (b)(3) through removal of CMI from copyrighted audiobook narrations); Am. Compl., Center for Investigative Reporting, Inc. v. OpenAI Inc., No. 1:24-cv-04872, at 28–32 (S.D.N.Y. filed Sept. 24, 2024) (alleging violations of Sections 1202(b)(1) and (b)(3) through removal of CMI from copyrighted news and media content); Second Am. Compl., Andersen v. Stability AI Ltd., No. 23-cv-00201, at 61, 62, 69, 79 (N.D. Cal. filed Oct. 31, 2024) (alleging violations of Section 1202(b)(1) through removal of CMI from copyrighted books); Pierce v. Photobucket, Inc., No. 1:24-cv-03432, at 43–46 (D. Colo. filed Dec. 11, 2024) (alleging violations of Sections 1202(b)(1) and (b)(3) through removal of CMI from copyrighted photographs).

[167] *Id.*; Andersen v. Stability AI Ltd., No. 23-cv-00201, 2024 WL 3823234, at *8 (N.D. Cal. Aug. 12, 2024).

[168] Kadrey v. Meta, Inc., No. 3:23-cv-03417 (N.D. Cal. filed Mar. 7, 2025) ECF 471 (declining to dismiss Section 1202(b)(3) claims from the plaintiff's third consolidated amended complaint).

[169] *See* Raw Story Media, Inc. v. OpenAI Inc., No. 1:24-cv-01514 at 6–7 (S.D.N.Y. Nov. 7, 2024) ECF 117 (dismissing Section 1202(b) claims for lack of a concrete injury as required for Article III Standing), ECF 137; Raw Story Media, Inc. v. OpenAI Inc., No. 1:24-cv-01514 at 2 (S.D.N.Y. Apr. 3, 2025) ECF 137 (denying plaintiffs' motion for leave to amend Section 1202(b) claims in complaint); Andersen v. Stability AI Ltd., No. 3:23-cv-00201 at 11–13 (N.D. Cal. Aug 12, 2024) ECF 223 (dismissing Section 1202(b)(1) and (b)(3) claims without leave to amend); The New York Times Co. v. Microsoft Corp., No. 1:23-cv-11195 at 1–2 (S.D.N.Y. Mar 26, 2025) ECF 485 (dismissing Section 1202(b)(1) and (b)(3) claims without leave to amend against all defendants in the *New York Times*, *Daily News*, and *Center for Investigative Reporting* related suits).

leave to amend.[170] In two suits, the Section 1202(b)(3) claims have been dismissed against a particular defendant, while the Section 1202(b)(1) claims have been allowed to proceed against that defendant.[171] Finally, in two suits, Section 1202(b) claims have been alleged but the defendant has yet to oppose them.[172] Claims have been dismissed without leave to amend for lack of Article III standing[173] and insufficient factual allegations of alteration or removal of CMI.[174] The fact-specific nature of Section 1202(b) claims makes it difficult (and perhaps unwise) to infer from these suits how other Section 1202(b) claims will progress.[175] However, it is certain that progression of the pending suits hinges upon answering significant interpretive questions about both the statute and threshold procedural requirements to bring suit.

---

[170] Tremblay v. OpenAI Inc., No. 3:23-cv-03223 at 6–8 (N.D. Cal. Feb. 12, 2024) ECF 104 (dismissing Section 1202(b)(1) and (b)(3) claims with leave to amend for failure to allege knowing removal or alteration of CMI and failure to allege distribution of works without CMI rather than mere reproduction of works without CMI); Concord Music Grp., Inc. v. Anthropic PBC, No. 5:24-cv-03811 at 9–12 (N.D. Cal. Mar. 25, 2025) ECF 322 (dismissing Section 1202(b)(1) and (b)(3) claims with leave to amend); Doe 1 v. GitHub, Inc., No. 4:22-cv-06823 at 14–16 (N.D. Cal. Jan 22, 2024) ECF 195 (dismissing Section 1202(b)(1) and (b)(3) claims with leave to amend); In re Google Generative AI Copyright Litigation, No. 5:23-cv-03440 at 1–2 (N.D. Cal. Jun 06, 2024) ECF 46 (dismissing Section 1202(b)(1) and (b)(3) claims with leave to amend).

[171] *See* The New York Times Co. v. Microsoft Corp., No. 1:23-cv-11195 at 1–2 (S.D.N.Y. Mar 26, 2025) ECF 485 (dismissing Section 1202(b)(3) claims without leave to amend against OpenAI Inc. in the *New York Times*, *Daily News*, and *Center for Investigative Reporting* related suits and denying dismissal of Section 1202(b)(1) claims against OpenAI Inc. in the *Daily News* and *Center for Investigative Reporting* related suits).

[172] *See* Compl., Pierce v. Photobucket, Inc., 1:24-cv-03432 at 43–47 (D. Colo. filed Dec. 11, 2024) (alleging violations of Sections 1202(b)(1) and (b)(3)); Mot. to Dismiss, Vacker v. ElevenLabs, Inc., No. 1:24-cv-00987 at 7–13 (D. Del. Dec. 6, 2024) (arguing dismissal of Section 1202(b)(1) and (b)(3) claims should be dismissed for lack of Article III standing and insufficient factual allegations to state a claim under Section 1202(b)).

[173] *See, e.g.*, Raw Story Media, Inc. v. OpenAI Inc., No. 1:24-cv-01514 at 2 (S.D.N.Y. Nov. 7, 2024) ECF 117 (dismissing Section 1202(b) claims for lack of Article III Standing), ECF 137; *infra* Part III.A.

[174] *See, e.g.*, Andersen v. Stability AI Ltd., No. 3:23-cv-00201 at 11–13 (N.D. Cal. Aug 12, 2024) ECF 223 (dismissing Section 1202(b)(1) and (b)(3) claims without leave to amend for failure to allege sufficient facts of alteration or removal of CMI for claims under Section 1202(b)(1) and (b)(3)).

[175] Additionally, the inconsistency between district court rulings on Article III standing to bring suit under Section 1202(b) suggests this uncertainty extends to threshold procedural inquiries. *Compare Raw Story Media, Inc.*, 2024 WL 4711729 (finding new organizations alleging violation of Section 1202(b) by an AI developer's removal of CMI and identifying information from their works lacked Article III standing to bring suit), *with* The Intercept Media, Inc. v. OpenAI Inc., No. 24-cv-1515, 2025 WL 556019 (S.D.N.Y. Feb. 20, 2025) (finding a media company pleaded a "concrete injury [sufficient for standing] that was of the kind long protected by American courts" through an AI developer's alleged removal of CMI from the media company's articles).

Current Section 1202(b) suits that do not implicate AI also raise a variety of interpretive questions about the provision's requirements. In *Oppenheimer v. Highland Falls Country Club*, a court in the Western District of North Carolina determined that Section 1202(b)(3) protection applies to physical copies of copyrighted works.[176] In *Oppenheimer*, the plaintiff photographer alleged violation of Section 1202(b) through the defendants' removal of the plaintiff's name, date, and copyright symbol included on his copyrighted photograph and use of the photograph on the defendant's website and in printed brochures the defendant distributed to the public.[177] The *Oppenheimer* court relied upon interpretation of the plain language of Section 1202(b)(3) in finding the printed works were protected.[178] The court identified that "digital" is not mentioned in the plain language of Section 1202(b)(3) and thus the non-digital, printed works were protected.[179] The *Oppenheimer* court also rejected the defendants' argument that CMI as defined in Section 1202(c) excludes physical or printed CMI.[180] The court noted that Section 1202(c)'s "inclusion clause" merely provides a digital copy as an example of a form of a copy.[181] As such, physical and printed copies of CMI fall within the scope of CMI as defined by Section 1202(c).[182]

One day prior to the decision in *Oppenheimer*, the court in *42 North LLC v. Brad Douglas, LLC* also found that protection under Section 1202(c) does not extend to CMI in non-digital form based on interpreting the language of Section 1202(c) in light of its legislative history.[183] In *42 North*, the plaintiff alleged violation of Section 1202(b) through the defendant's handmade permit drawings of the plaintiff's copyrighted architectural design drawings.[184] The *42 North* court followed a similar path as the *IQ Group* and *Textile Secrets* courts in investigating the policy motivators behind the adoption of Section 1202 and reached a similar conclusion.[185] Because the information included on the architectural design drawings did not operate "'to protect [an] automated system[] which protect and manage copyrights' in order to 'facilitate electronic and Internet commerce,'" it did not constitute CMI within the court's interpreted scope of Section 1202(c) and thus could not be CMI that was altered or removed in violation of the DMCA.[186] On Section 1202(b) issue, the court found that, even if the CMI fell within the scope of Section 1202(c), the defendant would not have violated Section 1202(b)

---

[176] *See* Oppenheimer v. Highland Falls Country Club, No. 1:24-cv-00133, 2024 WL 4683301, at *4 (W.D.N.C. Nov. 5, 2024).
[177] *Id.* at *2.
[178] *Id.* at *3.
[179] *Id.*
[180] *Id.*
[181] *Id.*
[182] *Id.*
[183] *42 Brand, LLC*, 2024 WL 4661396, at *2–4.
[184] *Id.* at *1.
[185] *Id.* at *2–4.
[186] *Id.* at *4.

because the hand-drawn permit drawings were not identical to the original architectural design drawings.[187]

III: OTHER LEGAL DOCTRINES THAT MAY IMPACT SECTION 1202(B) AND (C)

This Part details three legal doctrines that may impact contemporary courts' assessments of Section 1202(b) and (c) in the context of AI. First, the standing requirement of Article III appears poised to present challenges to bringing suits under Section 1202(b)(3). Second, broad references to "the law" in the statutory text of Section 1202(b) and (c) may provide an outlet for a viable fair use defense to Section 1202(b) claims. Third, if fair use is not a viable defense, forced inclusion of CMI to comply with Section 1202(b) may raise issues grounded in the First Amendment, such as compelled speech.

A. Article III Standing Under Section 1202(b)(3)

In *Raw Story Media, Inc. v. OpenAI Inc.*, Judge McMahon recently dismissed the plaintiff's complaint for lack of Article III standing to assert a violation of Section 1202(b)(1) without an allegation that the defendant disseminated copies of the plaintiff's copyrighted work with altered or removed CMI.[188] In *Raw Story Media,* the plaintiff alleged violation of Section 1202(b)(1) through the defendant's alleged use of the plaintiff's "breaking news features, investigative news articles and opinion columns published online" to train ChatGPT, the defendant's AI-powered large language model.[189] The plaintiffs alleged that "'thousands' of their copyrighted works were . . . stripped of their author, title, and copyright information, and input into . . . Open AI's training sets" and used

---

[187] *Id. But cf.* New Parent World, LLC v. True to Life Prods., Inc., No. cv-23-08089, 2024 WL 4277865, at *2–3 (finding Section 1202(b) does not require an allegedly infringing copy to be identical to the original work for a viable claim).

[188] Raw Story Media, Inc. v. OpenAI Inc., No. 1:24-cv-01514, 2024 WL 4711729, at *3–5 (S.D.N.Y. Nov. 7, 2024) (granting a motion to dismiss for lack of Article III standing and denying without prejudice a motion for leave to replead to renewal on a proper record); *see generally Big RulingL Judge McMahon dismisses Raw Story's complaint v. OpenAI on lack of standing for DMCA claim*, ChatGPT is Eating the World (Nov. 8, 2024), https://chatgptiseatingtheworld.com/2024/11/08/big-ruling-judge-mcmahon-dismisses-raw-storys-complaint-v-openai-on-lack-of-standing-for-dmca-claim/; Aaron Moss, *Will AI Copyright Claims Keep Standing After New Ruling?*, Copyright Lately (Nov. 10, 2024), https://copyrightlately.com/raw-story-copyright-lawsuit-standing/; *cf.* Jonathan Band, *TransUnion, Nicklin, and Preserving the Right to Embed*, Disruptive Competition Project (Aug. 11, 2021), https://project-disco.org/intellectual-property/081121-transunion-nicklin-and-preserving-the-right-to-embed/.

[189] *Id.* at *1.

to train ChatGPT, and that this violated Section 1202(b)(1).[190] The plaintiffs sought both actual or statutory damages and injunctive relief.[191]

The court found that plaintiff's Section 1202(b)(1) arguments failed due to a lack of Article III standing to pursue their claims for damages and an injunction.[192] Article III standing to bring a lawsuit for a statutory violation requires a plaintiff establish that they suffered a "concrete injury."[193] Specifically, "'to establish standing, a plaintiff must show (i) that he suffered an injury in fact that is concrete, particularized, and actual or imminent; (ii) that the injury was likely caused by the defendant, and (iii) that the injury would likely be redressed by judicial relief.'"[194] When assessing whether a harm is concrete, courts must assess whether "the alleged injury to the plaintiff has a close relationship to a harm traditionally recognized as providing a basis for a lawsuit in American courts" and requires plaintiffs to identify "a close historical or common-law analogue for their asserted injury."[195]

The court assessed the deficiencies in the plaintiffs' standing damages and injunctive relief piecemeal. First, the court identified that the plaintiffs lacked standing to pursue damages because "interference with property" did not function as a sufficient historical analogue.[196] Judge McMahon identified that she "[is] not convinced that the mere removal of identifying information from a copyrighted work–absent dissemination–has *any* historical or common-law analogue" of concrete harm.[197] Second, the court identified that the plaintiffs lacked standing to pursue injunctive relief because they "failed to allege facts tending to show that the risk of ChatGPT reproducing their work without the requisite inclusion of CMI was "substantial."[198] The plaintiffs failed to allege that the information in their publications is copyrighted as required to protect against future copyright infringement.[199] Moreover, the court found there was no substantial risk that the current operating version of ChatGPT would generate plagiarized information.[200]

In light of *Raw Story Media*, it's likely that Article III standing will likely play a role in future Section 1202(b) suits, particularly those that involve non-

---

190 *Id.*

191 *Id.*

192 *Id.* at *3.

193 *Id.* at *2 (citing Spokeo, Inc v. Robins, 578 U.S. 330, 341 (2016); Lujan v. Defenders of Wildlife, 504 U.S. 555, 561 (1992)).

194 *Id.* (citing TransUnion LLC v. Ramirez, 594 U.S. 413, 423 (2021)).

195 *Id.* (citing TransUnion LLC v. Ramirez, 594 U.S. 413, 424–25 (2021)).

196 *Id.* at *3.

197 *Id.* at *4.

198 *Id.*

199 *Id.* at *5.

200 *Id.* The court distinguished the current operating version of ChatGPT from older versions of ChatGPT that generated responses with significant amounts of plagiarized content. *Id.*

copyrightable works and plead only the removal or alteration of CMI in violation of Section 1202(b) without a claim of copyright infringement.

B. "The Law" as it Relates to Section 1202(b)

Second, fair use may operate as a defense to allegations of Section 1202(b) violations. Per the statute's language, Section 1202(b) safeguards against removal or alteration of CMI unless such removal or alteration as permitted by the copyright owner or "the law."[201] This undefined reference to "the law" could encompass permission to remove or alter CMI so long as such uses fall within the ambit of fair use outlined under 17 U.S.C. § 107.

The interplay between the DMCA and fair use has previously been explored with regard to provisions of the Act outside of Section 1202(b). On July 28, 2020, the U.S. Senate Committee on the Judiciary Subcommittee on Intellectual Property held a hearing titled, "How Does the DMCA Contemplate Limitations and Exceptions Like Fair Use?"[202] The hearing commentary primarily focused on the safe harbor provisions included in Section 512 of the Act and the "anti-circumvention" provision of Section 1201, but did not discuss the provisions of Section 1202.[203] The lack of consideration of fair use as a defense to Section 1202 claims makes the prospect ripe for discussion in light of the pending Section 1202(b) suits.

The fair use defense protects an author's use of another's original work provided the use is for purposes including criticism, comment, news reporting, teaching, scholarship, or research. The fair use defense is codified in Section 107 of the Copyright Act of 1976. When a court is tasked with gauging whether a particular use is fair, the statute provides four factors to guide the court's determination:

(1) The purpose and character of the use, including whether the use is of a commercial nature or is for nonprofit educational purposes;

---

[201] 17 U.S.C. § 1202(b).

[202] *How Does the DMCA Contemplate Limitations and Exceptions Like Fair Use? Before the S. Comm. on Intell. Prop.*, 116th Cong. (2020), https://www.judiciary.senate.gov/committee-activity/hearings/how-does-the-dmca-contemplate-limitations-and-exceptions-like-fair-use; *see generally* Katharine Trendacost & Corynne McSherry, *What Really Does and Doesn't Work for Fair Use in the DMCA*, Elec. Frontier Found. (July 31, 2020), https://www.eff.org/deeplinks/2020/07/what-really-does-and-doesnt-work-fair-use-dmca; Eileen McDermott, *What's Fair? Senate IP Subcommittee Contemplates Problems with Copyright Fair Use Regime*, IP Watchdog (July 30, 2020 7:15 AM), https://ipwatchdog.com/2020/07/30/whats-fair-senate-ip-subcommittee-contemplates-problems-with-copyright-fair-use-regime/id=123614/.

[203] *See, e.g.*, *How Does the DMCA Contemplate Limitations and Exceptions Like Fair Use? Before the S. Comm. on Intell. Prop.*, 116th Cong. (2020) (statements of Sherwin Siy, Lead Public Policy Manager at Wikimedia Foundation; Christopher Mohr, Vice President of Intellectual Property and General Counsel, Software and Information Industry Association).

(2) The nature of the copyrighted work;

(3) The amount and substantiality of the portion used in relation to the copyrighted work as a whole; and

(4) The effect of the use upon the potential market for or value of the copyrighted work.

If a court found "the law" as described in the language of Section 1202(b) encompasses the statutory fair use defense, activities that entail the alteration or removal of CMI and that fall within the kinds of uses protected by fair use may constitute fair uses and thus not be violations of Section 1202(b).

Particular activities that entail the removal or alteration of CMI are well-positioned to excuse violations of Section 1202(b) under the fair use defense. Instances of CMI removal or alteration to create copyrighted works that parody original works may have particularly compelling arguments for excusal as fair uses. This is largely because required retention of CMI identifying original authors in the works of others that comment on or criticize original works would risk associating original authors with criticism of their own works, an activity that is likely improbable.[204] Additionally, AI technologies that employ CMI removal and alteration for research purposes are suited for excusal as fair use. Academics and researchers commonly use such tools to conduct text data mining research and format and restructure data for subsequent analysis. Hypothetical fair use assessments of these removals of CMI would benefit from the fact that the removal and alteration of CMI is for research and potentially nonprofit educational purposes.

C. *First Amendment Issues Implicated in Section 1202(b)*

Finally, First Amendment issues implicated in Section 1202(b) may impact the constitutionality of the statute and thus limit its operation. Courts have long recognized that fair use operates as a "safety valve" to prevent copyright law from restricting the First Amendment freedoms of speech, expression, and the press.[205] This function of fair use is best explained through an example. Suppose an individual wants to write and publish a review of an author's book and include quotations of language from the book. In a world without the fair use defense, the individual cannot include the quotations in their review without violating the author's copyright in the book. As a result, the individual's First Amendment

---

[204] *Cf.* Campbell v. Acuff-Rose Music, Inc., 510 U.S. 569, 593 (1994) (finding that there is no derivative market for critical works because of the "unlikelihood that creators of imaginative works will license critical reviews or lampoons of their own productions.").

[205] *See* Harper & Row Publishers, Inc. v. Nation Enters., 471 U.S. 539, 558–59; *see generally* Melville B. Nimmer, Does Copyright Abridge the First Amendment Guarantees of Free Speech and Press?, 17 UCLA L. REV. 1180 (1970).

freedom of expression through inclusion of the quotations in the review would be unconstitutionally restrained. In a world with fair use, the individual can include the quotations without violating the author's copyright in the book because the use of the quotations in the review easily qualifies as commentary or criticism expressly protected by the fair use defense and the author's First Amendment rights remain unviolated.

If a court found "the law" as described in the language of Section 1202(b) encompasses the statutory fair use defense, the fair use safety valve would operate to prevent restriction of First Amendment rights by Section 1202(b), and the provision would remain constitutionally sound. Conversely, if a court found "the law" did not encompass the statutory fair use defense, First Amendment freedoms of speech, expression, and the press could be restricted by limitations imposed by Section 1202(b).

The anticircumvention and antitrafficking provisions in Section 1201 of the DMCA have previously been challenged as overbroad, unconstitutionally vague, and facial violations of the First Amendment.[206] In every challenge, federal district and appellate courts found the provisions were content neutral, constitutional when assessed under an intermediate scrutiny standard of review, and did not violate the plaintiffs' First Amendment rights.[207] Section 1202(b) has never been challenged on First Amendment grounds, and it is uncertain whether the same First Amendment challenges made to Section 1201 would fare any better if made against Section 1202(b). However, unlike Section 1201, Section 1202(b) may be susceptible to challenge under the compelled speech doctrine of the First Amendment.

The compelled speech doctrine provides that the government cannot force an individual to express a particular belief or "punish an individual for refusing to articulate, advocate, or adhere to the government's approved messages."[208] For example, the government cannot require children in public schools to salute the American flag since it is unconstitutional to require students to espouse particular symbolic messages put forward by the government.[209] Similarly, the government cannot require individuals to publicly display government speech, such as a state

---

[206] *See* Universal City Studios, Inc. v. Corley, 273 F.3d 329 (2d Cir. 2001) (holding antitrafficking provisions of the DMCA was not an unconstitutional restriction of speech under the First Amendment); United States v. Elcom, Ltd., 203 F. Supp 2d 111 (N.D. Cal. 2002) (holding the anticircumvention provision of the DMCA was not unconstitutionally vague, not an unconstitutional restriction of speech under the First Amendment, and not unconstitutionally overbroad); 321 Studios v. Metro Goldwyn Mayer Studios, Inc., 307 F. Supp. 2d 1085 (N.D. Cal. 2004) (holding the anticircumvention provisions of the DMCA were constitutional); Green v. United States Dept. of Justice, 111 F.4th 81 (D.C. Cir. 2024) (holding the anticircumvention and antitrafficking provisions of the DMCA were not overbroad in violation of the First Amendment and were not susceptible to a facial First Amendment challenge).

[207] *Id.*

[208] David L. Hudson, *Compelled Speech*, Free Speech Ctr. at Middle State Tenn. Univ. (last updated July 2, 2024), https://firstamendment.mtsu.edu/article/compelled-speech/.

[209] West Virginia Bd. of Edu. v. Barnette, 319 U.S. 624, 640–42 (1943).

motto on a license plate, since it is unconstitutional for the government to "require an individual to participate in the dissemination of an ideological message by displaying it on his private property in a manner and for the express purpose that it be observed and read by the public."[210]

Compelled speech caselaw to date suggests the compelled speech doctrine primarily protects against compulsion of political or ideological messages,[211] and the potential of the compelled speech doctrine to protect against compelled factual disclosures by individuals is comparatively less explored.[212] However, existing practices of government-enforced factual disclosures by individuals that are afforded no First Amendment protection suggest it may be difficult to allege that required inclusion of factual information like CMI constitutes compelled speech. For example, individuals are required to make factual disclosures providing the amount and sources of their income on their tax returns and disclosing their current home address information for inclusion in sex offender registries, yet neither of these disclosures have been found to constitute compelled speech.[213] As a result, a successful argument that required retention of CMI in creators' works constitutes compelled speech would likely have to hinge upon the effect of the inclusion of CMI on a creator's ideological message or beliefs as relayed in their copyrighted work.

IV: PRACTICAL CONCERNS WHEN DEALING WITH CMI

Section 1202 has risen in prominence across the many AI copyright lawsuits filed over the last two years, but the courts have yet to answer many critical

---

[210] Wooley v. Maynard, 430 U.S. 705, 713 (1977).

[211] *See Barnette*, 319 U.S. 624 (1943); *Wooley*, 430 U.S. 705 (1977); Hurley v. Irish-Am. Gay, Lesbian and Bisexual Grp. of Bos., 515 U.S. 557 (1995) (holding application of a public accommodation law which would require parade organizers to include the plaintiffs-appellees in a parade would alter the expressive content of the parade and thus violate the First Amendment); Rumsfeld v. Forum for Academic and Institutional Rights, Inc., 547 U.S. 47 (2006) (holding a Department of Defense policy that the Department to deny federal funding to educational institutions that prohibited military representatives access and assistance at the institutions for recruiting purposes was unconstitutional under the unconstitutional conditions doctrine because it required the institutions to choose between surrendering its First Amendment rights and losing federal funding for its university).

[212] *See* Alan K. Chen, Compelled Speech and the Regulatory State, 97 IND. L.J. 881, 892–96.

[213] *See id.* at 895; United States v. Sindel, 53 F.3d 874, 878 (8th Cir. 1995) (finding a requirement that the defendant disclose client information did not constitute compelled speech of an ideological belief in violation of the First Amendment); United States v. Arnold, 740 F.3d 1032, 1035 (5th Cir. 2014) (holding the registration requirement of the Sex Offender Registration and Notification Act did not constitute compelled speech in violation of the First Amendment).

questions about viable defenses or limitations on Section 1202(b) claims.[214] Creators and other users should therefore exercise caution. This is especially true if, as these cases are decided, courts should begin to lower existing barriers to Section 1202(b), such as the identicality requirement. This could have the effect of allowing these claims to survive past early stages of litigation, making resolution more costly and riskier, and Section 1202(b) claims more attractive to opportunistic plaintiffs or outright "copyright trolls."[215] Unlike a copyright infringement claim under Section 501, a Section 1202 claim requires no prerequisite copyright registration (and in fact may not require copyright ownership at all), but does provide plaintiffs with significant statutory damages if Section 1202 is found to be violated.[216] These features make the statute well-suited for abuse, especially where plaintiffs may be able to drag out litigation past the initial stages.[217] While some Section 1202(b) claims are undoubtedly legitimate, users should be wary of the potential for plaintiffs with less compelling or nonexistent Section 1202(b) claims to bring suit with nefarious intent.

So, what can users do? First, if at all possible, users should refrain from separating any information that could be construed as CMI from copyrighted works when re-using them to avoid possible liability under Section 1202(b)(1).[218] As discussed above, courts continue to be unclear about the scope of information encompassed in Section 1202(c).[219] In the context of creating and sharing copyrighted works, content such as titles, author names, organizational affiliations, and numerical citation information could be construed as CMI per the enumerated categories provided in Section 1202(c). Users should avoid separating

---

[214] *See, e.g.*, *Github*, , 2024 WL 4336532 (granting the plaintiff's motion to certify an order for interlocutory appeal to determine if Section 1202(b) imposes an identicality requirement). Similarly, courts have come down on different sides of whether Article III standing serves as a limitation to bringing a Section 1202(b) claim. *Compare* Raw Story Media, Inc. v. OpenAI Inc., No. 24-cv-01514, 2024 WL 4711729 (Nov. 7, 2024) (finding new organizations alleging violation of Section 1202(b) by an AI developer's removal of CMI and identifying information from their works lacked Article III standing to bring suit), *with* The Intercept Media, Inc. v. OpenAI Inc., No. 24-cv-1515, 2025 WL 556019 (S.D.N.Y. Feb. 20, 2025) (finding a media company pleaded a "concrete injury [sufficient for Article III standing] that was of the kind long protected by American courts" through an AI developer's alleged removal of CMI from the media company's articles).

[215] For general background on the evolution and practices of copyright trolls, *see generally* Matthew Sag, *Copyright Trolling: An Empirical Study*, 100 IOWA L. REV. 1105 (2014).

[216] *See* 17 U.S.C. § 1203(c)(3)(B) ("At any time before final judgment is entered, a complaining party may elect to recover an award of statutory damages for each violation of section 1202 in the sum of not less than $2,500 or more than $25,000.").

[217] *Cf.* Sag, *supra* note 216, at 1119 ("The problem with [copyright] statutory damages, as a matter of both design and application, is that the amounts awarded bear no relationship to the harm of infringement. . . . Statutory damages play a significant role in the profitability of copyright trolling. Without statutory damages, defendants might decide that their infringements are so trivial that the plaintiff will not bother to pursue them.").

[218] 17 U.S.C. § 1202(b), (c).

[219] *See supra* Part I.C.

these kinds of information from copyrighted works whenever possible, regardless of whether the works are being processed in a physical or digital format. Additionally, other information like organizational logos or hyperlinks to copyright notices could be construed as CMI. Although both of these were not found to constitute CMI in *IQ Group, Ltd. v. Weisner Publishing, LLC*,[220] the court in *Murphy v. Millennium Radio Group* expressly overruled the *IQ Group* interpretation of Section 1202.[221] As such, both logos and hyperlinks could constitute CMI as defined in Section 1202(c) and thus should receive the same careful treatment as the other information discussed above.

Second, users should know that distributing works that have removed or altered CMI raises potential liability under Section 1202(b)(2).[222] This is true regardless of whether the distributed copy is in a print or digital format. Practically speaking, doing so raises the visibility of such actions so naturally heightens risk. But additionally, distribution may make it more difficult to mount at least one successful defense: lack of standing based on failure to allege concrete harm, as was successfully argued in *Raw Story Media v. OpenAI Inc.*, relying on the Supreme Court's *TransUnion* decision.[223] While the *Raw Story* court found lack of harm for mere removal of CMI, under Section 1202(b)(1), distribution that puts copyrighted works in the hands of third-parties without CMI attached seems a much more tenuous case. This is because potential downstream distribution of copyrighted works without adequate tracking information to monitor authorized uses could more naturally be construed as a "concrete harm" that Section 1202 was enacted to specifically address.[224]

Organizations that develop AI technologies face somewhat higher stakes in their prospective liability under Section 1202(b).[225] Users that engage in occasional removal of CMI are better positioned to implement the suggestions provided above to avoid liability under Section 1202(b). However, organizations that remove CMI en masse, like AI developers, would likely have difficulty implementing the above suggestions since removal of CMI and other forms of identifying information is necessary for the effective creation and development of AI technologies. As a result, AI developers may feel at a loss as to how to protect against liability under Section 1202(b).

Ideally, AI developer defendants in Section 1202(b) suits would want to establish that they did not remove or alter CMI and thus did not violate Section 1202(b). While this is not feasible given the necessity of CMI removal and alteration for certain AI applications, especially during training stages, AI developer defendants can benefit from limitations imposed on Section 1202(b)

---

[220] 409 F. Supp. 2d 587 (D.N.J. 2006).

[221] Murphy v. Millennium Radio Grp., LLC, 650 F.3d 295, 304–06 (3d Cir. 2011).

[222] *See* 17 U.S.C. § 1202(b)(2).

[223] *See Raw Story Media, Inc.*, 2024 WL 4711729, at *3–5.

[224] *See* Information Infrastructure Task Force, *supra* note 28, at 191–92;

[225] *See generally* Alyn, *supra* note 12; Cacco, *supra* note 11.

claims under current caselaw. First, current and prior lawsuits assessing Section 1202(b) claims reveal that Section 1202(b) determinations are incredibly fact specific. As courts continue to come down on either side of Section 1202(b) issues in cases that look factually similar, there is little certainty as to how individual Section 1202(b) claims will be assessed.[226]

Third, AI developer defendants can leverage a number of defenses built into the requirements for a valid Section 1202(b) claim.[227] The double-scienter requirement necessitating plaintiffs prove a defendant intended to remove CMI and had knowledge that removal would further copyright infringement creates two hurdles to establish knowledge.[228] Defendants in jurisdictions that apply the double-scienter requirement can use this heightened standard to argue against having the knowledge required under Section 1202(b). Moreover, the identicality requirement provides another opportunity for defendants to argue against liability under Section 1202(b).[229] If a defendant's reproduction involves less-than-complete copies of copyrighted works, they can argue that failure to meet the identicality requirement renders the plaintiff's Section 1202(b) claim unviable.

CONCLUSION

Until recently, Section 1202 was a relatively quiet and seldom-used part of the Digital Millennium Copyright Act. No more. The surge of interest in Section 1202(b) claims brought by plaintiffs against developers of generative artificial intelligence technologies have put this provision in the spotlight. As recounted above, making a successful Section 1202 claim still faces many barriers, and no court has imposed Section 1202 liability in any of the AI copyright infringement lawsuits to date. But, given the potential for high statutory damages and the relatively routine ways in which many users remove and alter CMI, it is important that the courts carefully consider the limits of such claims.

[226] *Compare* Textile Secrets Int'l, Inc. v. Ya-Ya Brand Inc., 524 F. Supp. 2d 1184 (C.D. Cal. 2007), *with* McClatchey v. The Associated Press, No. 3:05-cv-145, 2007 WL 776103 (W.D. Pa. Mar. 9, 2007).

[227] *See supra* Part I.E.2; Part I.E.3.

[228] *See supra* Part I.E.2.

[229] *See supra* Part I.E.3.

PART III:
INTERVIEW

INTERVIEW OF
THERESA WEISENBERGER*AND CHAD RUTKOWSKI**

Conducted by ELIZABETH TOWNSEND GARD***

Chad Rutkowski and Theresa Weisenberger, both attorneys at BakerHostetler, are two leading voices in the conversations surrounding copyright and artificial intelligence. Elizabeth sat down in April 2025 for a conversation on how we might think about our current state.

Elizabeth Townsend Gard: Thank you so much for joining me. You are both so important to the current AI conversation. It's a thrill to have you here to chat. I really appreciate you being part of this.

Theresa Weisenberger: Thank you.

Chad Rutkowski: We appreciate being asked that Elizabeth? Obviously, it's near and dear to our heart. And I tell everybody that listens. You know the Copyright Society made me a copyright lawyer. but for the Copyright Society I wouldn't be doing any of this stuff.

Elizabeth Townsend Gard: Awesome. Okay? So I'm a historian, an oral historian by training. So we're going to start with a really simple thing which is for each of you to tell me your name, the date, and where you're calling from, and then I'm going to ask you each for a little biographical information again for preservation purposes. So, Theresa, should we start with you.

Theresa Weisenberger: So, Theresa Weisenberger, I'm calling from Atlanta, Georgia. I really wanted to say, like "longtime listener first time caller."

---

* Theresa Weisenberger is a Partner at BakerHostetler where she co-leads the Artifical Intelligence practice. She focuses her work in the areas of intellectual property and technology law, particularly in counseling on emerging technologies and its intersection with the evolving legal landscape. Theresa also serves as the Secretary and Vice President of Governance of the Copyright Society. *Theresa Weisenberger*, BAKERHOSTETLER, https://www.bakerlaw.com/professionals/theresa-m-weisenberger/.

** Chad Rutkoski is a Partner at BakerHostetler where he co-leads the Technology and IP Transactions and Outsourcing team. He is an expert on the intersection of copyright and technology, especially on copyright issues with AI and other softwares, and is the author of Lexis Practical Guidence notes on data licensing and Creative Commons licenses. Chad currently serves as the Chair of the Copyright Society's AI Subcommittee and previously developed the curriculum for the Copyright Society's AI programming series. *Chad Rutkowski*, BAKERHOSTETLER, https://www.bakerlaw.com/professionals/chad-a-rutkowski/.

*** Editor-in-Chief, Journal of the Copyright Society, and John E. Koerner Endowed Professor of Law, Tulane University Law School

I am a partner at BakerHostetler, where I co-lead the AI practice and our IP transactions group.[1] I have a background in electrical engineering, and early in my career I focused almost exclusively on patent law.[2] I address copyright and AI from a technology perspective. I'm particularly interested in how copyright law both protects and restricts the development of technology, and AI is an ideal case study. As part of my focus on AI, I maintain the AI Copyright Case Tracker where we monitor how copyright law is being applied in the context of the development and use of AI technology.[3] And I think that's it.[4]

Chad Rutkowski: So I'm Chad Rakowski. I'm a partner in the Philadelphia office of BakerHosteler.[5] My practice focuses on the intersection of copyright and technology. I write rather regularly on the copyright protections for data and copyright protections for software, and how that all relates and interrelates with AI. I've been writing about AI issues since 2016, when the Copyright Office issued its the Third Edition of its Compendium of U.S. Copyright Office Practices.[6] The Copyright Office was updating guidance on authorship issues, including AI authorship.[7] And I've been giving presentations on AI related topics

---

[1] BakerHostetler's Artifical Intelligence practice has provided a consortium of more than 40 companies with AI advice in a variety of areas, such as data collection, development of AI policies, and data privacy. The AI practice focuses on three main concerns: the use of AI in the legal field, the use of AI in the work and operations of clients, and the emerging legal and regulatory requirements for the use of AI. *Artificial Intelligence (AI)*, BAKERHOSTETLER, https://www.bakerlaw.com/services/artificial-intelligence-ai/.

[2] Theresa received her B.S. in Electrical Engineering from Mississippi State University in 2008 where she graduated *magna cum laude* and with a certificate in Engineering Entrepreneurship. *Theresa Weisenberger*, *supra* note 1.

[3] The AI Copyright Case Tracker monitors key pending litigation in the U.S. that raise copyright issues related to the creation or use of generative AI. Each case within the tracker includes an overview of the lawsuit, key filings that address the substantive legal issues, and a summary of the filings. Theresa M. Weisenberger, *Case Tracker: Artifical Intelligence, Copyrights and Class* Actions, BAKERHOSTETLER, https://www.bakerlaw.com/aicasetracker.

[4] Theresa is also the current Secretary/VP of Governance for the Copyright Society.

[5] *See Chad Rutkowski*, *supra* note 2.

[6] Chad's first article about AI discussed section 313.2 of the *Compendium of the U.S. Copyright Office Practices, Third Edition.* The article explored how AI technologies that can produce creative works challenge traditional ideas of authorship and ownership, as well as what the legal considerations are for protecting the copyright of AI-generated works. The full article can be found here: Chad A. Rutkowski, *The Monkey in the Machine*, BAKERHOSTETLER (Feb. 3, 2016), https://www.ipintelligencereport.com/blogs/the-monkey-in-the-machine/.

[7] Section 313.2 of *Compendium of the U.S. Copyright Office Practices, Third Edition* discussed Works That Lack Human Authorship, such as those produced by a machine. In that section the Copyright Office declared that it would not register machine created works if there was no creative input or innovation from a human author. U.S. COPYRIGHT OFFICE, COMPENDIUM OF U.S. COPYRIGHT OFFICE PRACTICES § 101 (3d ed. 2021), https://www.copyright.gov/comp3/docs/compendium.pdf.

and data ownership and copyright fair use for the Copyright Society and other organizations since 2018.[8] I'm the co-chair of the firm's Intellectual Property and Transactions Group, and co-chair of its AI group.[9] And I am the current chair of the Copyright Society's AI Programming Committee, and the co-chair of the American Bar Association, Copyright and Tech Committee, as well.

Elizabeth Townsend Gard: So do you just dream of AI issues like, do you ever get away from it?

Chad Rutkowski: For many years I felt like some of the disturbed folks that you might find in front of a 7-Eleven, trying to convince everybody that the end was coming. And I think the kindest compliment that I've gotten over the past two years was from our fellow Copyright society member and New York Chapter chair. James Trigg,[10] who is at Kilpatrick, who told me at a dinner in 2023 after our first Copyright Society AI Series panel, that for years he would listen to my presentations on data, copyright, and machine learning, and he would say to himself, "What is he talking about? And why do we care about this?" … And you know the compliment was that I was right, that this was something people needed to be paying attention to. And so here we are.

Elizabeth Townsend Gard: So help me help me understand, Chad, why did you start "paying attention" in 2016? What made you think about it in 2,016?

Chad Rutkowski: So in 2016 my practice was changing in a lot of different ways. I had been doing quite a lot of work in the patent space, although I don't have a technical degree. So I was getting a lot of exposure to issues around software architecture, software, coding, and software networking. And so I now had this sort of buildup of knowledge and my work in the patent space was beginning to diminish. So I had always had this interest in copyright law and decided that I wanted to figure out how to join those two things together, especially because nobody was really interested in the copyright space in tackling issues around code and data ownership. It was a bit of a backwater. I was focusing at the time on big data analytics, which was the buzzword.[11] You know the

---

[8] In 2020, Chad was a speaker for the Copyright Society's Content as Data and Data as Content program, where he spoke about how AI and machine learning interacts with copyright. *Content as Data and Data as Content: Copyright Issues in Machine* Learning, THE COPYRIGHT SOCIETY, https://copyrightsociety.org/event/content-as-data-and-data-as-content-copyright-issues-in-machine-learning/.

[9] *See Chad Rutkowski*, *supra* note 2.

[10] James Trigg is a Partner at Kilpatrick where he represents creators and brand oweners in the areas of copyright and trademake law. He has previously taught trademark and entertainment law as an Adjunct Professor at the Univeristy of Georgia School of Law. *James A. Trigg*, KILPATRICK TOWNSEND & STOCKTON, https://ktslaw.com/en/People/T/TriggJamesA.

[11] Big data analytics deals with extractig insights from large amounts of data and complex data sets by systematicly processing and analyzing the data. Tim Mucci and Cole Stryker, *What is Big Data Analytics?*, IBM, https://www.ibm.com/think/topics/big-data-analytics.

Gartner Hype cycle,[12] the issue *de jour* at the time. Related to that, I was beginning to learn more of the connection between data analytics and at least machine learning, a form of artificial intelligence. And so the ownership of data and the copyright issues that go around that were very much being discussed in that context back then, and that includes use of copyrighted content to train AI data models. We think of this as coming to the forefront with the prominence of ChatGPT at the end of 2022 and the beginning of 2023, but realistically, that was being discussed even back in 2016. So I was paying more attention to the AI space at the time. The hot technology was Google's Deep Dream, where you would take a photograph and plug it into the Google interface, and it would use the images that it was trained on to detect things like animals.[13] For example, is this a cat or is this a dog? And it would intentionally scramble the color palette of the photograph and map it to color palettes of animals that were in its image database and sort of create these funky psychedelic type outputs. And: that was sort of novelty art, there was no real apparent value in it, but it raised really interesting questions of authorship. Is there and author who is the author? Is it that you have selection authorship in picking the photograph that you sort of fed into the model or is Google the author because the software does the lion's share of the work? And so, as I began to think about those issues, the Copyright Office issued the Third Edition of the Compendium. The Compendium stated that works created by animals (at the time the Naruto monkey case was all the rage) and the Copyright Office sort of addressed that tangentially in the Compendium and saying, for example, a photograph taken by a monkey is not copyrightable.[14] And then in the same sentence–I think it was comma–works created solely by machines are not copyrightable, and that I found to be found to be bothersome right that the technology was likely to develop in ways we hadn't foreseen yet, that it was going to become an important technology, and to compare what AI was

---

[12] The Gartner Hype Cycle is a graphical representation of the maturity, adoption, and social application of specific technologies over time. The illustration helps organizations understand the potential value of emerging technologies within the context of their industry. The Cycle has five distinct phases: Technology Trigger, Peak of Inflated Expectations, Trough of Disillusionment, Slope of Enlightenment, and Plateau of Productivity. *Gartner Hype Cycle*, GARTNER, https://www.gartner.com/en/research/methodologies/gartner-hype-cycle.

[13] Deep Dream is a computer vision program created by Google that alters images to create surreal, dreamlike visuals. The program was designed to understand how neaural networks perceive and process images, and it was trained on millions of photos to classify and recognize patterns. Deep Dream was about to use its training to interpret and manipulate images to amplify patterns that would result in otherworldly images. *Deep Dream: An In-Depth Exploration*, GEEKSFORGEEKS (Aug. 1, 2024), https://www.geeksforgeeks.org/deep-dream-an-in-depth-exploration/.

[14] Section 313.2 of *Compendium of the U.S. Copyright Office Practices, Third Edition* declared that works that did not have a human author could not be copyrightable and specifically gave the example that a photograph taken by a monkey could not be protected. *See supra* note 10.

likely to do to what a monkey did was not likely to capture the nuances. So I wrote a blog post cleverly titled the "Monkey in the Machine."[15] sort of teased out some of these issues and some of the scholarship, that was out there at the time. Annemarie Bridy, who was a Stanford professor at the time, who is now heading copyright at Google,[16] was addressing some of these issues, and I relied quite heavily on some of her scholarship and thought leadership.[17]

Elizabeth Townsend Gard: And Theresa, how did you get involved and thinking about AI?

Theresa Weisenberger: Like I said earlier, I have a tech background, and I started my career doing patent prosecution and patent litigation. My industry focus was primarily software with the Supreme Court decision in *Alice v. CLS Bank,*[18] the patentability of software was really pulled back. A lot of our clients were left trying to figure out how to protect their investment in software.

Around 2016, I was at an outside counsel conference for one of our clients, and I had just started working at the firm, and I get cornered by this guy, Chad, that starts proselytizing about how copyright is the solution to all of our problems and that it's going to be what protects software going forward. And he had this great analogy explaining how the non-literal elements of software are protected just like plot and characters. He talked about Harry Potter. I just started at this firm as an associate, and I got this partner overly excited about copyright law in a room full of patent attorneys. That scared me off for a little bit.

But over timeI heard him talk over and over about copyright and its value for software. When I was hanging out with patent attorneys, when clients asked "How do we protect our software?" They didn't have a good answer. Copyright protection was often dismissed out of hand based on the misconception that infringement requires that source code be copied verbatim–which reminded me of Chad's Harry Potter analogy,. And so I dug a little bit further into this area. And that's how I started working more closely with Chad.

My AI practice began to grow around the same time, both as I was drafting patents to protect machine learning algorithms and the Patent Office was reluctant to issue any software patents.

I did a secondment at a company that had developed technology for running its operations, including AI technology for identifying contaminants in their supply and for identifying potential real estate acquisitions based off of publicly

---

[15] *See* Rutkowski, *supra* note 9.

[16] Annemarie Bridy is Senior Copyright Counsel at Google and a Nonresidential Fellow at the Stanford Law School Center for Internet and Society. Annemarie is the former Allan G. Shepard Professor of Law at the Univeristy of Idaho, having taught courses relating to intellectual property and interformation law. *Annemarie Bridy*, YALE LAW SCHOOL, https://law.yale.edu/annemarie-bridy.

[17] *See generally* Annemarie Bridy, *Coding Creativity: Copyright and the Artificially Intelligent Author*. 2012 STAN. TECH. L. REV. 5 (2012).

[18] Alice Corp. v. CLS Bank Int'l, 573 U.S. 208 (2014).

available data. And what was interesting about that work is that it came right at that time where we were kind of trying to figure out how to advise clients on patenting versus copyright. So I had to dig really far into actually at the specifics of how the technology worked, while I have an engineering degree, I did not specialize in AI. Back when I was in school, I don't think you could specialize in AI. That was kind of my segue into the AI stuff.

And then, to be honest, I got more involved in copyright because of the Copyright Society, and it's not exactly the same story as Chad's. It's not that I became a copyright attorney because of the Copyright Society. I became a copyright attorney because I wanted to work with the people in the Copyright Society. It was such a fun, intelligent organization that delves into really squishy problems, and once I overcame that learning curve, it became a bigger part of my focus.

Elizabeth Townsend Gard: Love it So how would you describe the moment we're at? How have we progressed? How do you describe who we are at the moment?

Theresa Weisenberger: Before 2022, we already had AI technology integrated into our systems; we just weren't calling it "AI." It wasn't as interesting to talk about data analytics or the machine learning algorithms. But once 2022 hit and AI became the hot topic, largely in part to the public reaction to ChatGPT. There in AI exploded, , and everybody wanted to integrate AI into everything, sometimes regardless of whether AI was the best solution to the particular business challenge. And from the legal perspective, from our clients, we were getting more questions about the risks of AI in general. The tech industry and the government both struggled with not only how to identify those risks, but how to allocate liability and responsibility appropriately. We are all still trying to figure out the right kind of language to use to discuss AI–there is no single definition of "AI" or even "generative AI" or "large language model" that provides enough clarity to regulate this technology. What we've seen in the EU AI Act,[19] in some of the state laws is that they're encompassing more than generative AI–whether intentionally or not. So that while ChatGPT brought to the forefront generative AI and the issues that come up with that,[20] we're now seeing more scrutiny and more regulation of non-generative AI than we had seen before. It's not that AI is a new problem; t it's just got renewed interest.

[19] Regulation (EU) 2024/1689 of the European Parliament and of the Council of 13 March 2024 laying down harmonised rules on artificial intelligence (Artificial Intelligence Act) and amending certain Union legislative acts. A copy of the Act can be found here: https://eur-lex.europa.eu/legal-content/EN/TXT/PDF/?uri=OJ:L_202401689.

[20] Some of the legal concerns that arise with generative AI include questions over intellectual property rights, copyright protections, personal data and confidentiality, and contractual terms. *The legal implications of Generative AI*, DELOITTE, https://www2.deloitte.com/us/en/pages/consulting/articles/generative-ai-legal-issues.html.

Elizabeth Townsend Gard: Interesting, interesting. And Chad, other thoughts about this moment? Where are we? Can you help us understand the historic context? How did we get to where we are, and where are we at the moment?

Chad Rutkowski: So I bracket AI into essentially two different buckets: 1) what I call boring AI, and 2) generative AI, which is exciting and all the rage. Boring AI though is what Theresa was talking about, which is the machine learning data driven trying to tease out insights out of your data. Data analytics sort of falls into one of three columns:

- descriptive analytics: You've got a bunch of information.. What is it saying? What is the state of play?
- predictive analytics: We know what the data says. We have some, degree of pattern detection, and we can say that you know the current state is this, but the future state will likely be this, based on, historical information or other factors.
- prescriptive analytics, the gold standard.

I had dealt with that for years in healthcare and detecting population health management trends. There's a spike in diabetes cases in this particular community. Let's deploy nutritional information, and there to try to drive down the hospitalizations or drive down the healthcare costs by proactively giving preventive type treatments. Or Fintech. You look at what the risk profiles are in issuing loans. But at the same time, GPT2 was being created and GPT 3 was being created, at the Copyright Society, we put on a panel.[21] I guess it was in 2020, where we had a Professor Hector Postigo at Temple University, demonstrate GPT.[22] And we created a Yeats poems because I was an Irish literature major. So I asked him, "Can you make some AI generated Yeats poems?" and they were pretty good. They sounded sort of in the style of Yeats.

Elizabeth Townsend Gard: Just curious. How did the Copyright Society react to all of that? Because that, I imagine that would be slightly frightening.

Chad Rutkowski: Yeah, and there was a fair amount of consternation. And we were starting an AI steering committee at the time and some other folks. Monica Corton and Bhamati Viswanathan really wanted, from the rights holder

---

[21] On November 23, 2020, the Copyright Society hosted Nadia Baksh, Hector Postigo, Paul Reinitz, and Chad Rutkowski for a panel discussion on emerging machine learning programs and their effects on the legal field. The panel explored how machine learning can transform existing content into new forms and the data markets behind such tools, as well as an examination of relevant legal issues such as fair use and authorship. *Content as Data and Data as Content: Copyright Issues in Machine* Learning, THE COPYRIGHT SOCIETY, https://copyrightsociety.org/event/content-as-data-and-data-as-content-copyright-issues-in-machine-learning/.

[22] Hector Postigo is an Associate Professor at Temple University where he researches new digital media, cultural production, and technologically mediated activism. He is the author of The Digital Rights Movement and the co-editor of Managing Privacy through Accountability. *Id.*

side, the content owner side, to monitor. We had Paul Reinitz from Getty, who was eventually was involved in the *Getty v. Stability* AI lawsuit. He spoke alongside of us with Hector and and Nadia Steele. I had a slide that said, "Data is AI fuel."[23] And that in the AI world, content is data and data is content. And what I meant by that was is that you may not think of stories, or paintings as data. But to a data scientist, they assign different values. Break it down by the pixel, you know. Break it down by paragraphs. The notion of tokens is to try to detect patterns of how language works, how expression works. So to a data scientist, the content is data in that sense. And things like collections of information, for example: temperature data that might be thrown off of an industrial piece of refining equipment or a chiller. It's not content, but when you can collect that together all of a sudden, that collection becomes incredibly valuable and important. So the data sort of becomes content. And when you ask a data scientist, "How much data do you need in order to do their jobs?" The answer is always "more." And we see that with the notion of LLM collapse and data drift,[24] and we can talk in a moment about. But in terms of how did we get here? I would say that you know the innovations that drove things that we've kind of become used to right natural language processing that gives us, things like Siri, and machine learning algorithms that give us autonomous vehicles. There's been an enormous amount of work in this space going on in the background for the past 15 to 20 years. There was a paper that Google had put out, *Attention Is All You Need*, where they talked about transformer models. [25] That sort of set woke the world up to the possibility of transformer models and led to a lot of the academic work that drove open AI at the time, including the GPT2 and 3 models,[26] and the LAION database

---

[23] The idea that data is the fuel for AI comes from the fact that data is the foundation given to AI engines that enables it to learn patterns, make predictions, and improve over time. AI engines are trained on large datasets to recognize patterns which allow them to adapt to become more accurate and reliable. *Why Data is the Fuel for AI*, COLLECTIVE INTELLIGENCE (Nov. 21, 2024), https://www.collectiveintelligence.com/why-data-is-the-fuel-for-ai/.

[24] The idea of LLM collapse and data drift comes from when AI models are trained off their own output or other generated data, which leads to long-term learning problems. The models then degrade in quality and generative data that drifts further away from fact. This false data can then be used to train other models which will increase the issue and can eventually cause the models to collapse. *New research warns of potential 'collapse' of machine learning* models, UNIVERSITY OF OXFORD (July 25, 2024), https://www.cs.ox.ac.uk/news/2356-full.html.

[25] Transformer models are a type of deep learning architecture that are highly intelligence at processing sequential data by understanding the relationships among the different parts of the input. Ashish Vaswani et al., Attention Is All You Need (June 12, 2017) (unpublished manuscript), https://arxiv.org/abs/1706.03762.

[26] GPT-2 and GPT-3 are generative pre-trained transformer models that were developed by OpenAI in 2019 and 2020. GPT-2 was the predecessor to GPT-3, with GPT-3 being the larger and more capable model of the two. *GPT-2 (GPT2) vs GPT-3 (GPT3): The*

models.[27] And at some level, this was a technology looking for a problem. We know these models can create output. But what is it good for? What are we going to use it for? And so you know the advent of ChatGPT, in November of 2022, that set off a lot of light bulbs that "Wow, this stuff actually works." It's actually: still clunky, but kind of good. And we've just watched this, sort of evolutionary telescoping scaling, this exponential growth has been amazing.. Like Moore's Law, that computing power doubles every year or so. You just have this compression of advancement. That same principle, I think, has occurred in the past two years where the stuff that was kind of good has become really good. And so where I think we're at right now is we're in several places at once. We're in a hype cycle.

I don't think that AI is akin to NFTs. I don't think that AI is akin to Pets.com and eToys.[28] And just like the Internet bubble, I think there's going to be somewhat of a contraction or rolling back, but I don't think it's going to be as severe as what we saw with the Internet in 1999 and 2000, with that bubble bursting.[29] I also don't think it's going to be as severe as what we've seen with NFTs or the "metaverse".

Elizabeth Townsend Gard: I'm just going to pause. I'm thinking of people 30 years from now. Can you help us understand what you mean by the Internet bubble and the NFT bubble, and why? It's different. Why, you think this moment is different?

Chad Rutkowski: Sure. So in the late 1990s, it was very similar to what we're seeing with AI right now. In the beginnings of the Internet, which was largely a chat room type system set up between university students to be able exchange research papers and then rolled out commercially. And so this means of using computers to have more immediate interaction and then began to find commercial applications. So we had a sort of birth of e-commerce in the late nineties, and that led to enormous amounts of speculation, and enormous amounts of investment that wasn't necessarily borne out in profits. So you had a lot of darlings of the early Internet era, including pets.com, and Yahoo. And a lot of them just collapsed. And it led a lot of people to say, "Oh, the Internet was fake."

OpenAI Showdown, EXXACT (Feb. 3, 2021), https://www.exxactcorp.com/blog/Deep-Learning/gpt2-vs-gpt3-the-openai-showdown.

[27] The Large-scale Artificial Intelligence Open Network (LAION) is a non-profit organization that provides tools, datasets, and models for machine learning research. LAION, https://laion.ai (last visited May 18, 2025).

[28] *See* pets.com and eToys.com.

[29] In the late 1990s there was a period of rapid growth in internet-based companies due to an increase in technological advancements and investor enthusiasm. This enthusiasm led to a stock surge but many of the surging companies lacked solid business models. The dot-com bubble burst in early 2000 which led to massive fancial losses and the collapse of many startups. *The Late 1990s Dot-Com Bubble Implodes in 2000*, GOLDMAN SACHS, https://www.goldmansachs.com/our-firm/history/moments/2000-dot-com-bubble.

The promise of it all was not it was always cracked up to be. I don't know about you, Elizabeth, but I continue to use the Internet every day…

Elizabeth Townsend Gard: We're doing it right–

Chad Rutkowski: Right now.

Elizabeth Townsend Gard: That's right.

Chad Rutkowski: Yeah.

Elizabeth Townsend Gard: And that the influx of capital and energy and excitement over it was kind of out of control, it seems. And so you're saying that a lot of those companies didn't make it. And then it kind of settled down. And you're saying the same thing happened with NFTs. I'm curious, when I look at the numbers of what's being invested in AI companies, it is staggering. It's not even conceivable how many billions of dollars a particular company has. And I'm sure that's because of the data and all kinds of other things. But how do we understand the investment that's happening now with AI companies as opposed to those startup Internet companies, that Internet phase? Is it exactly the same? Or is it a little bit different? It seems like there's less of them, but that the money they're getting is just incredible. And they're sprouting up very quickly. Am I right about that? It just seems kind of different.

Chad Rutkowski: What I would say is it takes a lot of money to run this stuff, and we'll see how long that stays true. Now that we have new entrants like China's DeepSeek,[30] and others that are challenging that. But the amount of infrastructure computing power that it takes to create AI outputs requires: a lot of the money. And so it does sort of naturally creates a limited number of players, because there's a natural barrier to entry.

Elizabeth Townsend Gard: I'm curious. Does it take a lot of money to run it or to build it? I'm thinking of the story of AT&T. It takes them 100 years to get to where they are, and then they get broken up. But Skype can build upon the AT&T infrastructure and thrive in years.[31] Are the companies we see now having to build a lot, and that's where the money is? Or is it because the running of it is so expensive, is it going to get less expensive as we go? How do we understand? Kind of infrastructure versus, like the day-to-day operations of this kind of stuff?

---

[30] DeepSeek is a Chinese artificial intelligence company founded in 2023 by Liang Wenfeng. The company has developed several open-source AI models that have been praised for their efficiency and performance. Kelly Ng et al., *DeepSeek: The Chinese AI app that has the world talking*, BBC (Feb 4, 2025), https://www.bbc.com/news/articles/c5yv5976z9po#.

[31] Skype was a telecommunications application released in the early 2000s that allowed users to communicate with other via the internet. *About Skype*, MICROSOFT, https://www.skype.com/en/about/. As of May 5, 2025, Skype has officially been retired by Microsoft. *Skype is retiring in May 2025: What you need to know*, Microsoft, https://support.microsoft.com/en-us/skype/skype-is-retiring-in-may-2025-what-you-need-to-know-2a7d2501-427f-485e-8be0-2068a9f90472#:~:text=As%20of%20May%205th%2C%202025,same%20core%20features%20and%20more.

Theresa Weisenberger: It will get less expensive both to use and develop AI technology as we go on. What Chad said earlier about needing all of the data to create these LLMs, if companies like Deep Seek who are focuses on develop more efficient technology without compromising its functionality are successful,, then we can see a decrease in the cost of maintaining these or running these systems. A big part of it is how much electricity and computing power is needed to operate. It is much more environmentally costly to have prompt generative AI tool to provide search results than it is to run a typical search on a search engine. If the semiconductor chips can become more efficient, and if we can make the LLMs themselves more efficient, I think we will see a decrease in the environmental impact and the cost. But right now we're still in t the early Internet days–right before the.com bubble burst–where we're paying for generative AI tools based on "tokens" used, like when AOL would give you Internet access for a certain number of minutes a month.

Elizabeth Townsend Gard: So am I right that 2022 is an important marker, but that things came before that. How do we understand the November 2022 release of ChatGPT?

Theresa Weisenberger: That was when AI became tangible to the general public. It was being used before, and of course it was being developed long before that, but AI was something that we really didn't have good language or examples to talk about in ordinary conversation before ChatGPT.

Chad Rutkowski: And it marked the changeover from boring AI to fun AI! Right? To generative AI. I can't tell you how many of our clients at the time in late 2022 and early 2023 told us, "Oh, we want to use ChatGPT to sort resumes or detect cancer. Help us manage and use ChatGPT." Now, maybe now, right there, there's different services and plugins. But they didn't realize that "You're talking about the boring AI that you've been using for the past ten years." So what we dealt with a lot in early 2023 was this conflation of AI. We spent a lot of time having conversations like this. 'Let's slow down. Let's talk about what you're really doing, and that you're not even using ChatGPT, that's not what you mean, even though that's what made you think of it." That moment at the end of 2022, and the first quarter of 2023, we grabbed a lot of people's imaginations, made AI interesting and required a lot of education.

Elizabeth Townsend Gard: Okay, then, 2023, we get the lawsuits. It's like the year of the lawsuits. Help us understand what's happening. Did the authors and the artists, and everyone not know? Were they just becoming aware of Generative AI? Is that why it happens in 2023? Why in 2023 do we see this huge amount of lawsuit litigation happening?

Chad Rutkowski: Oh, I know exactly– money. Because you know, we saw investment. Microsoft investing in OpenAI. We've seen Google and Amazon investing in Anthropic. And some of these other companies. We've seen Google trying to create its own versions, Meta trying to create its own versions. So suddenly, there was commerciality to this, and potential deep pockets. And whereas beforehand it was all this is nothing commercial, a lot of research communities and nonprofits like Common Crawl.

We know what the vast bulk of data that GPT and certainly GPT 2 GPT 3 were trained on. There are a lot of claims that the AI companies are so non-transparent about what they trained on. But in 2019 US Patent and Trademark Office issued a request for comments on all things AI and IP.[32] Initially it was focused on patents, and that was because Steven Thaler claimed in the summer of 2019 that AI had created a patent for him, and it set the world ablaze right like that was the first AI hype cycle, even before ChatGPT came out. His assertion that AI should be recognized essentially with human-like rights and a patent should issue as if AI was an employee, an agent, as the basis of ownership.[33] So in that request for comments, OpenAI responded to that and explained what they were doing and laid out the basis for most of the data set training data sets in Gpt3, which included Common Crawl.[34] Common crawl had lots of books in it, and there was no mystery to that. That's again at the time that I was giving these presentations with the Copyright Society,[35] but I also gave them to the American Bar Association. Both the Patent and Trademark Office and the Copyright Office held AI days as well.[36] They had day long presentations about these issues. At the time, the Rembrandt project was at the height of AI technology.[37] That they could create new Rembrandts because the AI was trained on Rembrandt paintings. And what was this going to mean for new tools coming forward. There was a lot of interest in it. A lot of it was sort of academic interest. A lot of it was trying to understand what the industrial business use cases were going to be. And you know there were a number of people on top of it from the get-go. One of the things that

---

[32] Request for Comments on Patenting Artificial Intelligence Inventions, 84 FR 44889 (Aug. 27, 2019), https://www.federalregister.gov/documents/2019/08/27/2019-18443/request-for-comments-on-patenting-artificial-intelligence-inventions

[33] Thaler v. Vidal, 43 F.4th 1207 (Fed. Cir. 2022), https://www.cafc.uscourts.gov/opinions-orders/21-2347.OPINION.8-5-2022_1988142.pdf.

[34] Common Crawl is an engine that crawls the web and provides its archives and datasets to the public for free. Mission, COMMON CRAWL, https://commoncrawl.org/mission. A copy of OpenAI's comments to the PTO can be found here: https://cdn.openai.com/policy-submissions/OpenAI%20Comments%20on%20Intellectual%20Property%20Protection%20for%20Artificial%20Intelligence%20Innovation.pdf.

[35] *See Content as Data and Data as Content*, *supra* note 24.

[36] The Copyright Office and the World Intellectual Property Organization co-sponsored a symposium on Copyright in the Age of Artificial Intelligence in February of 2020. Information and recordings of the event can be found here: https://www.copyright.gov/events/artificial-intelligence/.

[37] The Rembrandt Research Project is a collaboration by a group of art historians to produce a comprehensive catalogue of Rembrandt's creative works as well as research on the artist himself. *About Us*, REMBRANDT RESEARCH PROJECT, https://www.rembrandtresearchproject.org/about-us/.

I did for the American Bar Association at this time is help the ABA write its response to the PTO's request for comments in 2019,[38] very similar to what the Copyright Office did in 2023, with, its notice of inquiry. And Mary Rasenberger of the Authors Guild, Josh Simmons from Kirkland, Steven Chow, and Dave Green, who is now at Github, worked on it with me, and we wrote a position paper to the PTO.[39] So we knew this was coming. We knew that adoption of these tools was going to occur rapidly. It was the roll out of a commercial product that starts the lawsuits.

Elizabeth Townsend Gard: Yeah, that makes, I mean as an outsider. That also sort of makes sense. I mean, if you're bragging about the money that's coming in. People are going to start to feel like, "Hey, what? You're using my stuff and that's not fair. And why don't we get licenses?" So 2022 is the public recognizes Generative AI, and by 2023, many lawsuits are filed.[40] Theresa, when does your firm start tracking these Generative AI lawsuits, and help us understand where the tracker comes in? You've got one of the best trackers out there for AI cases.[41] Related to this, how many cases are there? We can't figure out how you count them. We've decided that there's no way to actually know how many they are, because everybody counts them differently. Is that true? And tell us a little bit about that.

Theresa Weisenberger: That is definitely true. I looked at the beginning of your working draft of your article [AI Litigation v. Licensing], and it shows how many different ways to count how many cases there are. I can't figure it out either, and a lot of it is more art than science.

Elizabeth Townsend Gard: That's so amazing. Usually, you're like, "Well, how many cases are there?" 42. But in this case, it isn't because they keep getting consolidated, but everybody has their different numbers and which ones they care about, and which ones get ignored. It's really weird.

Theresa Weisenberger: Not only are they getting consolidated, but we've also seen copycat cases filed. In *Tremblay v. OpenAI* and *Silverman v. OpenAI* .The complaints are almost identical. The plaintiffs are different, and so the value of tracking those cases was a judgment call as far as bandwidth and everything else. And eventually those cases ended up getting consolidated into In re: *OpenAI ChatGPT Litigation.* And then it was a little bit easier to track.

I started this case tracker in 2023. I'm looking at the website now, I think when I started it, there were 3 or 4 cases filed. I was getting asked by my clients,

---

[38] A copy of the ABA's comments can be found here: https://www.aallnet.org/wp-content/uploads/2020/01/RE-IP-Protection-for-AI-Innovation-010720.pdf.

[39] *ABA responds to Copyright Office Notice of Inquiry on AI and Copyright*, BAKERHOSTETLER (Nov. 6, 2023), https://www.bakerlaw.com/insights/aba-responds-to-copyright-office-notice-of-inquiry-on-ai-and-copyright/.

[40] *See generally* Drew Berg, *Exploring Generative AI Lawsuits Timeline*, TRIALLINE (Mar. 14, 2024), https://blog.trialline.net/generative-ai-lawsuits-timeline/.

[41] *Case Tracker*, *supra* note 5.

"What is this case? What are they focused on? What data sets are they focused on? And what are the theories of the parties, and how are the courts evaluating them?" They weren't all straightforward. We've seen a lot of focus on CMI claims under Section 1202(b). We've seen some interesting common law claims that have sometimes survived motions to dismiss and sometimes been found to be preempted by the Copyright Act. When I started the case tracker, it was because I kept going back to PACER over and over, looking at these complaints, looking at the motions to dismiss, and I wanted a central place to keep them. And I thought it would be good for clients to have access and the public to have access to. So that's it. It really is designed to be a neutral reporting.

Elizabeth Townsend Gard: It is, and it's amazing. When you look at our paper, we just keep quoting your site like we just like I had to keep telling them you have to go see other stuff like you can't just do this one site because it's you. Do you feel that it's trustworthy? It's thorough. It's up to date. It understandable. Having now engaged in it with the students for a couple of months, it's been really interesting to see.

Theresa Weisenberger: That was intentional. I've got a blog that covers all of these different cases, and as more cases were filed, we needed to include them without running afoul of any existing relationships with the parties involved. So we intentionally summarize, but do not opine on, the case developments. When my clients were asking the implications of these cases to their businesses. I wanted them to come directly to me.

Elizabeth Townsend Gard: I hope you continue it. And I hope we preserve it somehow. Because I think it's a really important moment of tracking what's happening. So all of this litigation that begins in 2023. I imagine we've never seen anything like this in copyright. Am I right that, like the level of like the flurry of copyright infringement cases, and the CMI stuff which has never really been a thing in any significant way. This is unprecedented in copyright. Have we seen this before?

Chad Rutkowski: The Perfect 10,[42] the thumbnail cases and some of the early Internet cases…

Theresa Weisenberger: And the class action aspect is unique. There have been copyright class action cases before this, but not proliferation that we've seen with AI.

Elizabeth Townsend Gard: Right. Like all the copyright professors, we have to know about class actions and all the class action professors are like we have to know about copyright. We're not happy about this. You all stay in your lanes, you know. It makes our jobs harder. Yeah, it's pretty funny Okay. So 2023 lots of lawsuits, 2024 licensing deals: the amount of licensing deals that are happening was staggering. What do you think of this turn? So I was talking to copyright lawyer Eric Schwartz yesterday about historical stuff on the copyright law, and he said some of the things that got put into the copyright law were

[42] Perfect 10, Inc. v. Amazon.com, Inc., 508 F.3d 1146 (9th Cir. 2007).

bargaining chips for negotiations. Do you think the lawsuits were bargaining chips for licensing deals and how do we understand what occurred in 2024?

Theresa Weisenberger: When these cases first started getting filed in early 2023, we did work for clients interested in procuring content licenses from publishers. Licensing content for LLMs raises a whole host of issues that neither the publishers or the LLM providers were in a position to answer. The potential licensors wanted use restrictions, as they didn't want the model to end up being used to create downstream competing products. But that's not how LLMs work, so potential licensees were not able to agree these restrictions. We did see a stall in communications. I do think that for some of the big plaintiffs, ultimately licensing their content was probably the goal. They knew that this technology wasn't going away, so they can at least make sure that they got some type of compensation. For some of the other plaintiffs, I don't think that's true.

Elizabeth Townsend Gard: Yeah, I mean, I think what's really interesting is you get these sort of the actor/writer/artist side of it "You're going to replace me." You got all this all the SAG/AFTRA/Writer's Guild strike stuff, which we haven't even talked about. What struck me was when Openai was funding four newsrooms for Axios. AI money becomes the Savior potentially of news organizations. That was that I was not expecting that part that, like that, was a kind of flip in the story that seemed kind of interesting to me. Am I getting the story right? Is that kind of the narrative now of like these licensing deals are going to support ways of allowing news to continue?

Chad Rutkowski: It, I think so. Let me also hasten to add that I'm not sure whether even to call these things licenses is a pain point and a bargained for term. Because on some level, to call it a license is to acknowledge that you need a license as opposed to an access right. And there's plenty of sort of academic articles out there that suggests that fair use is not a defense. Rather, it's an affirmative right.

Elizabeth Townsend Gard: That's right, and that is all still working its way through the courts. So we have this notion. It's this, I was talking to my students. It feels like the litigation is kind of moving the sway [slowly], and then what the licenses are just whipping through. The newest case kind of really got me, which was Advanced Local Media v. Cohere.[43] In that case the publishers are saying, "Look, we already have licensing deals. Now you're infringing because we have the licensing deals." It was like this really interesting moment of like, making the licensing deals and then using it as a litigation strategy to sue people that didn't get a license for you from you.

Chad Rutkowski: And that's why there was resistance. There's a real issue here. As to you know who the proponent of the access. AI is always going to be hungry for more and more content to protect against what we call LLM collapse or data drift, where we get less accurate answers. Where the reasoning is impeded, there's always going to be this sort of need for dynamic ingestion. So I don't know.

[43] Advanced Local Media v. Cohere, No. 1:25-cv-01305 (S.D.N.Y. filed Feb. 13, 2025).

That realistically, from a technological perspective, that scraping and crawling and access to data in the wild is ever going to stop. I don't think that these business deals are going to sort of solve the AI problem. I think they're going to be part of the ecosystem, but they're not going to be the only part. And so you have to look at what the sort of business case the business logic, the business proposition is for controllers of content and AI developers and AI companies. And I think there's a couple of those steel points. You know. One is avoiding litigation. Another is, having access, the more that controllers of content: can provide data that is clean, that is usable, that is free from bias that is robust. That actually is a value. And for AI companies that means something that's worth paying for. And there's public opinion That, as you're saying, Elizabeth, AI as the Savior of the news organizations that that's going to play into it as well.

But I think one thing that we all need to be mindful of is there's a difference between a copyright owner and the controller of content. I'm using that term purposefully right. The controller of content might be an aggregator like a Getty images. That, like a music publisher might be a platform right. The Copyright society in 2 weeks is going to have one session on these content deals in the AI space, and one that we're hoping we believe one of the speakers is going to be Reddit. And Reddit's interesting. They don't own anything. They don't purport to own anything that their users create, but they're licensing access right to that content. So you know it, it matters that's going to matter in the fair use context, Like, for these class action suits. That is a collection of individual artists, and the value prop for licensing one author's work is enormously different from getting access to a data set that might be owned by Getty. Right. Getty may not have rights to the underlying photographs, but wouldn't necessarily own them. So are you a compilation owner? Are you an individual content owner? You know an individual work owner rather. Take JK Rawling where her books are often held up as prominent in some of these AI models. If AI models spit out a Rawlings book, well that's bad data science. It's called memorization. That's just because it wasn't deduped.[44] It doesn't actually have any real value. No, AI company is going to say, "Oh, you're JK Rowlings. Let me give you 10 million dollars because you're going to teach my AI model so well that you know it's worth more." It's not worth different than any other collection of 800 or 8,000 pages of literature.

Theresa Weisenberger: The Harry Potter books are some of the most frequently pirated content on the Internet. So that's one of the reasons why it's hung up as an example over and over is because multiple copies of it have been included in the data sets that are used to train these models.

Elizabeth Townsend Gard: Interesting.: Do you think we'll ever see copyright holders, the photographers suing the platforms like Getty that they're making these big deals?

---

[44] 'Dedupe' is an abbreviation for 'deduplication,' which is when unnecessary copies or parts of a file are eliminated from a dataset. *Dedupe*, CEGAL, https://www.cegal.com/en/dictionary/dedupe.

Theresa Weisenberger: I think that we've seen that in *Anderson v. Stability AI*. DeviantArt was a defendant based on what they were doing with user-uploaded content: One of the arguments was that they had changed their terms of use, so that they had the right to do with your content as they did. And you know there's debate over whether they provided adequate notice and whether the training data went back to content that existed before then.

The most interesting case that has addressed this issue or that will address this issue is *Pierce v. Photobucket* in Colorado.[45] Photobucket was where everybody put all of their images maybe ten years ago.[46] And its really kind of become this undervalued graveyard of photographs. Now that we're looking at online content differently. It is so valuable to AI development. Photobucket is all of a sudden sitting on a lot more valuable asset than they were a few years ago, and they have been sued by a few [of the photographers] as a putative class action. Photobucket was sued, not on the basis that it has actually licensed user content yet for AI development, but that plaintiffs believe based on recent Photobucket activity that such licensing it's coming down the pike.

Elizabeth Townsend Gard: Fascinating, fascinating. Okay, I know we've been here already for a while. Let me ask you 2 quick questions. Help us understand what your thoughts are on fair use arguments. I'm curious about the *Ross* case, and I'm also curious about the cases that are doing the 1202 decisions that are coming out, and how you all are thinking about that.

Theresa Weisenberger: So on the *Ross* case,[47] it was hugely important that copyright infringement in the context of creating AI models was an issue of first impression for any court. And these summary judgment decisions were particularly significant, because after first denying summary judgment, the court invited the parties to rebrief the issues, and ultimately the court changed its mind. But how the recent summary judgment decision is being interpreted and how it's going to end up affecting these other cases is going to be a lot more interesting. As the opinion states, what we're talking about in *Thompson, Reuters v. Ross* is not generative AI. It's not necessarily a one-to-one comparison about whether one use is fair or not. The court found that they were creating a competing product, unlike t these other cases. There isn't some type of assumption that Stability AI is creating a competing product to the content owners.

Elizabeth Townsend Gard: Okay. Let's pivot. The Copyright Office has come out with two out of now three reports relating to AI. I'm curious what your

---

[45] Pierce v. Photobucket, Inc., No. 1:24-cv-03432 (D. Colo. filed Dec. 11, 2024).

[46] Photobucket is a company founded in 2003 that offers online backup cloud storage services for digital media. *Photobucket Reviews, Ratings & Features 2025*, GARTNER, https://www.gartner.com/reviews/market/photo-management-software/vendor/photobucket/product/photobucket#.

[47] Thomson Reuters v. Ross Intel., No. 1:20-cv-613-SB, 2025 U.S. Dist. LEXIS 24296 (D. Del. Feb. 11, 2025).

thoughts are. Did we learn anything new? There's a lot of effort being put into this. So I'm curious what you think.

Chad Rutkowski: When the first report came out, it almost seemed coordinated, although I think we've been assured that it wasn't, with the legislation that that was positive at the same time. And I think it really spoke to concerns over deep fakes and the need to address digital replicas.[48] But in this political environment, I just don't see you know any meaningful legislation going forward. So it's to me the first report was more a policy statement or a clarifying statement that this needs to be handled by Congress and you ought to get on this.

Elizabeth Townsend Gard: Do you think that because of our political climate, at the moment that the States will take it up that we'll see more state engagement in the deep fake problem.

Theresa Weisenberger: Yes. I was looking at the deep fake problem, which has been on states' radars at least as far back as 2021. Louisiana that had laws specifically targeting deep fakes in certain criminal contexts.[49] But with this surge of AI we've seen j that the federal government is not in a position right now to actually meaningfully legislate, at least on these topics. We have seen step states step up to address AI issues the same way they stepped up to address data privacy, like California did with the California Consumer Privacy Act.[50] We will continue to see states tackle AI issues in similar ways. Last year we saw a ton of bills proposed, and, I want to say, maybe a third of the states didn't pass [proposed AI legislation],[51] and we're as early in the legislative season for 2025, but new AI bills have already been proposed. A lot of the states are also going to follow on to what we've seen happening with the EU AI Act.[52] Parties are looking towards the language and the restrictions of the EU AI Act not only to comply with the EU and future state AI legislation,, but also incorporate similar restrictions and rights into their contracts in which they are either providing or using AI

---

[48] The term 'digital replica' can refer to an image, video or audio recording that has been digitally created or edited to depict an individual, also known by the term 'deepfake.' Digitial replicas can be both authorized or unauthorized content. Alexander Touma et al., *Overview of the U.S. copyright office's AI digital replicas ("deepfakes") report*, A&O SHEARMAN (Aug. 2, 2024), https://www.aoshearman.com/en/insights/ao-shearman-on-tech/overview-of-the-us-copyright-offices-ai-digital-replicas#. The first report on AI from the Copyright Office can be found at the following: U.S. Register of Copyrights, Copyright and Artificial Intelligence Part 1: Digital Replicas, (July 2024), https://www.copyright.gov/ai/Copyright-and-Artificial-Intelligence-Part-1-Digital-Replicas-Report.pdf.

[49] La. Rev. Stat. § 14:73.13 (2023), https://www.legis.la.gov/legis/Law.aspx?d=1336015.

[50] Cal. Civ. Code § 1798.100 et seq.

[51] *See Tracking U.S. state artificial intelligence* legislation, HUSCH BLACKWELL, https://www.huschblackwell.com/2024-ai-state-law-tracker.

[52] *See* Regulation (EU) 2024/1689, *supra* note 22.

technology, so even if the states don't legislate, the parties can agree by contract how the AI issues should play out.[53]

Elizabeth Townsend Gard: Interesting. I love it. And then part two from the Copyright Office?.

Chad Rutkowski: I have a lot to say on that, and you know I'm working on a blog article to address it. I

I'm looking forward to the Copyright Office's revised guidance on registration. You know that was hinted at in the second report. I was a little surprised to there was quite a lot of emphasis and reliance on Professor Jane Ginsburg's law review article, "Machines and Authors"[54] and she had a co-author. A good bit of that article focused on a type of copyright authorship. An author is not just this sort of artist in the garret that has this brilliant idea spring from the top of their head and end up on a page–that's classic authorship and certainly one form of the author. But the law recognizes other types of authors. Obviously, compilation authorship. But what I find interesting is what we call mastermind authorship and it's why we give authorship rights, ownership rights to production companies right in the *Al-Mohammed* case, the *Casa Duce* case. These are entities that may not have had a single creative thought, but they superintended the arrangements. They brought together the various creative elements. As a hallmark of some of those cases is what I call a veto. There's a major focus in the *Kashtanova* registration decision.[55] And again, in this second report over control over predictability, you'd never know what the AI is going to hand back to you. At one point, it was described in the report as spinning a roulette wheel over and over again, and: there may be some truth to that. But it's kind of true with humans, too. They never know what they're going to hand back to you. And you know the production studio has the veto. This goes in, and that doesn't right. I get to decide what the final product looks like, whether to accept it or not, whether fire the director, or to bring another scriptwriter.. The actors–bring another set of actors on until I get it right, and it meets some degree of mental conception. The production company wants the film to be what it wants it to look like. And you know I, personally don't see any major difference in that type of iteration with what we have in a Theatre de Opera. You know where they iterated 600 times in MidJourney to get to that concept. And I was disappointed that you know there's

---

[53] *See generally Model Contractual Clauses for AI Procurement in the EU: Key Takeaways for AI Companies*, Cooley (Mar. 20, 2025), https://cdp.cooley.com/model-contractual-clauses-for-ai-procurement-in-the-eu-key-takeaways-for-ai-companies/.

[54] Jane C. Ginsburg & Luke A. Budiardjo, *Authors and Machines*, 34 BERKELEY TECH. L. J. 343 (2019).

[55] The US Copyright Office granted Kris Kashtanova's graphic novel "Zarya of the Dawn" limited copyright protections, which was a signficiant step in the development of copyright standards for works created through generative AI platforms. Tom Hals & Blake Brittain, *Insight: Humans vs. machines: the fight to copyright AI art*, REUTERS (Apr. 1, 2023), https://www.reuters.com/default/humans-vs-machines-fight-copyright-ai-art-2023-04-01/.

a lot of discussion about joint authorship. And how the cases are analogous to the situation. But no discussion about mastermind authorship, even though that was in the Ginsburg law review article. The other thing that I found a little disappointing is that it seems like Mid Journey is driving all the policy here, that image generation, and you know the concerns of visual artists which are super important, but not the only use. You look at. from what I understand, for what Theresa and I think, see in our business, and from what we benchmark with other practitioners, 80% of the adoption. The real uses of these tools are in code generation, in source code, software code generation. So to have no discussion and the authorship rights in this context [is disappointing]. When you're using CodeWhisperer, you're using Copilot is problematic, because what I think it does is set up for a situation of civil disobedience. If I disclaim the AI authorship here, that's you're done right, you're not able to unring that bell or I can decide to take on the expense of fighting the copyright officer. The PTO. I think, takes that approach right. The PTO seems like it has a much more deferential approach, and you'll fight it out in court. And we deal with this all the time. When I give these talks I take my phone out and I'll go like that. And I'll say, do I have a copyright in the photograph?. You know we're going back to *Burrow-Giles*.[56] We're going right back to that. I didn't pick the lighting. I didn't position you. I own the phone. Am I the author? I don't know but you know what I'm going to get: I'm gonna get a registration on that photograph. I want to spend the money to enforce it. It will get this determined by the courts as to whether or not I'm an author.

Elizabeth Townsend Gard: I don't know. It just starts to really unravel part of the physics of copyright that we all know so well by not really addressing it at the moment. So I find it interesting, and I like the idea of the mastermind that we are.

I have just loved our time together. You are both the two of the smartest people on the planet on this stuff, and we're so lucky that the Copyright Society has you as the members and so involved, and that you're willing to have an interview, and that we can do this. So anything else before we end that we haven't covered that you'd like to cover, because I mean again, we could talk forever.

Chad Rutkowski: I'll just as quickly as I can, you mentioned *Thomson Reuters v. Ross*.[57] I have a blog article out on it, but you know one thing that threw me for a loop a little bit was on the derivative argument.. The infringement that supposedly occurred was there was a creation of bulk memos where the head notes were reproduced entirely, and then a database created from that in order to train…

Elizabeth Townsend Gard: And to compete with the originals.

Chad Rutkowski: I think that you know this is going to sound convenient, but I think a positive: fair use decision would have been very problematic for content owners. But I don't think that this decision is equally problematic for AI

---

[56] Burrow-Giles Lithographic Co. v. Sarony, 111 U.S. 53 (1884).

[57] *See* Thomson Reuters v. Ross Intel., No. 1:20-cv-613-SB, 2025 U.S. Dist. LEXIS 24296 (D. Del. Feb. 11, 2025).

developers. And the reason is because the general purpose nature of large language models. This is what I call a small model. Competition here was direct. One of the things I think some of the AI cases suffer from is this notion you're creating a competing product and materials. Well, at what level? It's not that competition problem is with specific works. If you create an AI model, you know that creates the specific same work and competes. That's the thing: if it's competition in the vague, sort of universal sense of it, well, that's not what the case law focuses on.

You know one thing that I think was missed in the decision, and I think it has got to become more prominent is this notion of extraction. You know we have a case wire data from 2005 about taking a database and downloading it temporarily to extract unprotectable information. I think that there's a corollary between what data scientists do with content, although, I don't mean it to minimize the importance of creativity, and I think would appall most people to think of their works of art as just simply being containers of information. There is a fair use argument to be made that if you're simply downloading the express content temporarily to extract unprotectable patterns, facts, information that could be fair use. There's a really interesting journal article called "The Freedom to Extract and Copyright Law," written by Molly Schaeffer von Howling just this past month.[58] That sort of collects those cases, addresses it. So that's you know that that to me is one of the things I think is most interesting about *Ross*.

Elizabeth Townsend Gard*:* So interesting, and there really hasn't been any kind of conversation, I think, about the *Salinger* case of the unauthorized derivative novel, Sixty Years Later. It'll be interesting to see what happens the moment that someone tries to create their own JK. Rowling novel and sells it, using generative AI tools.

Chad Rutkowski: I hasten to add to and to amplify the point that you're making, Elizabeth, which is where you look at the technology matters. So we know about large language models, foundation models. Think of those as like sort of, you know, the giant flywheel. And then you have more fine tuning, you have rag. The better use analysis in a general-purpose foundation model is likely to be quite different than when you are fine tuning, or you're using rag or tag, or any one of these different types of training models. So you really need to understand the technology, you need to understand what's happening. You know what the alleged infringer did, how they did it. I think that's you know it's going to become very grand.

Elizabeth Townsend Gard: But so important.. So our family made a fake Christmas letter and then asked ChatGPT to put it in the style of Sally Bowles and it knew exactly who Sally Bowles was, and we didn't have to say from *Cabaret.* And again, it sort of makes me think about the protectability of characters and

---

[58] *See* Molly S. Van Houweling, *The Freedom to Extract in Copyright Law*, 103 N.C. L. REV. 445 (2025), https://scholarship.law.unc.edu/cgi/viewcontent.cgi?article=7009&context=nclr.

derivative works and all that. And what you're saying, what does these systems have to do on the back end to not have that a thing. And, as you're saying, what is the responsibility of the technology in that Sally Bowles Christmas letter? And what is on the person that asked for it?

Theresa Weisenberger: And how much of that style is protectable? Copyright law does not prohibit me learning to imitate an artist's style–

Elizabeth Townsend Gard: But what is the style? When is it style, and when is it expression? I don't know the answer to that right.

Theresa Weisenberger: If we could correctly provide the answer to that, I we would be very wealthy lawyers…

Elizabeth Townsend Gard: Right, totally.

Theresa Weisenberger: And I think that we have seen similar issues addressed in the cases evaluating the public domain status of Sherlock Holmes..[59] We've got Sherlock's Holmes as a character in the public domain at one point, while some of the later-developed traits of his character remained subject to copyright. of his characteristics, how much of those actually are in the public domain, and how much of them were created after the fact. When you start slicing up copyright protection of a character whose personality evolved over a long period of time, to determine whether an allegedly infringing work portrays the public domain characteristics of Sherlock or those still subject to copyright, it gets muddled very quickly. .

Elizabeth Townsend Gard: Right. But the LLMs aren't distinguishing between something that's in the public domain and Sally Bowles, that is still under copyright..

Theresa Weisenberger: Oh, no! I'm just saying what part of a character is protected will be challenging. These are analogous to issues AI developers face when separating out protectible and unprotectable elements of copyrighted works that may be included in AI outputs. Researchers have experimented with how much the AI outputs can be restricted–like refusing to answer prompts that blatantly ask for infringing content (like the text of a news article)--without being overly restrictive, like the filtering of raw facts. And there are harder questions when generative AI is used to analyze a work–while literary criticism is squarely within the context of fair use, for example, it's hard to quantify when discussion of a work rises to the level of infringement.

Elizabeth Townsend Gard: Thank you again for this interview. You're a great team, and you're both amazing. And thank you again for all your time. I really appreciate it.

Chad Rutkowski: You bet! Thanks for inviting us. Take care!

---

[59] Carter Ostrowski, *Sherlock Holmes: To What Extent Can a Character's Feelings Be Copyrighted?*, UNIVERISTY OF CINCINNATI LAW REVIEW, https://uclawreview.org/2020/11/18/sherlock-holmes-to-what-extent-can-a-characters-feelings-be-copyrighted/#_ftn1.

PART IV: LATE BREAKING NEWS

COPYRIGHT AND AI, PART III
US. COPYRIGHT OFFICE REPORT

On May 9, 2025, the U.S. Copyright Office released the third part of the Copyright and AI Report, subtitled "Generative AI Training." This was a "pre-publication version." And it was released in the midst of controversy – the Librarian of Congress being fired just before its release, and the Register of Copyright fired just after. Aaron Moss has allowed us to reprint his blog post of May 11, 2025 (two days after the report released), "Five Takeaways the Copyright Office's Controversial AI Report."

Then, on May 22, 2025, Shira Perlmutter, the Register of Copyright, filed a lawsuit for unlawful firing against Todd Blanche, Paul Perkins, Sergio Gor, Trent Morse, the Executive Office of the President, and Donald Trump. Full disclosure: Perlmutter is a long-time member of the Journal's advisory board. And of course, Aaron Moss also wrote a blog post about the firing and the lawsuit, and so we asked again for permission to reprint. For the sake of newsworthiness and the historical record, we have included the full complaint as part of this issue.

FIVE TAKEAWAYS FROM THE COPYRIGHT OFFICE'S CONTROVERSIAL NEW AI REPORT

by AARON MOSS*
Originally published May 11, 2025
Copyright Lately[1]
Reprinted by the Journal with Permission

The Copyright Office released a "pre-publication version" of its long-awaited AI and fair use report just a day before the Register of Copyrights was dismissed. Inside the timing, the fallout, and what it all means.

Late Friday afternoon—a time traditionally reserved for burying news and slipping out of the office—the U.S. Copyright Office quietly dropped a "pre-publication" version of Part 3 of its highly anticipated artificial intelligence study (read it here).[2] The 108-page report provides the Office's detailed take on how U.S. copyright law, particularly the fair use doctrine, should apply to the use of copyrighted works to train generative AI models. To be clear, "pre-publication versions" of Copyright Office reports aren't standard practice. And the timing of this one was no accident. The report's release was sandwiched between two

---

* Aaron Moss is a partner in the Entertainment, Intellectual Property, and Litigation practice groups at Mitchell Silberberg & Knupp LLP (MSK). For more, see https://www.msk.com/attorneys-aaron-moss. He is also the author of the blog COPYRIGHT LATELY and a member of the Copyright Society.

[1] COPYRIGHT LATELY, http://www.copyrightlately.com (last visited May 27, 2025)

[2] U.S. COPYRIGHT OFFICE, COPYRIGHT AND ARTIFICIAL INTELLIGENCE PART 3: GENERATIVE AI TRAINING (PRE-PUBLICATION VERSION) https://www.copyright.gov/ai/Copyright-and-Artificial-Intelligence-Part-3-Generative-AI-Training-Report-Pre-Publication-Version.pdf (2025).

extraordinary firings. The day before it was posted on the Copyright Office's website, the Trump administration abruptly dismissed Dr. Carla Hayden, the longtime Librarian of Congress who had appointed Register of Copyrights Shira Perlmutter. [3] Then, on Saturday—less than 24 hours after the report went live—Perlmutter was fired by the administration as well.[4] While some have speculated that the report itself triggered Perlmutter's dismissal, it's more likely that the Office raced to release the report before a wave of leadership changes could delay—or derail—its conclusions.

Whether this report survives as "official" policy is uncertain. It may even be rescinded by the time you read this post. But its 50,000-plus words remain very much alive—alongside more than 40 generative AI copyright cases now pending in federal courts across the country. Judges, law clerks, and policymakers will read them. And on several hotly contested issues, the report speaks with unusual clarity—often siding with creators over the tech platforms whose tools are backed by an increasingly aggressive executive branch. Several of those platforms are now lobbying the Trump administration to declare it categorically lawful to use copyrighted works for AI training.[5]

I don't typically veer into political commentary in this space. That said, the Register of Copyrights isn't supposed to be a political position. It's not a presidential appointment, and the Copyright Office sits within the Library of Congress—not the executive branch—raising serious questions about the legality of the Register's dismissal. What really can't be questioned is that Shira Perlmutter served the Copyright Office with honor and distinction, guiding it into the modern age—and into the uncharted territory of AI. Her removal underscores just how much was at stake in getting this report out the door—and how much it may come to define her legacy.

Though lengthy, the report is worth reading in full, especially in light of the broader context surrounding its release. In the meantime, here are my five biggest takeaways.

1. Copying Starts Early—and May Linger in the Weights

Unsurprisingly, the Copyright Office acknowledges that building a training dataset using copyrighted works "clearly implicate[s] the right of

[3] Andrew Limbong, *Librarian of Congress firing is latest move in upheaval of U.S. cultural institutions*, NPR (May 9, 2025 4:36 PM EST), https://www.npr.org/2025/05/09/nx-s1-5393737/carla-hayden-fired-library-of-congress-trump.

[4] Scott MacFarlane, *Trump fires director of U.S. Copyright Office, sources say*, CBS NEWS (May 10, 2025 9:04 PM EST), https://www.cbsnews.com/news/trump-fires-director-of-u-s-copyright-office-shira-perlmutter-sources/.

[5] Cecilia Kang, *Emboldened by Trump, A.I. Companies Lobby for Fewer Rules*, N.Y. TIMES (March 24, 2025).

reproduction"[6]—making it presumptively infringing unless a defense like fair use applies. Developers typically create multiple copies of protected works throughout the training process: downloading, reformatting, transferring between systems, and incorporating them into training datasets. And when a trained model later generates outputs that reproduce or closely resemble copyrighted content, several of the copyright owner's exclusive rights may be implicated then as well.

The more interesting and controversial question is what happens inside the model itself. Specifically, can the model's "weights"[7]—the numerical parameters that encode what it has learned—constitute a copy? According to the report, the answer is yes, in some cases. If a model can output verbatim or nearly identical content from the training data—even without being prompted—that expression "must exist in some form in the model's weights." In such cases, the Office concludes, "there is a strong argument that copying the model's weights implicates the right of reproduction for the memorized examples."[8]

The implications are significant. If protectable expression is embedded in the weights, then "subsequent copying of the model weights, even by parties not involved in the training process, could also constitute prima facie infringement."[9] That means distributing, fine-tuning, or deploying a model could expose not just the original developers but also downstream users to liability under both reproduction and derivative work rights.[10] Liability would ultimately turn on whether the model retains substantial protectable expression—but the Office's analysis clearly opens a path for claims beyond the training stage.

> **KEY QUOTE:** *"Whether a model's weights implicate the reproduction or derivative work rights turns on whether the model has retained or memorized substantial protectable expression from the work(s) at issue. . . [T]he use of those works in preparing a training dataset and training a model implicates the reproduction right, but copying the resulting weights will only infringe where there is substantial similarity."*[11]

2. Training May Be Transformative—But It Depends on How the Model Is Used

---

[6] U.S. Copyright Office, *supra* note 2 at 26.
[7] *Id.* at 5.
[8] *Id.* at 28.
[9] *Id.*
[10] Aaron Moss, *Derivative Work*, Copyright Lately, https://copyrightlately.com/glossary/derivative-work/.
[11] U.S. Copyright Office, *supra* note 2 at 30.

Where a model engages in copying that constitutes prima facie infringement, the next key question is whether a defense like fair use applies. The Office's first-factor analysis—the purpose and character of the use—closely tracks the Supreme Court's reasoning in *Warhol v. Goldsmith*: whether a use is transformative depends not just on the training process, but on how the resulting model is ultimately used.[12]

At one end of the spectrum are research-driven or closed-system applications, where the model performs tasks unrelated to the expressive goals of the source material. For instance, training on books to support a content moderation tool—a system used to detect and filter harmful or inappropriate content—is "highly transformative," in the Office's view.[13] At the other end are use cases where the model produces outputs "substantially similar to copyrighted works in the dataset."[14] Fine-tuning an image model on screenshots from an animated series to generate lookalike character art isn't transformative—it's a substitute for the original.[15]

Most uses fall in between. A model trained on sound recordings to generate new music might not copy any one track outright but still serves the same audience and purpose—entertainment—which the Office views as only "modestly transformative."[16] But if the same model were used to restore archival audio, the altered purpose would tip more strongly toward fair use.[17]

The Office also highlights the role of technical guardrails. Developers who implement safeguards to limit a model's ability to reproduce copyrighted material may reduce the risk of market substitution—making a finding of fair use more likely.[18] Although, per *Warhol*, if those safeguards are lifted or fail, the fair use analysis may need to be reevaluated.

> **KEY QUOTE:** "*[W]hile it is important to identify the specific act of copying during development, compiling a dataset or training alone is rarely the ultimate purpose. Fair use must also be evaluated in the context of the overall use.*"[19]

3. Training Isn't "Non-Expressive"—and It's Not Human Learning, Either

---

[12] Aaron Moss, *Let's Go Hazy: Making Sense of Fair Use After Warhol,* COPYRIGHT LATELY, May 22, 2023, https://copyrightlately.com/making-sense-of-copyright-fair-use-after-warhol/

[13] U.S. COPYRIGHT OFFICE, *supra* note 2 at 41.

[14] *Id.* at 46.

[15] *Id.* at 44.

[16] *Id.* at 41 n. 235.

[17] *Id* at 41

[18] *Id.* at 59.

[19] *Id.* at 36-37.

As part of its first-factor analysis, the Office directly confronts two common defenses: that AI training is "non-expressive,"[20] and that it mimics human learning.[21] Given how frequently these arguments appear in litigation and commentary, they're worth calling out on their own.

First, the report rejects the idea that training is merely statistical.[22] Language models, it explains, don't just process word frequencies—they learn "how [words] are selected and arranged at the sentence, paragraph, and document level," which it calls "the essence of linguistic expression."[23] Similarly, image models trained on aesthetic works absorb creative patterns specifically to generate expressive outputs. When a model is designed to replicate or reassemble expressive content, the training process can't be dismissed as non-expressive.[24]

Second, the Office pushes back on the human learning analogy.[25] Fair use doesn't automatically cover every act done in the name of learning.[26] As the report puts it, a student "could not rely on fair use to copy all the books at the library to facilitate personal education."[27] Humans also absorb information imperfectly and idiosyncratically. AI systems, by contrast, ingest exact digital copies and process them at "superhuman speed and scale"[28]—a difference the Office considers fundamental to the fair use analysis.

> **KEY QUOTE:** "*Humans retain only imperfect impressions of the works they have experienced . . . Generative AI training involves the creation of perfect copies with the ability to analyze works nearly instantaneously.*"[29]

4. Copying Everything Usually Hurts—But Context Can Tip the Scale

The third fair use factor examines how much of a copyrighted work was used—and whether that amount was reasonable given the use's purpose. That presents a challenge for AI developers, whose models often ingest millions of works in full.[30] Wholesale reproduction typically weighs against fair use.[31]

---

[20] *Id.* at 44.
[21] *Id.*
[22] U.S. COPYRIGHT OFFICE, *supra* note 2 at 45.
[23] *Id* at 47.
[24] *Id.*at 47-48.
[25] *Id.*
[26] U.S. COPYRIGHT OFFICE, *supra* note 2 at 48.
[27] *Id.*
[28] *Id.*
[29] *Id.*
[30] *Id.* at 55.
[31] *Id.* at 55.

But as the Copyright Office emphasizes, context matters.[32] Courts have allowed full-work copying where it enabled transformative tools—like search engines or plagiarism detectors—that provide information *about* the underlying works.[33] In those cases, the Office explains, full reproduction was "definitionally necessary" to achieve their functionality.[34]

Generative AI, by contrast, isn't limited to providing information about the training data. As the Office puts it, "the use of entire copyrighted works is less clearly justified" here than it was in the Google Books or image thumbnail cases.[35]

Even so, the Office acknowledges the technical realities of modern AI development. It cites research suggesting that "internet-scale pre-training data, including large amounts of entire works, may be necessary to achieve the performance of current-generation models."[36] So while full copying "ordinarily weighs against fair use," that presumption may be mitigated if developers can show the copying was functionally necessary to a transformative purpose—and if the resulting model includes effective guardrails to prevent the output of protected expression.[37]

> **KEY QUOTE:** "*[T]he third factor may weigh less heavily against generative AI training where there are effective limits on the trained model's ability to output protected material from works in the training data.*"[38]

5. Market Dilution May Be the Most Important—and Novel—Harm

Perhaps the report's most consequential—and controversial—takeaway is its expansive reading of the fourth fair use factor: the effect of the use on the potential market for the copyrighted work. The Office identifies three categories of potential market harm caused by generative AI training:

- **Lost licensing opportunities**: Where rights holders could have been paid to include their works in training datasets.[39]

- **Lost sales**: When a model generates outputs substantially similar to a protected work in the training set.[40]

---

[32] *Id* at 55.
[33] U.S. Copyright Office, *supra* note 2 at 56.
[34] *Id.*
[35] *Id.* at 57.
[36] *Id.*
[37] *Id.* at 57.
[38] U.S. Copyright Office, *supra* note 2 at 59.
[39] *Id.* at 66.
[40] *Id.* at 62.

- **Market dilution**: When AI-generated content floods the market with new works that, even if not directly infringing, compete with or diminish the value of the original training materials through sheer volume or stylistic imitation.[41]

It's this third theory—market dilution—that's likely to generate the most debate. The Office warns that "the speed and scale at which AI systems generate content pose a serious risk of diluting markets for works of the same kind as in their training data."[42] Even when outputs aren't substantially similar to any particular work, "stylistic imitation made possible by [the original work's] use in training may impact the creator's market."[43]

But this theory is legally untested. As the Office acknowledges, it's "uncharted territory," and no court has yet embraced it as a reason to deny fair use.[44]

Whether they will remains to be seen. The Copyright Office doesn't make law—it offers guidance that courts may consider under *Skidmore* deference, which depends entirely on the strength and persuasiveness of the Office's reasoning.[45] And while the Office draws from deep subject-matter expertise, courts will likely demand more than policy concerns or anecdotal examples—especially when asked to extend fair use doctrine into new territory. Of all the positions advanced in the report, this one may prove the most vulnerable to revision—or rejection—depending on the ultimate fate of the Office's report.

> **KEY QUOTE:** "*The speed and scale at which AI systems generate content pose a serious risk of diluting markets for works of the same kind as in their training data.*"[46]

THE BOTTOM LINE

The Copyright Office isn't picking winners or losers in the 40-plus AI copyright cases now pending in court, and its report repeatedly emphasizes that fair use turns on the specific facts of each case. But taken as a whole, the analysis reads as broadly favorable to copyright owners—most notably in its endorsement

---

[41] *Id.* at 64.
[42] *Id* at 65.
[43] *Id* at 56.
[44] U.S. COPYRIGHT OFFICE, *supra* note 2 at 65
[45] *Skidmore v. Swift & Co.*, WIKIPEDIA, https://en.wikipedia.org/wiki/Skidmore_v._Swift_%26_Co.
[46] U.S. COPYRIGHT OFFICE, *supra* note 2 at 65.

of a novel market dilution theory that no court has yet adopted. That position arrives amid a politically charged shake-up of the Office's own leadership.

Beyond fair use, the 108-page report explores licensing infrastructure, collective bargaining proposals, and broader policy reforms. For creators and rights holders pushing back against unauthorized AI training, it offers a detailed—and often forceful—rebuttal to sweeping fair use defenses.

But whether courts will adopt the Office's reasoning—or whether the report will even remain official policy under new leadership—is very much an open question.

As always, I'd love to hear what you think. Drop me a comment below or @copyrightlately on social media. In the meantime, I'm holding onto the full report…for safekeeping… because you never know how long it'll stay up on the Copyright Office's website.

PERMULLTER'S LAWSUIT IS ABOUT MORE THAN JUST GETTING HER JOB BACK

by AARON MOSS*

Originally published May 26, 2025
Copyright Lately
Reprinted by the Journal with Permission

Can the White House remove the Register of Copyrights? Shira Perlmutter says no—and warns the stakes go far beyond her job.

When Shira Perlmutter filed suit last week against senior White House and Justice Department officials—along with President Trump himself—much of the media coverage framed the case as an effort to reclaim her job as Register of Copyrights.[1] And it's true that Perlmutter is seeking reinstatement, arguing that her May 10 ouster from the top role at the U.S. Copyright Office was "blatantly unlawful."[2] But her motion for a temporary restraining order (read here) lays out a broader purpose: to block what she portrays as an Executive Branch power grab—one that's already disrupting operations, stalling critical policy work, and threatening the independence of the agency tasked with administering the nation's copyright laws.[3]

In other words, for Perlmutter, this isn't a garden-variety employment dispute. It's about safeguarding the integrity of the Copyright Office itself.
The Trump Administration sees things differently. In an opposition filed late today (read here), the government defends Perlmutter's removal as lawful and—while not directly disputing many of the institutional disruptions she alleges—argues that those are not her harms to assert.[4] According to the filing, Perlmutter has "no right to perpetual service as Register of Copyrights"—and no legal claim

---

* Aaron Moss is a partner in MSK's Entertainment, Intellectual Property. For more, see https://www.msk.com/attorneys-aaron-moss. He is also the author of the blog, CopyrightLateley, and a member of the Copyright Society.

[1] Andrew Limbong, *Fired Copyright Office head sues Trump administration over removal*, WBEZ CHICAGO, May 23, 2025, https://www.npr.org/2025/05/23/nx-s1-5408982/register-of-copyrights-lawsuit-trump.

[2] Complaint For Declaratory and Injunctive Relief at 2, Perlmutter v. Blanche, No. 25-cv-1659 (D.D.C. May 22, 2025).

[3] Motion for a Temporary Restraining Order at 6, Perlmutter v. Blanche, No. 25-cv-1659 (D.D.C. May 22, 2025).

[4] Defendants' Opposition To Plaintiff's Motion for A Temporary Restraining Order at 6, Perlmutter v. Blanche, No. 25-cv-1659 TJK (D.D.C. May 26, 2025) https://copyrightlately.com/pdfviewer/perlmutter-v-blanche-opposition-to-tro/?auto_viewer=true#page=&zoom=auto&pagemode=none.

to remain in office simply because the agency might operate differently without her.

On Wednesday, May 28, U.S. District Judge Timothy J. Kelly will hear arguments on Perlmutter's TRO motion. It promises to be an extraordinary proceeding to cap what's already been an extraordinary month for the Copyright Office. Perlmutter claims the White House is orchestrating an unprecedented and unconstitutional takeover of a legislative branch agency by installing senior DOJ officials atop both the Library of Congress and the Copyright Office. If allowed, she warns, the move would undermine the Office's structural independence, compromise the confidentiality of congressional research and copyright deposits, and put congressionally mandated projects in peril—including its fourth and final report on copyright and artificial intelligence.
As we head into Wednesday's hearing, here's what you need to know.

EVENTS LEADING TO THE LAWSUIT

The drama started on May 8, when President Trump abruptly fired Librarian of Congress Dr. Carla Hayden in a two-sentence email. Under internal Library rules, Hayden's deputy—40-year Library veteran Robert Newlen—succeeded her as Acting Librarian.[5] The next day, the Copyright Office released a pre-publication version of Part 3 of its report on generative AI and fair use, a project nearly two years in the making.

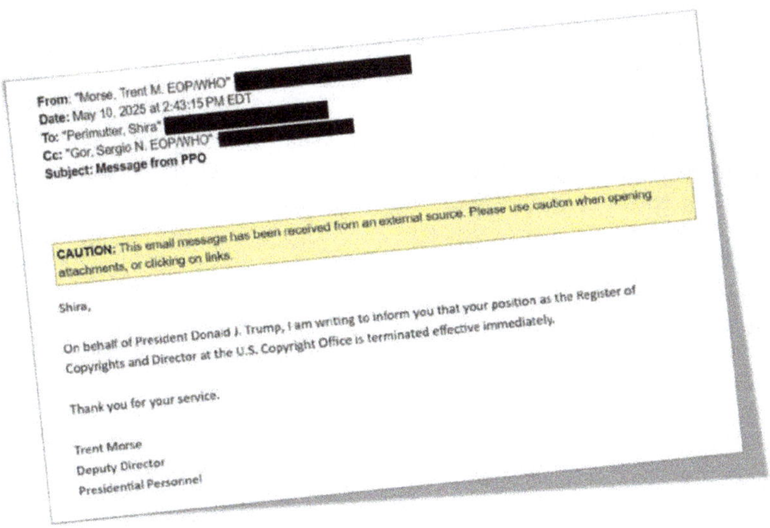

From: "Morse, Trent M. EOP/WHO"
Date: May 10, 2025 at 2:43:15 PM EDT
To: "Perlmutter, Shira"
Cc: "Gor, Sergio N. EOP/WHO"
Subject: **Message from PPO**

CAUTION: This email message has been received from an external source. Please use caution when opening attachments, or clicking on links.

Shira,

On behalf of President Donald J. Trump, I am writing to inform you that your position as the Register of Copyrights and Director at the U.S. Copyright Office is terminated effective immediately.

Thank you for your service.

Trent Morse
Deputy Director
Presidential Personnel

[5] Andrew Limbong, *Librarian of Congress firing is latest move in upheaval of U.S. cultural institutions,* NPR (May 9, 2025), https://www.npr.org/2025/05/09/nx-s1-5393737/carla-hayden-fired-library-of-congress-trump.

"Thank you for your service": Register Perlmutter was notified of her dismissal in a two-sentence email on Saturday, May 10.

Things escalated over the weekend. Perlmutter received an email from a White House personnel official informing her that she, too, was being removed—effective immediately—from her role as Register of Copyrights.[6] The White House asserted that Deputy Attorney General Todd Blanche had been appointed Acting Librarian under the Federal Vacancies Reform Act (FVRA), and that Blanche had designated DOJ official Paul Perkins to replace Perlmutter as Acting Register. But when Perkins and fellow DOJ official Brian Nieves arrived at the Library of Congress on the morning of May 12 with paperwork claiming their new roles, Library staff refused to recognize their authority.[7] Capitol Police were called, and the two officials ultimately left without incident.[8]

Perlmutter filed suit on May 22, arguing that neither the President nor Blanche has the legal authority to remove or replace her as Register.[9] Her motion seeks to preserve the status quo while the court determines whether her removal was lawful.[10]

WHAT THE TRO SEEKS—AND WHY IT MATTERS

Perlmutter's legal argument is straightforward: only the Librarian of Congress—not the President—has the authority to appoint or remove the Register of Copyrights.[11] Because the Librarian appointed her, she argues, only a lawfully appointed Librarian can remove her.[12] The Trump administration's reliance on the FVRA doesn't hold up, she claims, because the Act applies only to executive agencies—and the Library of Congress, as a legislative-branch institution, isn't one.[13] Perlmutter maintains that Blanche's purported appointment as Acting Librarian was invalid, and that any actions he took—including naming Perkins as Acting Register—have no legal effect.[14]

---

[6] Scott MacFarland, *Trump fires director of U.S. Copyright Office, sources say*, CBS NEWS (May 10, 2025), https://www.cbsnews.com/news/trump-fires-director-of-u-s-copyright-office-shira-perlmutter-sources/.

[7] Maya C. Miller and Evlin Barrett, *Trump Installs Top Justice Dept. Official at Library of Congress, Prompting a Standoff*, NY TIMES (May 12, 2025), https://www.nytimes.com/2025/05/12/us/politics/trump-library-of-congress.html.

[8] *Id.*

[9] Complaint For Declaratory and Injunctive Relief, *supra* note 2.

[10] *Id.* at 2.

[11] *Id.*

[12] *Id.*

[13] *Id.*

[14] Complaint For Declaratory and Injunctive Relief, *supra* note 2 at 2.

The administration strongly disagrees.[15] It argues that the Library does fall within the FVRA's scope—or, at minimum, that the President has independent Article II authority to remove federal officers and install temporary replacements.[16] But even if Perlmutter were right on the law, the government insists her TRO still fails—because the injuries she cites don't belong to her. "Plaintiff would not be irreparably harmed if she were reinstated and the Library was not exactly as when she left it," the filing tersely states.[17]

Meanwhile, the Copyright Office risks becoming collateral damage in the constitutional crossfire—with daily operations clouded by uncertainty and its institutional credibility hanging in the balance.

OPERATIONAL PARALYSIS

Perlmutter's motion describes a state of internal confusion as to who's lawfully in control of the Library of Congress and the U.S. Copyright Office—confusion she says is preventing the Office from fulfilling key statutory duties.[18] One immediate consequence is its inability to complete the fourth and final part of its report on copyright and artificial intelligence, which will address potential liability for AI-generated outputs.[19] While a pre-publication version of Part 3 was released the day before her removal, Perlmutter asserts that she can't issue the final installment without confirmation that she remains the lawful Register.[20] "If another person is appointed to Plaintiff's role," the motion states, "her ability to perform these duties will become at best unclear and at worst impossible."

There are also signs that the leadership vacuum at the Copyright Office may already be affecting some of its core day-to-day operations—most notably its copyright registration program, which processes hundreds of thousands of applications annually. While staff continue to accept and examine submissions, it remains unclear whether the Office can validly issue registration certificates without a properly appointed Register. Under Section 410(a) of the Copyright Act, "[w]hen, after examination, the Register of Copyrights determines that . . . the material deposited constitutes copyrightable subject matter . . . the Register shall register the claim and issue to the applicant a certificate of registration under the seal of the Copyright Office."[21] The plain language suggests that only the

---

[15] Defendants' Opposition To Plaintiff's Motion for A Temporary Restraining Order, *supra* note 4 at 1.

[16] *Id.* at 1.

[17] *Id.* at 21.

[18] Complaint For Declaratory and Injunctive Relief, *supra* note 2 at 7.

[19] *Id.*

[20] U.S. Copyright Office, Copyright and Artificial Intelligence Part 3: Generative AI Training (Pre-Publication Version) https://www.copyright.gov/ai/Copyright-and-Artificial-Intelligence-Part-3-Generative-AI-Training-Report-Pre-Publication-Version.pdf (2025).

[21] 17 U.S.C. § 410

Register can finalize registrations—raising questions about whether certificates issued without a lawfully-designated Register's stamp of approval while this dispute is pending would be valid.

STALLED POLICY WORK

Perlmutter's motion also suggests that the leadership disruption will stall or jeopardize several major statutorily required initiatives. In addition to Part 4 of the Copyright and AI study, these include:

1. **Enterprise Copyright System (ECS):** A multi-year effort to unify the Office's registration, recordation, public records, and licensing services into a single digital platform. ECS aims to replace outdated systems like eCO and eliminate paper-based workflows.[22]

2. **Fee Study:** The Copyright Office is required to periodically assess and adjust the fees it charges for public services.[23] The Register must ensure that any proposed changes are fair and equitable, and that they give proper consideration to the broader objectives of the copyright system.

3. **Copyright Claims Board (CCB) Review**: Created by the CASE Act of 2020, the CCB offers a streamlined, voluntary forum for resolving smaller copyright disputes.[24] The Copyright Office is currently conducting a required review of the Board's operations, including its effectiveness and accessibility.[25]

4. **Music Modernization Act (MMA) Redesignation:** Under the MMA, the Office is required to reassess and potentially redesignate the Mechanical Licensing Collective (MLC) and the Digital Licensee Coordinator (DLC), which manage blanket mechanical licenses and digital royalty distribution.[26]

---

[22] COPYRIGHT OFFICE MODERNIZATION, https://www.copyright.gov/copyright-modernization/Copyright-Office-Modernization-Update.pdf (June 2022).
[23] 17 U.S.C. § 708.
[24] Aaron Moss, *Felony Streaming and CASE Act Pass: What You Need to Know,* COPYRIGHTLATELY (Dec. 22, 2020), https://copyrightlately.com/felony-streaming-bill-and-case-act/.
[25] CASE Act Study, 90 Fed. Reg. 11625 (Mar. 10, 2025), https://www.federalregister.gov/documents/2025/03/10/2025-03795/case-act-study.
[26] Periodic Review of the Designations of the Mechanical Licensing Collective and Digital Licensee Coordinator, 89 Fed. Reg. 20 (Jan. 30, 2024),

Perlmutter asserts that Perkins' claim to be Acting Register has already interfered with her ability to oversee and advance these initiatives—and, if not enjoined, will continue to obstruct the Office's ability to fulfill its statutory responsibilities.

RISKS TO CONFIDENTIALITY AND LEGISLATIVE INDEPENDENCE

Finally, Perlmutter asserts that the attempted takeover by Executive Branch officials poses a deeper threat to the Copyright Office's role as a neutral advisor to Congress.[27] Her motion argues that placing DOJ personnel atop both the Library of Congress and the Copyright Office would compromise the agency's ability to provide independent policy guidance and assist lawmakers in their legislative and oversight functions.[28] That work, she contends, needs to remain insulated from Executive Branch influence to preserve the constitutional separation of powers.[29]

As part of her broader separation-of-powers argument, Perlmutter also warns of the risk of unauthorized Executive Branch access to confidential materials.[30] The Copyright Office maintains a vast archive of unpublished works submitted for registration—screenplays, manuscripts, musical compositions, and proprietary software—many of which are protected by statute from public disclosure.[31] The Library of Congress, meanwhile, houses private research prepared by the Congressional Research Service for Members of Congress. Perlmutter argues that unlawful Executive access to this information would cause immediate and irreversible harm, jeopardizing the value of copyright deposits, undermining the integrity of the registration system, and eroding the public's trust in the Office as a secure and neutral institution.[32]

THE BOTTOM LINE

Shira Perlmutter casts her lawsuit as a battle to preserve the integrity and independence of the Copyright Office—not just her own position at its helm.[33] The Trump Administration sees it differently, calling Perlmutter's removal entirely proper. Moreover, the legal standard for a temporary restraining order is

---

https://www.federalregister.gov/documents/2024/01/30/2024-01781/periodic-review-of-the-designations-of-the-mechanical-licensing-collective-and-digital-licensee.

[27] Complaint For Declaratory and Injunctive Relief, *supra* note 2 at 11.

[28] *Id.* at 5.

[29] *Id.* at 6.

[30] *Id.* at 10.

[31] *Id.* at 7.

[32] Complaint For Declaratory and Injunctive Relief, *supra* note 2 at 6.

[33] *Id.* at 10-11

clear, they argue, and Perlmutter hasn't shown the kind of personal, irreparable harm that would justify emergency relief.[34]

If the court grants the TRO, Perlmutter will temporarily resume her role while the legal issues play out. If not, the administration's appointees will remain in control—for now—amid ongoing questions about the Office's direction and independence—just as major policy debates over generative AI and licensing structures reach a critical stage.

Perlmutter's case raises a significant constitutional question: Does the President have the authority to remove and replace officers of an agency historically viewed as part of the Legislative Branch—or is the Copyright Office, as the administration now argues, effectively an executive entity subject to presidential control? But equally important—and perhaps even more immediate—is whether the Copyright Office can effectively fulfill its responsibilities while this dispute unfolds.

As always, I'd love to hear what you think. Drop me a note in the comments below or @copyrightlately on social media.

Thank you again, Aaron Moss, for allowing us to reprint both of these blog pieces as part of 72(2).

[34] Defendants' Opposition to Plaintiff's Motion for A Temporary Restraining Order, *supra* note 4 at 5.